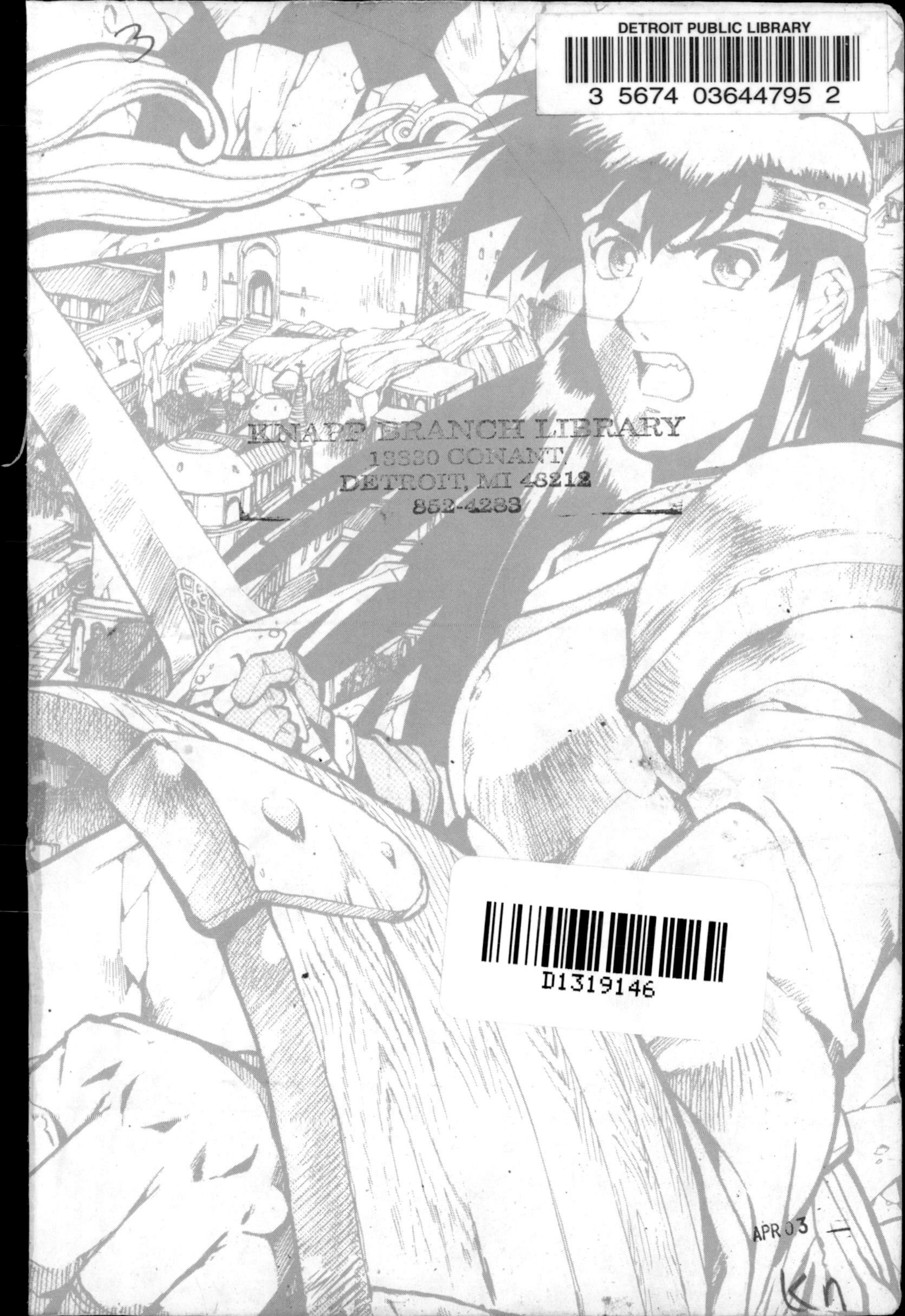

# Record of Lodoss War

## Chronicles of the Heroic Knight

### BOOK TWO

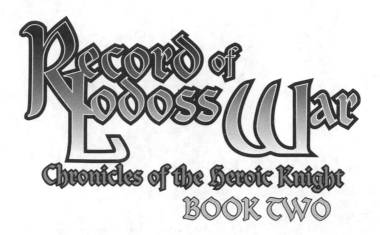

# Chronicles of the Heroic Knight
## BOOK TWO

## Ryo Mizuno • Masato Natsumoto

**CPM**®
**MANGA**
New York, New York

# Ryo Mizuno Writer
# Masato Natsumoto Artist

## Laura Jackson and Yoko Kobayashi
Translators
## Mark Griffin Retouching and Lettering
## Veronica Casson Designer
## Frank Pannone Project Manager
## Mike Lackey Print Production Manager
## Stephanie Shalofsky Vice President, Production
## John O'Donnell Publisher

**World Peace Through Shared Popular Culture™**
www.centralparkmedia.com
www.cpmmanga.com
AOL: Japanimation Station® Keyword: Japanimation
www.bigappleanimefest.com

*Record of Lodoss War: Chronicles of the Heroic Knight - Book Two*. Published by CPM Manga, a division of Central Park Media Corporation. Office of publication – 250 West 57th Street, Suite 317, New York, NY 10107. Original Japanese version "Record Of Lodoss War-Eiyuu Kishiden-Volume 2" ©1998 Ryou Mizuno/ Group SNE/ Kadokawa Shoten/ Masato Natsumoto. Originally published in Japan in 1998 by Kadokawa Shoten Publishing Co. Ltd. English translation rights arranged with KADOKAWA SHOTEN PUBLISHING CO. LTD.,Tokyo through TOHAN CORPORATION, Tokyo. English version ©2002 Central Park Media Corporation. CPM Manga, Japanimation Station and logos are registered trademarks of Central Park Media Corporation. All rights reserved. Big Apple Anime Fest and logo are trademarks of Big Apple Anime Fest Corporation. Price per copy $15.95, price in Canada may vary. ISBN: 1-58664-850-0. Catalog number: CMX 63102G. UPC: 7-19987-00631-7-00211. Printed in Canada. Second Printing

# Record of Lodoss War
# Chronicles of the Heroic Knight
## Book Two

In the first volume of *Record of Lodoss War: Chronicles of the Heroic Knight*, we were introduced to Spark, an apprentice knight. The last surviving male of the Fire Clan, Spark is in line to become the next King of Flaim, and is enthusiastic about assuming the full responsibilities of knighthood.

Before a sumptuous banquet thrown by King Kashu of Flaim, Spark is introduced to the legendary Parn and Deedlit, veterans of the fabled War of Heroes. Here Spark asks King Kashu why he hasn't been knighted yet. Insulted by Spark's presumption, Kashu dismisses the young apprentice.

Spark wanders the castle grounds dejectedly until he comes upon Dark Elves attempting to breach the locked treasury doors. Instead of calling for help, Spark attempts to stop their invasion himself, and fails. The Dark Elves escape with the Crystal Ball of Souls, a legendary object that the evil sorcerer Vagnado intends to use to resurrect Kardis, the Goddess of Destruction.

King Kashu charges Spark with the responsibility of recovering the Crystal Ball and assigns him an eclectic crew of mercenaries, magician, and a dwarven priest. Following the trail of the Dark Elves, our heroes enter the South Fort of Flaim where they meet two warriors, Laina and Randy, who claim to have seen the thieves firsthand. Unbeknownst to our heroes, both are thieves themselves.

When Randy is killed by the Dark Elves' treachery, Laina joins Spark on his quest for the Crystal Ball of Souls. But who is the mysterious cloaked woman following our heroes, and what role will she play in the upcoming adventure?

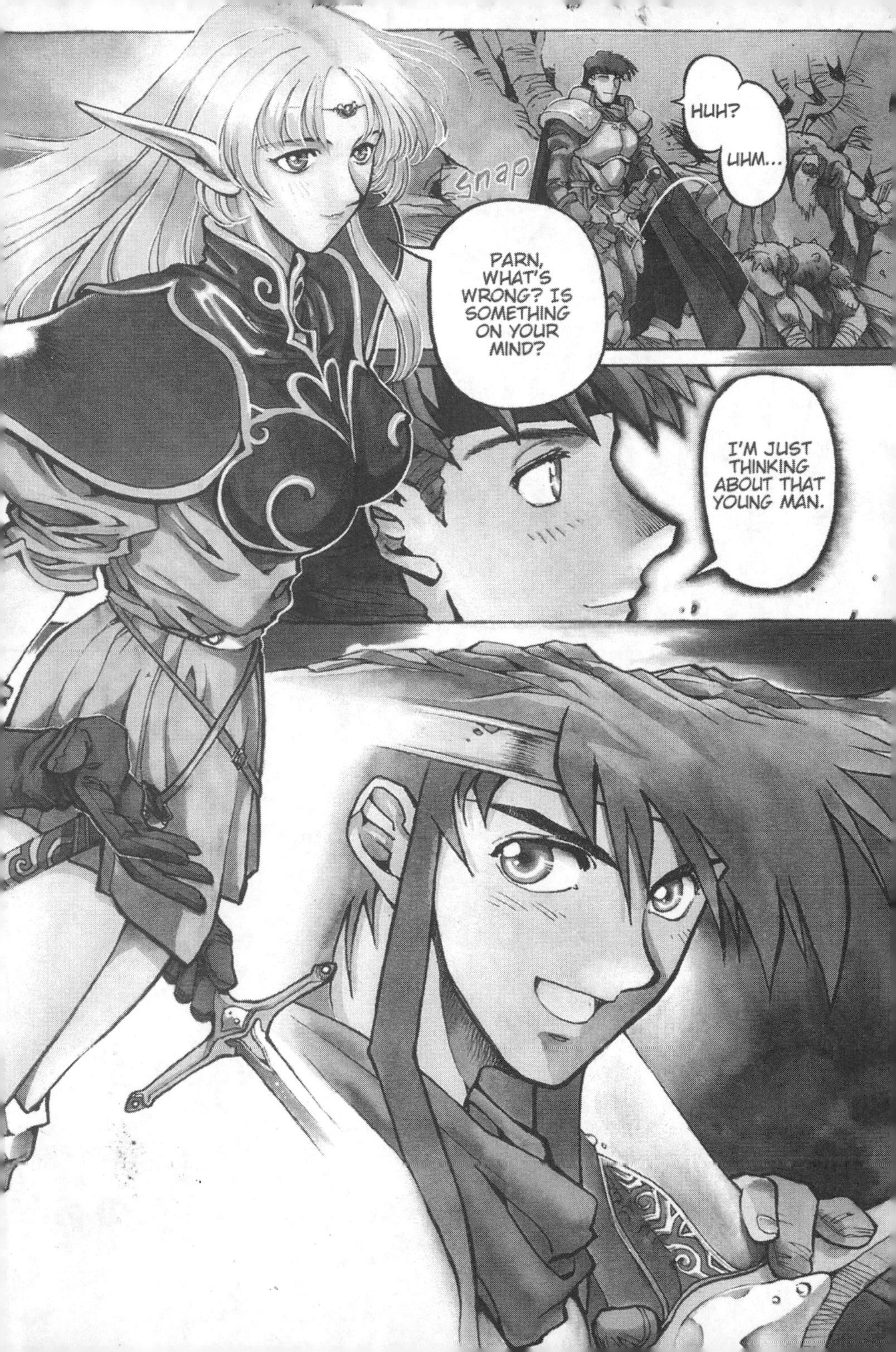

PARN, WHAT'S WRONG? IS SOMETHING ON YOUR MIND?
snap
HUH?
UHM...
I'M JUST THINKING ABOUT THAT YOUNG MAN.

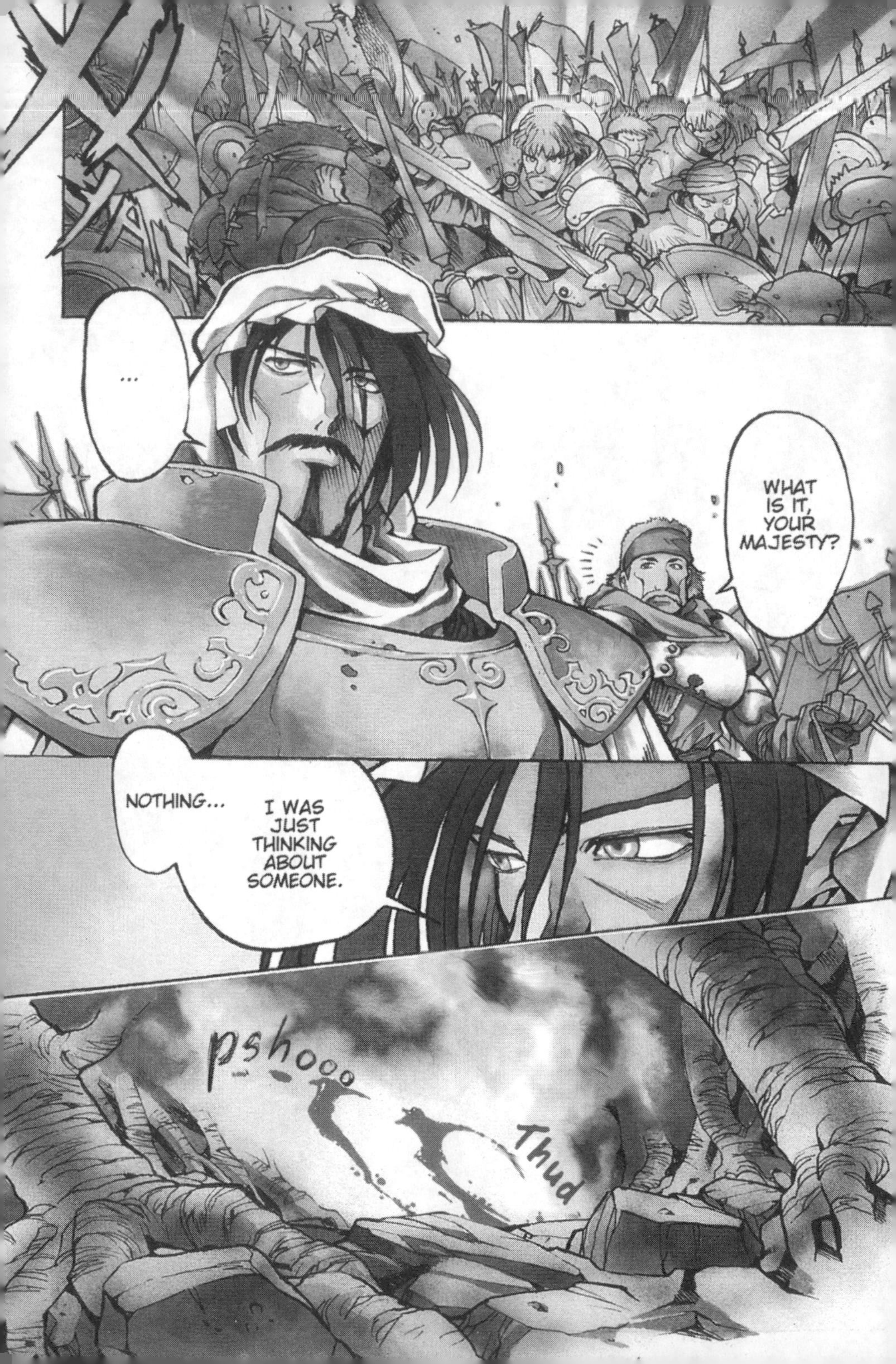
...
WHAT IS IT, YOUR MAJESTY?
NOTHING... I WAS JUST THINKING ABOUT SOMEONE.
pshooo
Thud

# Melody Of Light And Dark

EPISODE 6

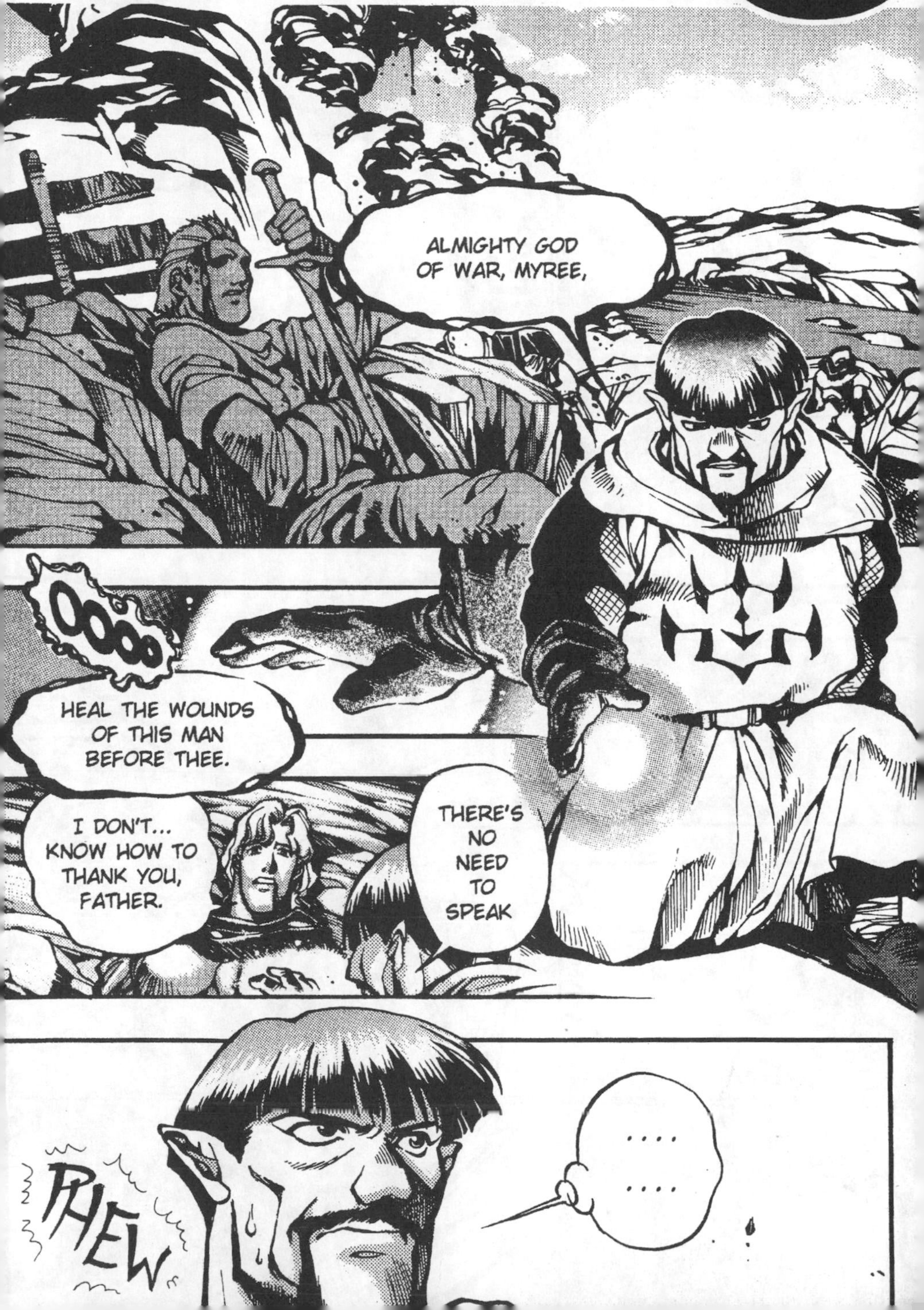
ALMIGHTY GOD OF WAR, MYREE,
OOOO
HEAL THE WOUNDS OF THIS MAN BEFORE THEE.
I DON'T... KNOW HOW TO THANK YOU, FATHER.
THERE'S NO NEED TO SPEAK
PHEW
....
....

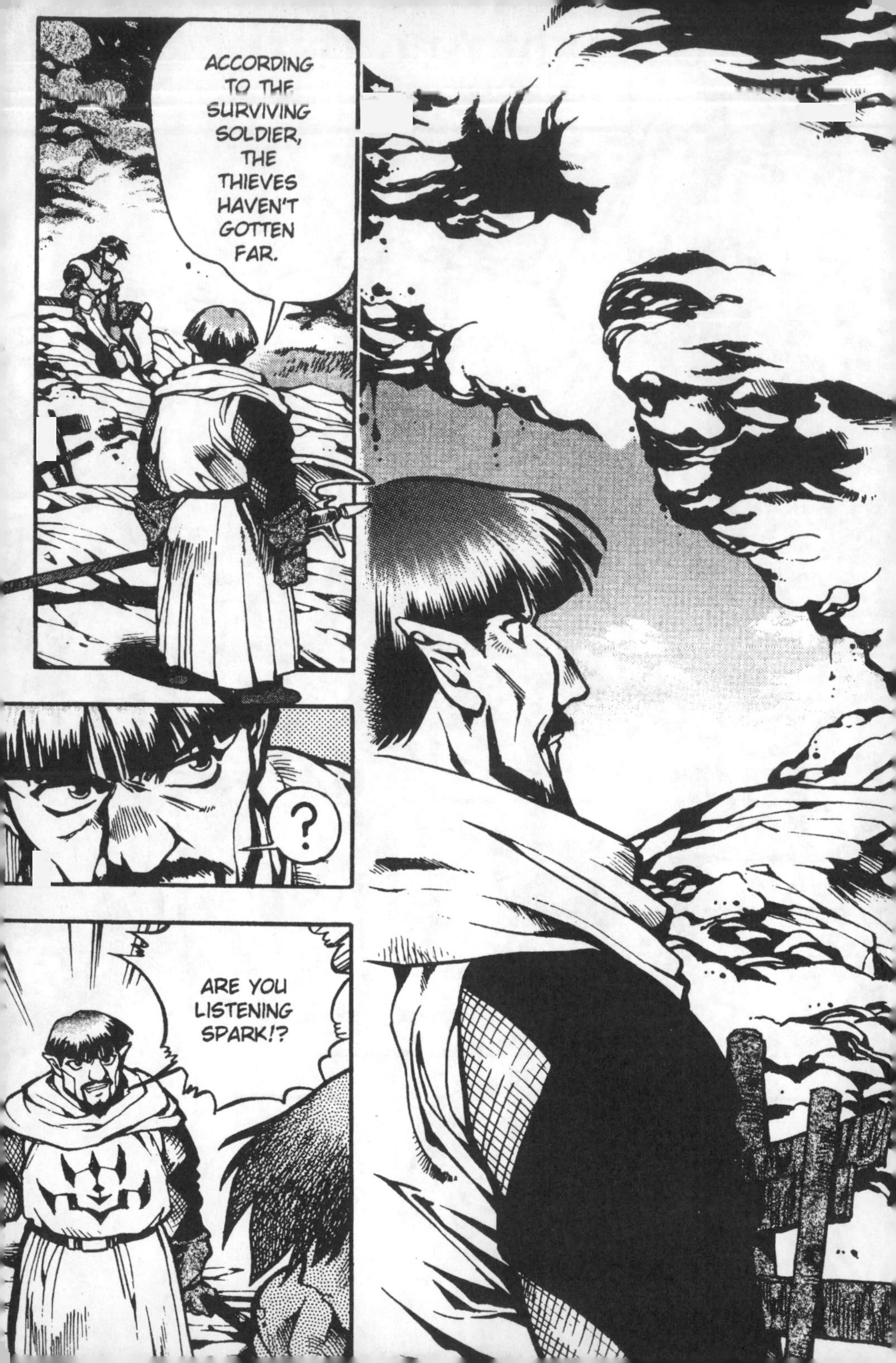
ACCORDING TO THE SURVIVING SOLDIER, THE THIEVES HAVEN'T GOTTEN FAR.
?
ARE YOU LISTENING SPARK!?

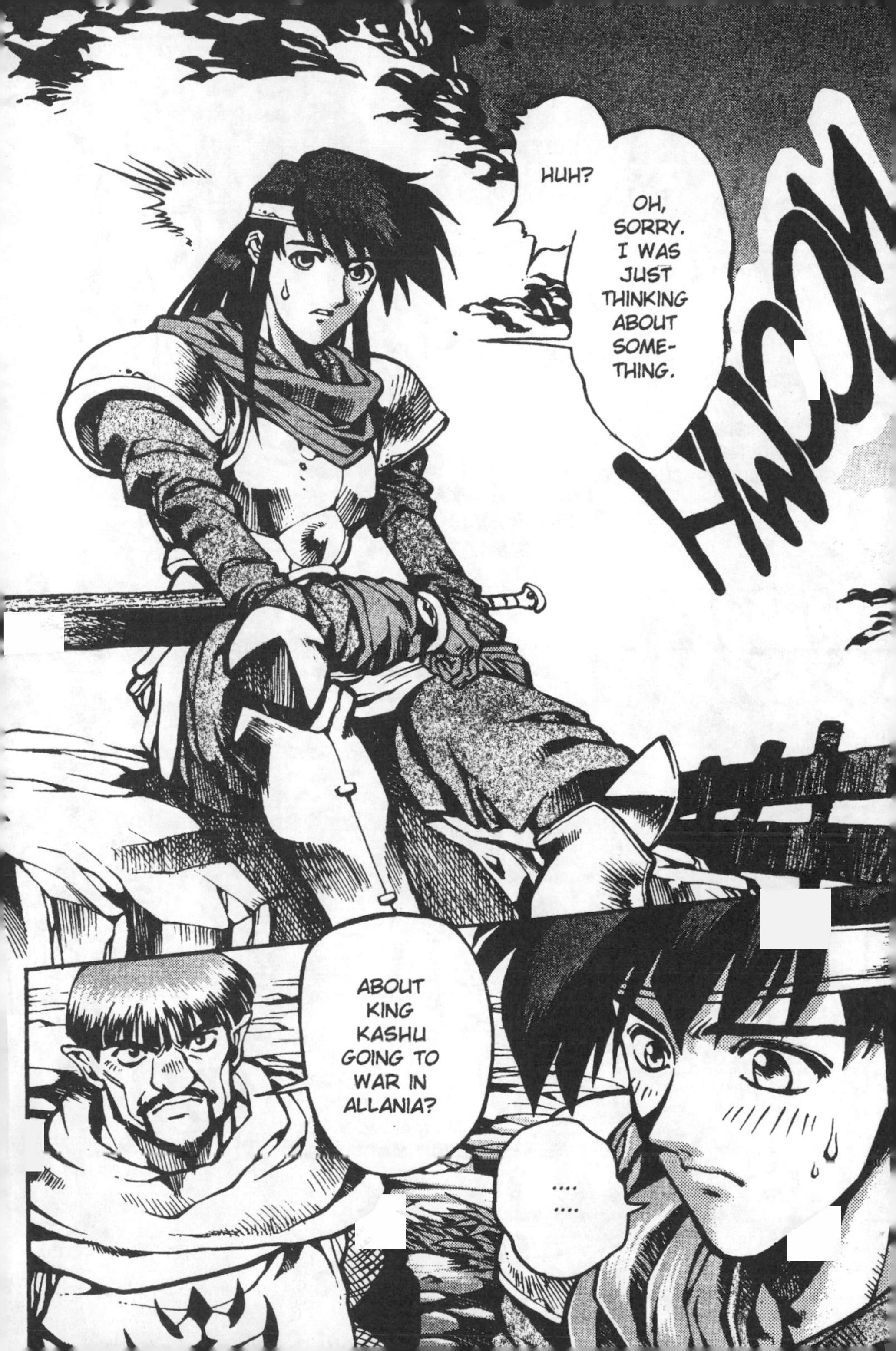
HUH?
OH, SORRY. I WAS JUST THINKING ABOUT SOME-THING.
ABOUT KING KASHU GOING TO WAR IN ALLANIA?
.... ....

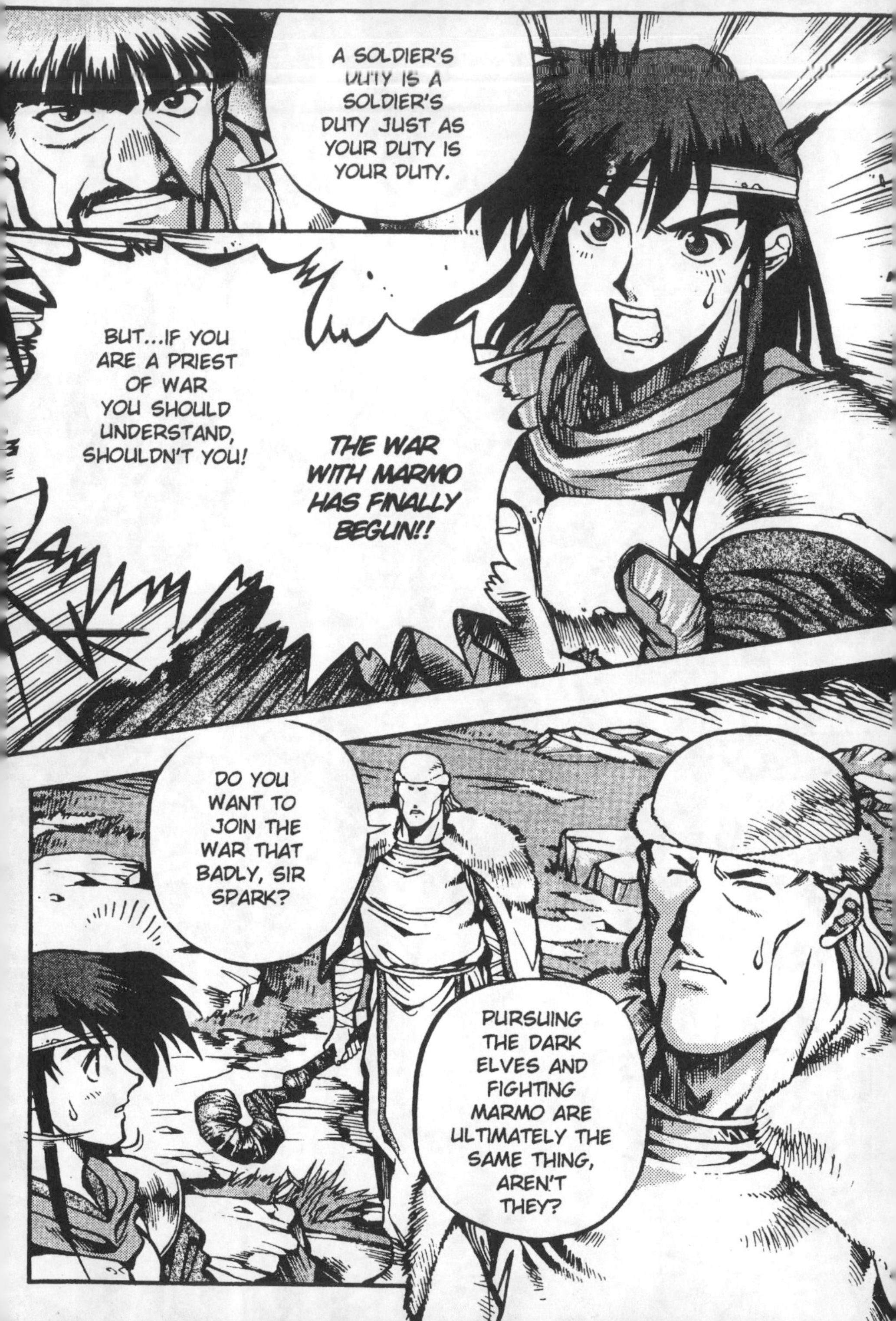
A SOLDIER'S DUTY IS A SOLDIER'S DUTY JUST AS YOUR DUTY IS YOUR DUTY.
BUT...IF YOU ARE A PRIEST OF WAR YOU SHOULD UNDERSTAND, SHOULDN'T YOU!
THE WAR WITH MARMO HAS FINALLY BEGUN!!
DO YOU WANT TO JOIN THE WAR THAT BADLY, SIR SPARK?
PURSUING THE DARK ELVES AND FIGHTING MARMO ARE ULTIMATELY THE SAME THING, AREN'T THEY?

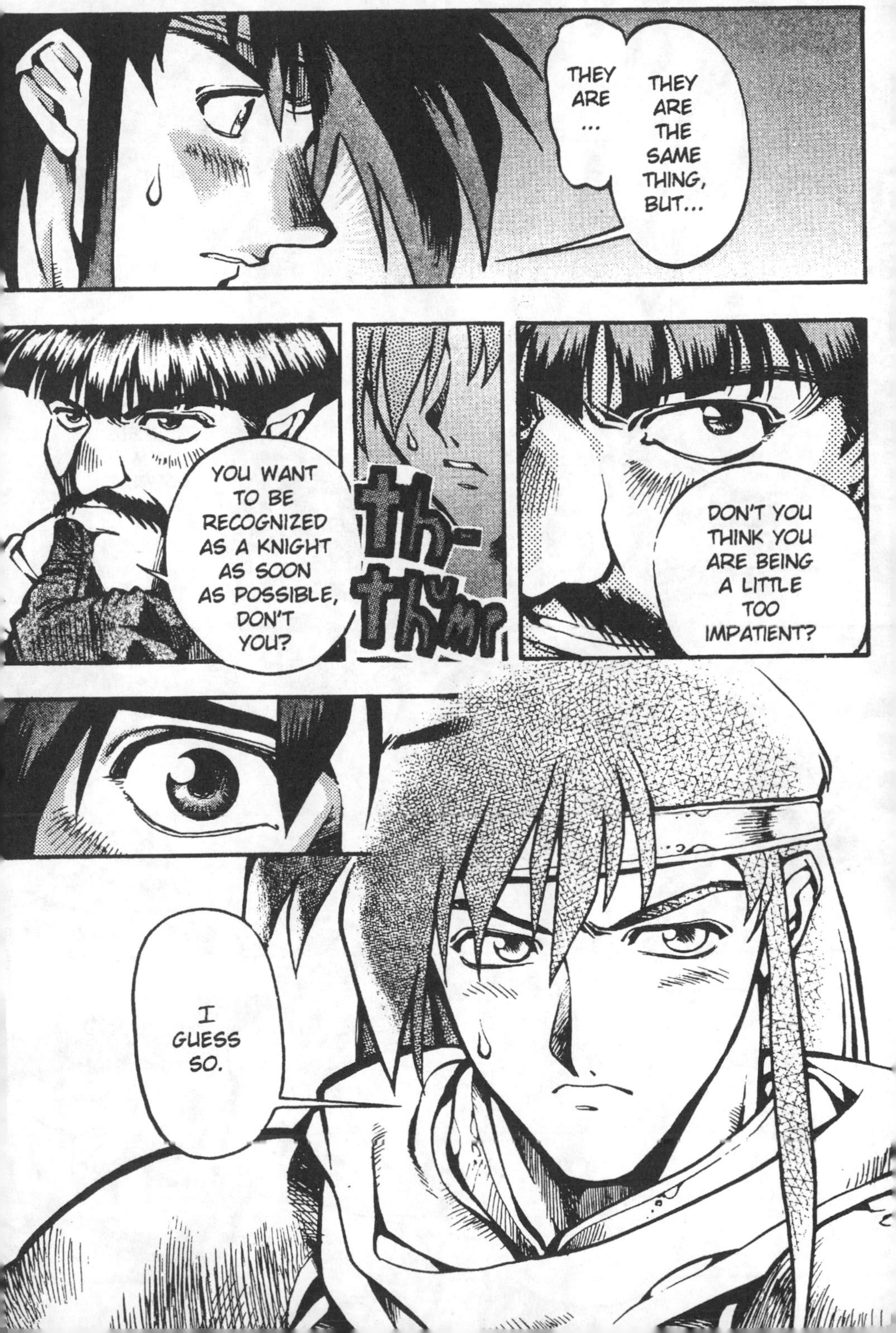
THEY ARE ...
THEY ARE THE SAME THING, BUT...
YOU WANT TO BE RECOGNIZED AS A KNIGHT AS SOON AS POSSIBLE, DON'T YOU?
DON'T YOU THINK YOU ARE BEING A LITTLE TOO IMPATIENT?
I GUESS SO.

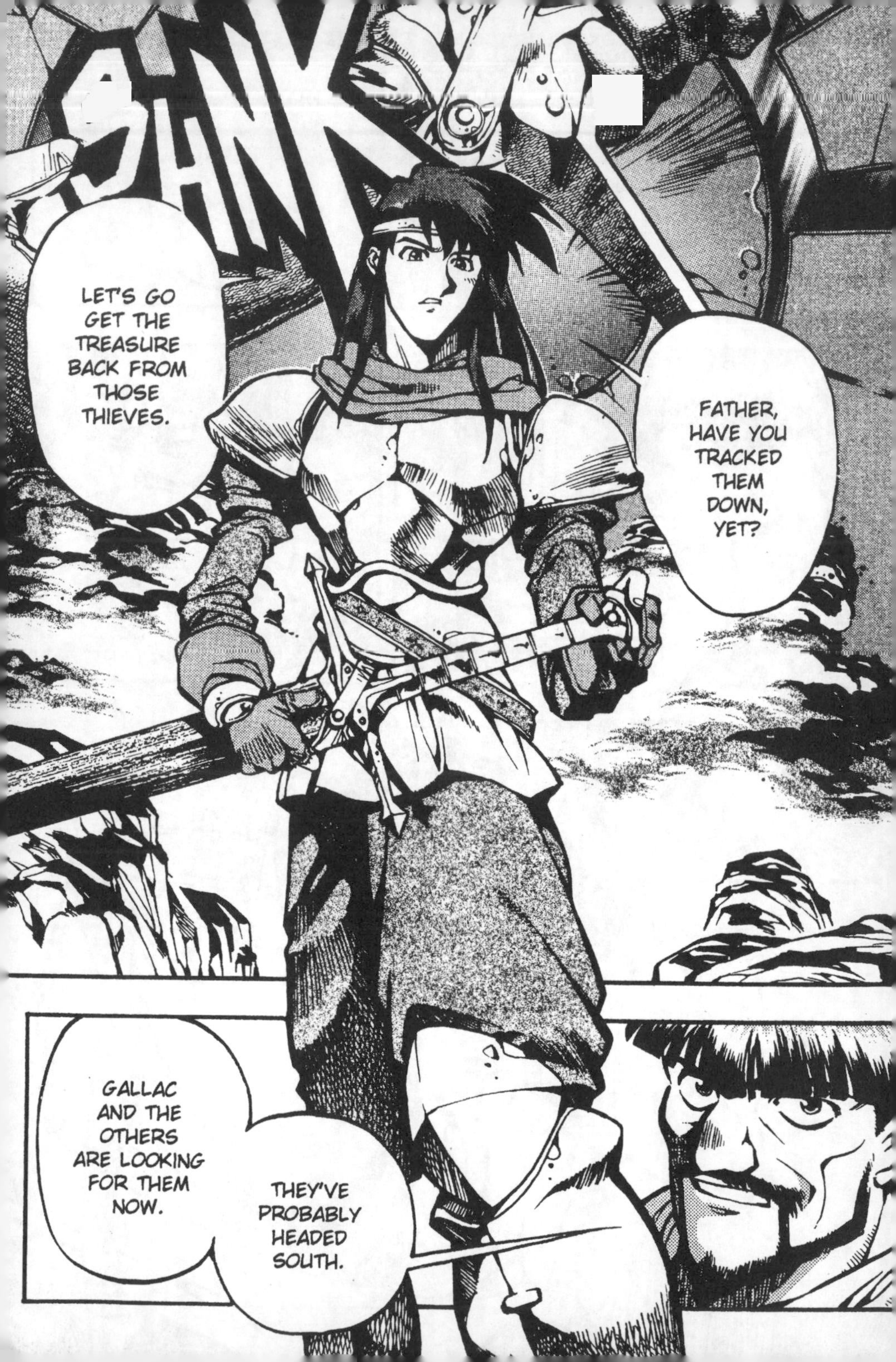

LET'S GO GET THE TREASURE BACK FROM THOSE THIEVES.
FATHER, HAVE YOU TRACKED THEM DOWN, YET?
GALLAC AND THE OTHERS ARE LOOKING FOR THEM NOW.
THEY'VE PROBABLY HEADED SOUTH.

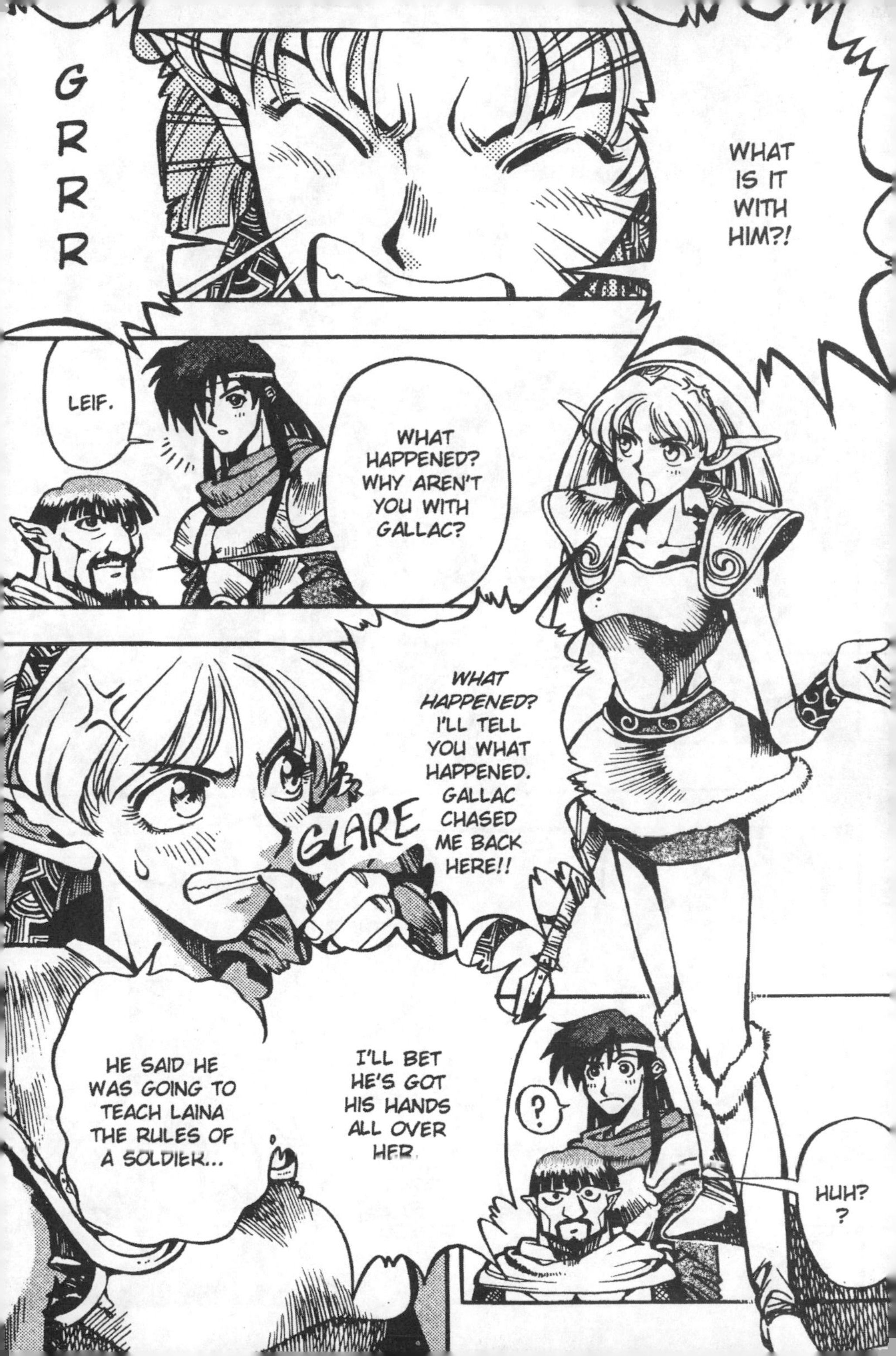
GRRR
WHAT IS IT WITH HIM?!
LEIF.
WHAT HAPPENED? WHY AREN'T YOU WITH GALLAC?
WHAT HAPPENED? I'LL TELL YOU WHAT HAPPENED. GALLAC CHASED ME BACK HERE!!
GLARE
HE SAID HE WAS GOING TO TEACH LAINA THE RULES OF A SOLDIER...
I'LL BET HE'S GOT HIS HANDS ALL OVER HER.
?
HUH? ?

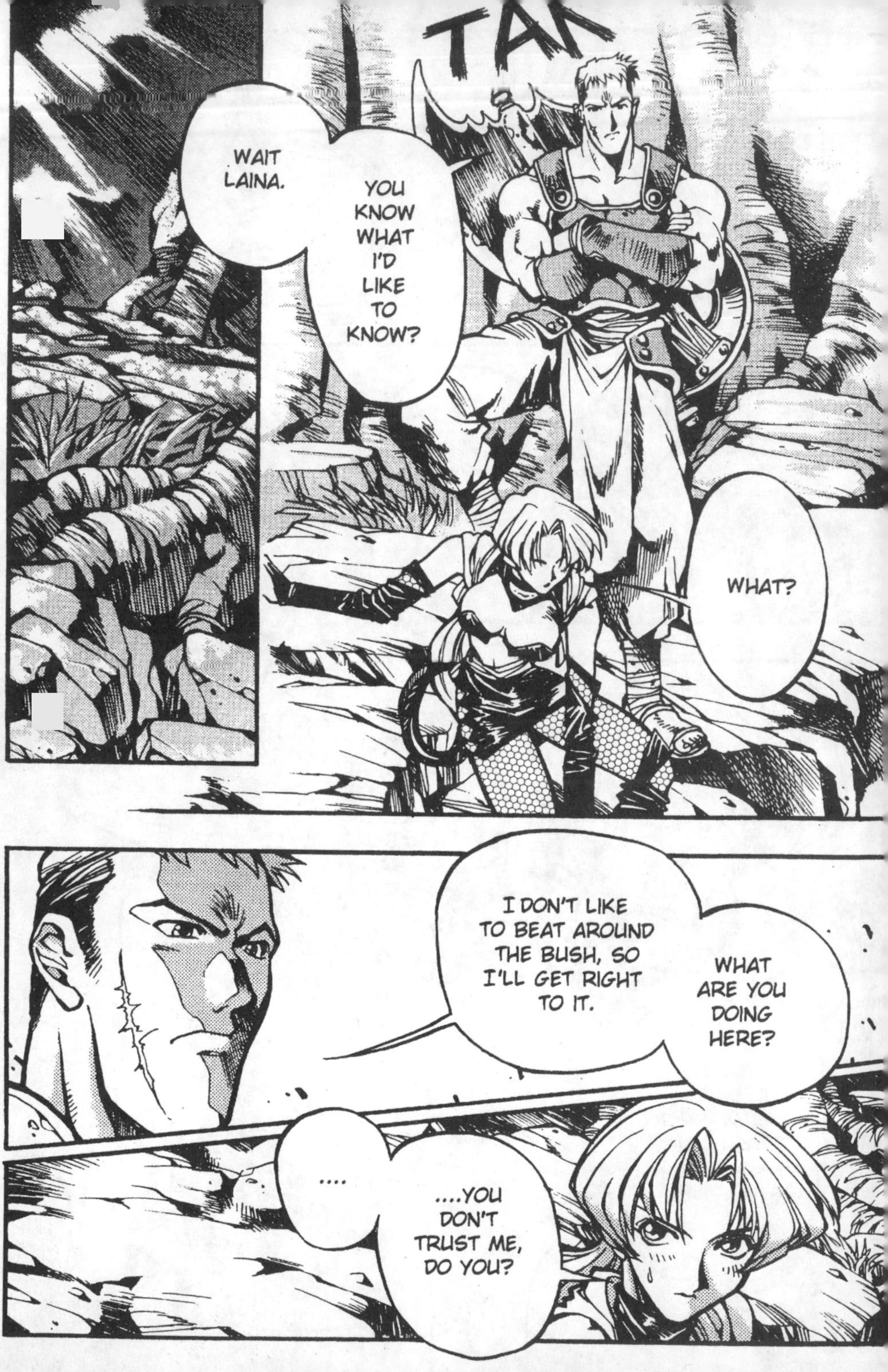
TAP
WAIT LAINA.
YOU KNOW WHAT I'D LIKE TO KNOW?
WHAT?
I DON'T LIKE TO BEAT AROUND THE BUSH, SO I'LL GET RIGHT TO IT.
WHAT ARE YOU DOING HERE?
....
....YOU DON'T TRUST ME, DO YOU?

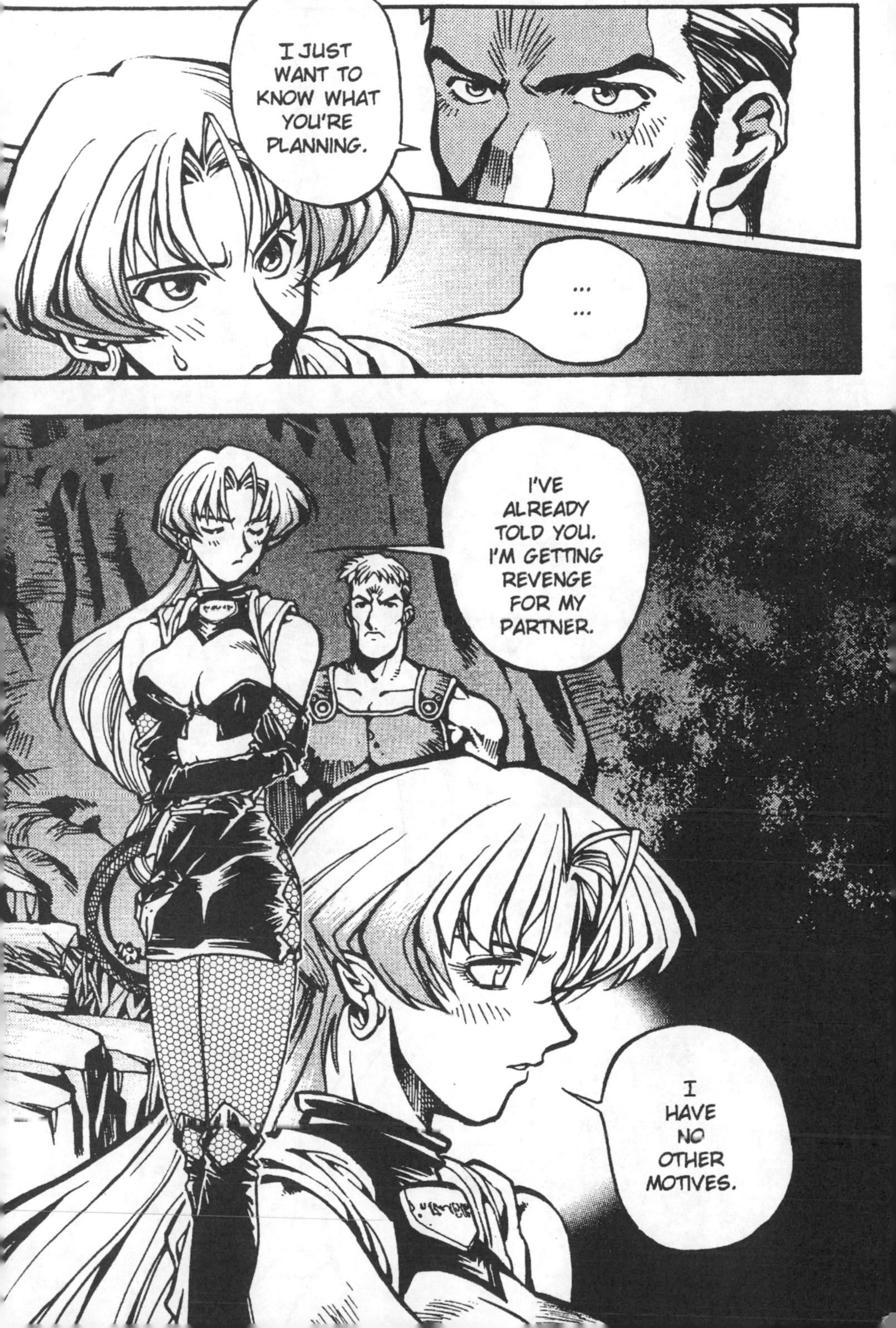
I JUST WANT TO KNOW WHAT YOU'RE PLANNING.
... ...
I'VE ALREADY TOLD YOU. I'M GETTING REVENGE FOR MY PARTNER.
I HAVE NO OTHER MOTIVES.

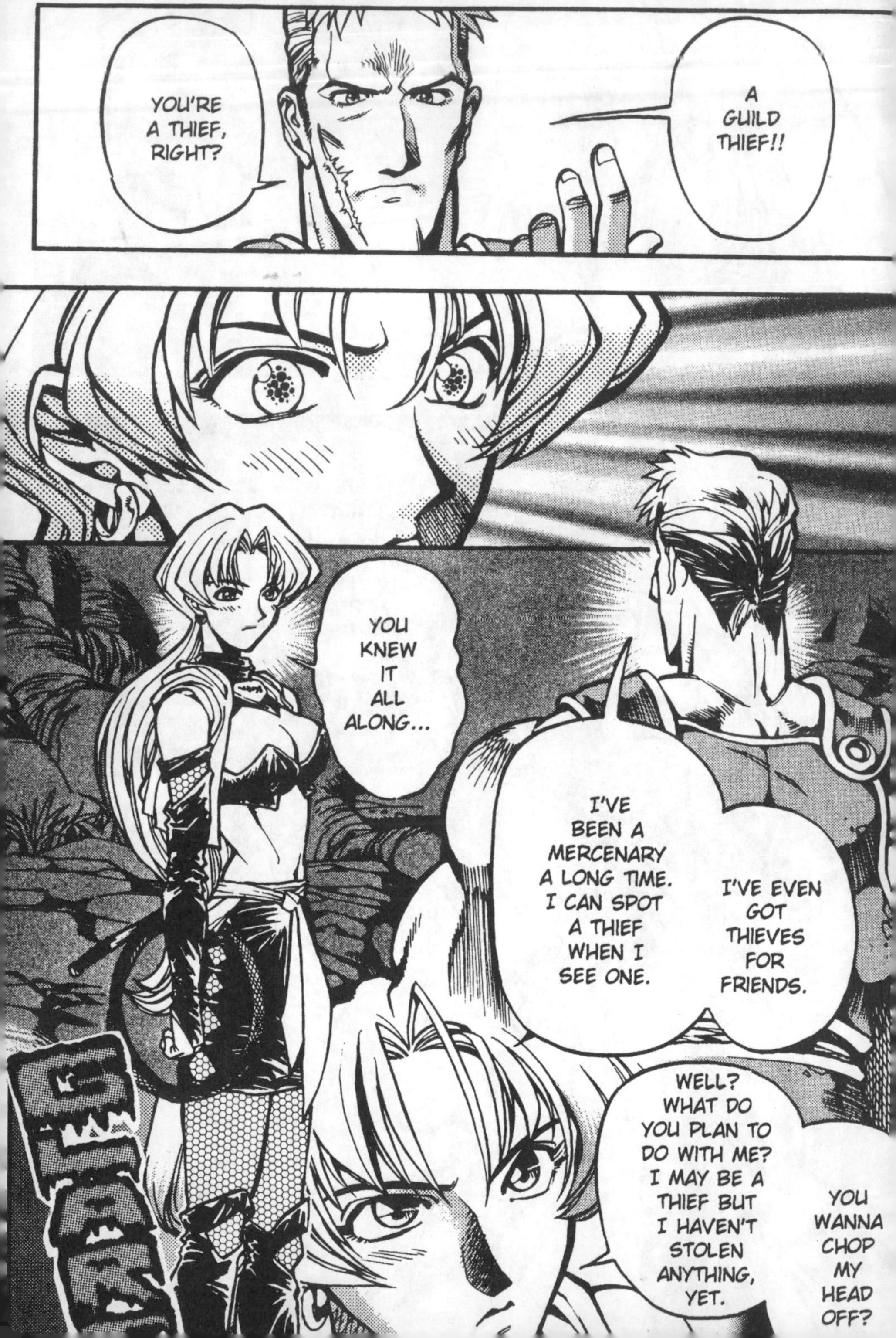
YOU'RE A THIEF, RIGHT?
A GUILD THIEF!!
YOU KNEW IT ALL ALONG...
I'VE BEEN A MERCENARY A LONG TIME. I CAN SPOT A THIEF WHEN I SEE ONE.
I'VE EVEN GOT THIEVES FOR FRIENDS.
WELL? WHAT DO YOU PLAN TO DO WITH ME? I MAY BE A THIEF BUT I HAVEN'T STOLEN ANYTHING, YET.
YOU WANNA CHOP MY HEAD OFF?

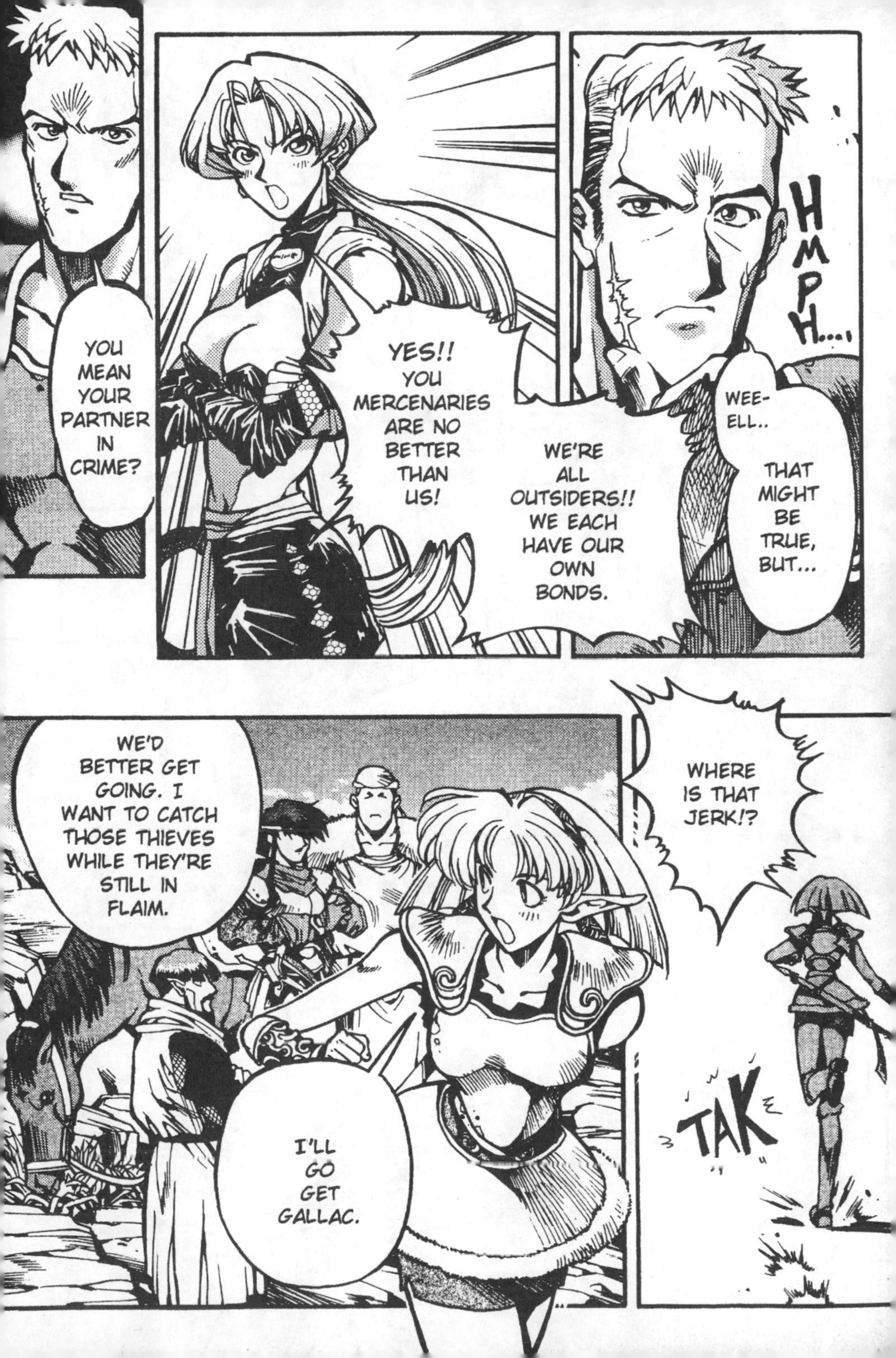
YOU MEAN YOUR PARTNER IN CRIME?
YES!! YOU MERCENARIES ARE NO BETTER THAN US!
WE'RE ALL OUTSIDERS!! WE EACH HAVE OUR OWN BONDS.
HMPH...
WEE-ELL..
THAT MIGHT BE TRUE, BUT...
WE'D BETTER GET GOING. I WANT TO CATCH THOSE THIEVES WHILE THEY'RE STILL IN FLAIM.
I'LL GO GET GALLAC.
WHERE IS THAT JERK!?
TAK

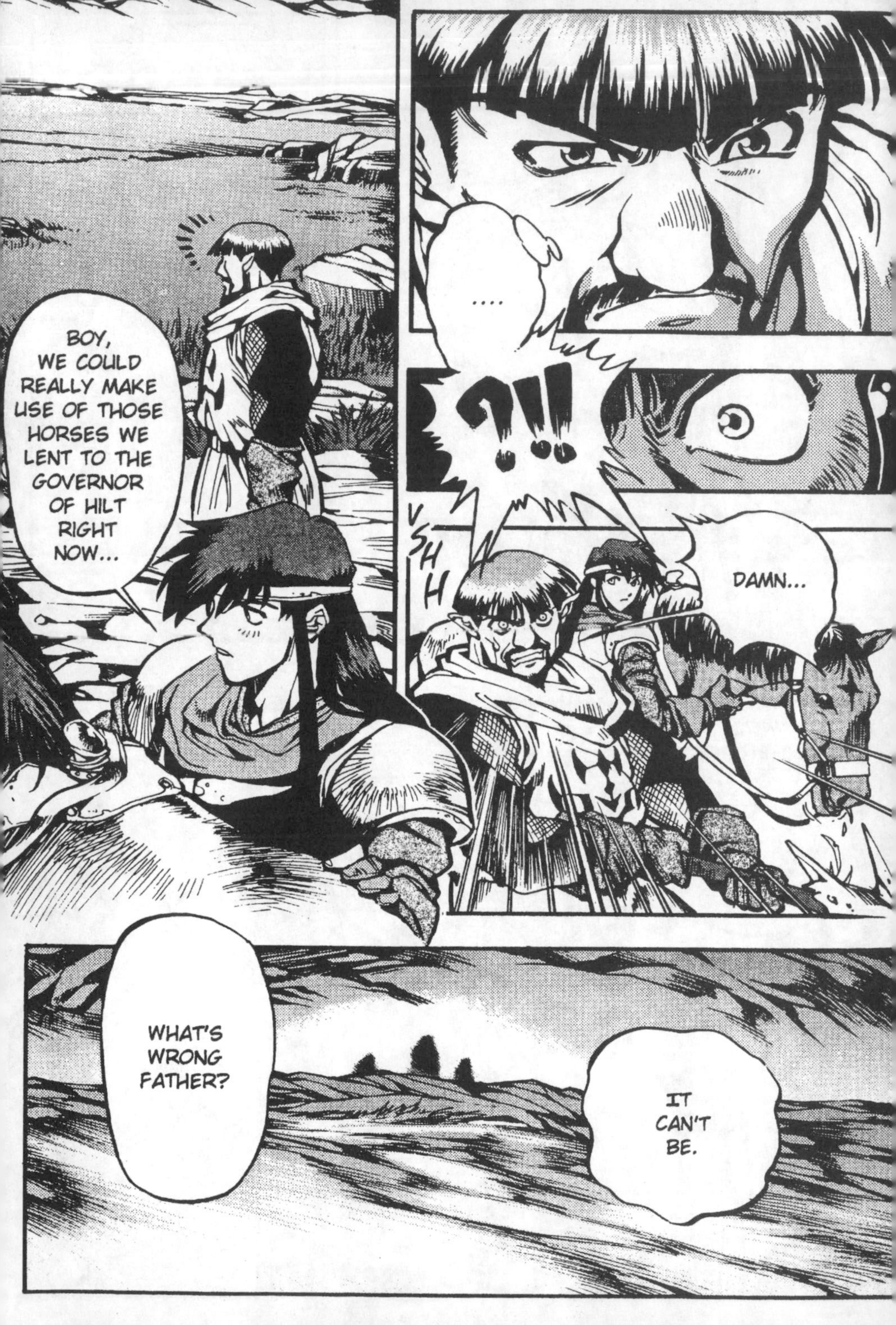
BOY, WE COULD REALLY MAKE USE OF THOSE HORSES WE LENT TO THE GOVERNOR OF HILT RIGHT NOW...
....
?!!
VSHH
DAMN...
WHAT'S WRONG FATHER?
IT CAN'T BE.

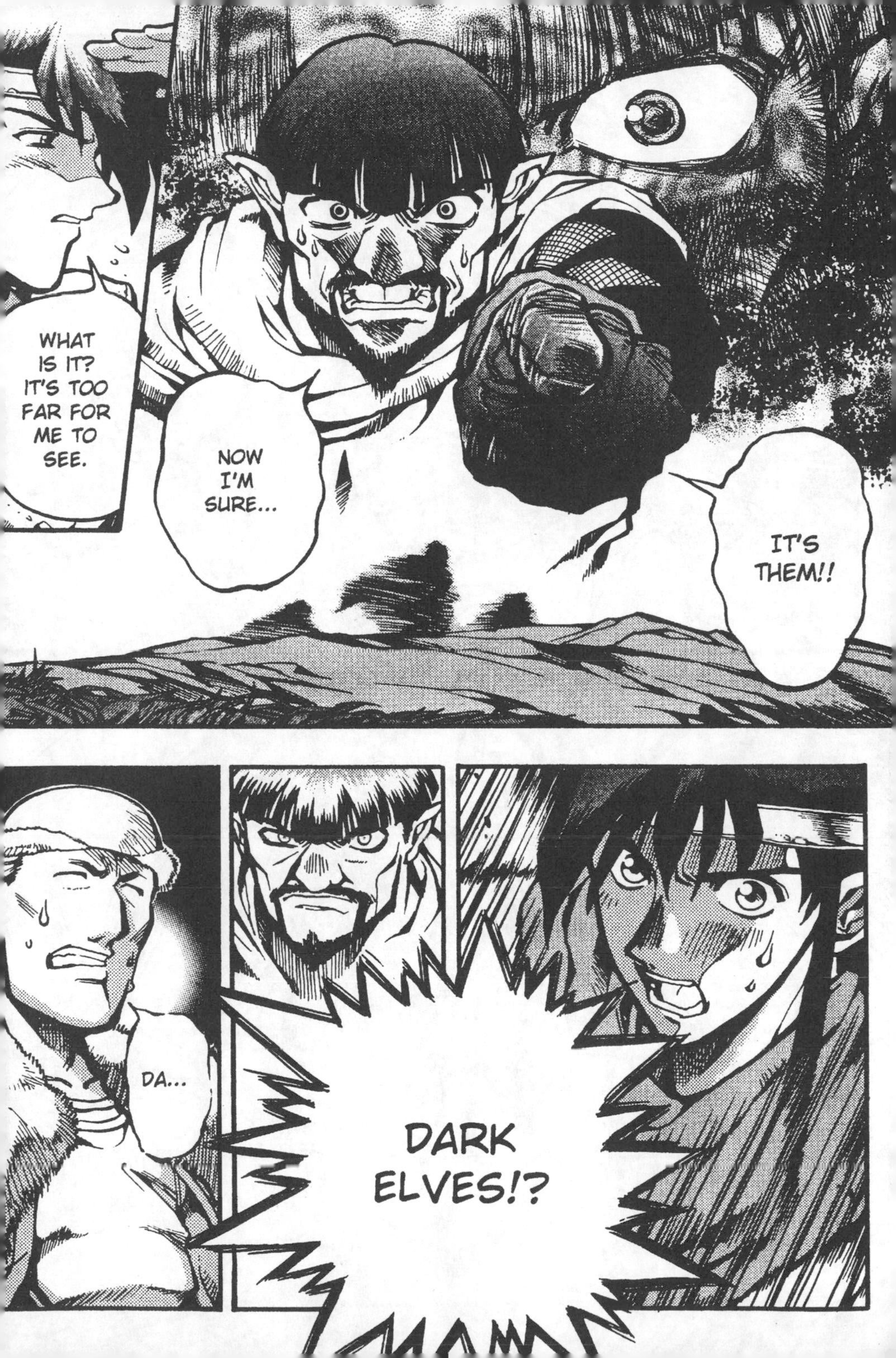
WHAT IS IT? IT'S TOO FAR FOR ME TO SEE.
NOW I'M SURE...
IT'S THEM!!
DA...
DARK ELVES!?

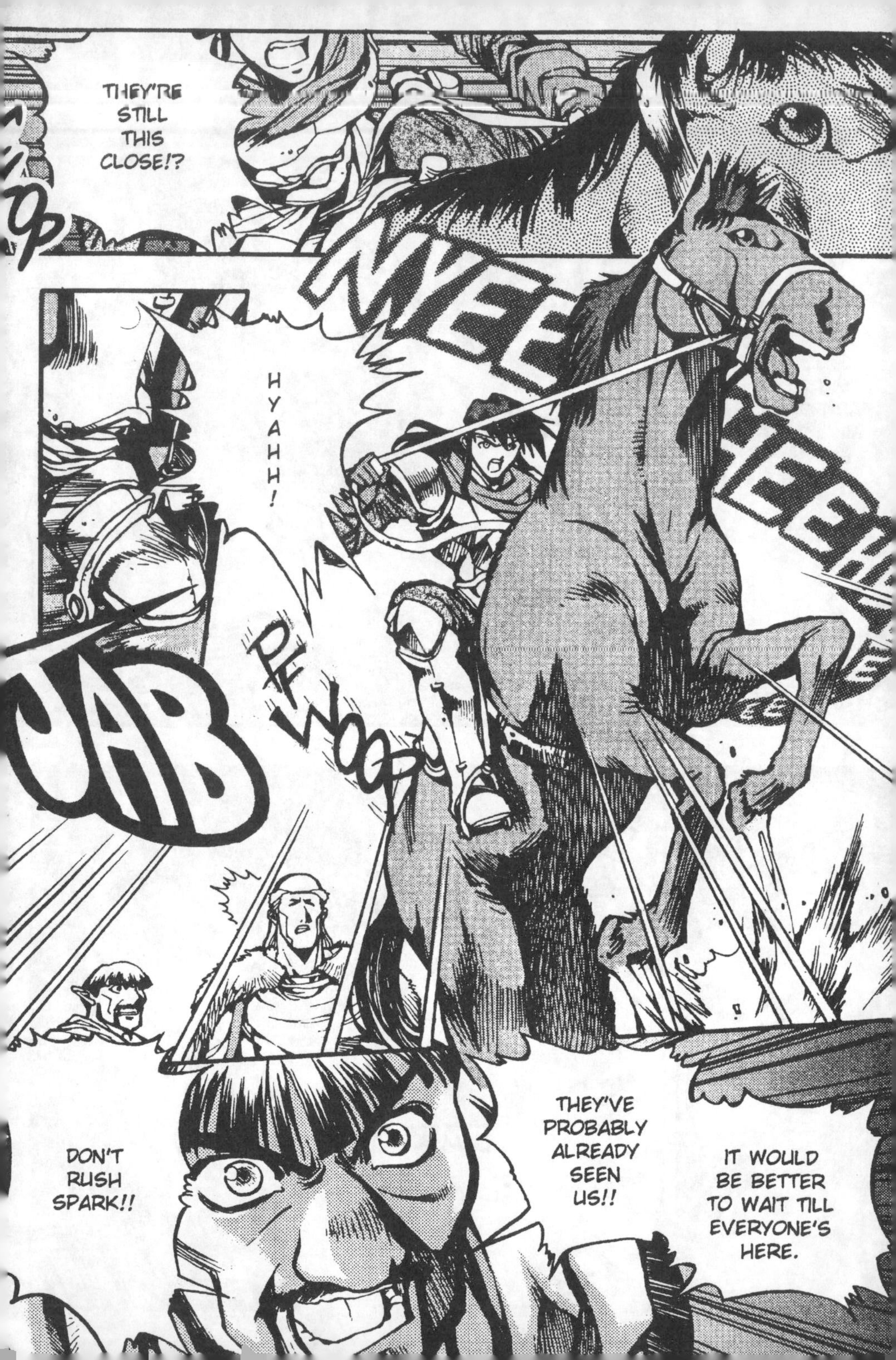
THEY'RE STILL THIS CLOSE!?
FWOOP
NYEEEEEEEE
HYAHHH!
CHAB
PFWOOP
DON'T RUSH SPARK!!
THEY'VE PROBABLY ALREADY SEEN US!!
IT WOULD BE BETTER TO WAIT TILL EVERYONE'S HERE.

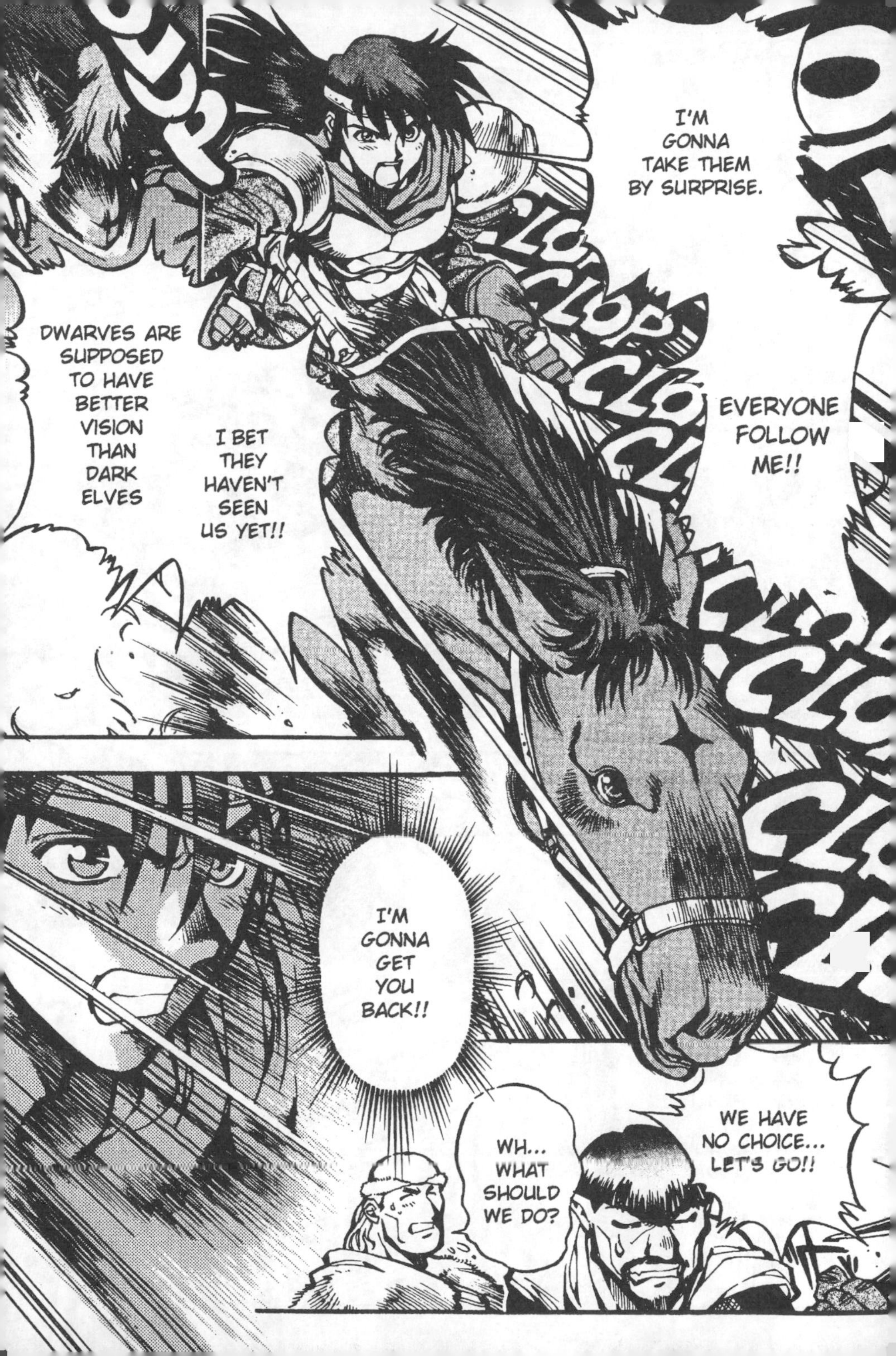
I'M GONNA TAKE THEM BY SURPRISE.
DWARVES ARE SUPPOSED TO HAVE BETTER VISION THAN DARK ELVES
I BET THEY HAVEN'T SEEN US YET!!
CLOP CLOP
EVERYONE FOLLOW ME!!
I'M GONNA GET YOU BACK!!
WH... WHAT SHOULD WE DO?
WE HAVE NO CHOICE... LET'S GO!!

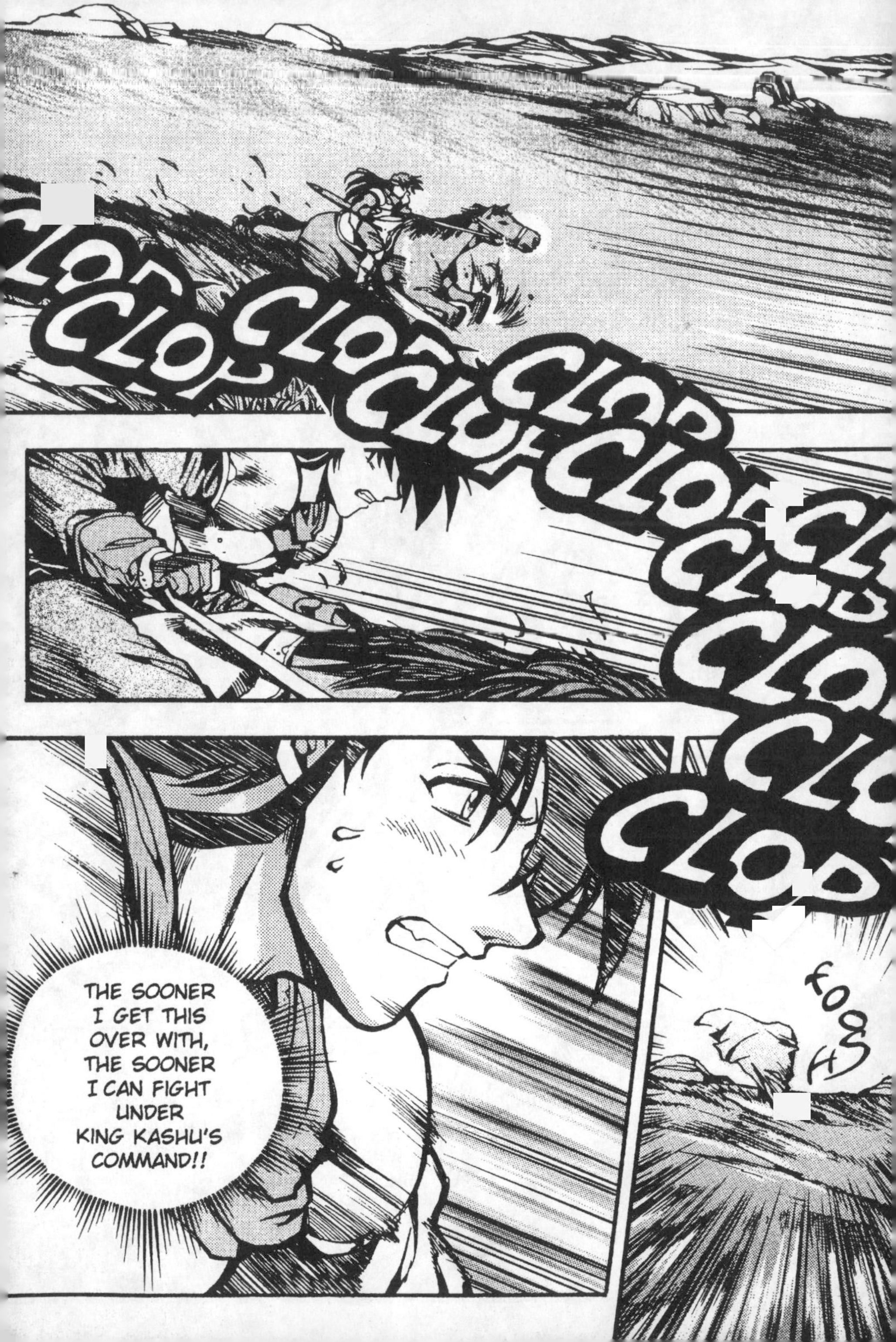
CLOP CLOP CLOP CLOP
CLOP CLOP CLOP CLOP CLOP CLOP
THE SOONER I GET THIS OVER WITH, THE SOONER I CAN FIGHT UNDER KING KASHU'S COMMAND!!
FOOSH

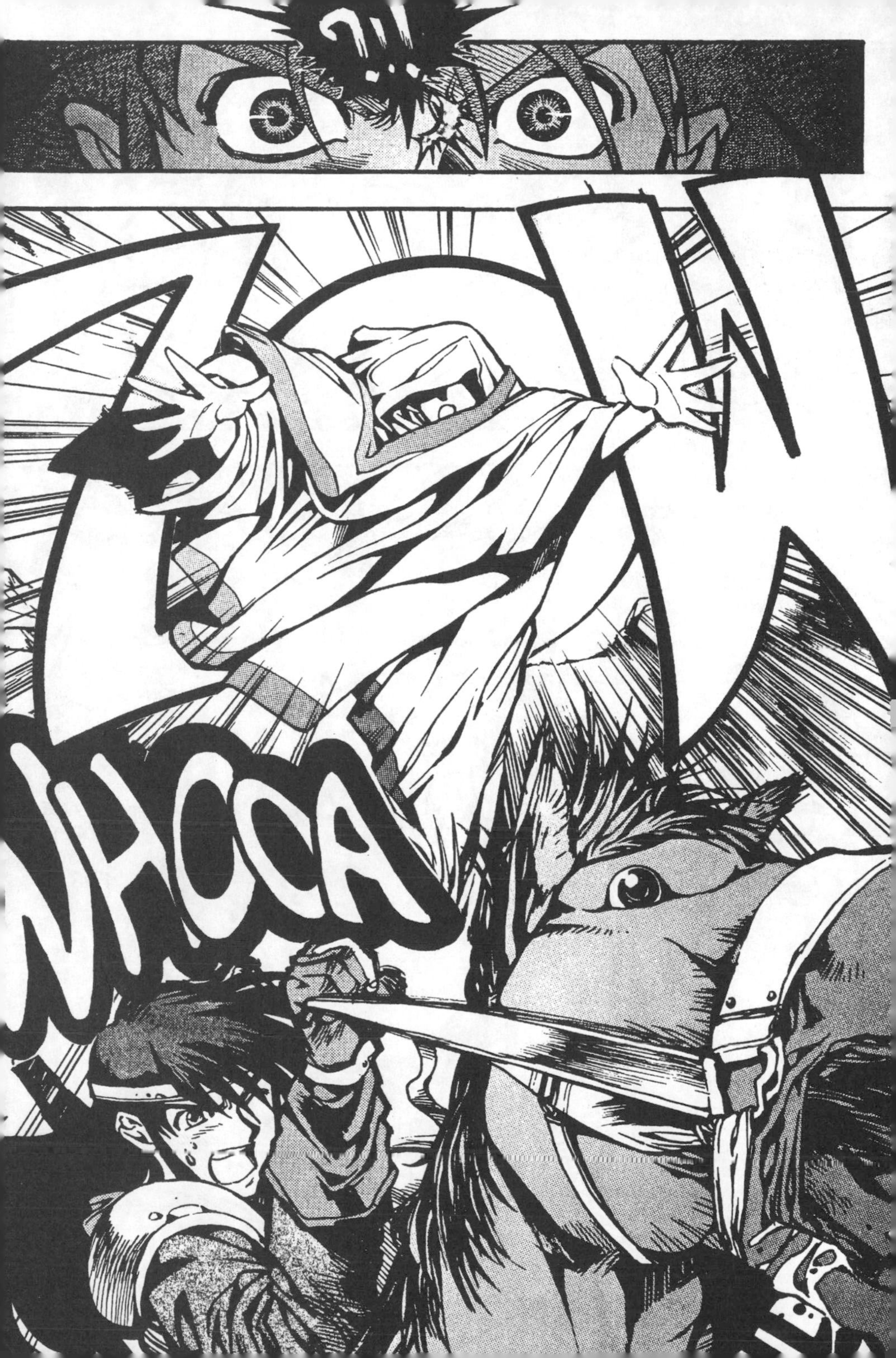
ZOW

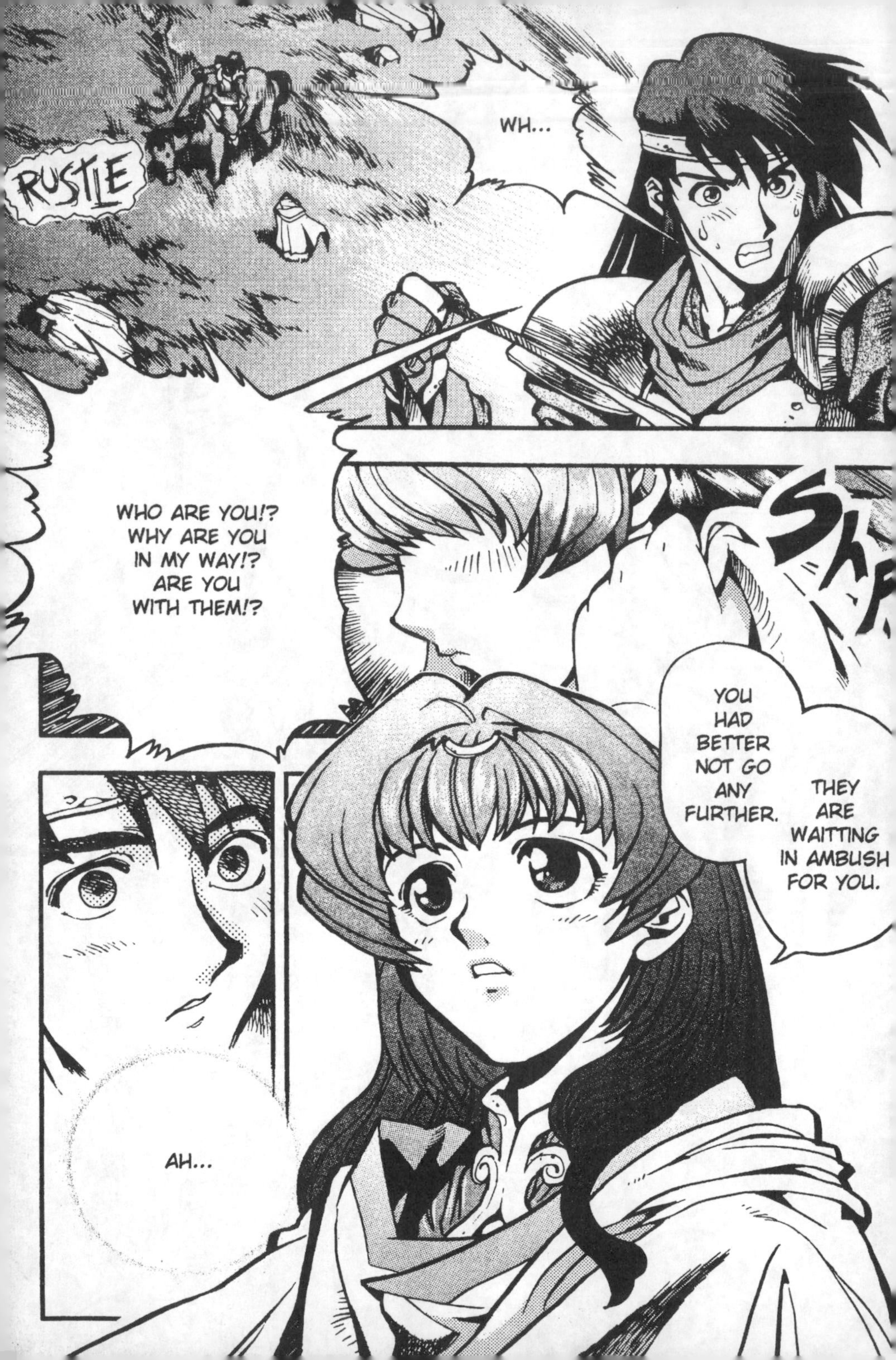
RUSTLE
WH...
WHO ARE YOU!? WHY ARE YOU IN MY WAY!? ARE YOU WITH THEM!?
AH...
YOU HAD BETTER NOT GO ANY FURTHER.
THEY ARE WAITTING IN AMBUSH FOR YOU.

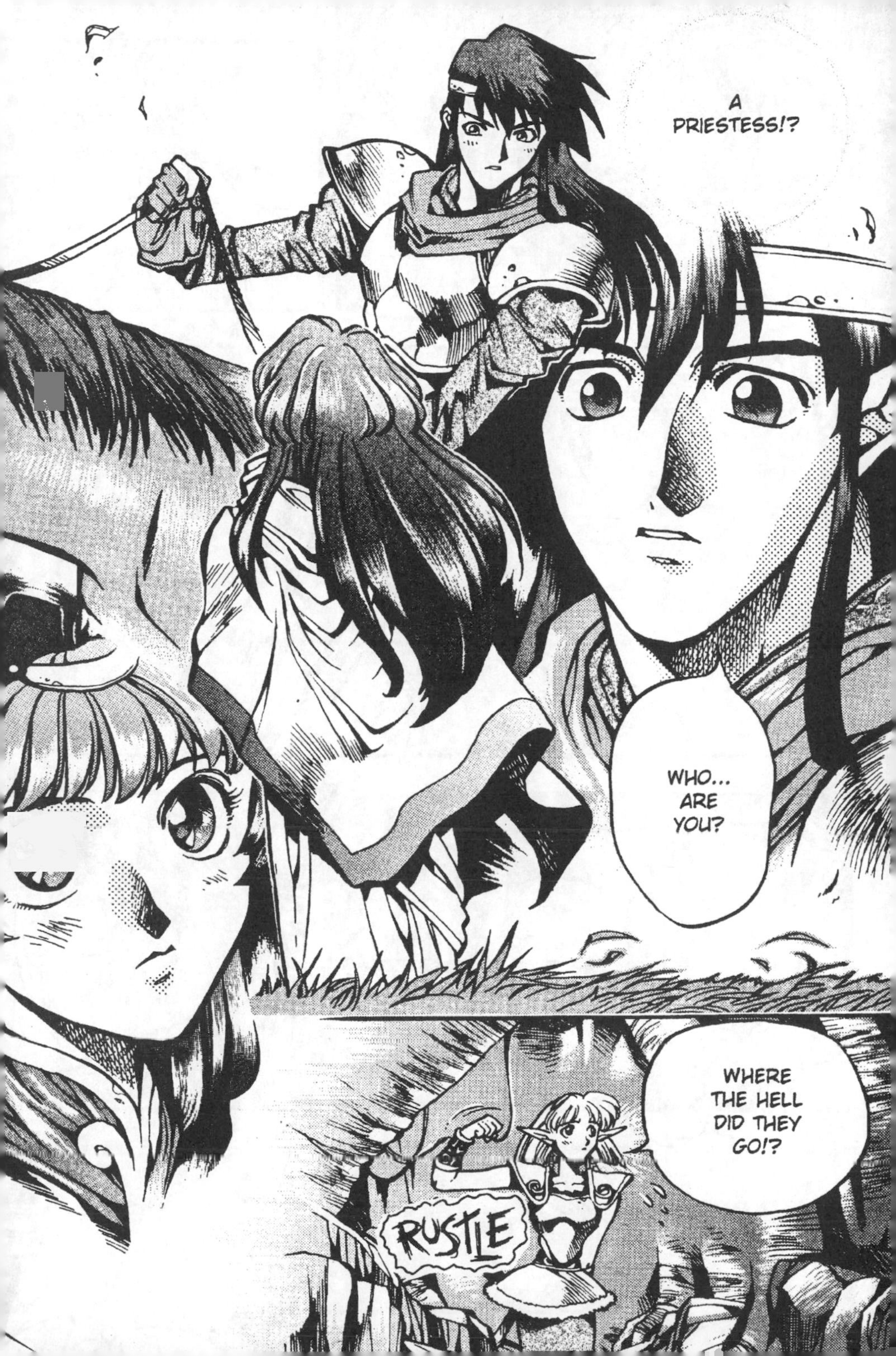
A PRIESTESS!?
WHO... ARE YOU?
WHERE THE HELL DID THEY GO!?
RUSTLE

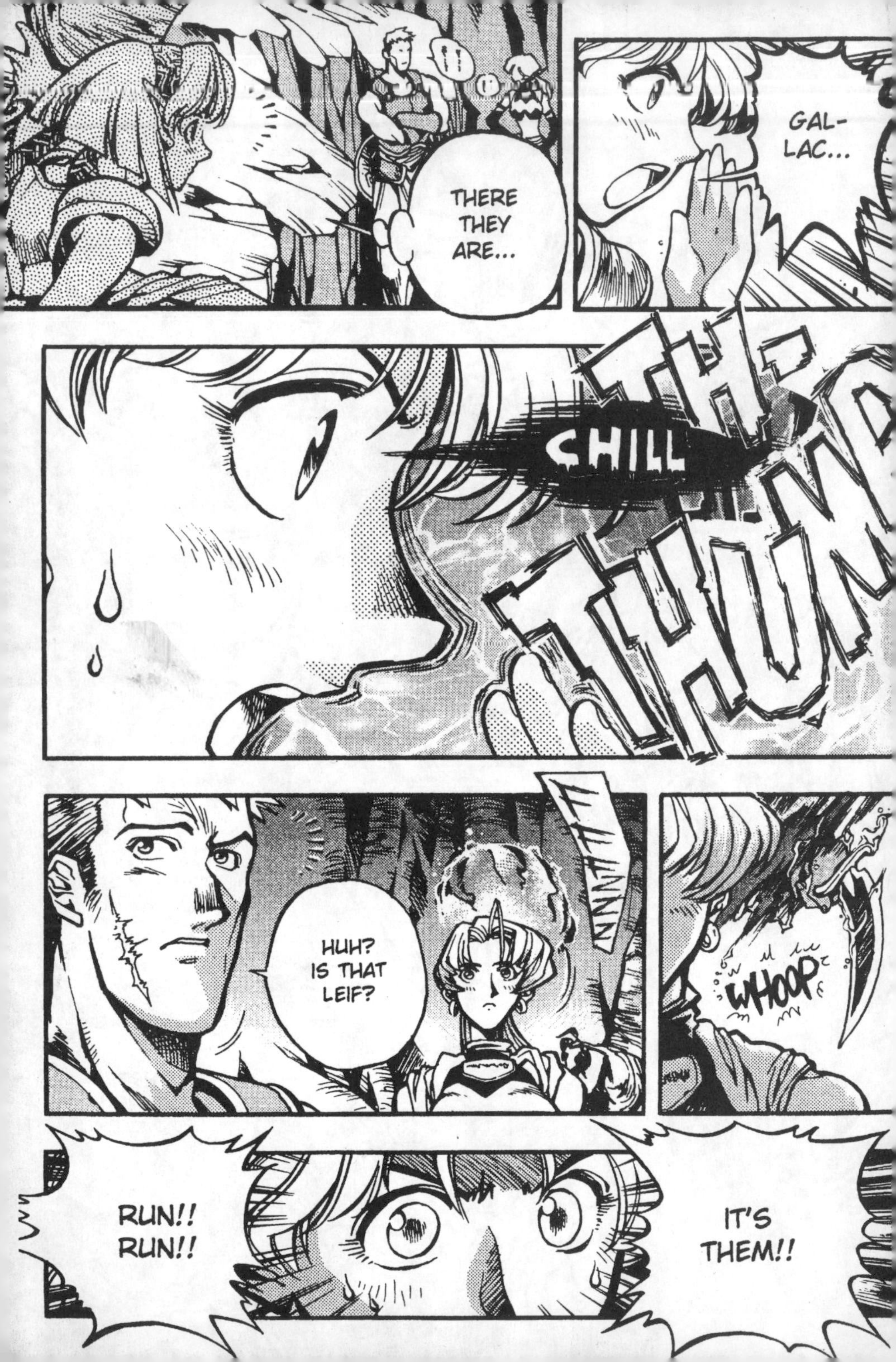
!!
!!
THERE THEY ARE...
GAL-LAC...
CHILL
THUMP
HUH? IS THAT LEIF?
WHOOP
RUN!! RUN!!
IT'S THEM!!

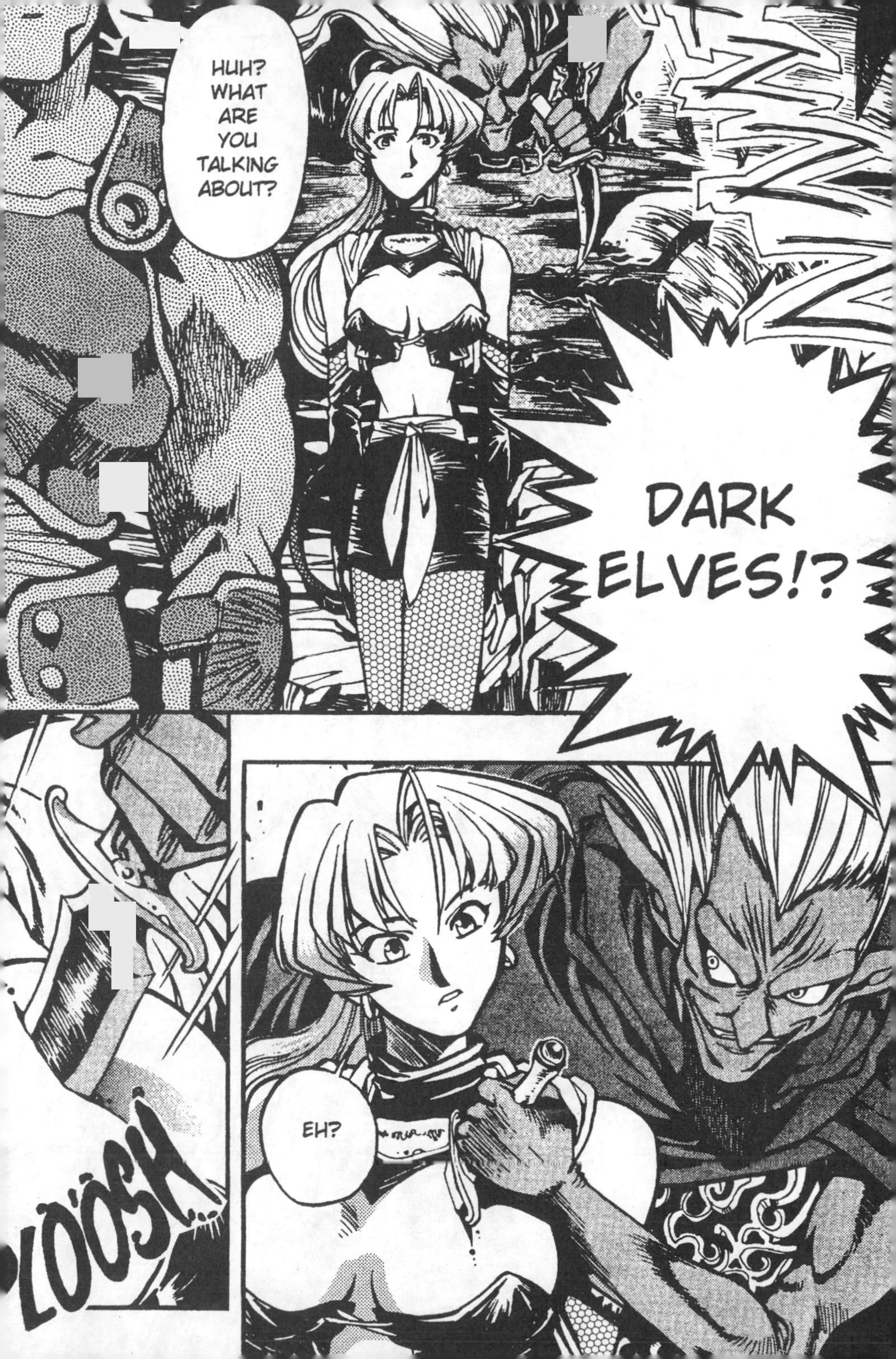
HUH? WHAT ARE YOU TALKING ABOUT?
DARK ELVES!?
OOSH...
EH?

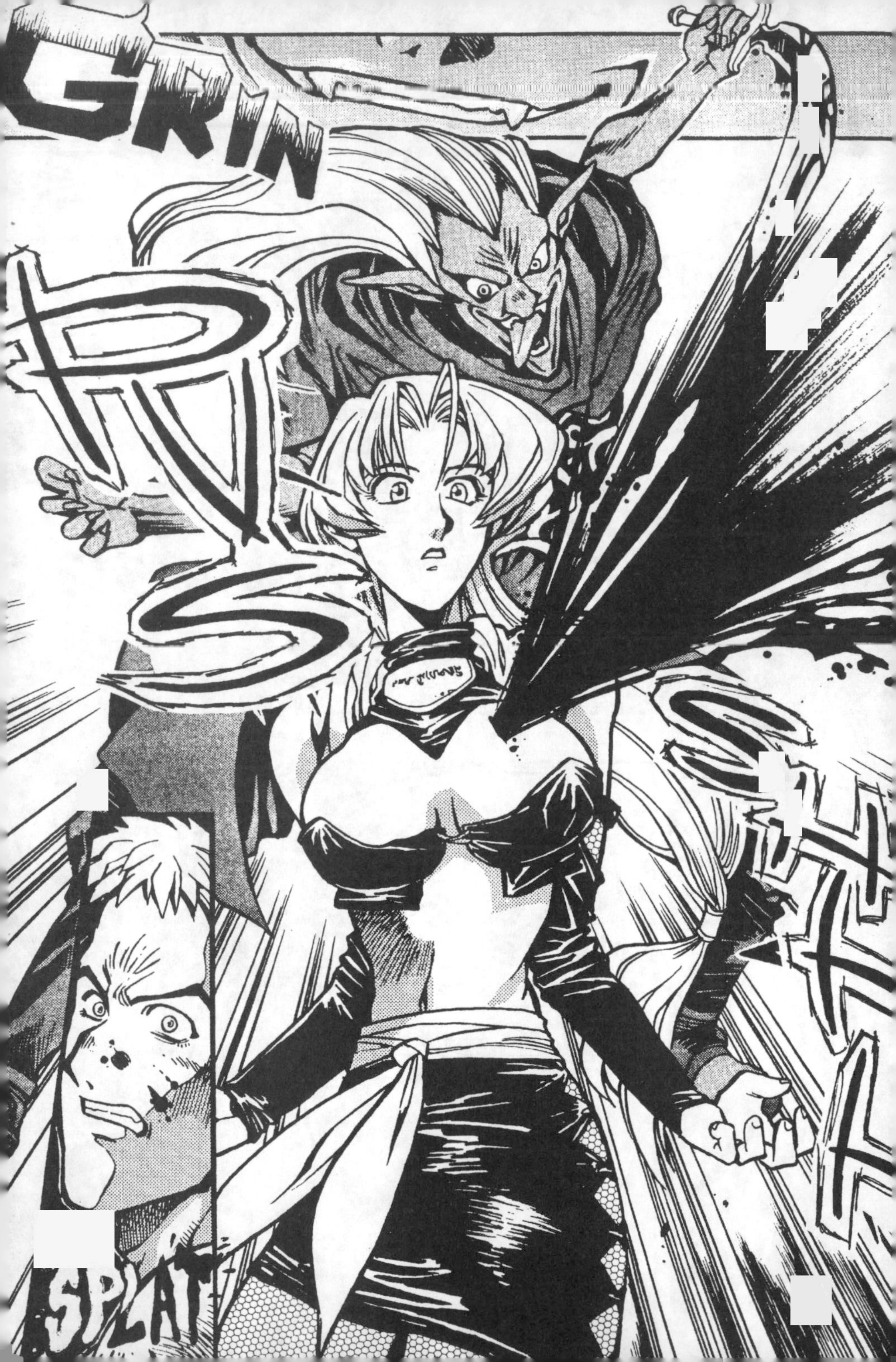
GRIN
SPLAT

# Melody Of The Lady In White

EPISODE 7

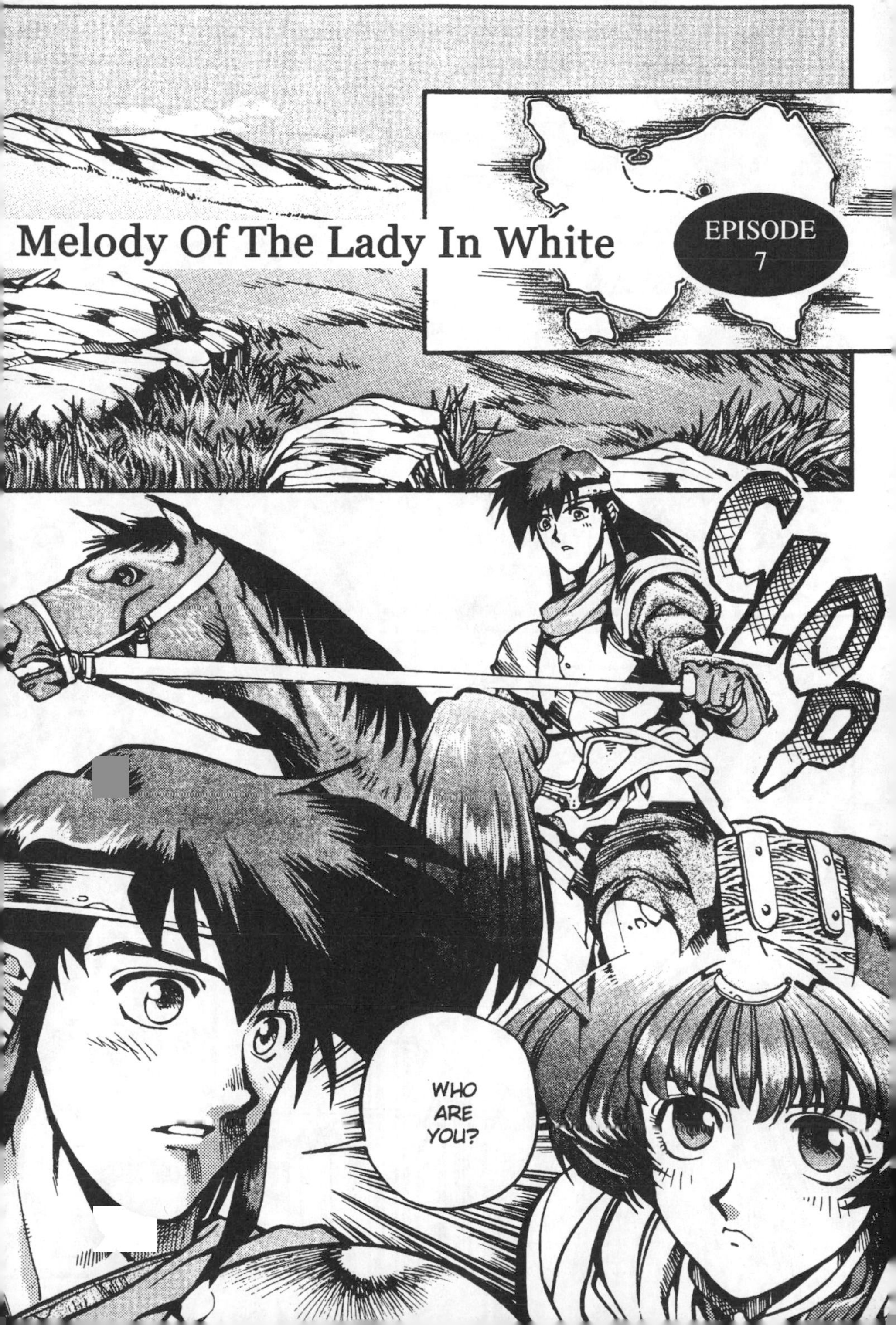
CLOP
WHO ARE YOU?

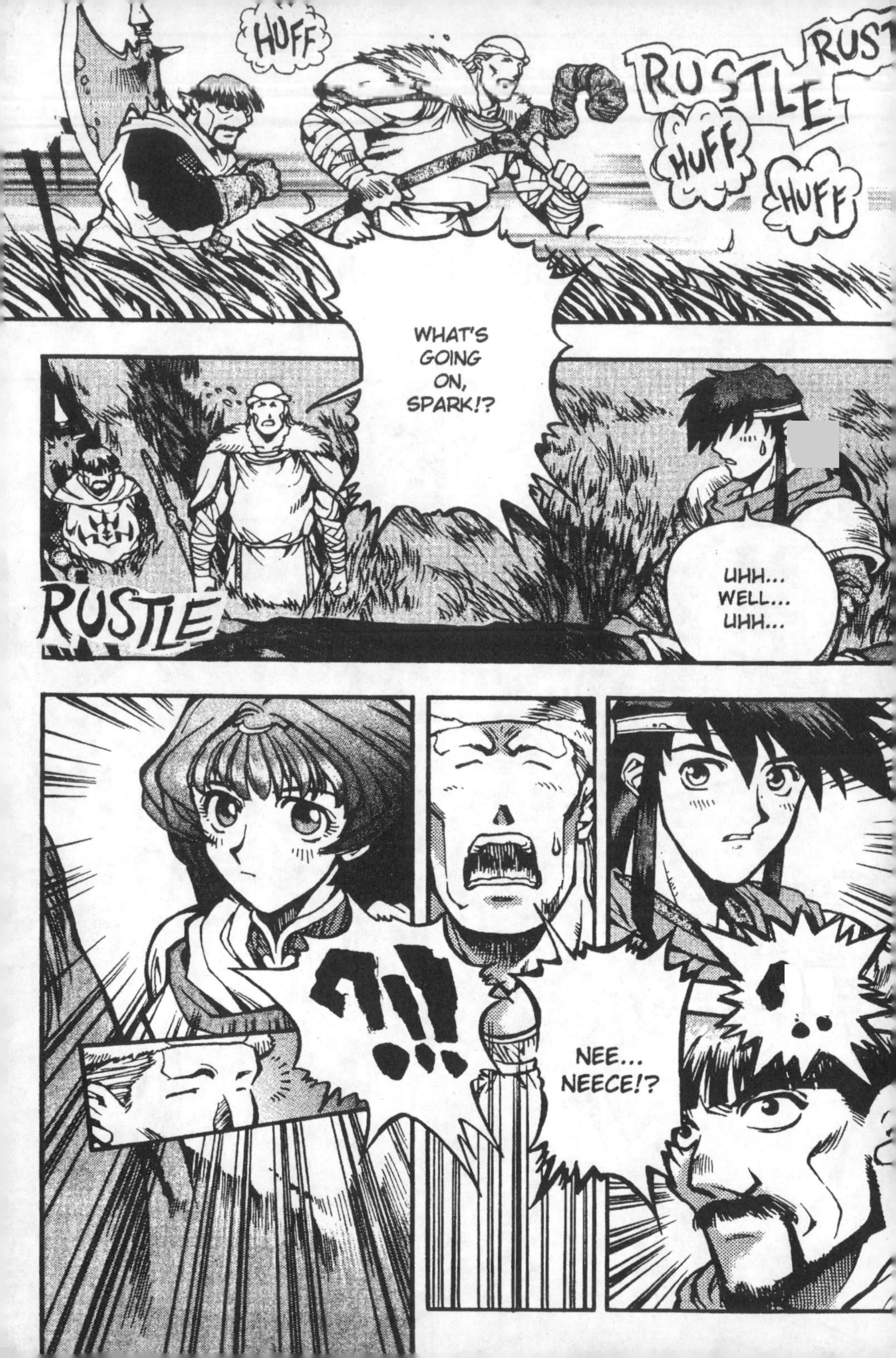
HUFF
RUSTLE
RUST
HUFF
HUFF
WHAT'S GOING ON, SPARK!?
RUSTLE
UHH... WELL... UHH...
!!
NEE... NEECE!?

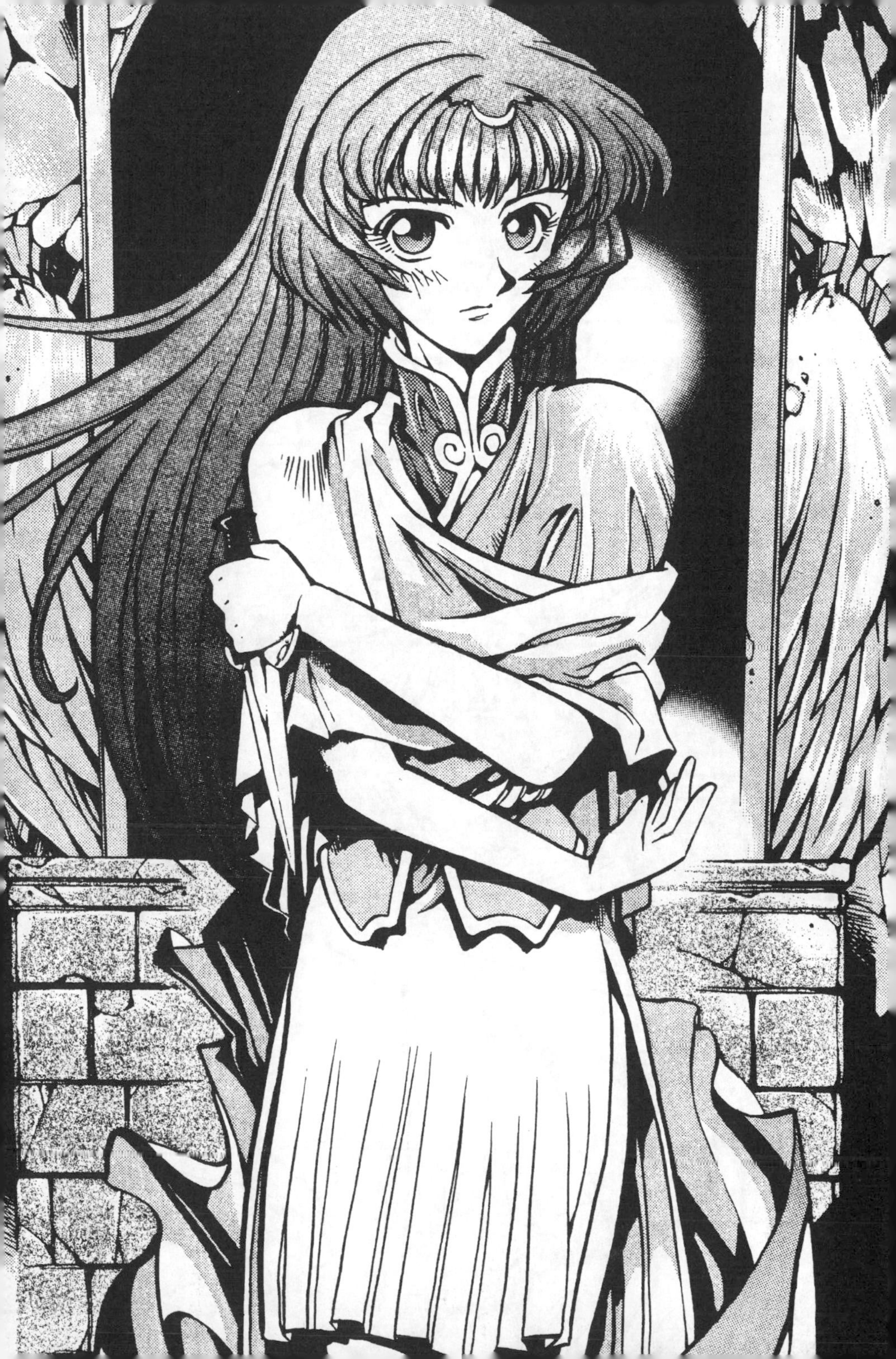

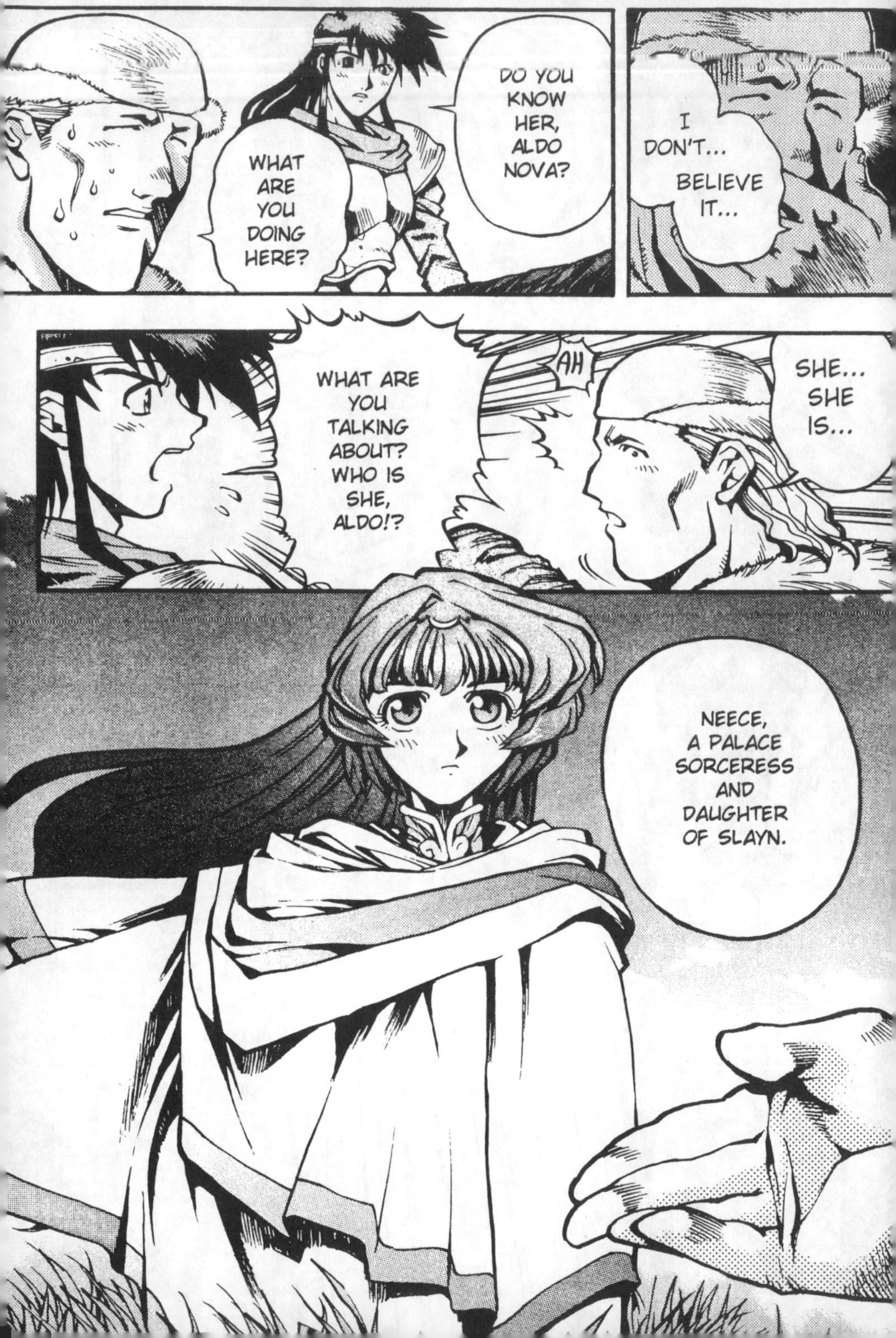
WHAT ARE YOU DOING HERE?
DO YOU KNOW HER, ALDO NOVA?
I DON'T... BELIEVE IT...
WHAT ARE YOU TALKING ABOUT? WHO IS SHE, ALDO!?
AH
SHE... SHE IS...
NEECE, A PALACE SORCERESS AND DAUGHTER OF SLAYN.

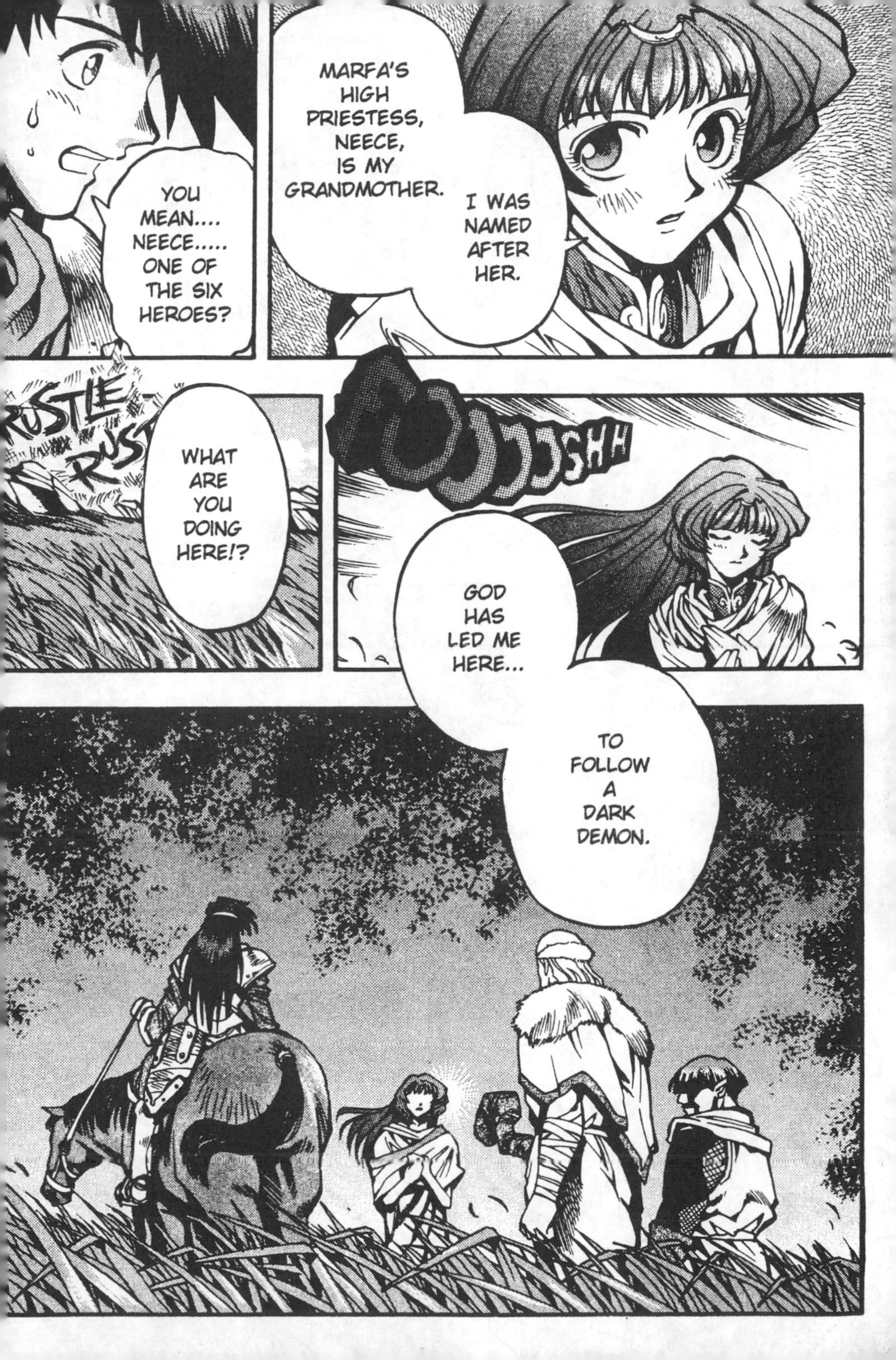
YOU MEAN.... NEECE..... ONE OF THE SIX HEROES?
MARFA'S HIGH PRIESTESS, NEECE, IS MY GRANDMOTHER.
I WAS NAMED AFTER HER.
RUSTLE RUST
WHAT ARE YOU DOING HERE!?
FWOOOOSHH
GOD HAS LED ME HERE...
TO FOLLOW A DARK DEMON.

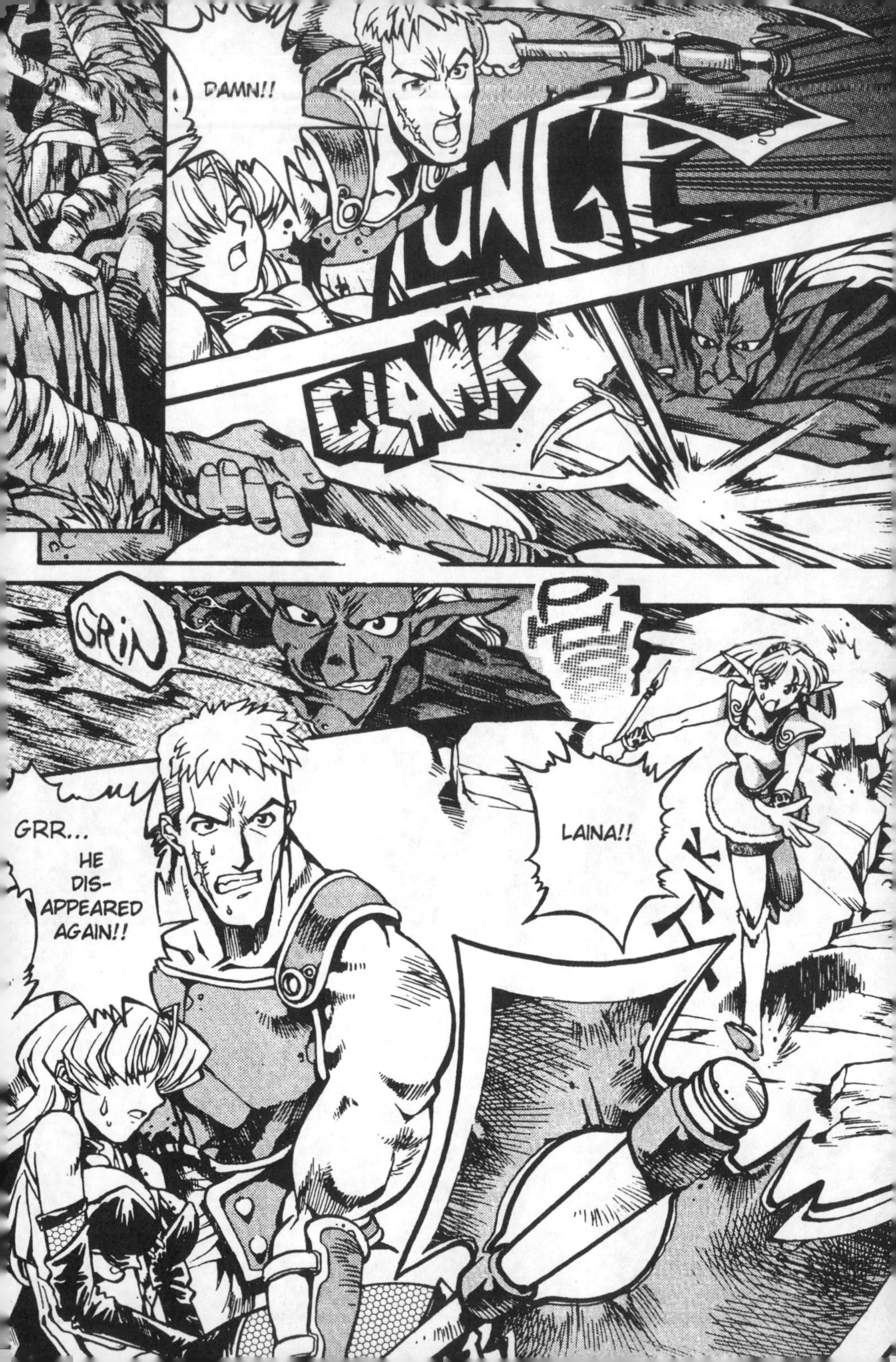
DAMN!!
CLANK
GRIN
GRR... HE DIS-APPEARED AGAIN!!
LAINA!!
TAK

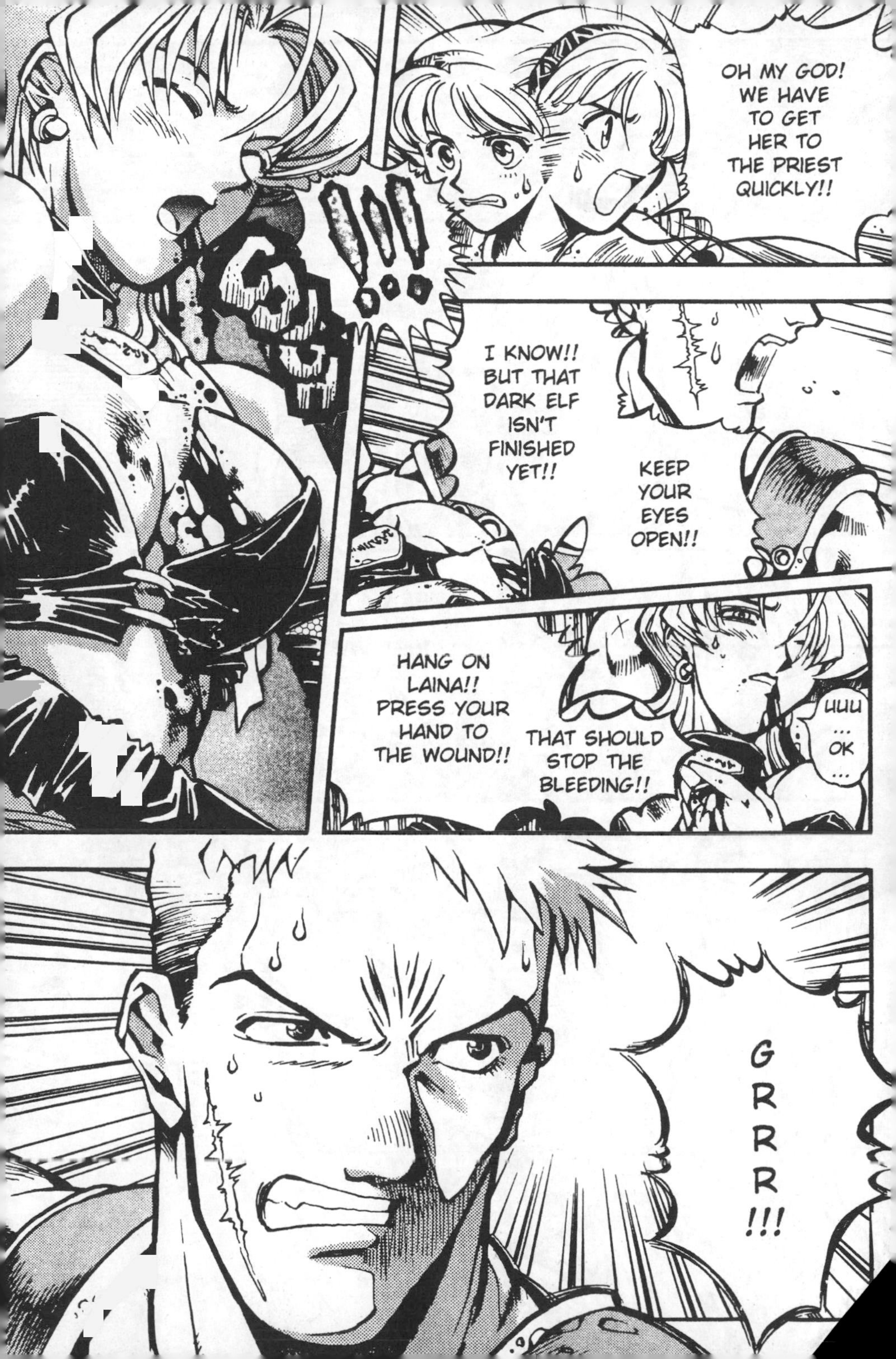

OH MY GOD! WE HAVE TO GET HER TO THE PRIEST QUICKLY!!
I KNOW!! BUT THAT DARK ELF ISN'T FINISHED YET!!
KEEP YOUR EYES OPEN!!
HANG ON LAINA!! PRESS YOUR HAND TO THE WOUND!!
THAT SHOULD STOP THE BLEEDING!!
uuu ... OK ...
GRRR!!!

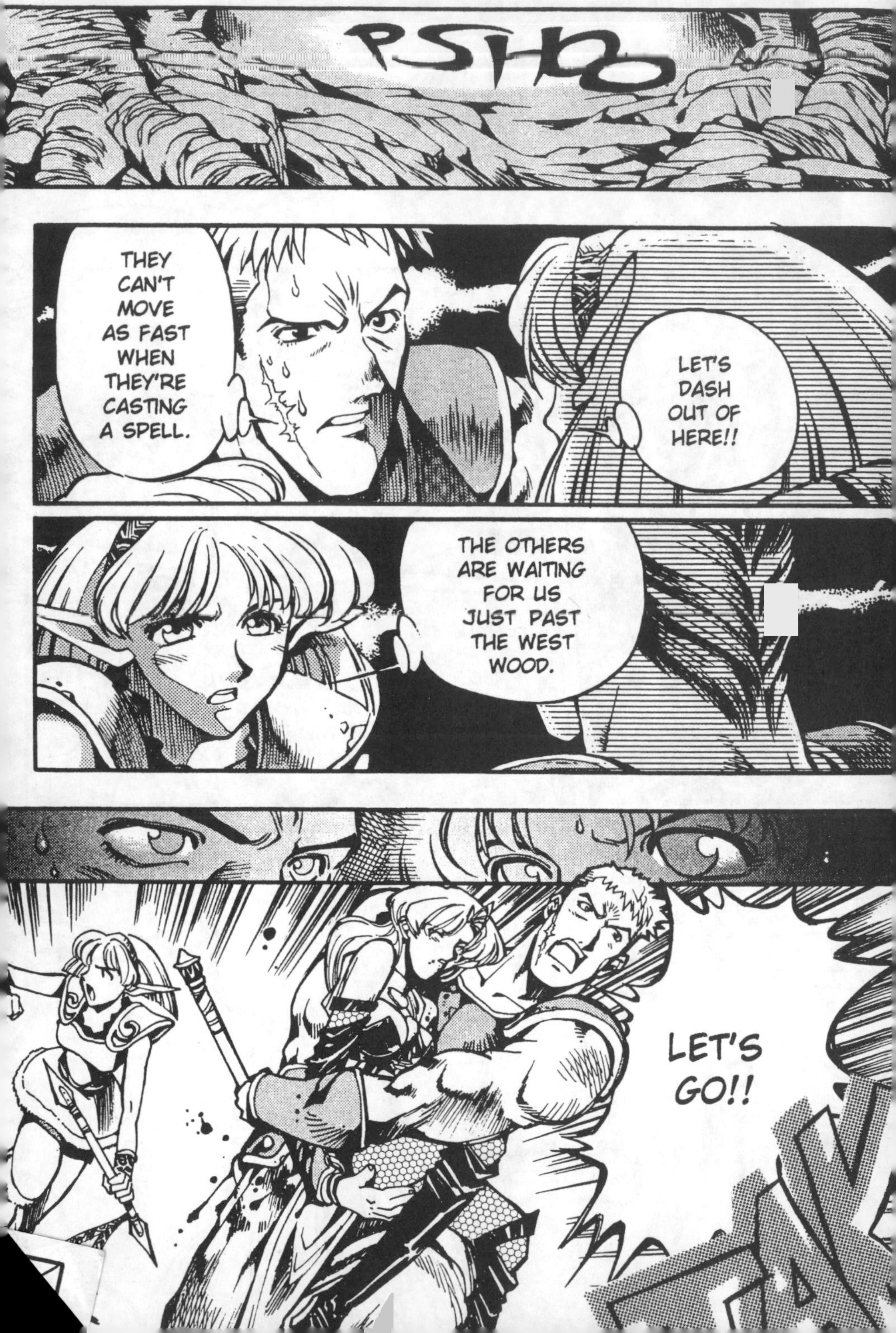
PSHOO
THEY CAN'T MOVE AS FAST WHEN THEY'RE CASTING A SPELL.
LET'S DASH OUT OF HERE!!
THE OTHERS ARE WAITING FOR US JUST PAST THE WEST WOOD.
LET'S GO!!

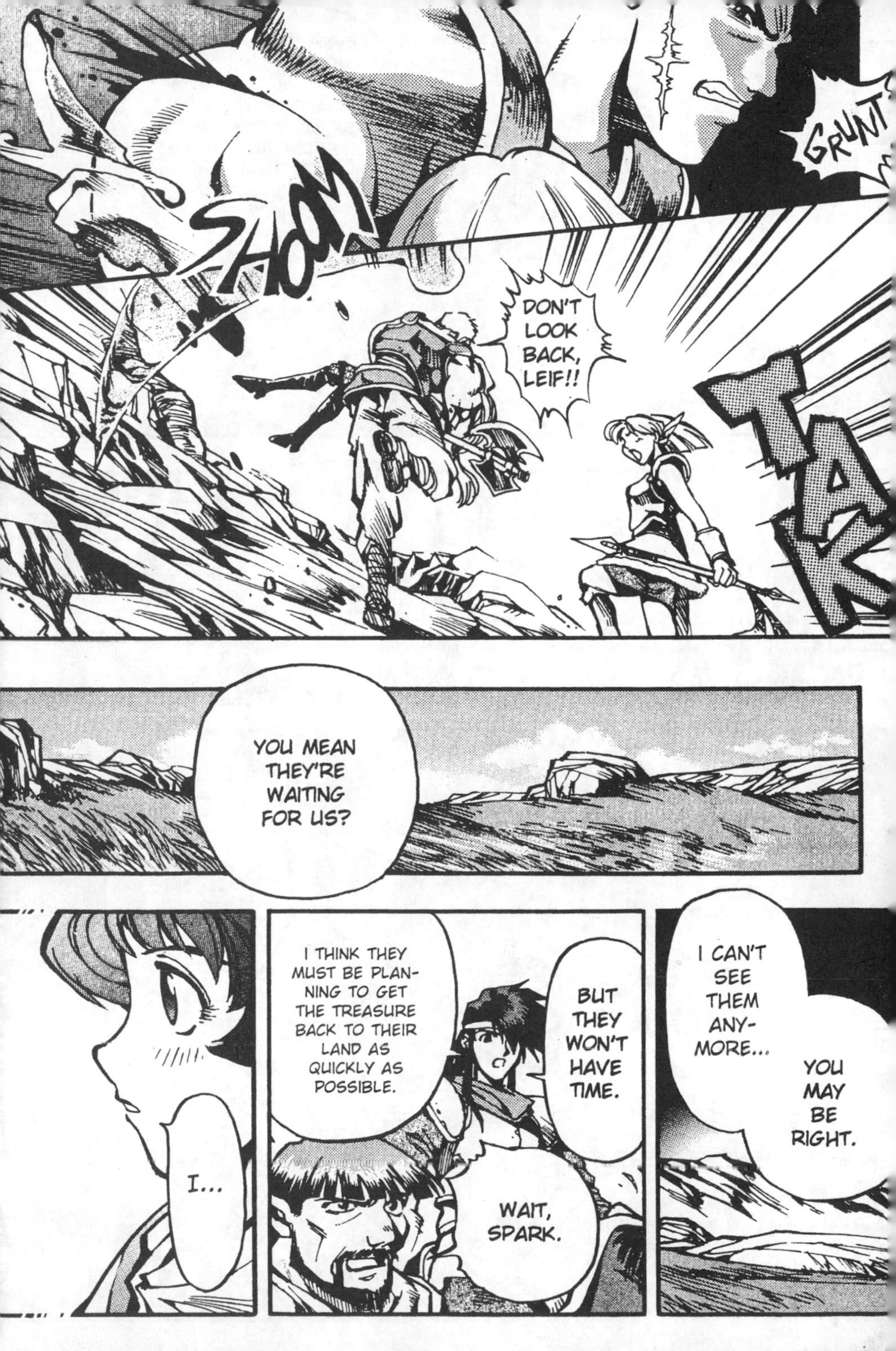
SHOOM!
GRUNT
DON'T LOOK BACK, LEIF!!
TAK
YOU MEAN THEY'RE WAITING FOR US?
I...
I THINK THEY MUST BE PLAN-NING TO GET THE TREASURE BACK TO THEIR LAND AS QUICKLY AS POSSIBLE.
BUT THEY WON'T HAVE TIME.
WAIT, SPARK.
I CAN'T SEE THEM ANY-MORE...
YOU MAY BE RIGHT.

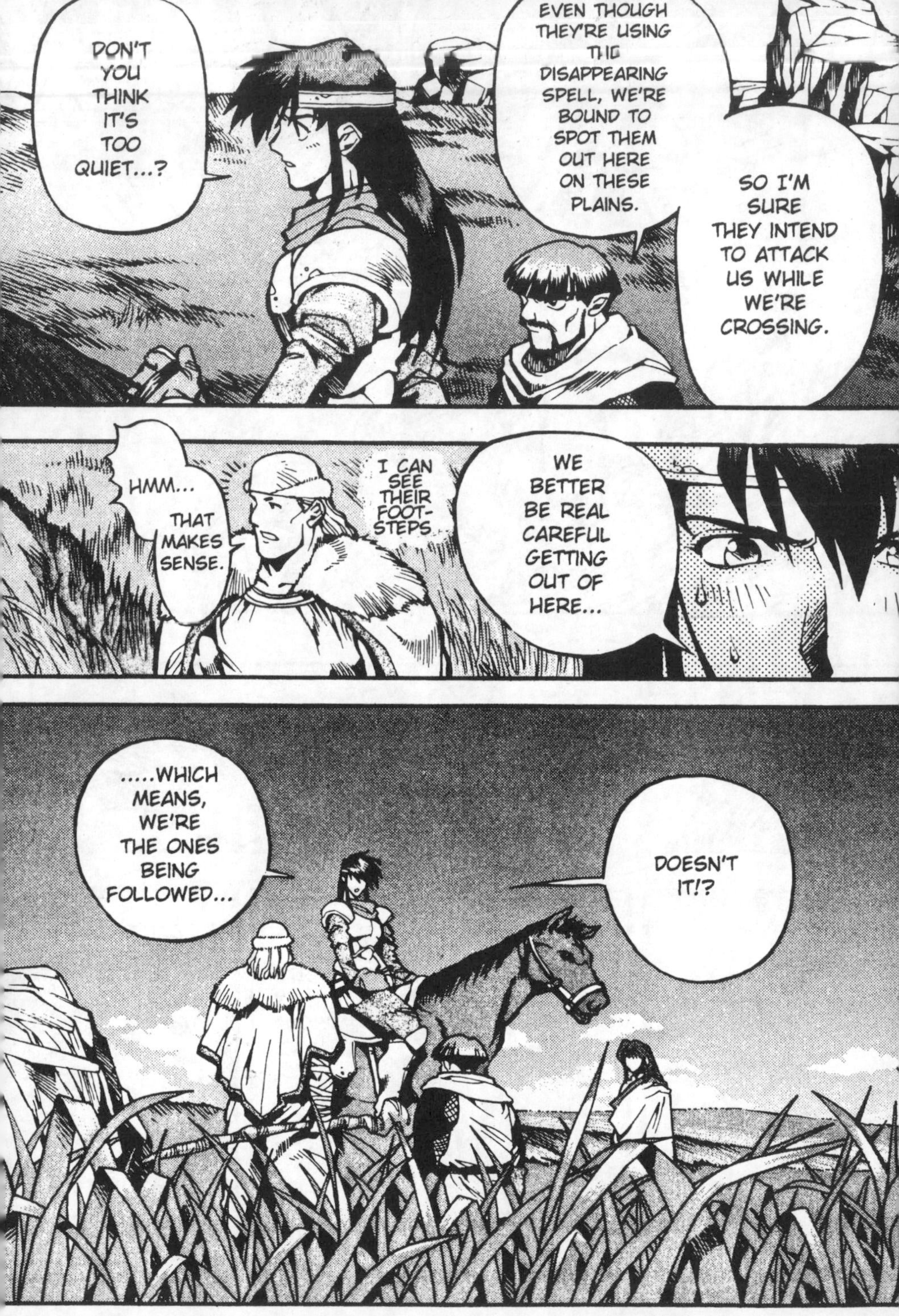
DON'T YOU THINK IT'S TOO QUIET...?
EVEN THOUGH THEY'RE USING THE DISAPPEARING SPELL, WE'RE BOUND TO SPOT THEM OUT HERE ON THESE PLAINS.
SO I'M SURE THEY INTEND TO ATTACK US WHILE WE'RE CROSSING.
HMM...
THAT MAKES SENSE.
I CAN SEE THEIR FOOT-STEPS
WE BETTER BE REAL CAREFUL GETTING OUT OF HERE...
.....WHICH MEANS, WE'RE THE ONES BEING FOLLOWED...
DOESN'T IT!?

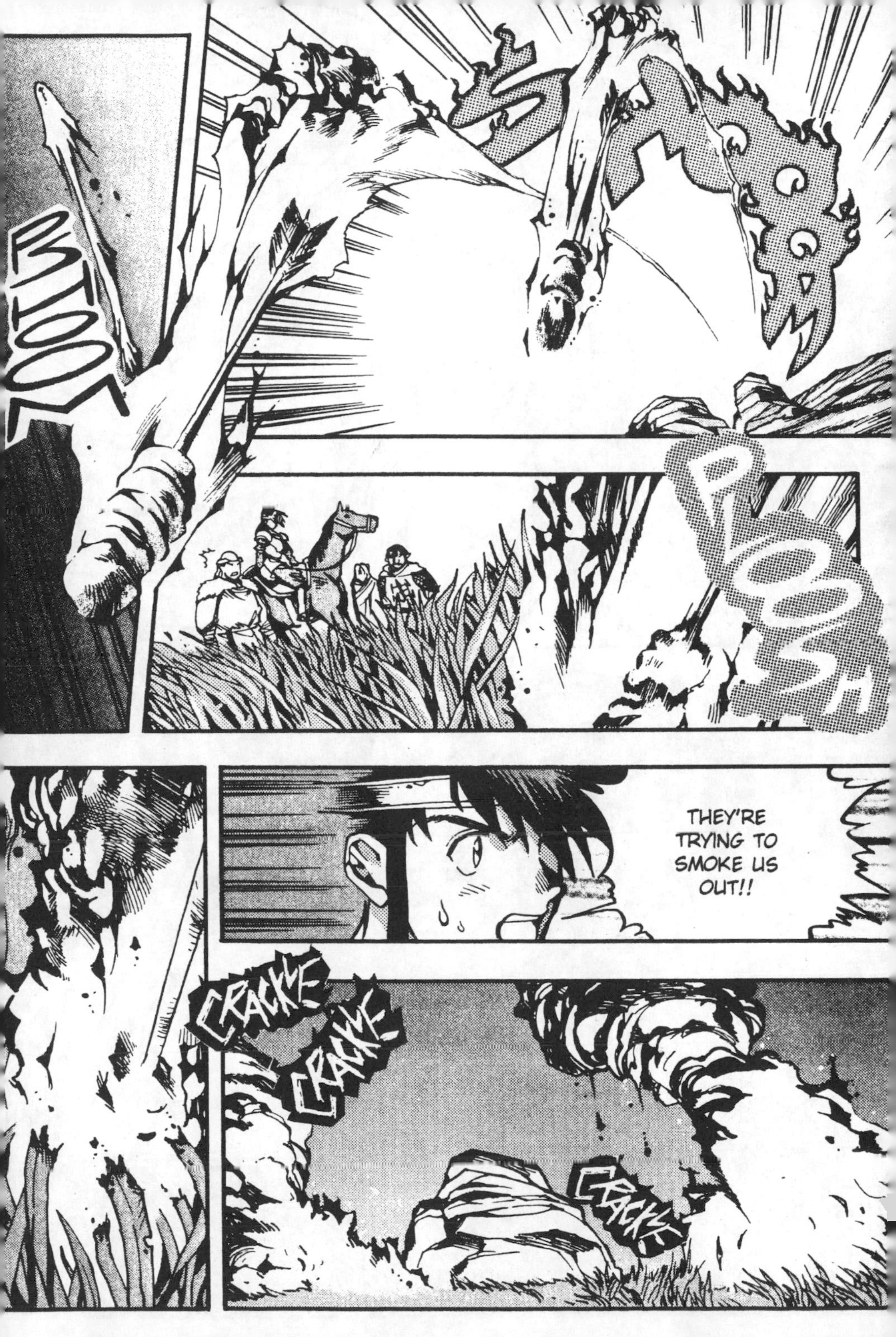
PWOOSH
THEY'RE TRYING TO SMOKE US OUT!!
CRACKLE
CRACKLE
CRACKLE

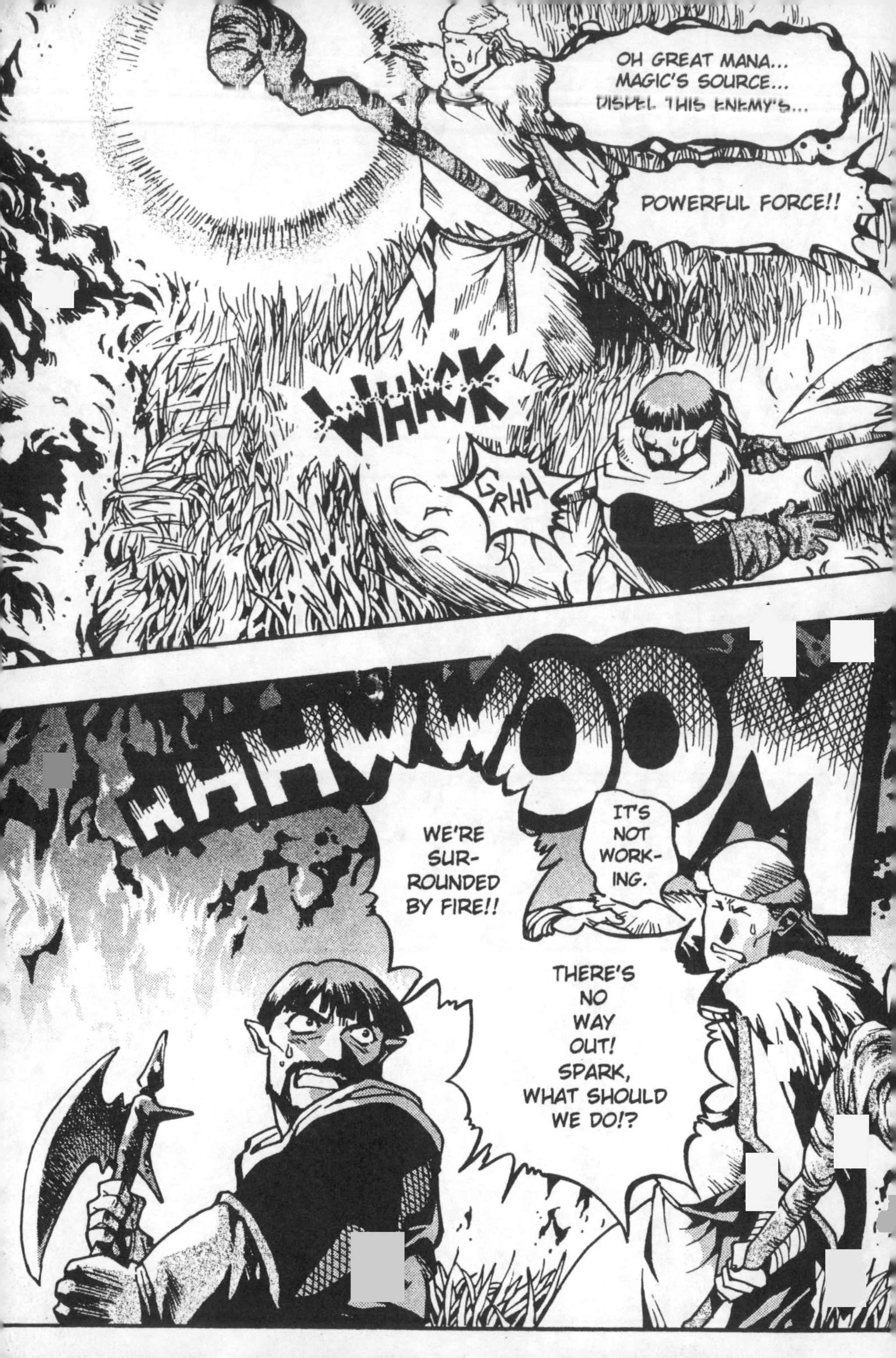
OH GREAT MANA... MAGIC'S SOURCE... DISPEL THIS ENEMY'S...
POWERFUL FORCE!!
WHACK
GRHH
WE'RE SUR-ROUNDED BY FIRE!!
IT'S NOT WORK-ING.
THERE'S NO WAY OUT! SPARK, WHAT SHOULD WE DO!?

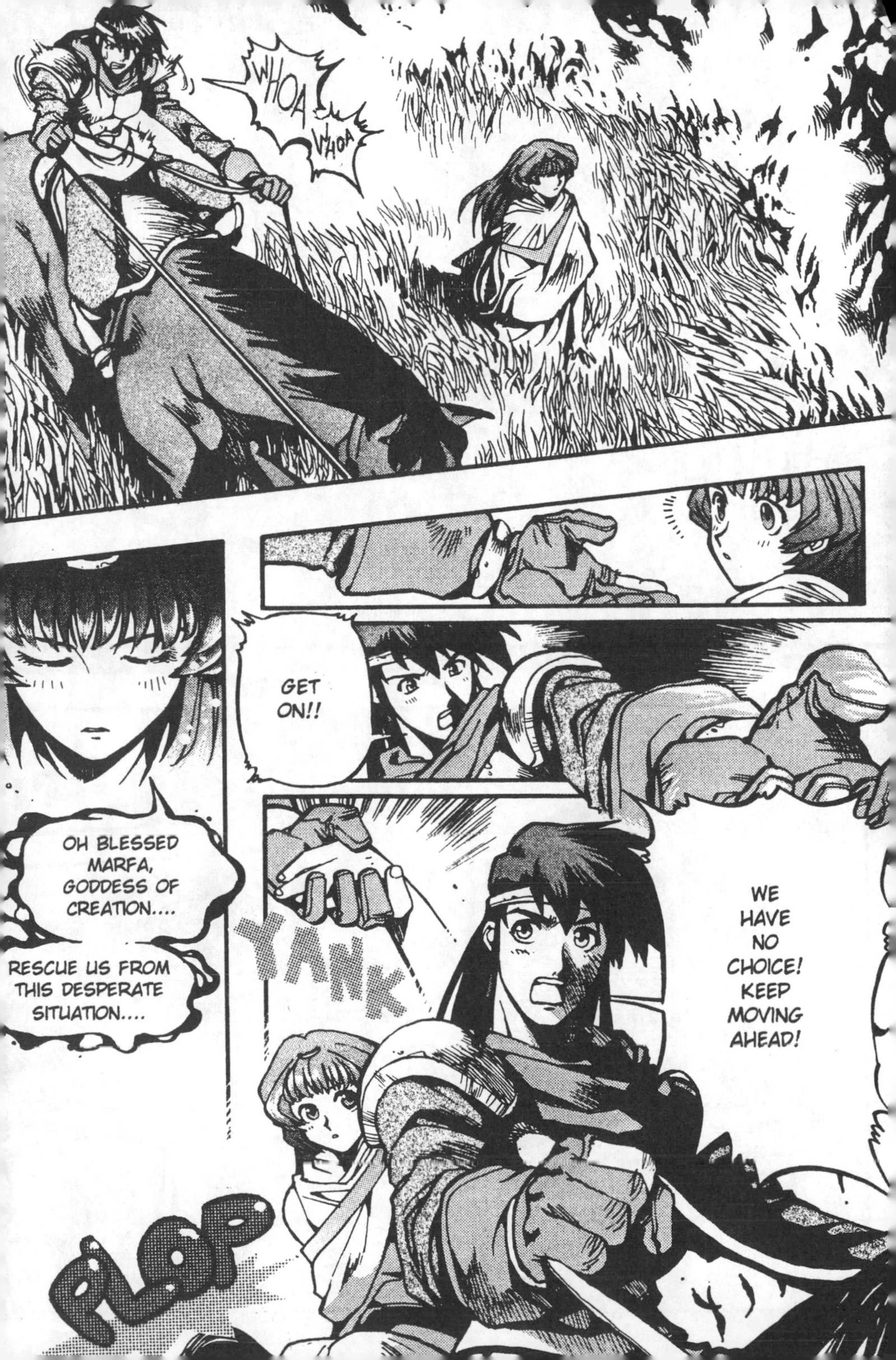
WHOA
WHOA
OH BLESSED MARFA, GODDESS OF CREATION....
RESCUE US FROM THIS DESPERATE SITUATION....
GET ON!!
YANK
WE HAVE NO CHOICE! KEEP MOVING AHEAD!
PLOP

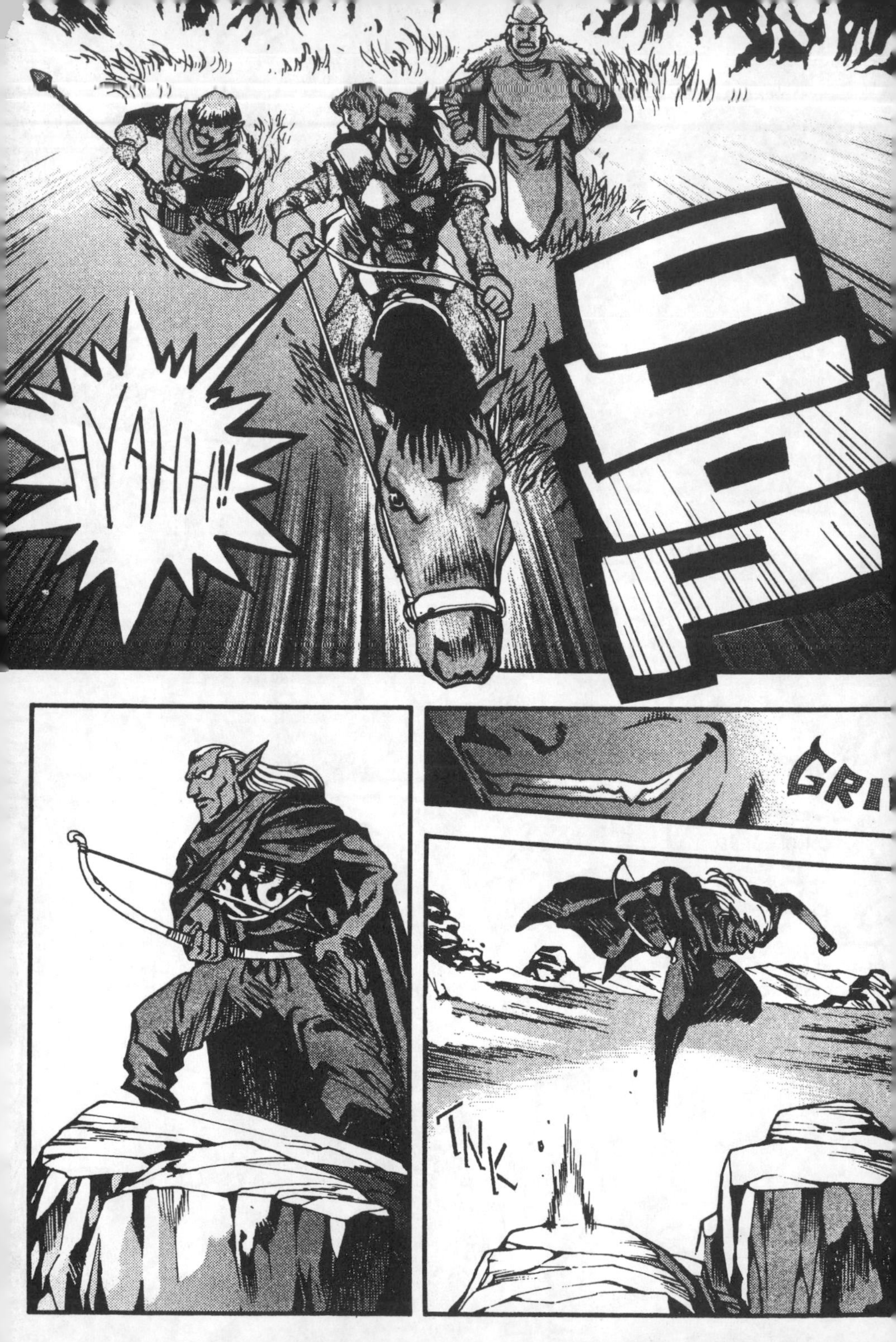
HYAHH!!
GRI
TINK

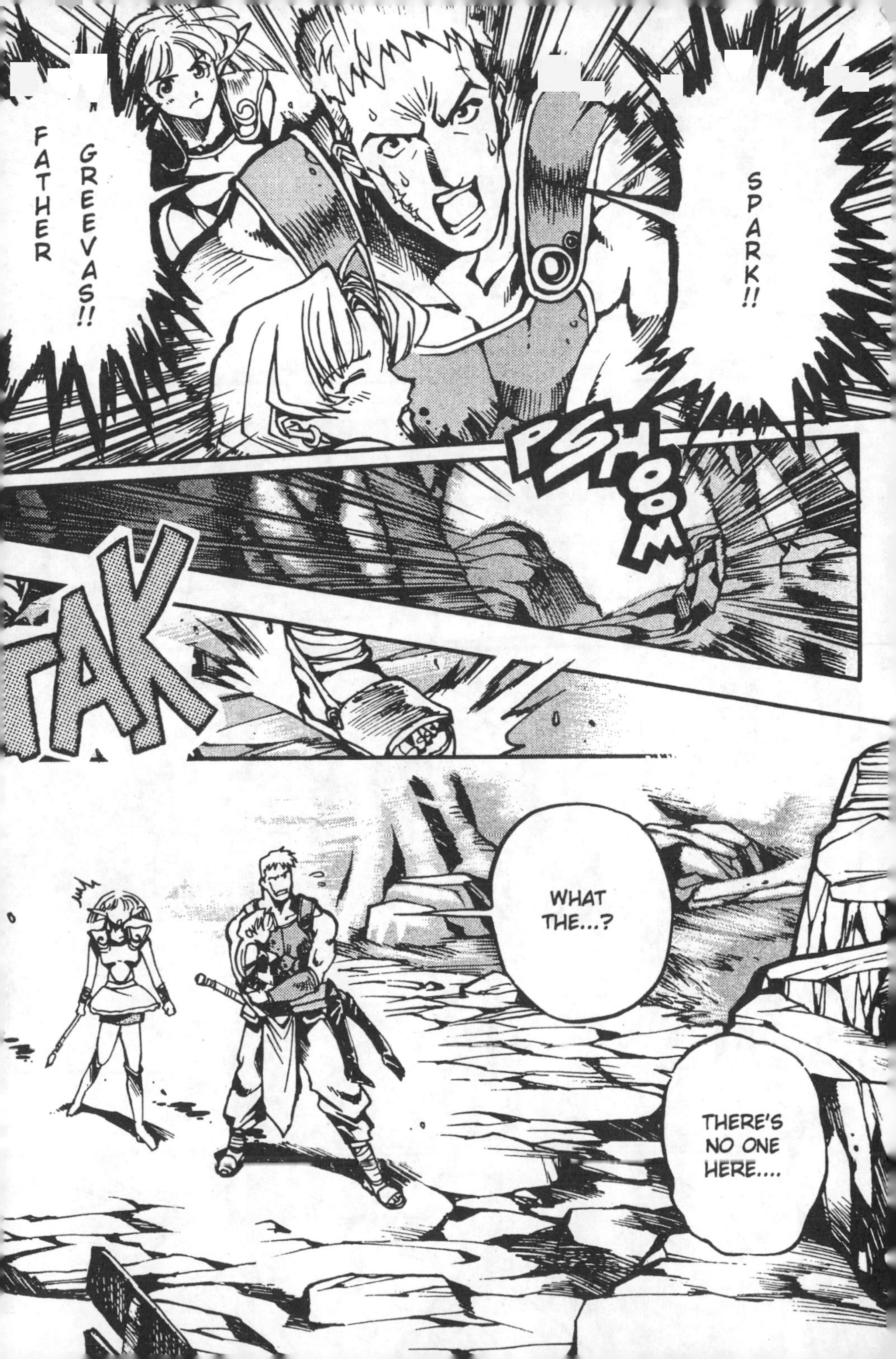
FATHER GREEVAS!!
SPARK!!
PSHOOM
TAK
WHAT THE...?
THERE'S NO ONE HERE....

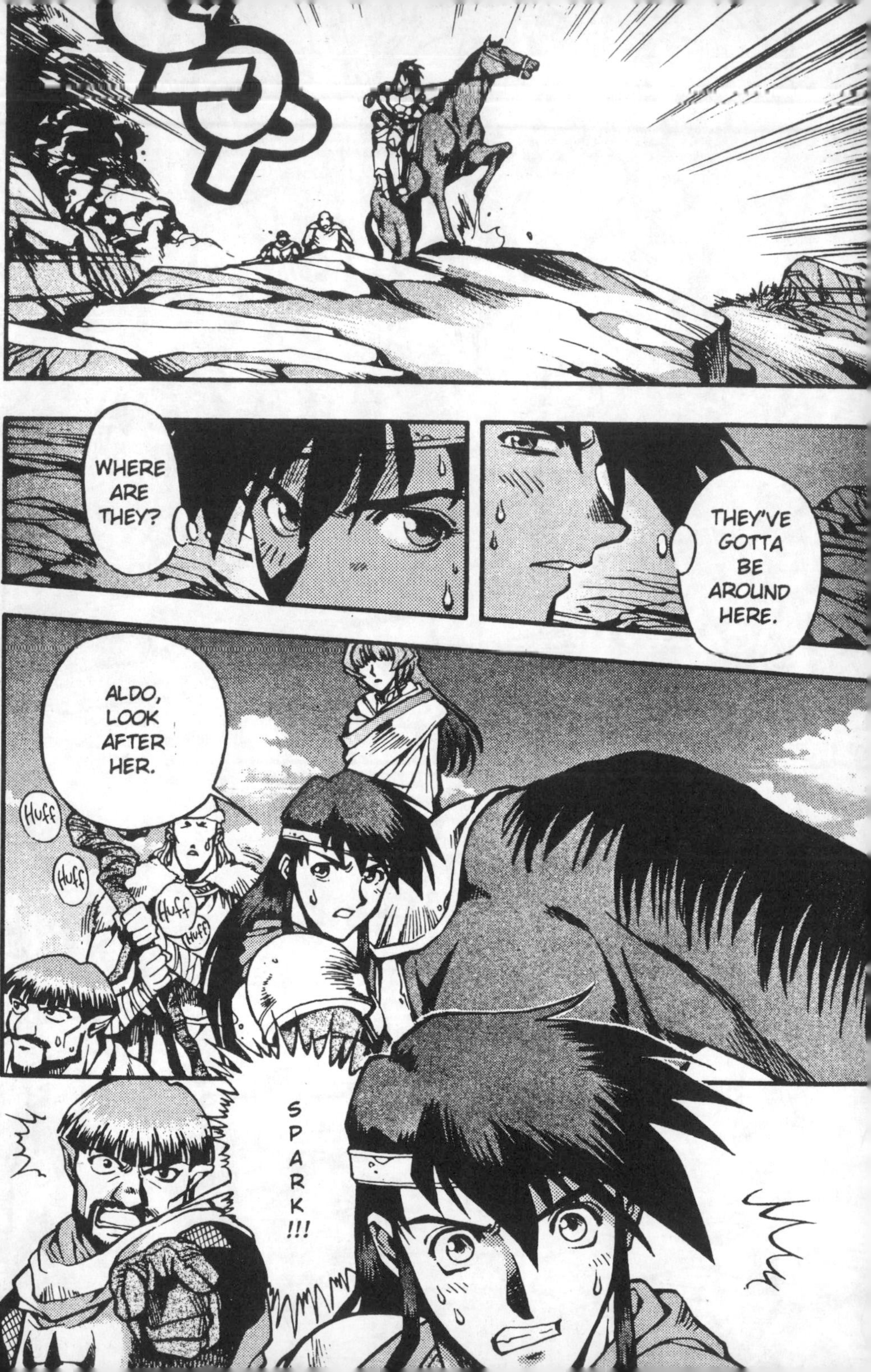
CLOP
WHERE ARE THEY?
THEY'VE GOTTA BE AROUND HERE.
ALDO, LOOK AFTER HER.
Huff
Huff
Huff
Huff
SPARK!!!

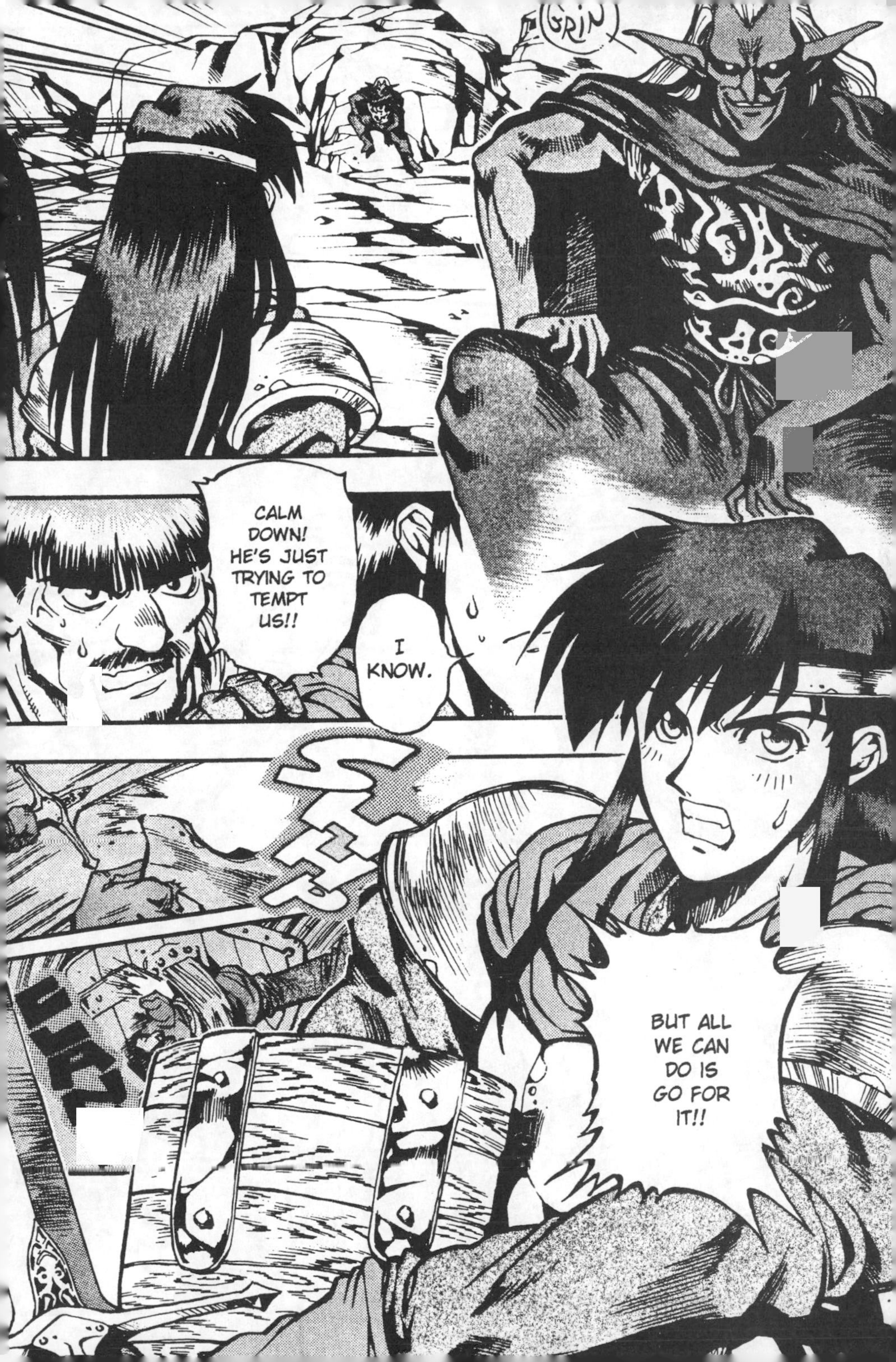
GRIN
CALM DOWN! HE'S JUST TRYING TO TEMPT US!!
I KNOW.
BUT ALL WE CAN DO IS GO FOR IT!!

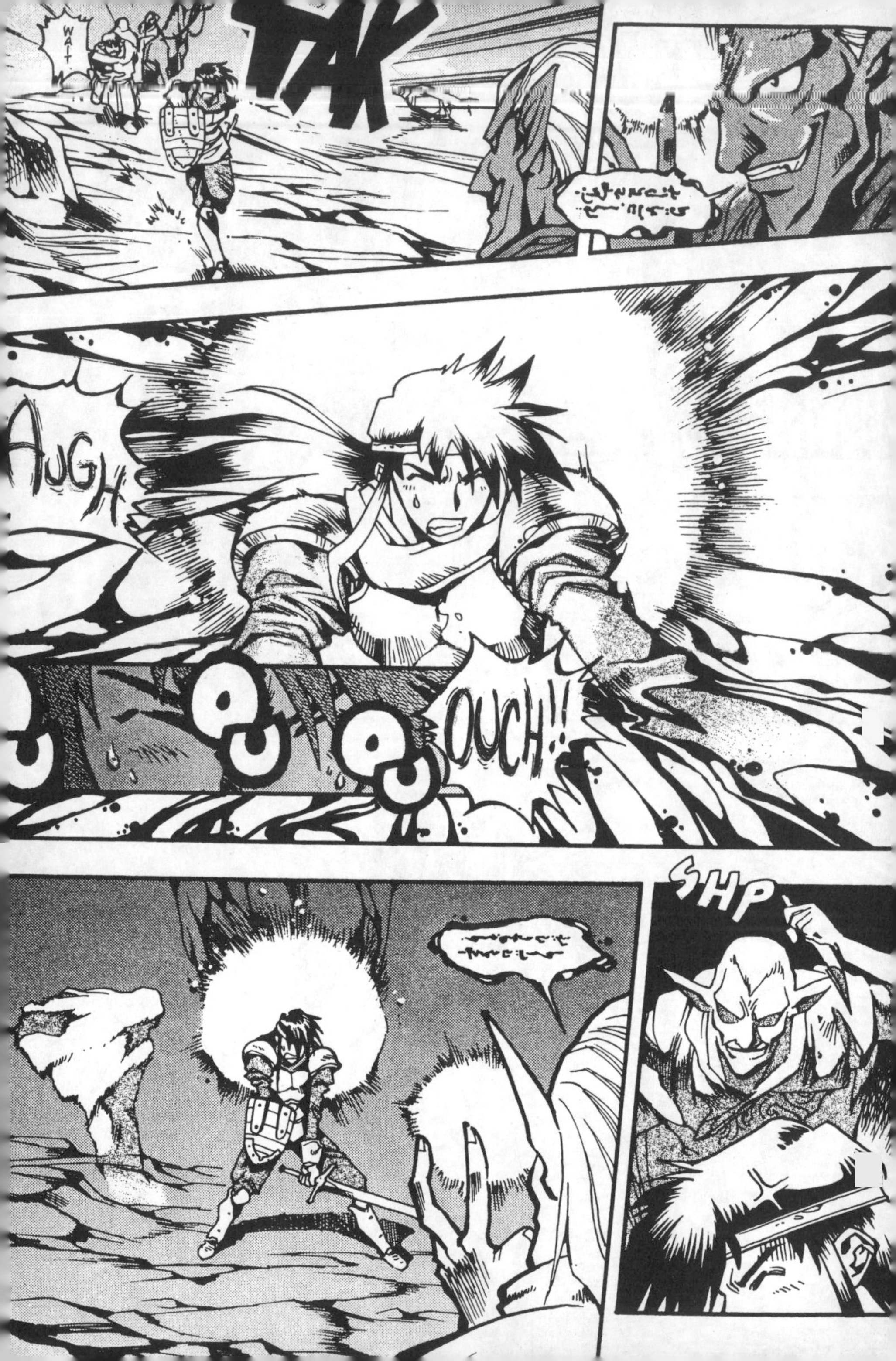
WAIT
TAK
AUGH
OUCH!!
SHP

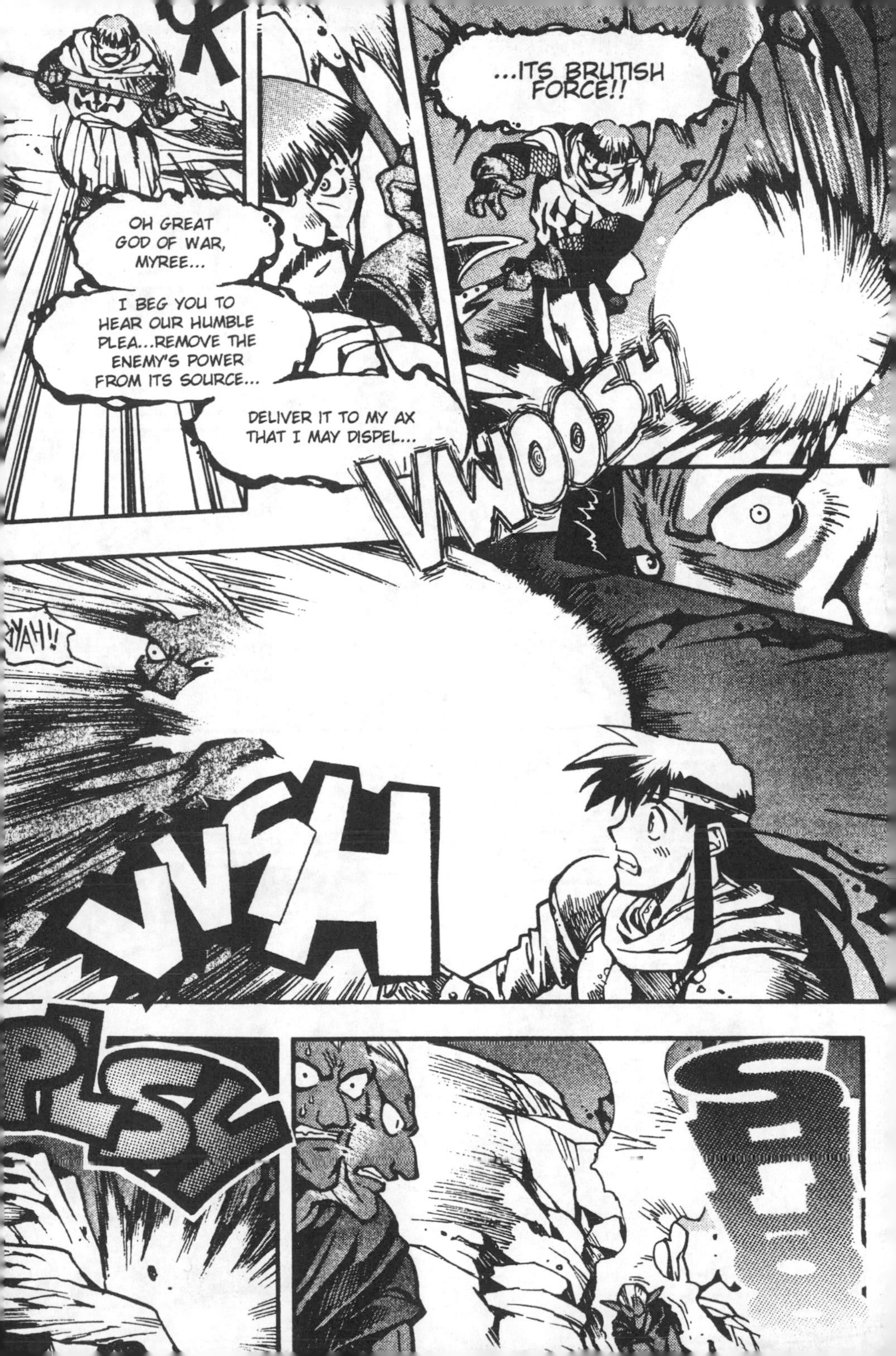
OH GREAT GOD OF WAR, MYREE...
I BEG YOU TO HEAR OUR HUMBLE PLEA...REMOVE THE ENEMY'S POWER FROM ITS SOURCE...
DELIVER IT TO MY AX THAT I MAY DISPEL...
...ITS BRUTISH FORCE!!
VWOOSH
YAH!!
VWSH
PLSH

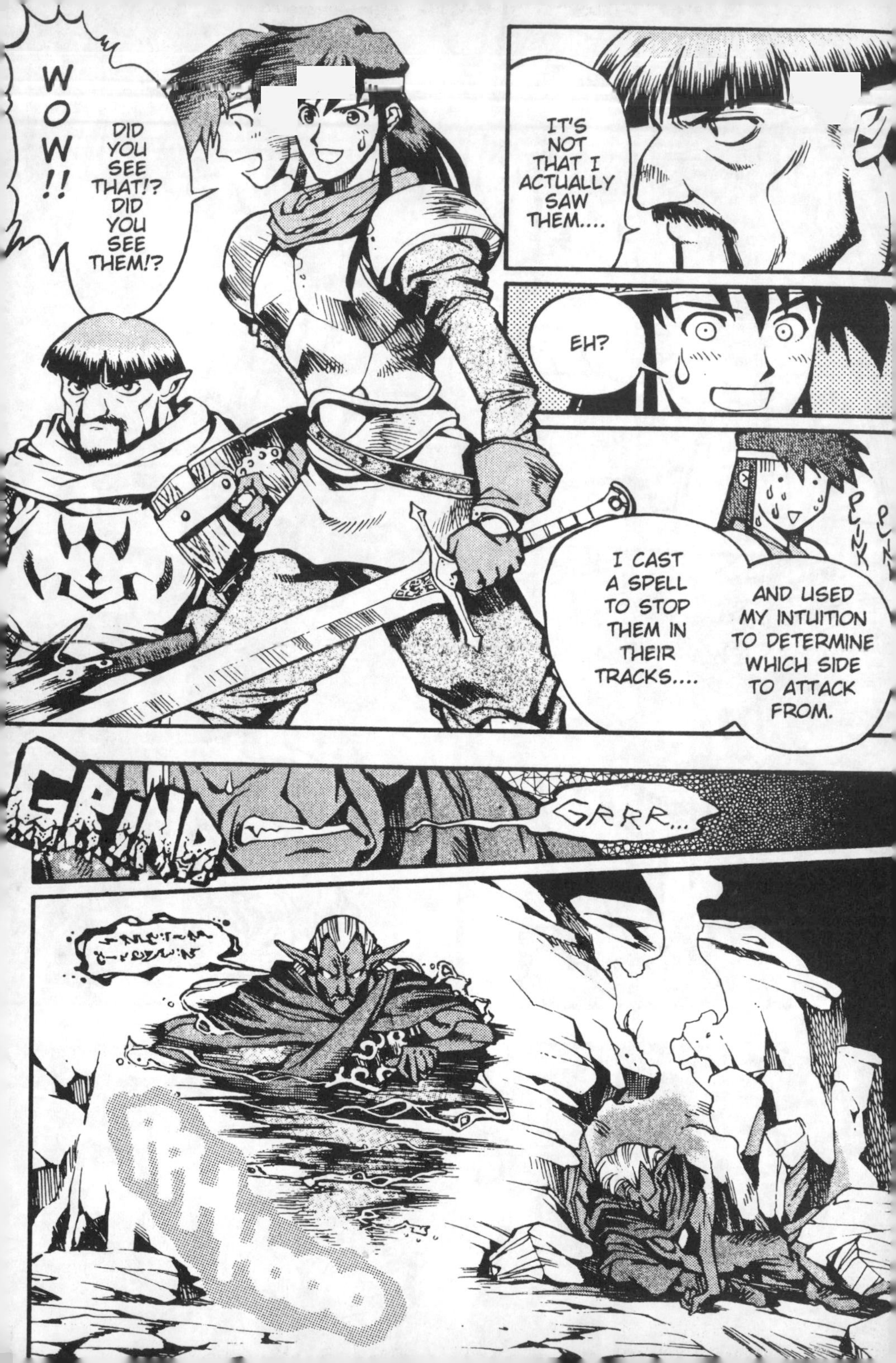
WOW!!
DID YOU SEE THAT!? DID YOU SEE THEM!?
IT'S NOT THAT I ACTUALLY SAW THEM....
EH?
I CAST A SPELL TO STOP THEM IN THEIR TRACKS....
AND USED MY INTUITION TO DETERMINE WHICH SIDE TO ATTACK FROM.
GRIND
GRRR...

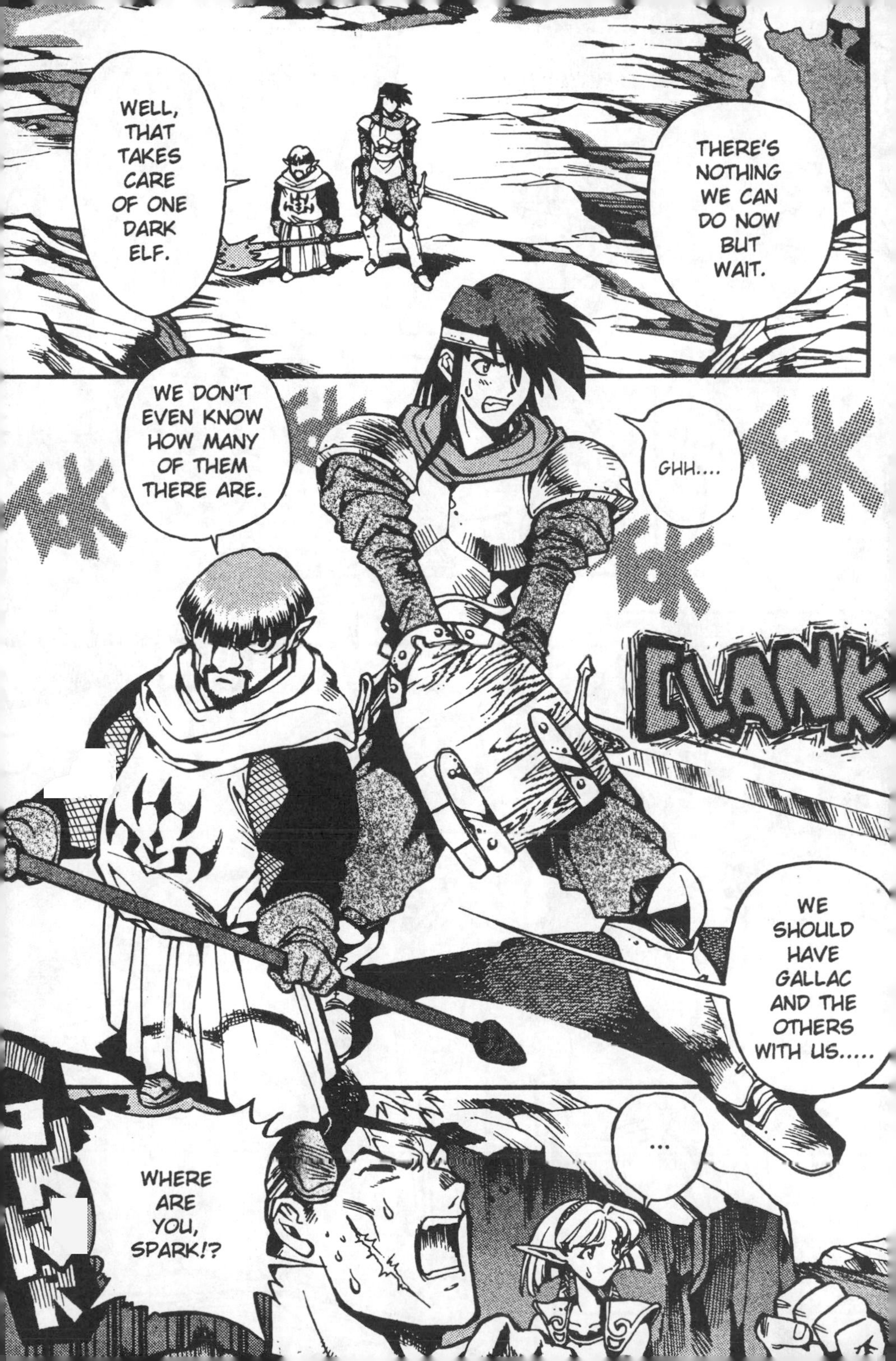
WELL, THAT TAKES CARE OF ONE DARK ELF.
THERE'S NOTHING WE CAN DO NOW BUT WAIT.
WE DON'T EVEN KNOW HOW MANY OF THEM THERE ARE.
GHH....
CLANK
WE SHOULD HAVE GALLAC AND THE OTHERS WITH US.....
WHERE ARE YOU, SPARK!?
...

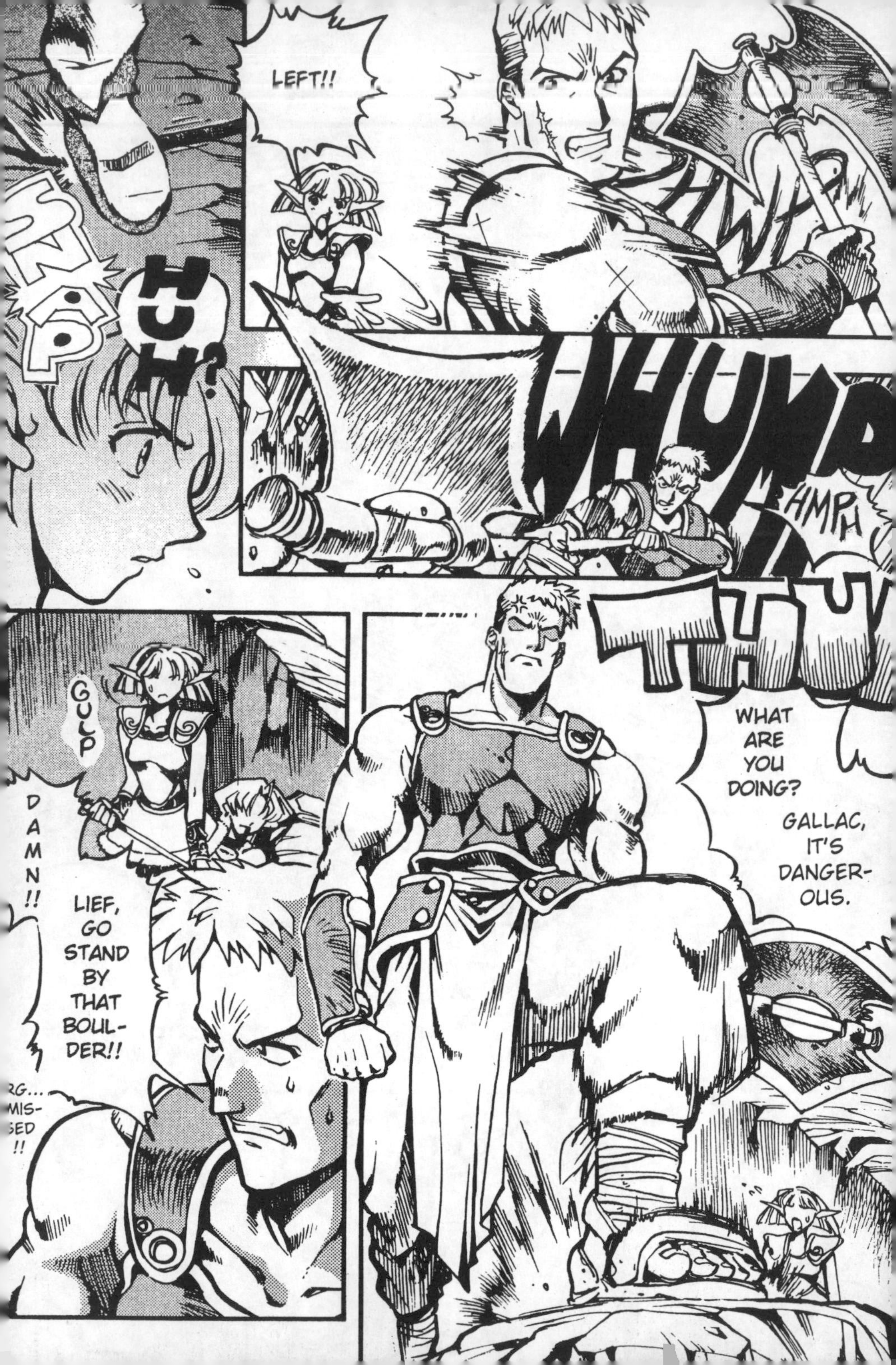

SNAP
HUH?
LEFT!!
WHUMP
HAMPH
GULP
DAMN!!
LIEF, GO STAND BY THAT BOULDER!!
RG... MISSED!!
THU
WHAT ARE YOU DOING?
GALLAC, IT'S DANGEROUS.

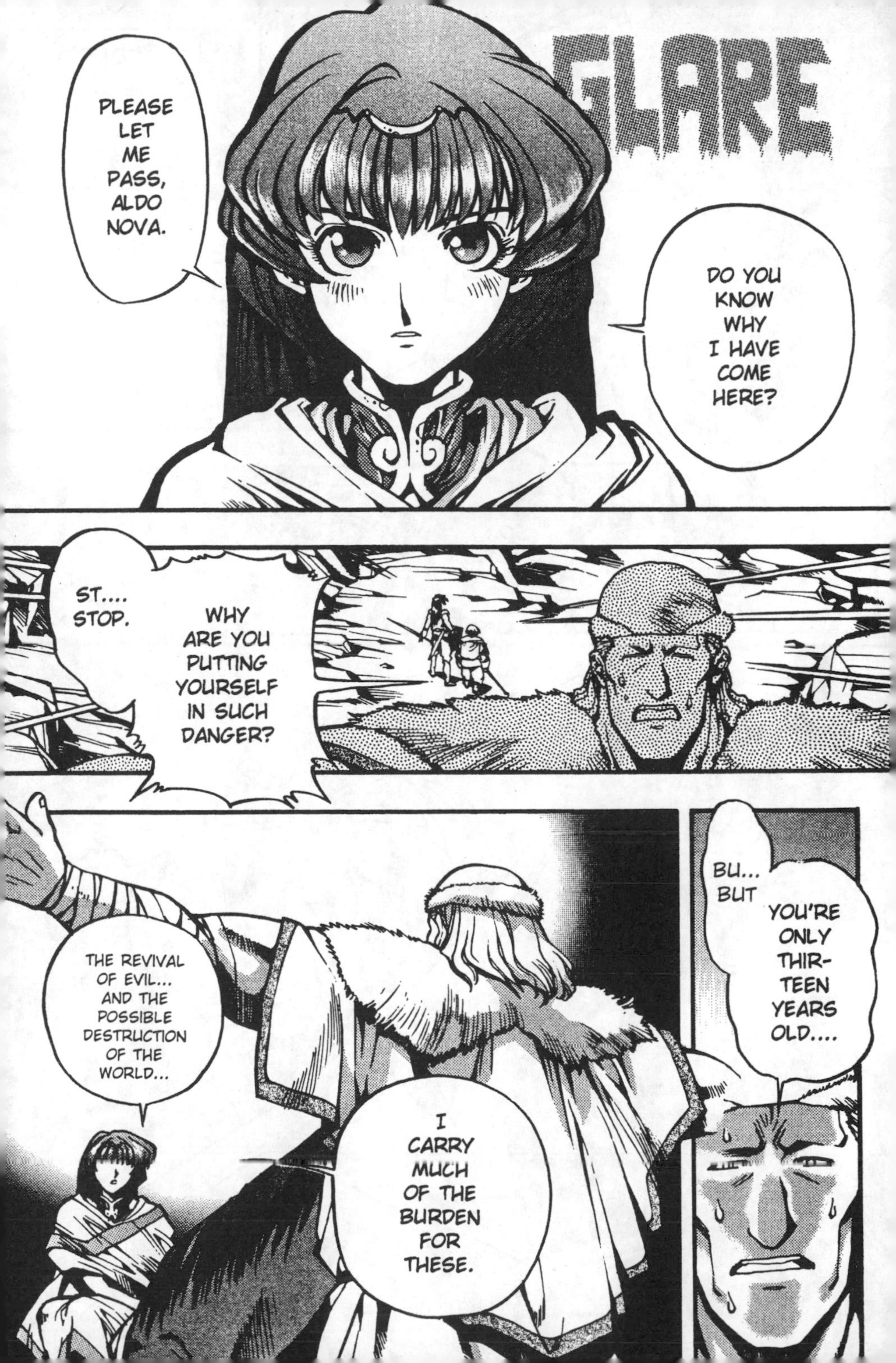
PLEASE LET ME PASS, ALDO NOVA.
GLARE
DO YOU KNOW WHY I HAVE COME HERE?
ST.... STOP.
WHY ARE YOU PUTTING YOURSELF IN SUCH DANGER?
THE REVIVAL OF EVIL... AND THE POSSIBLE DESTRUCTION OF THE WORLD...
I CARRY MUCH OF THE BURDEN FOR THESE.
BU... BUT
YOU'RE ONLY THIR-TEEN YEARS OLD....

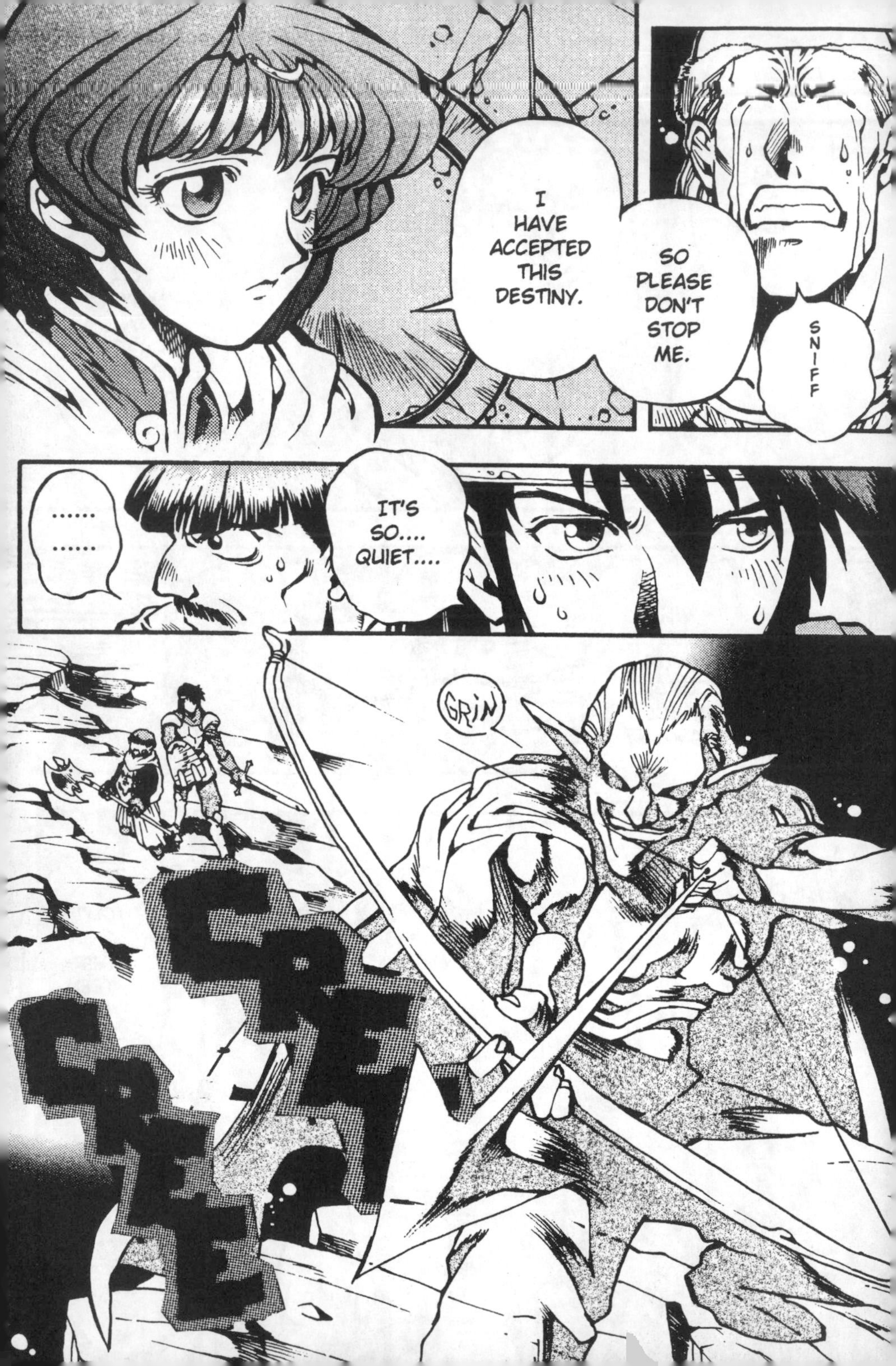
I HAVE ACCEPTED THIS DESTINY.
SO PLEASE DON'T STOP ME.
SNIFF
......
......
IT'S SO.... QUIET....
GRIN

# Things We Must Do To Survive

EPISODE 8

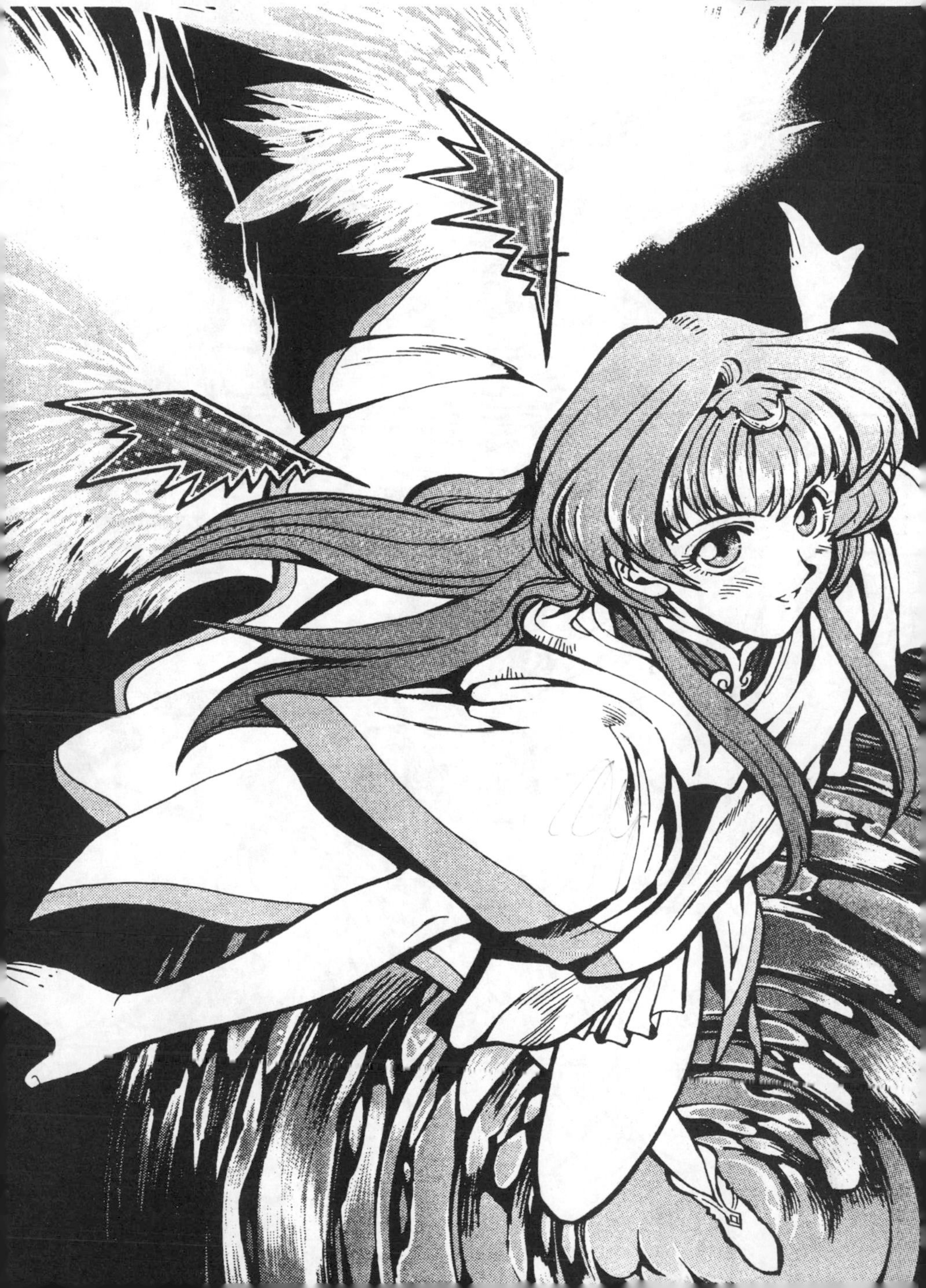

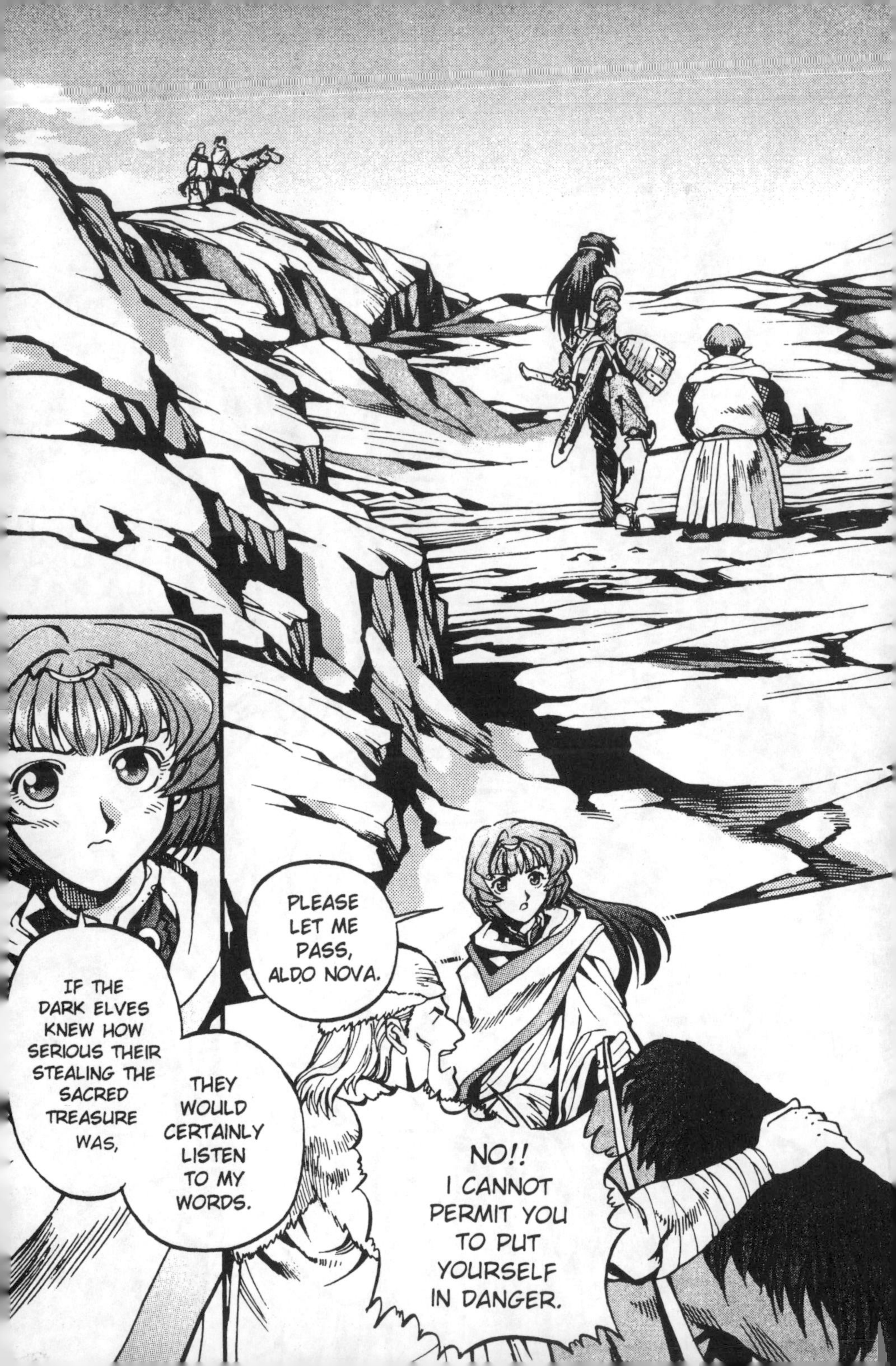
PLEASE LET ME PASS, ALDO NOVA.
IF THE DARK ELVES KNEW HOW SERIOUS THEIR STEALING THE SACRED TREASURE WAS,
THEY WOULD CERTAINLY LISTEN TO MY WORDS.
NO!! I CANNOT PERMIT YOU TO PUT YOURSELF IN DANGER.

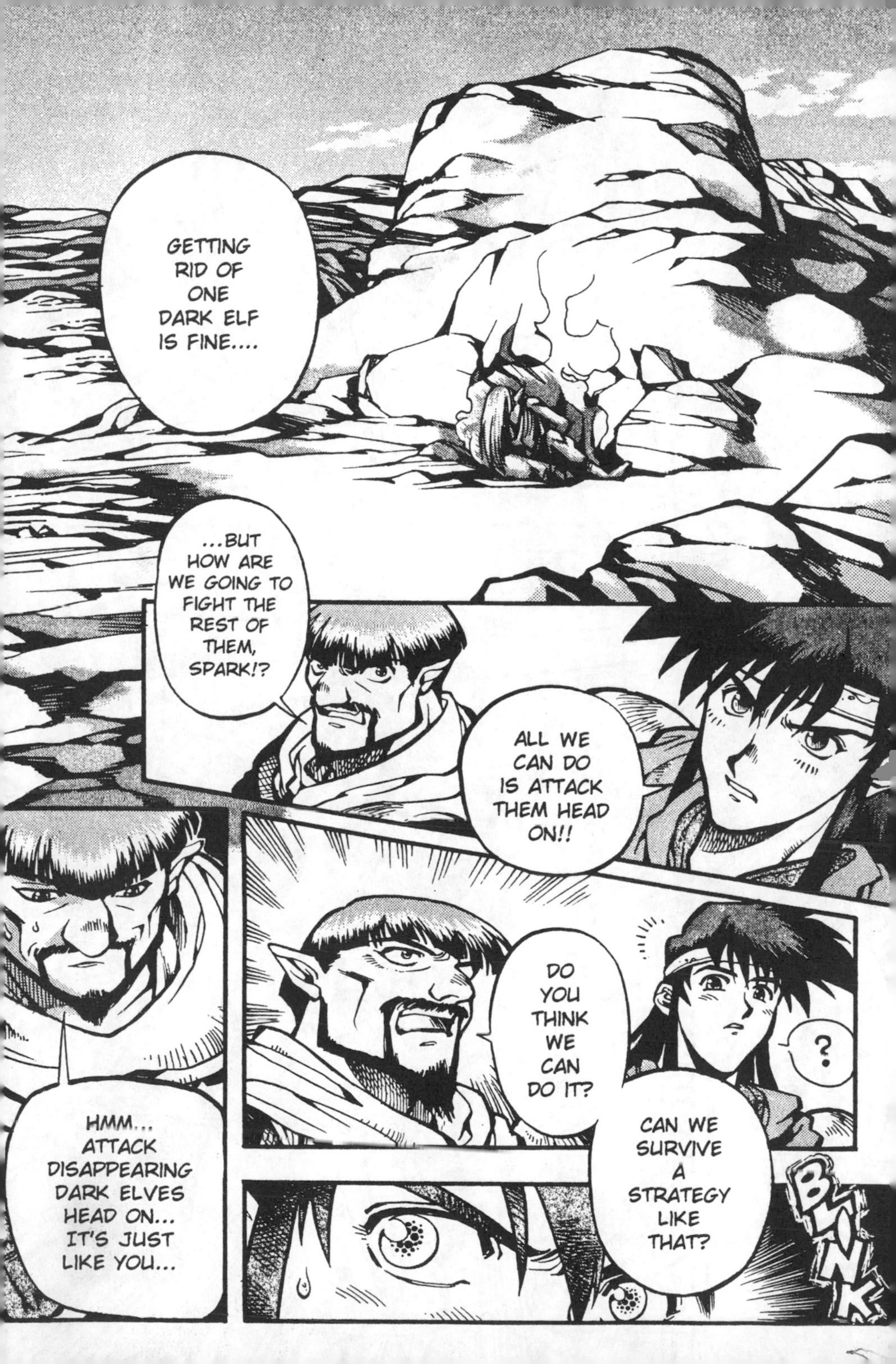
GETTING RID OF ONE DARK ELF IS FINE....
...BUT HOW ARE WE GOING TO FIGHT THE REST OF THEM, SPARK!?
ALL WE CAN DO IS ATTACK THEM HEAD ON!!
HMM... ATTACK DISAPPEARING DARK ELVES HEAD ON... IT'S JUST LIKE YOU...
DO YOU THINK WE CAN DO IT?
?
CAN WE SURVIVE A STRATEGY LIKE THAT?
BLINK

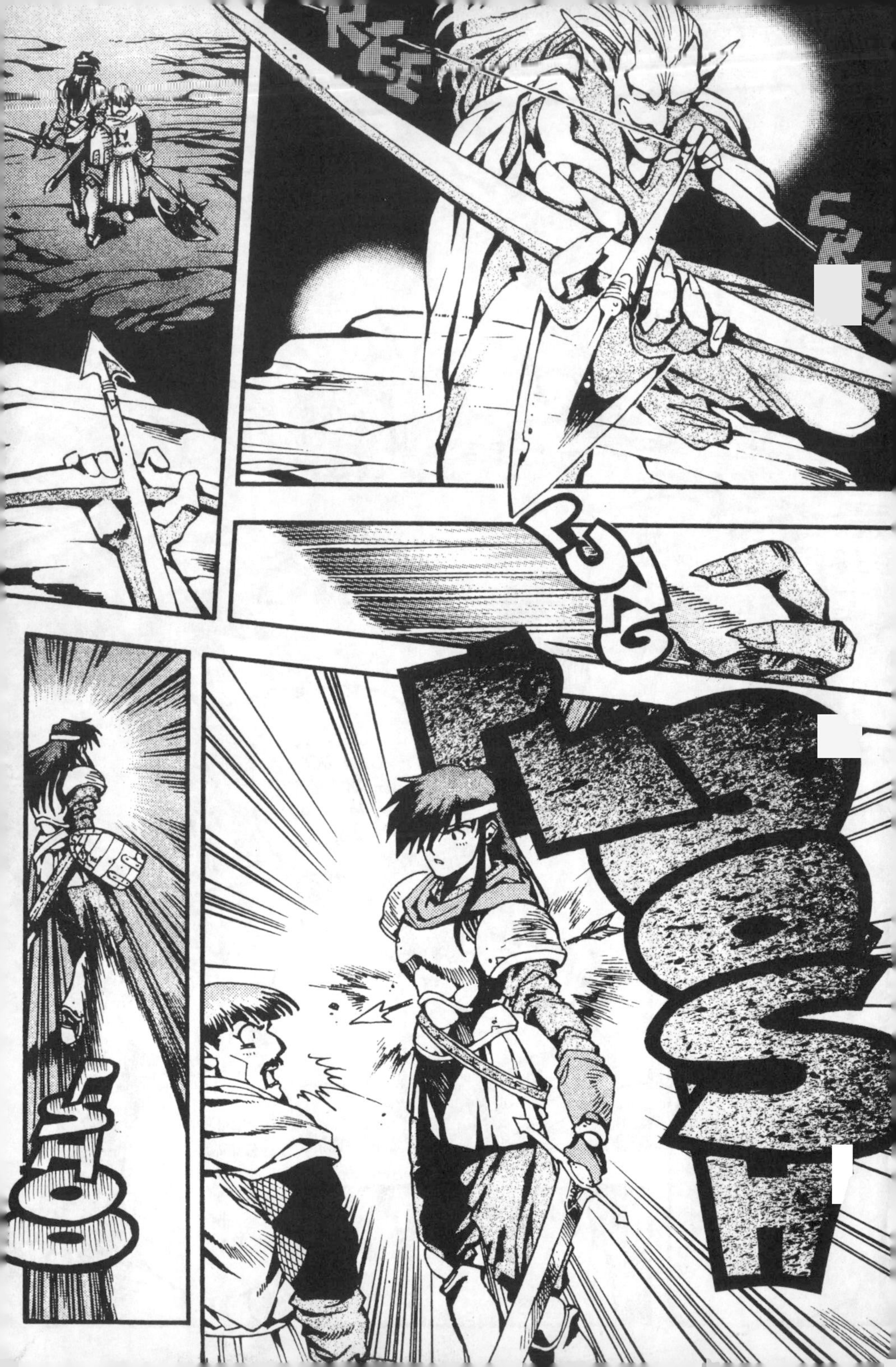
KREE
TUNG
FOOSH!

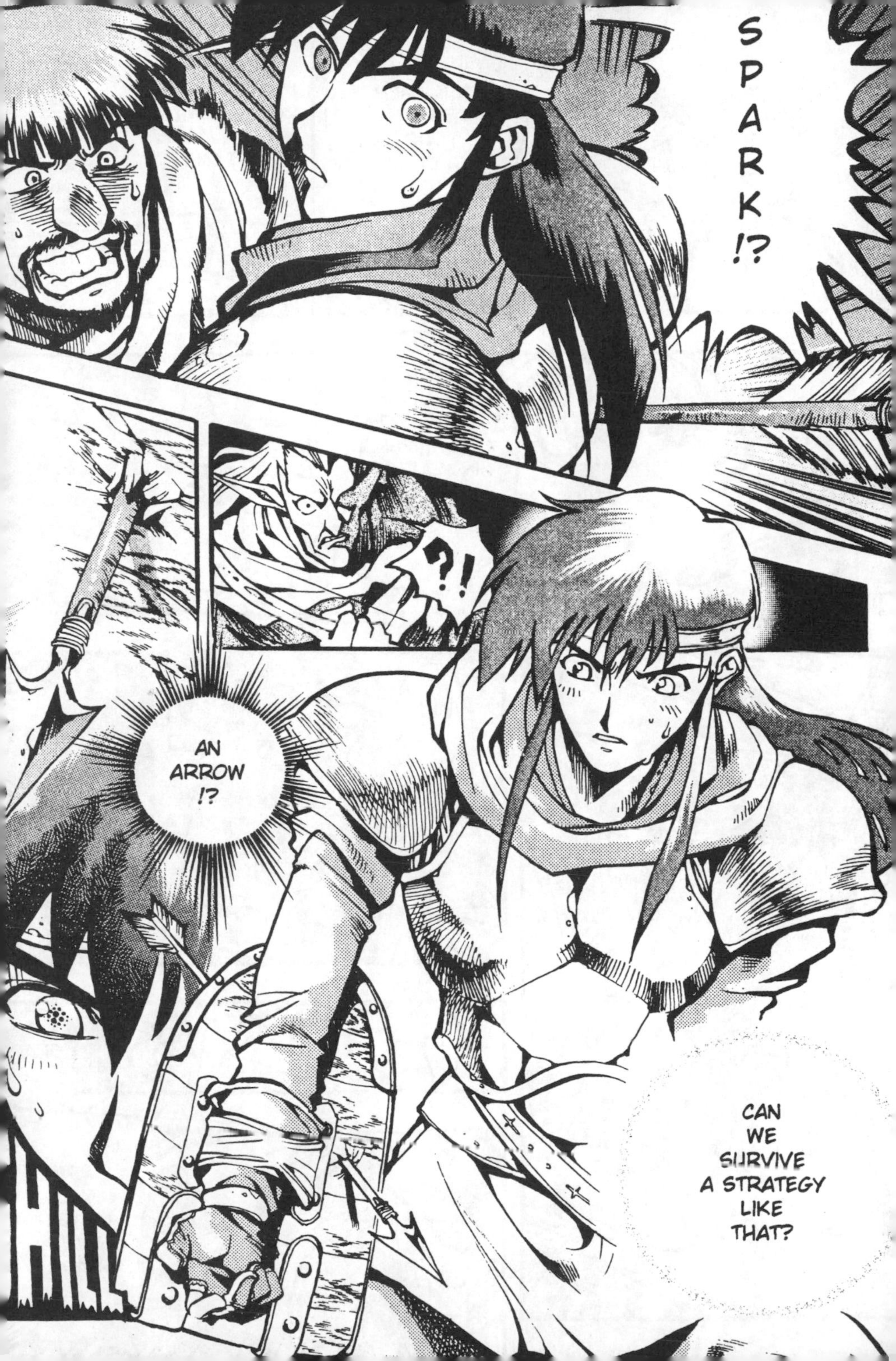
SPARK!?
?!
AN ARROW !?
CAN WE SURVIVE A STRATEGY LIKE THAT?

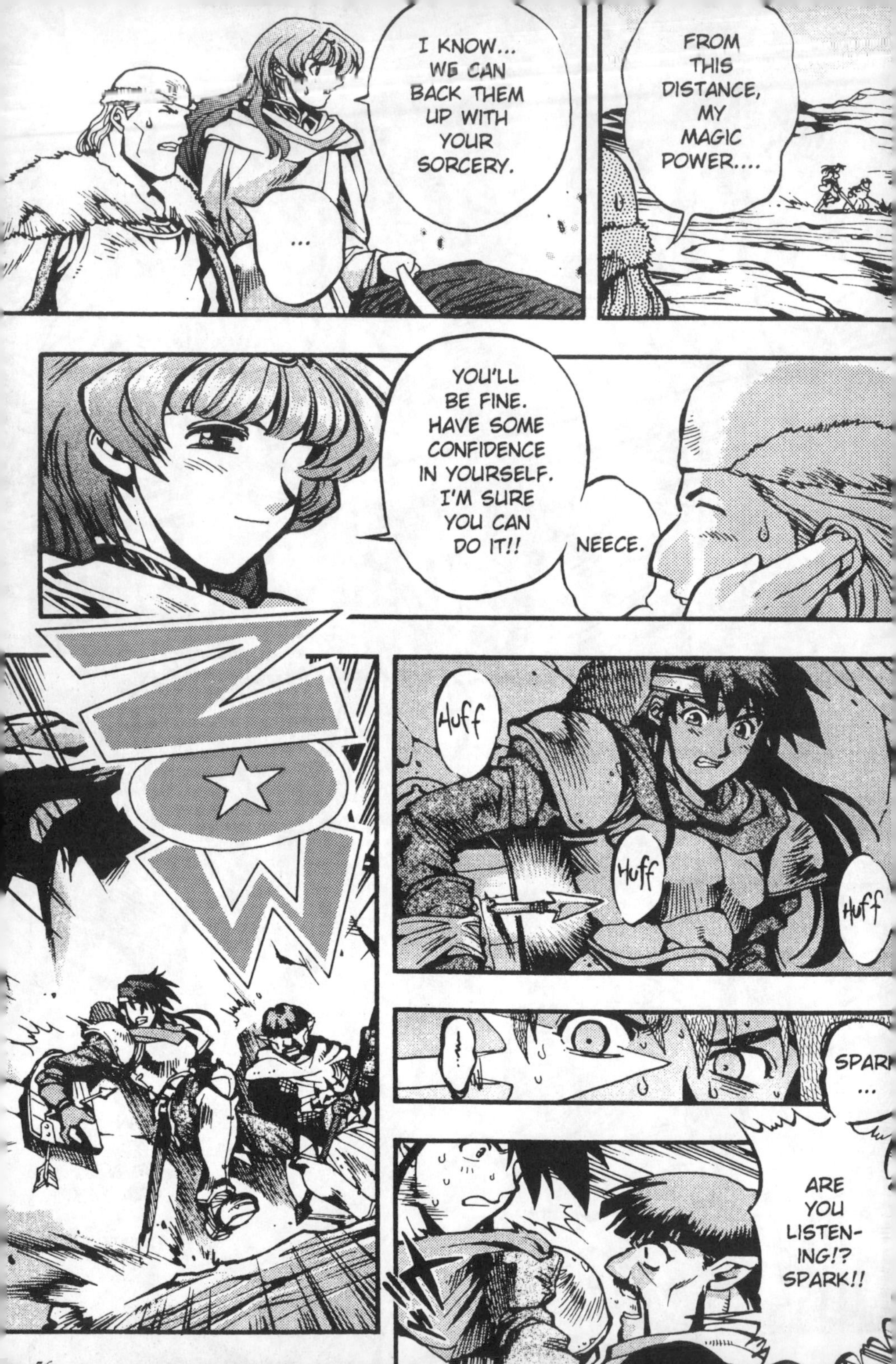

I KNOW... WE CAN BACK THEM UP WITH YOUR SORCERY.
...
FROM THIS DISTANCE, MY MAGIC POWER....
YOU'LL BE FINE. HAVE SOME CONFIDENCE IN YOURSELF. I'M SURE YOU CAN DO IT!!
NEECE.
ZOW
Huff
Huff
Huff
!
SPARK ...
ARE YOU LISTEN-ING!? SPARK!!

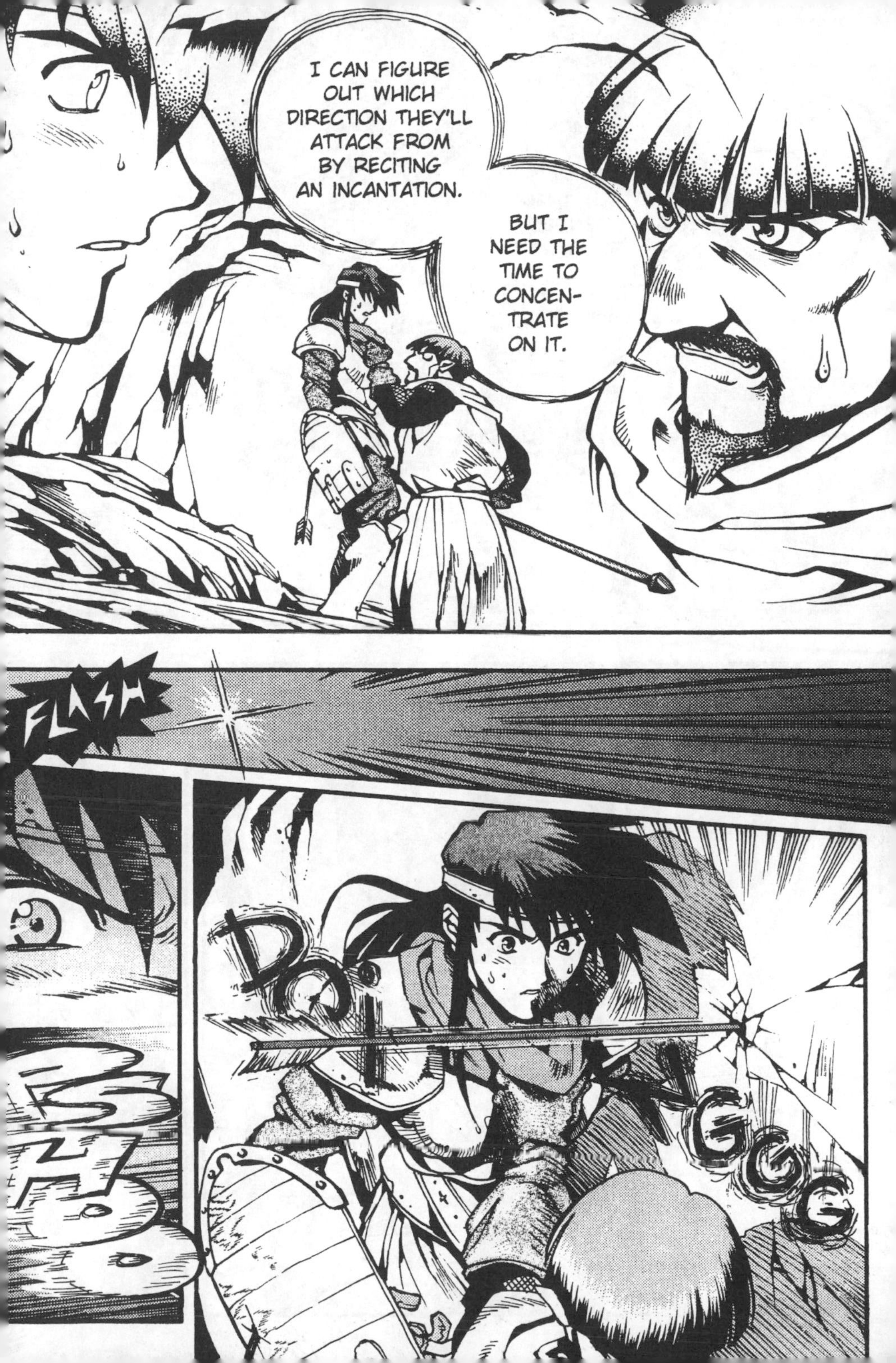
I CAN FIGURE OUT WHICH DIRECTION THEY'LL ATTACK FROM BY RECITING AN INCANTATION.
BUT I NEED THE TIME TO CONCEN-TRATE ON IT.
FLASH
DOO
GOGG

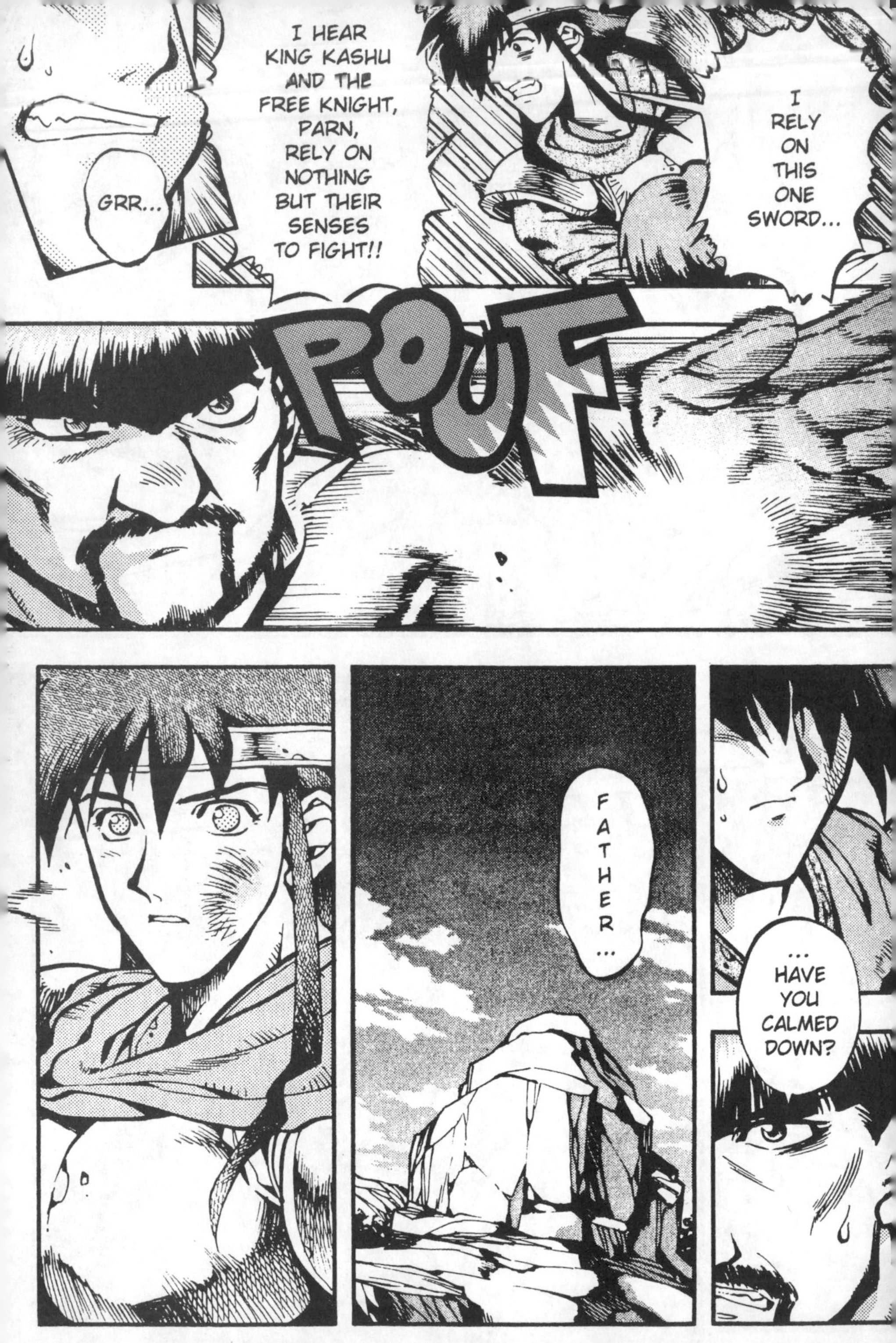
GRR...
I HEAR KING KASHU AND THE FREE KNIGHT, PARN, RELY ON NOTHING BUT THEIR SENSES TO FIGHT!!
I RELY ON THIS ONE SWORD...
POUF
FATHER...
... HAVE YOU CALMED DOWN?

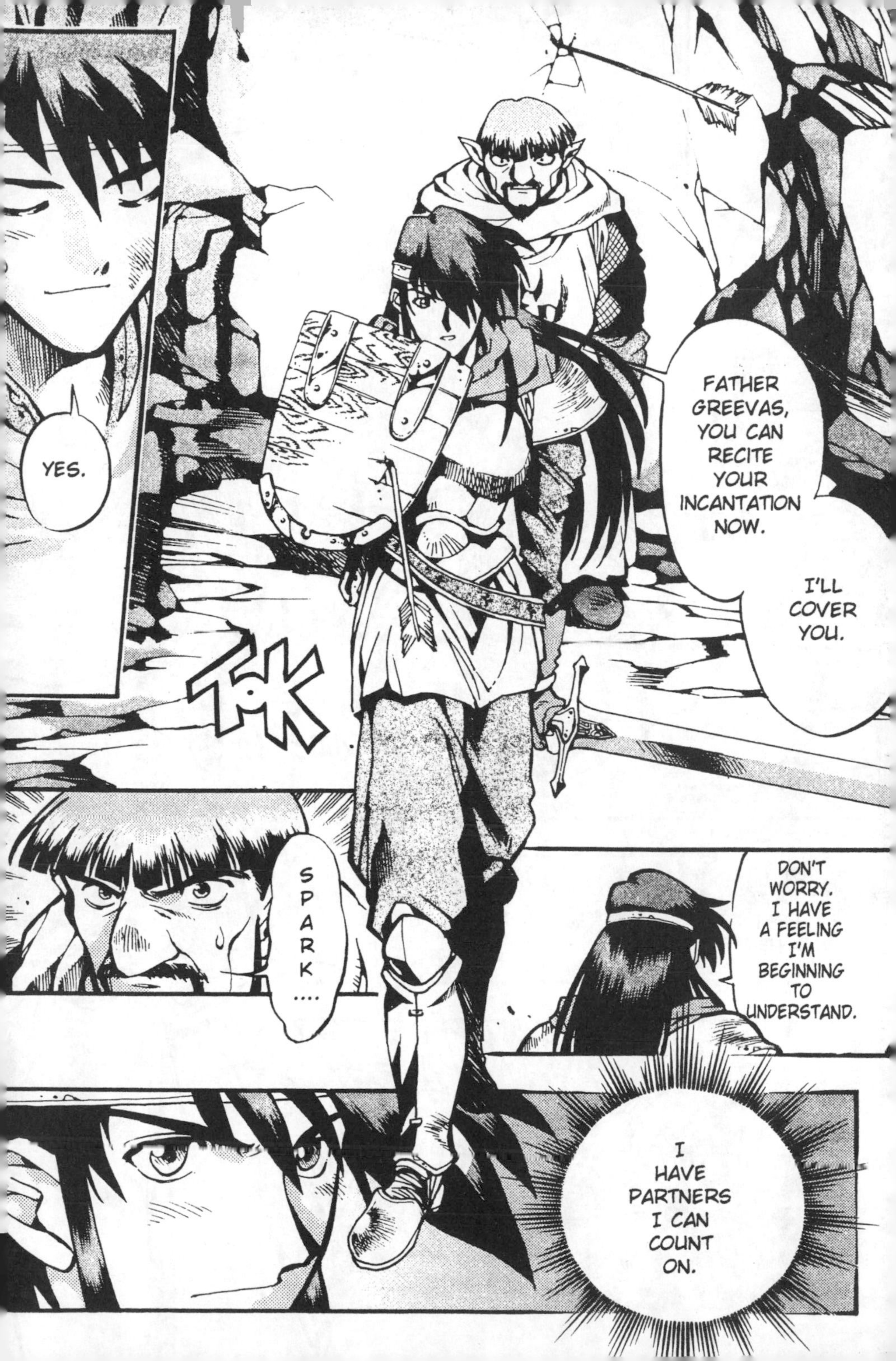
YES.
FATHER GREEVAS, YOU CAN RECITE YOUR INCANTATION NOW.
I'LL COVER YOU.
TOK
SPARK....
DON'T WORRY. I HAVE A FEELING I'M BEGINNING TO UNDERSTAND.
I HAVE PARTNERS I CAN COUNT ON.

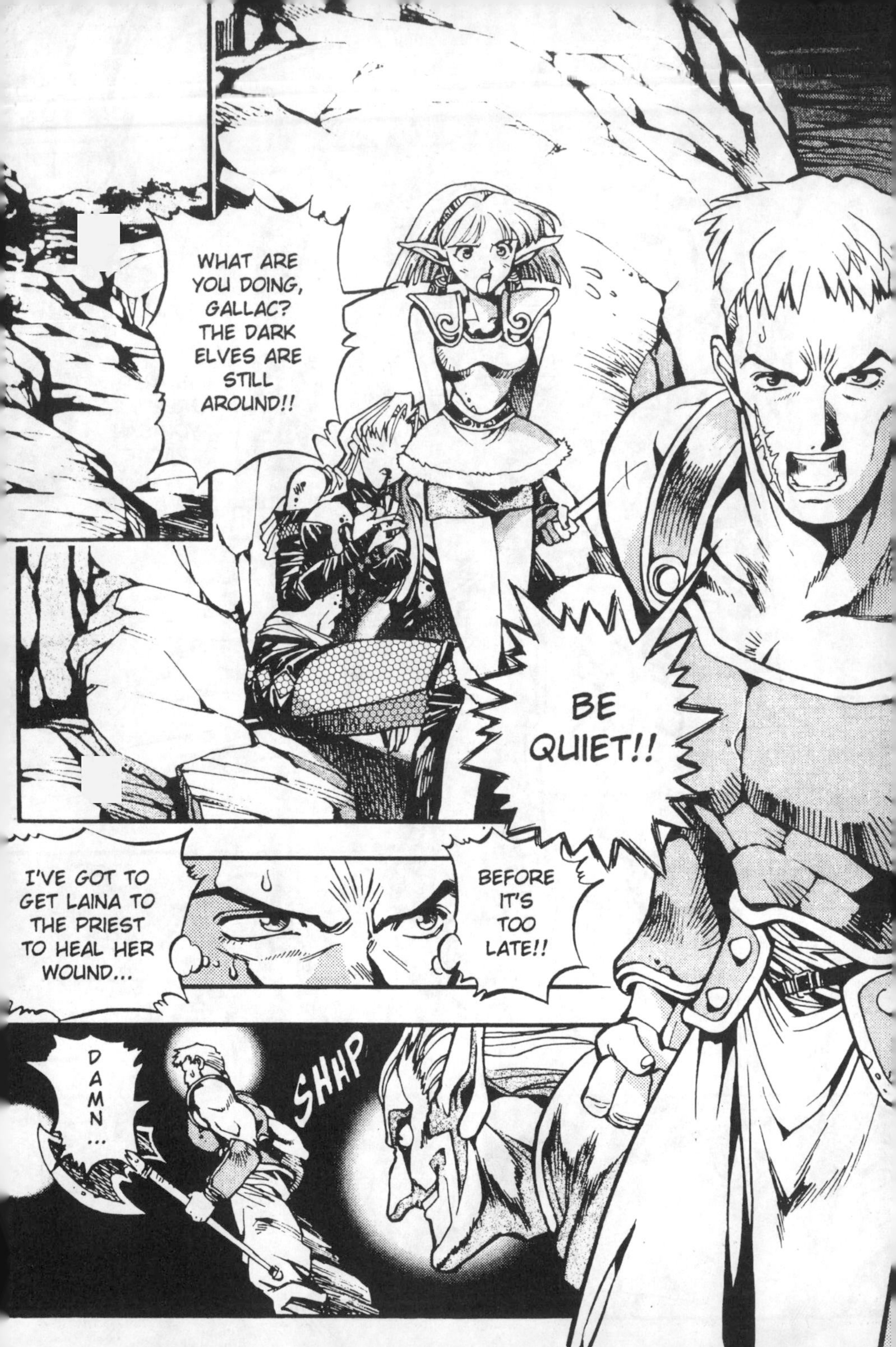
WHAT ARE YOU DOING, GALLAC? THE DARK ELVES ARE STILL AROUND!!
BE QUIET!!
I'VE GOT TO GET LAINA TO THE PRIEST TO HEAL HER WOUND...
BEFORE IT'S TOO LATE!!
DAMN...
SHHP

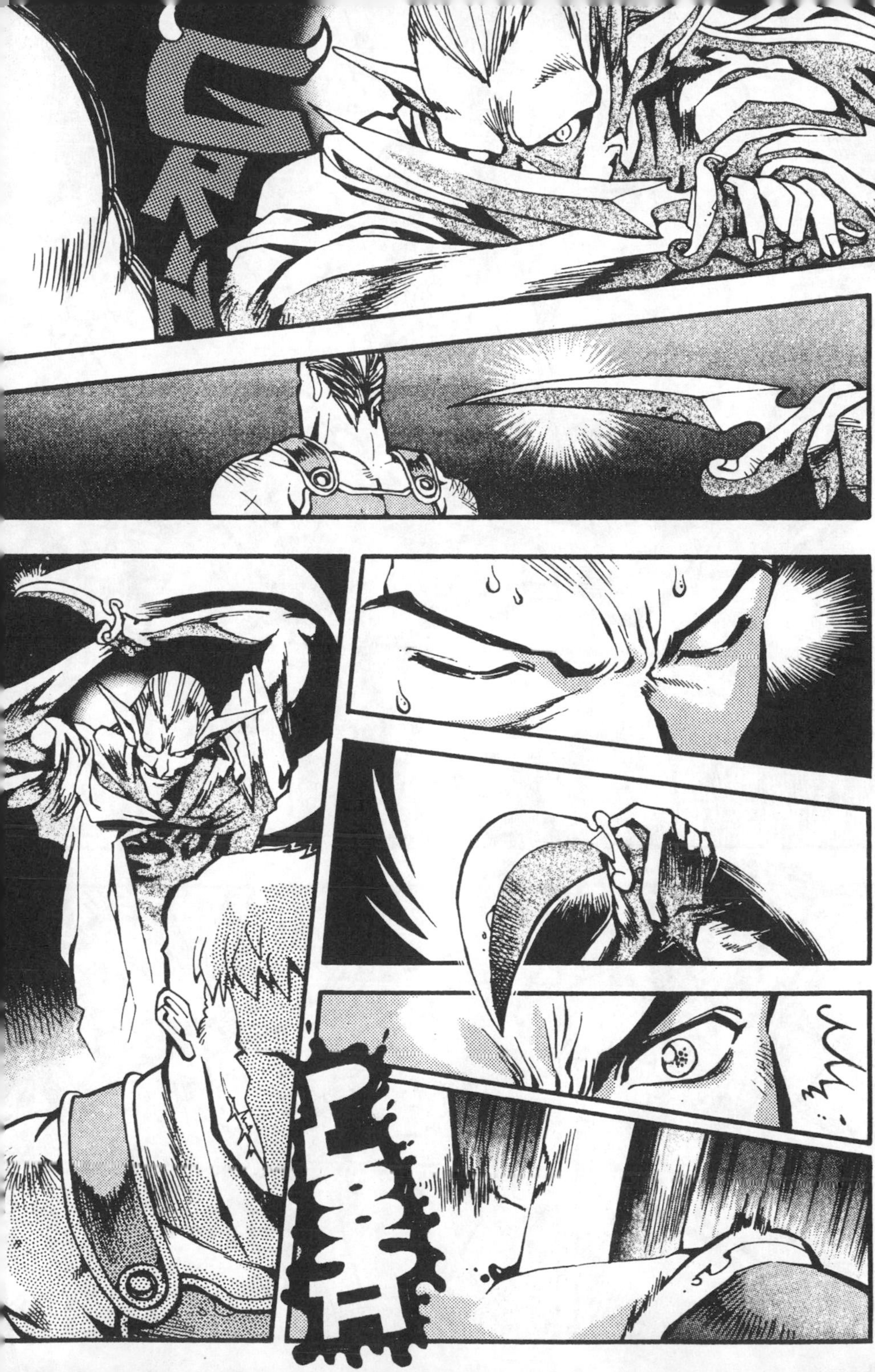

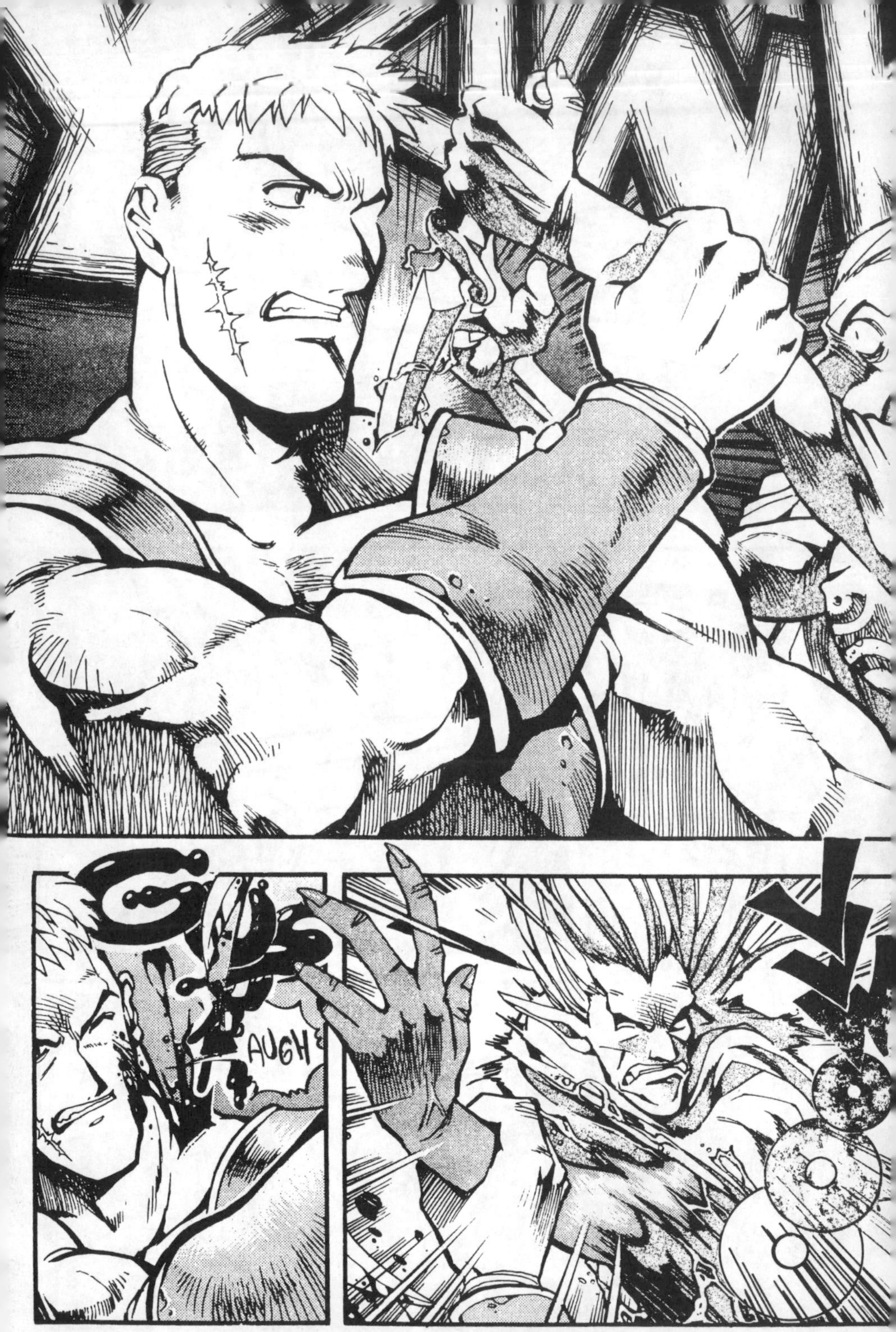
AUGH

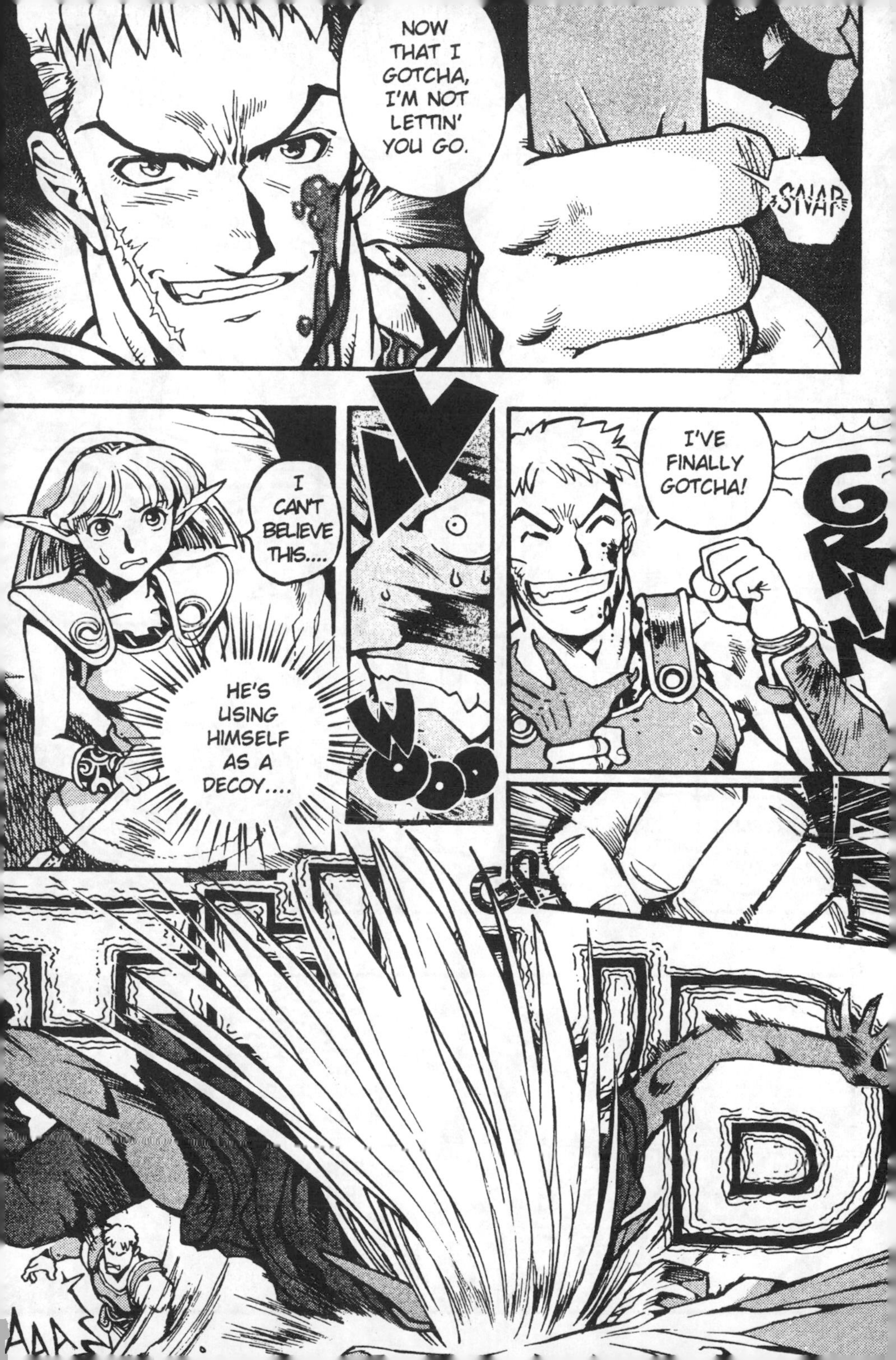
NOW THAT I GOTCHA, I'M NOT LETTIN' YOU GO.
SNAP
I CAN'T BELIEVE THIS....
HE'S USING HIMSELF AS A DECOY....
I'VE FINALLY GOTCHA!
GRIN
AAA

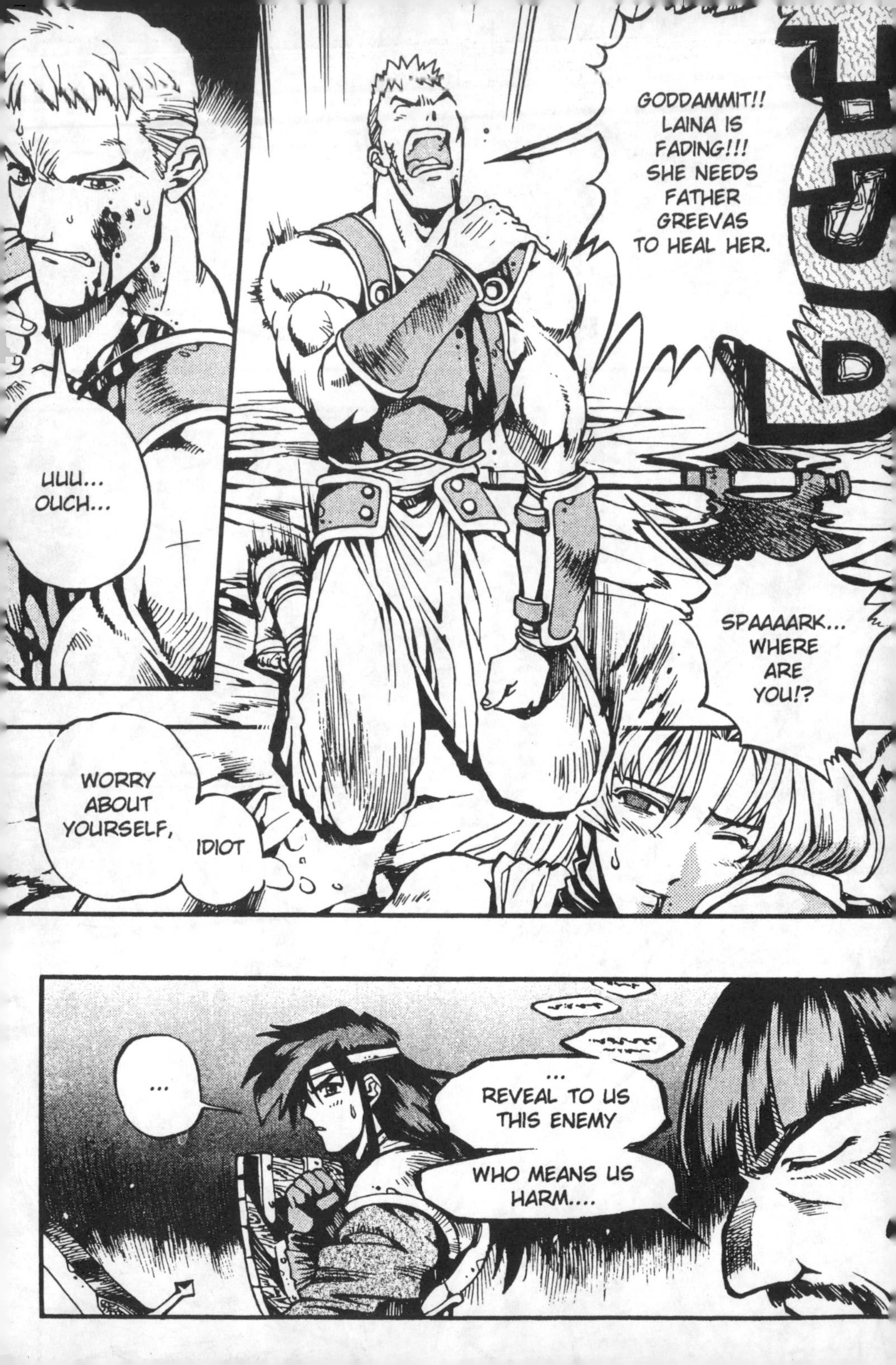
UUU... OUCH...
GODDAMMIT!! LAINA IS FADING!!! SHE NEEDS FATHER GREEVAS TO HEAL HER.
WORRY ABOUT YOURSELF, IDIOT
SPAAAARK... WHERE ARE YOU!?
...
... REVEAL TO US THIS ENEMY
WHO MEANS US HARM....

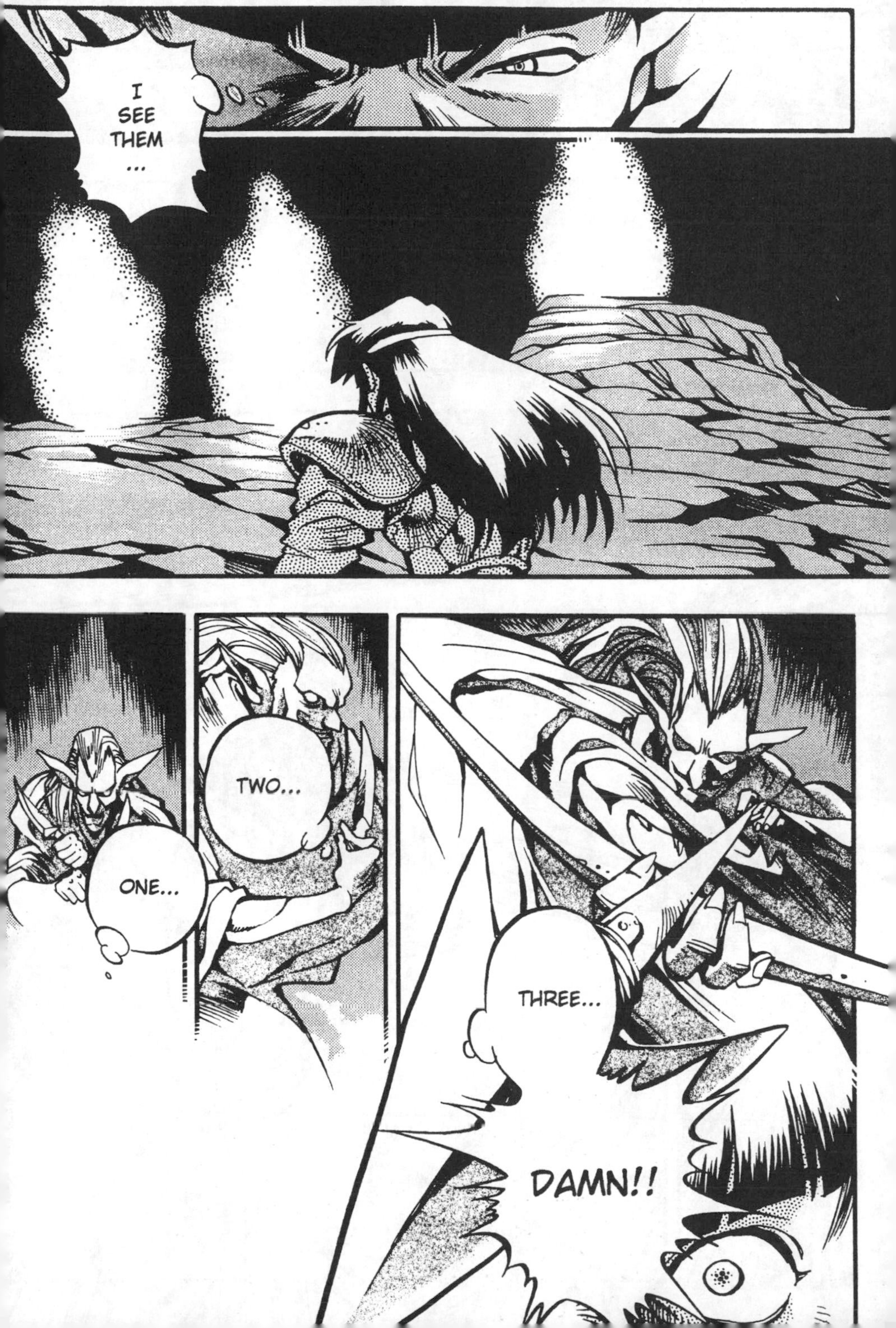

I SEE THEM ...
ONE...
TWO...
THREE...
DAMN!!

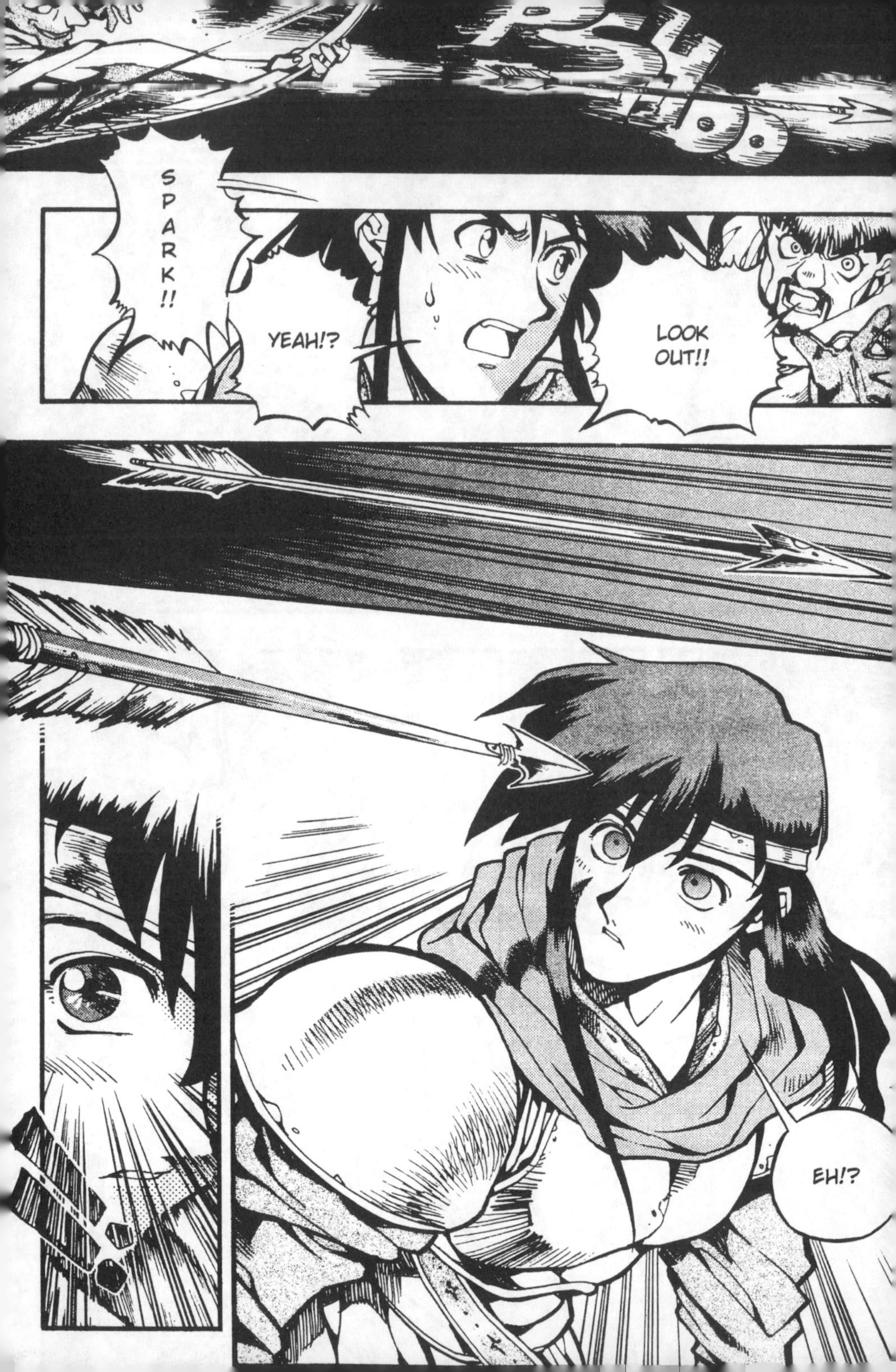
SPARK!!
YEAH!?
LOOK OUT!!
EH!?

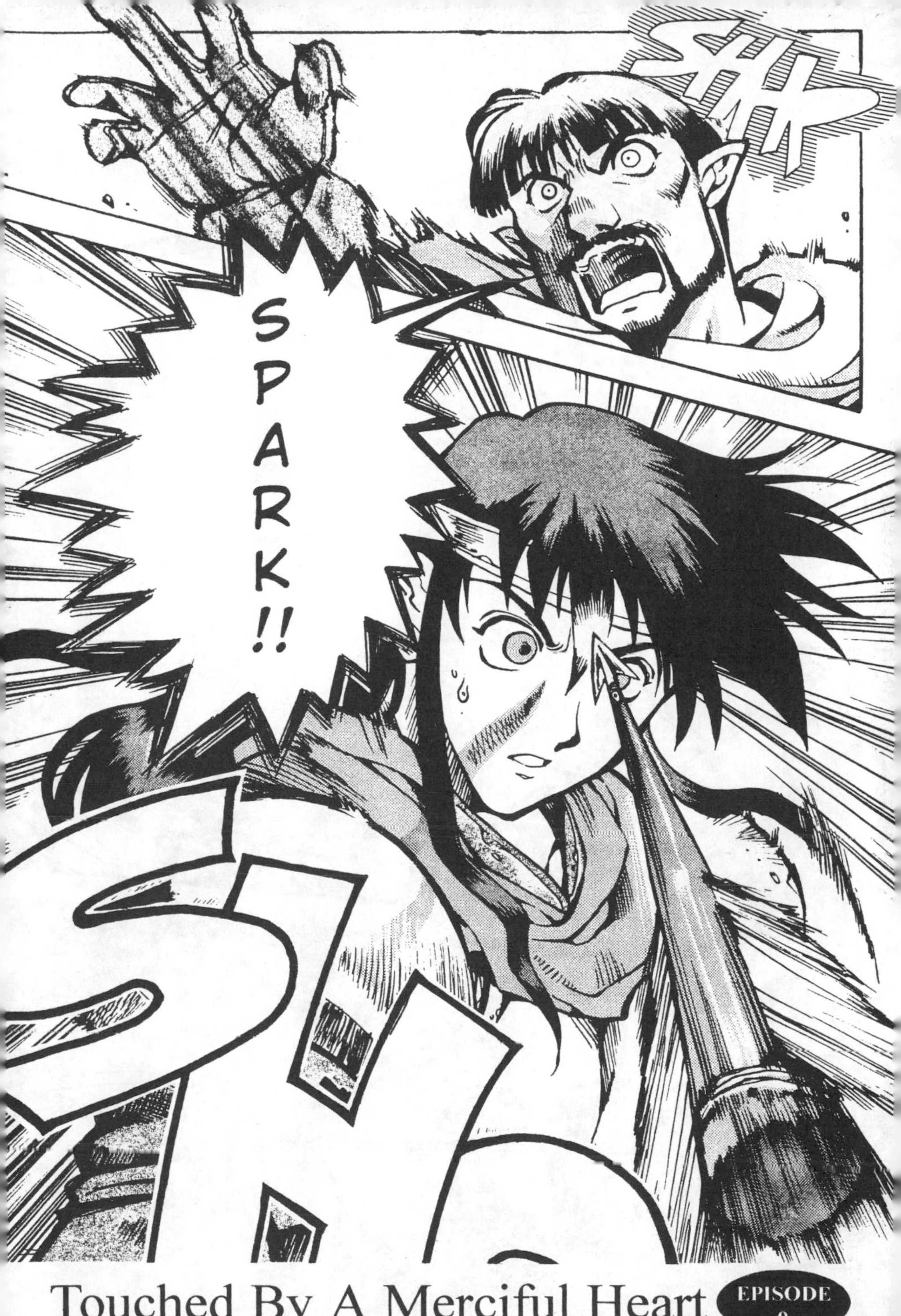
SPARK!!

# Touched By A Merciful Heart

EPISODE 9

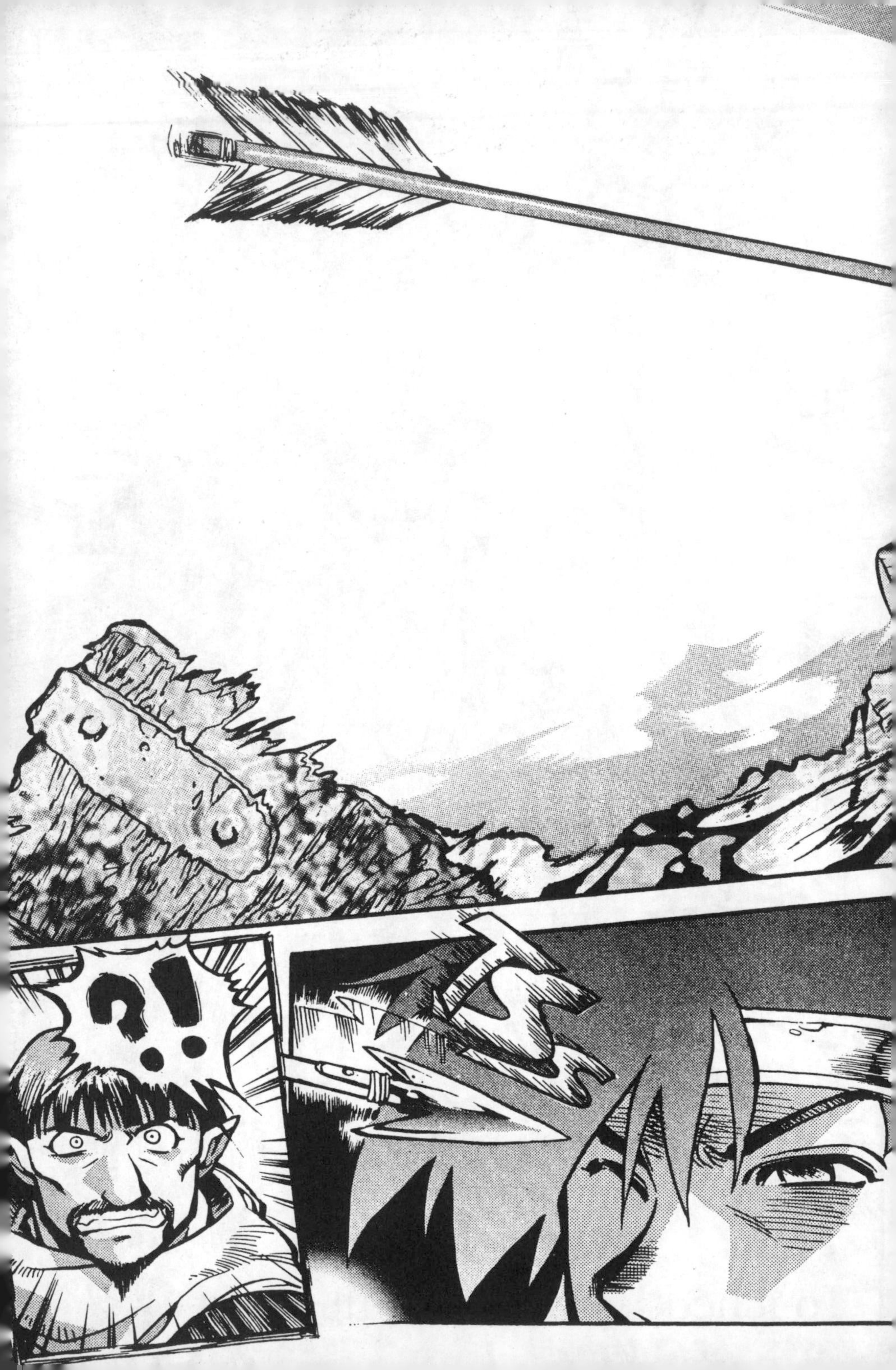
?!

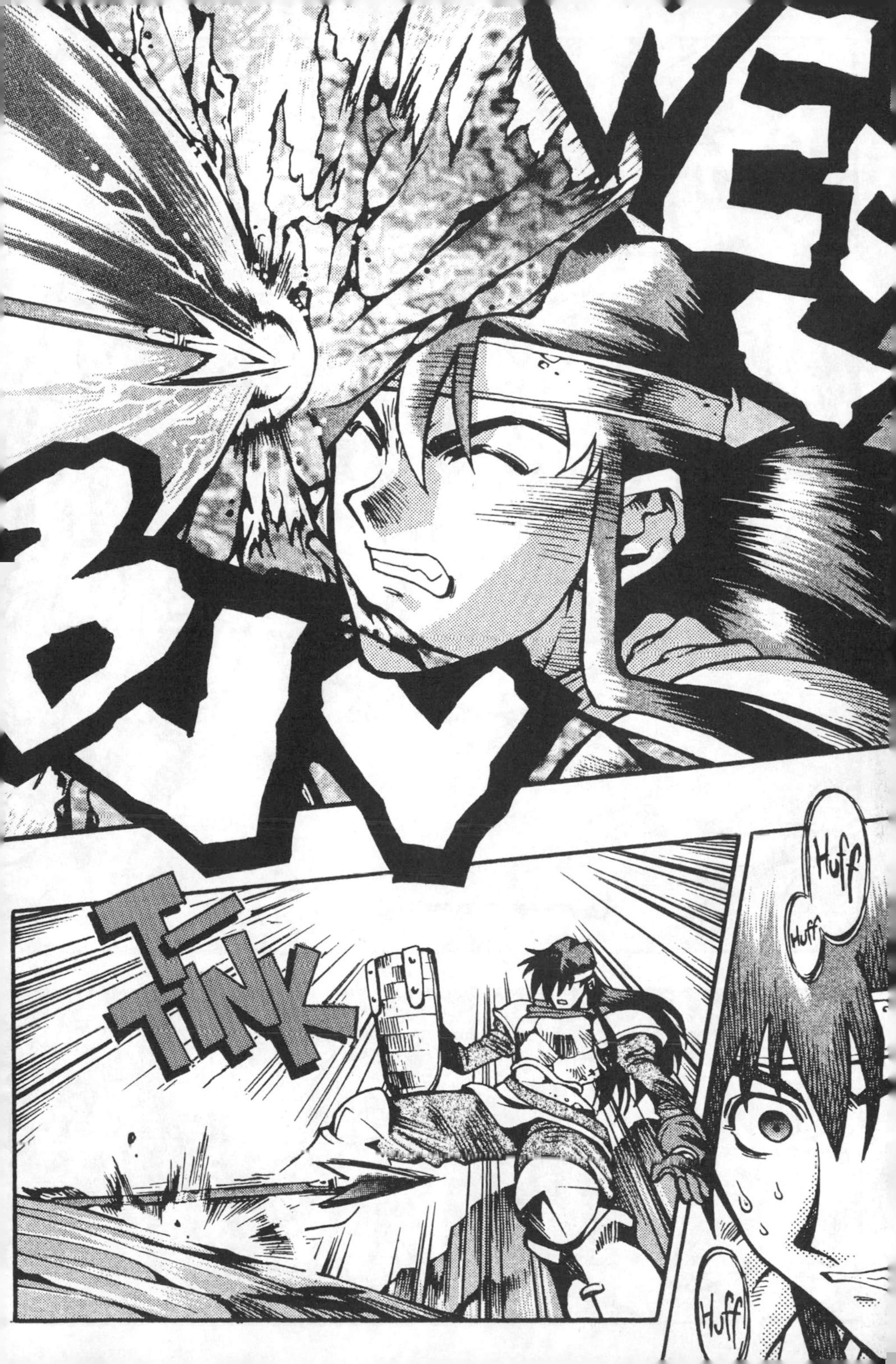
T-TINK
Huff
Huff
Huff

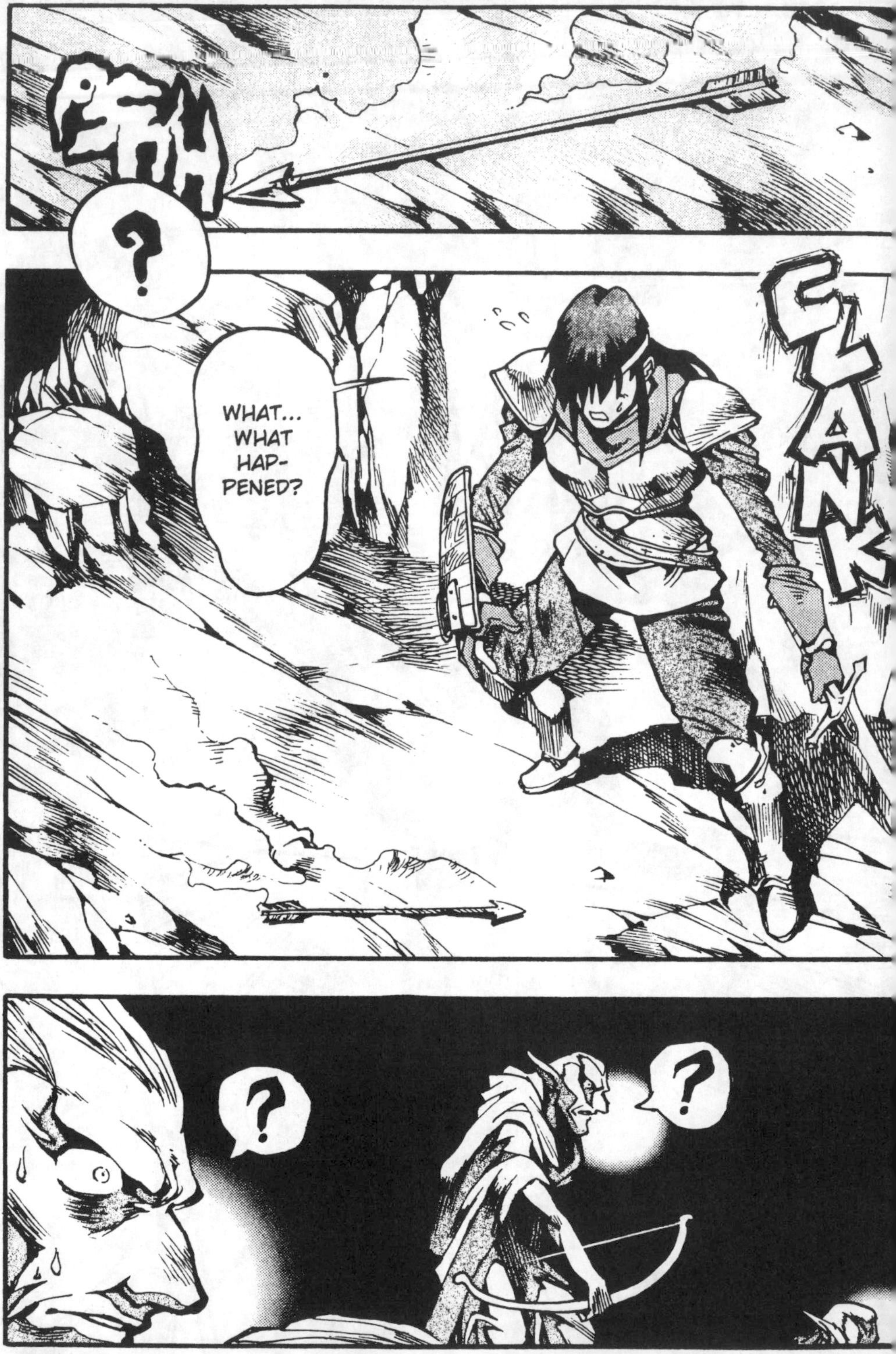
?
WHAT... WHAT HAP-PENED?
CLANK
?
?

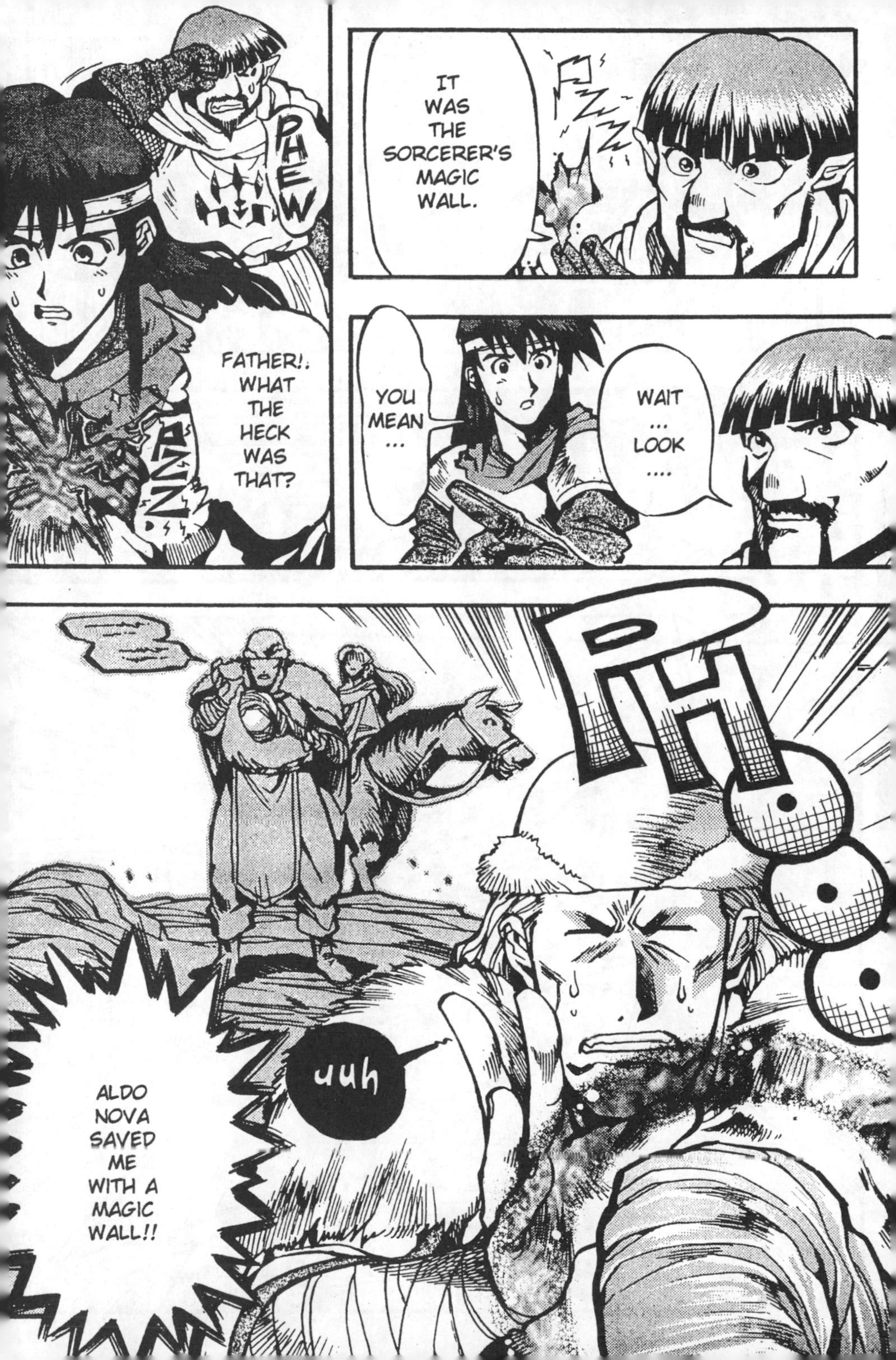
PHEW
FATHER!. WHAT THE HECK WAS THAT?
IT WAS THE SORCERER'S MAGIC WALL.
YOU MEAN ...
WAIT ... LOOK ....
PH...
uuh
ALDO NOVA SAVED ME WITH A MAGIC WALL!!

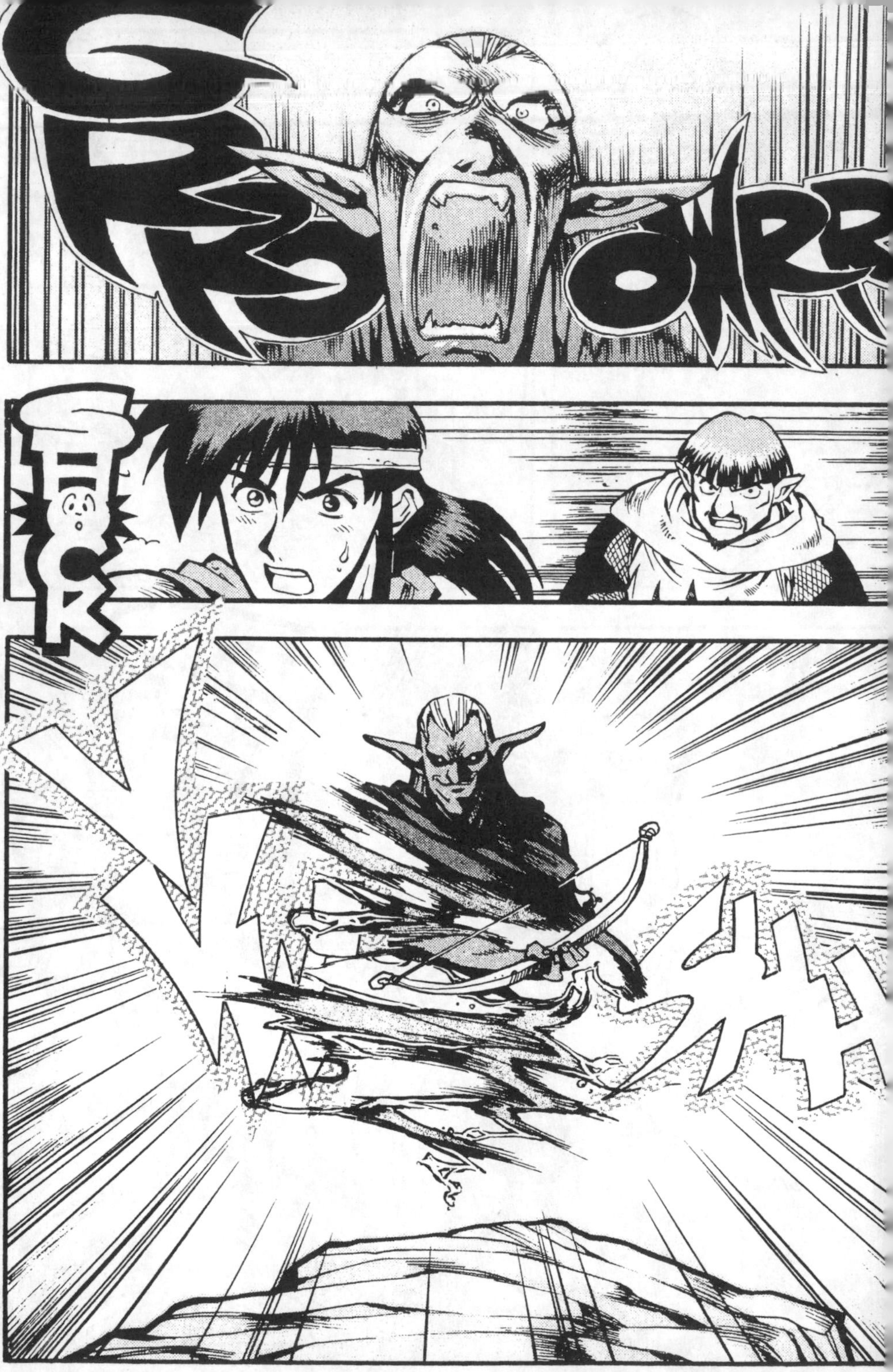

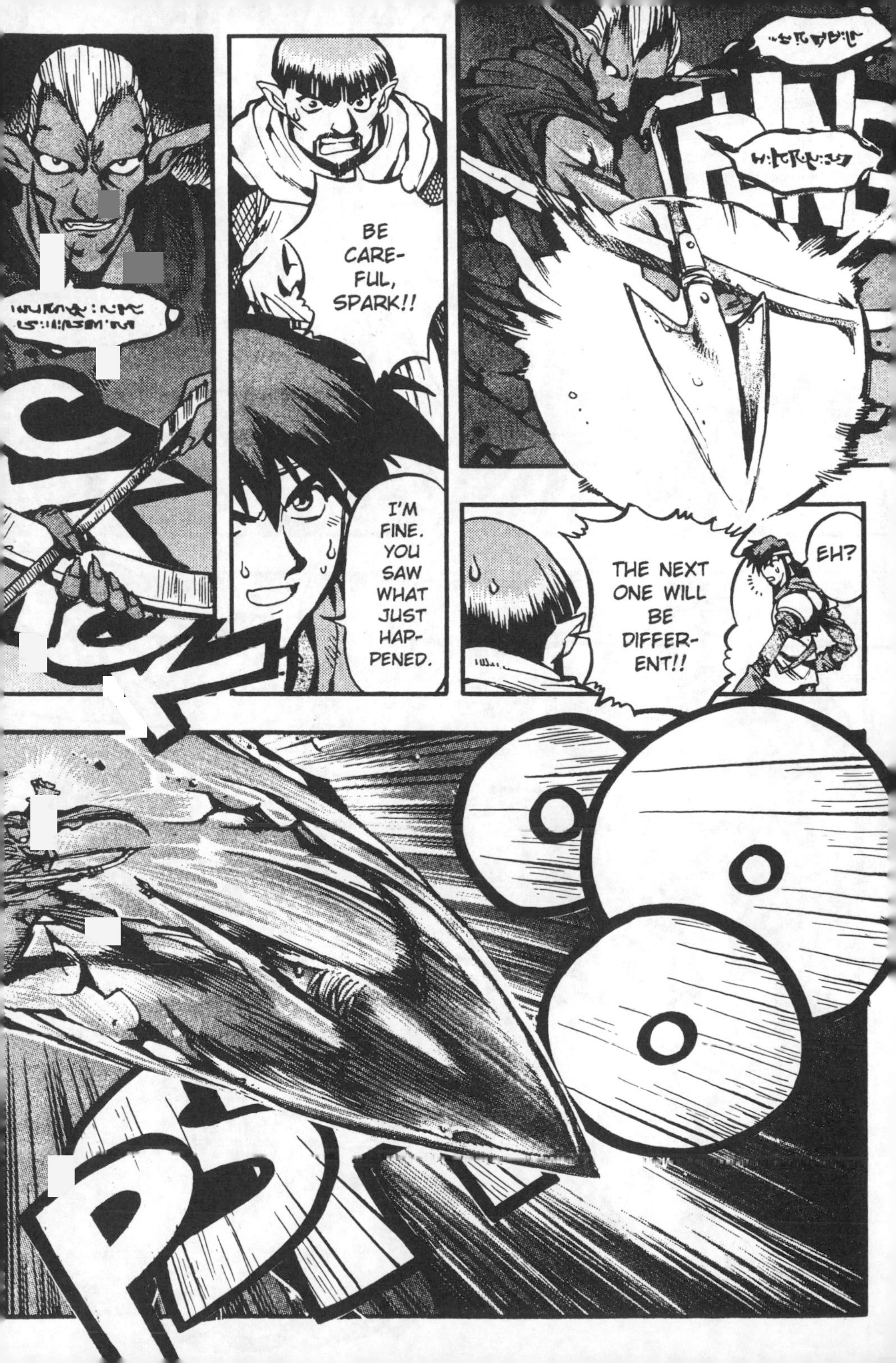
BE CAREFUL, SPARK!!
I'M FINE. YOU SAW WHAT JUST HAPPENED.
THE NEXT ONE WILL BE DIFFERENT!!
EH?

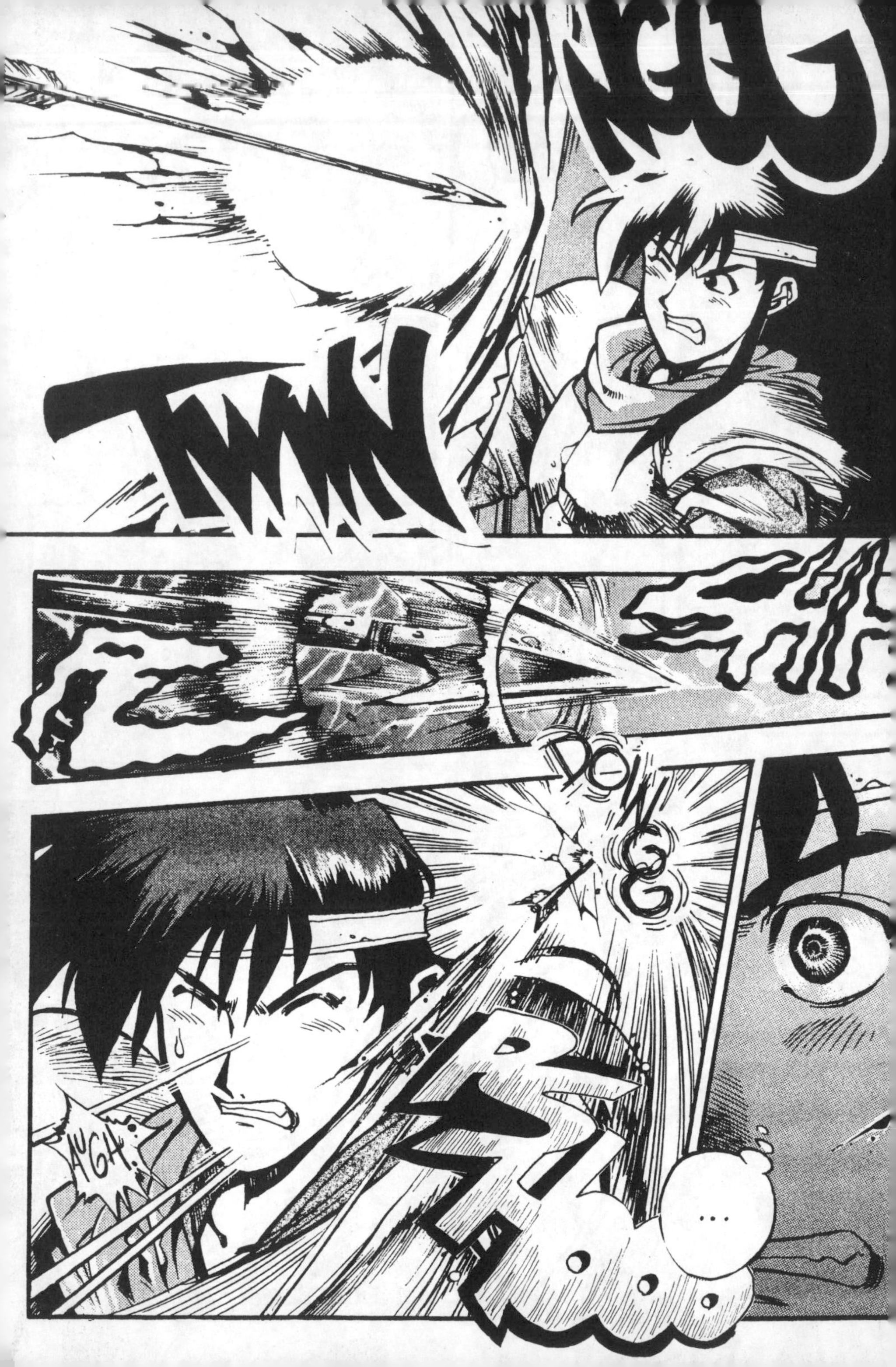
AUGH!
...

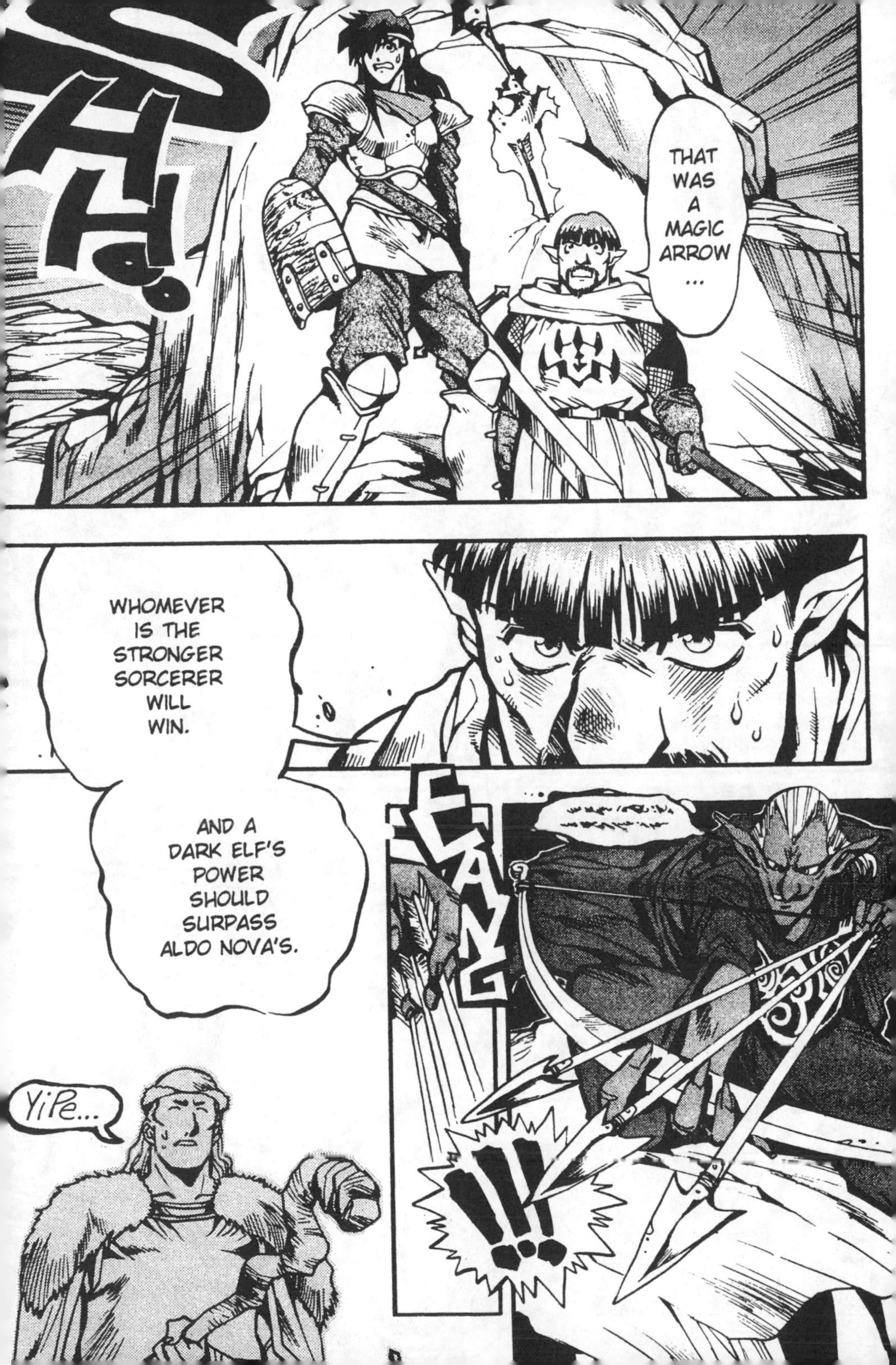
THAT WAS A MAGIC ARROW ...
WHOMEVER IS THE STRONGER SORCERER WILL WIN.
AND A DARK ELF'S POWER SHOULD SURPASS ALDO NOVA'S.
YiPe...
!!!

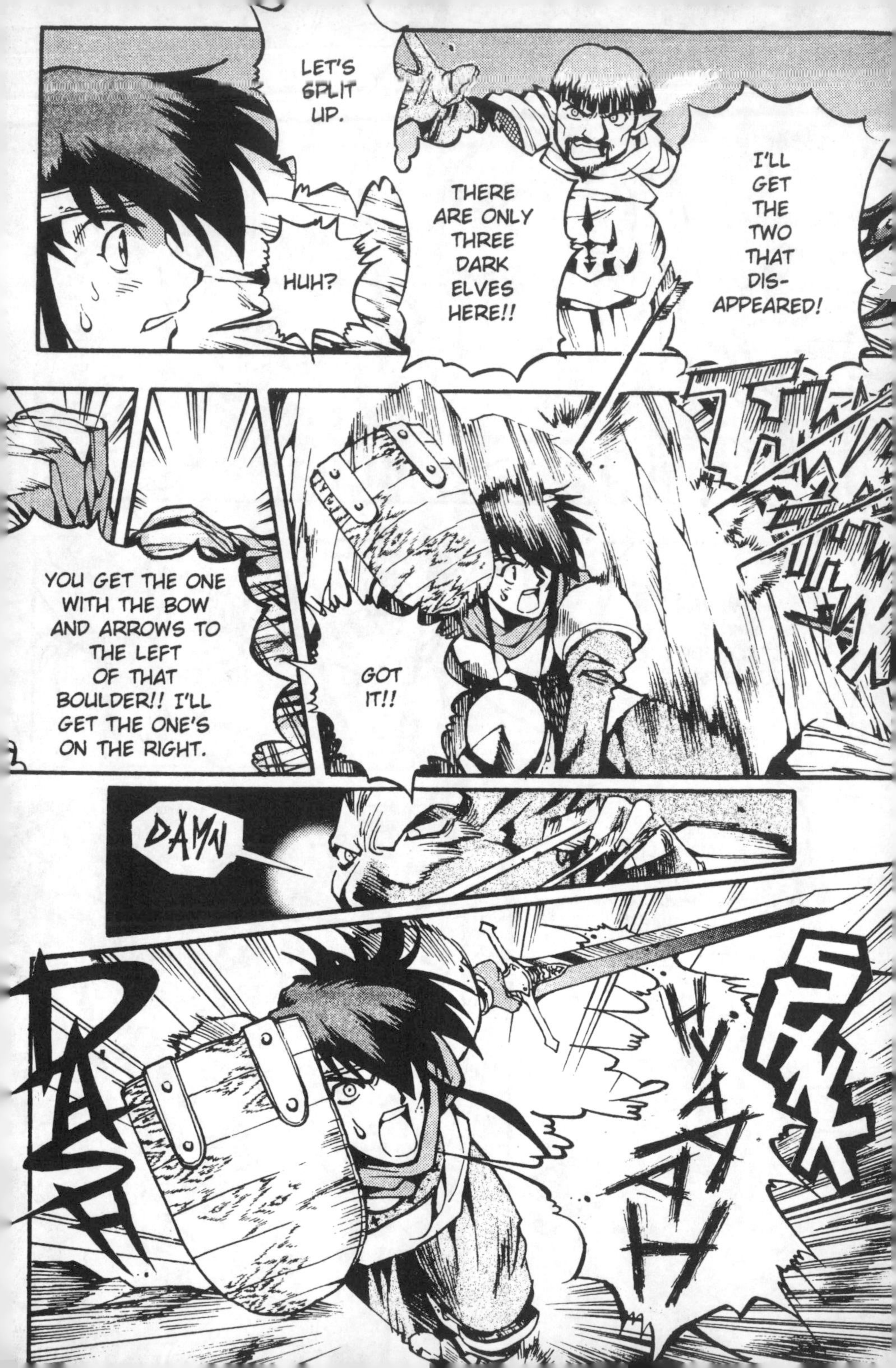
LET'S SPLIT UP.
HUH?
THERE ARE ONLY THREE DARK ELVES HERE!!
I'LL GET THE TWO THAT DIS-APPEARED!
YOU GET THE ONE WITH THE BOW AND ARROWS TO THE LEFT OF THAT BOULDER!! I'LL GET THE ONE'S ON THE RIGHT.
GOT IT!!
DAMN
DASH
HYAAAH

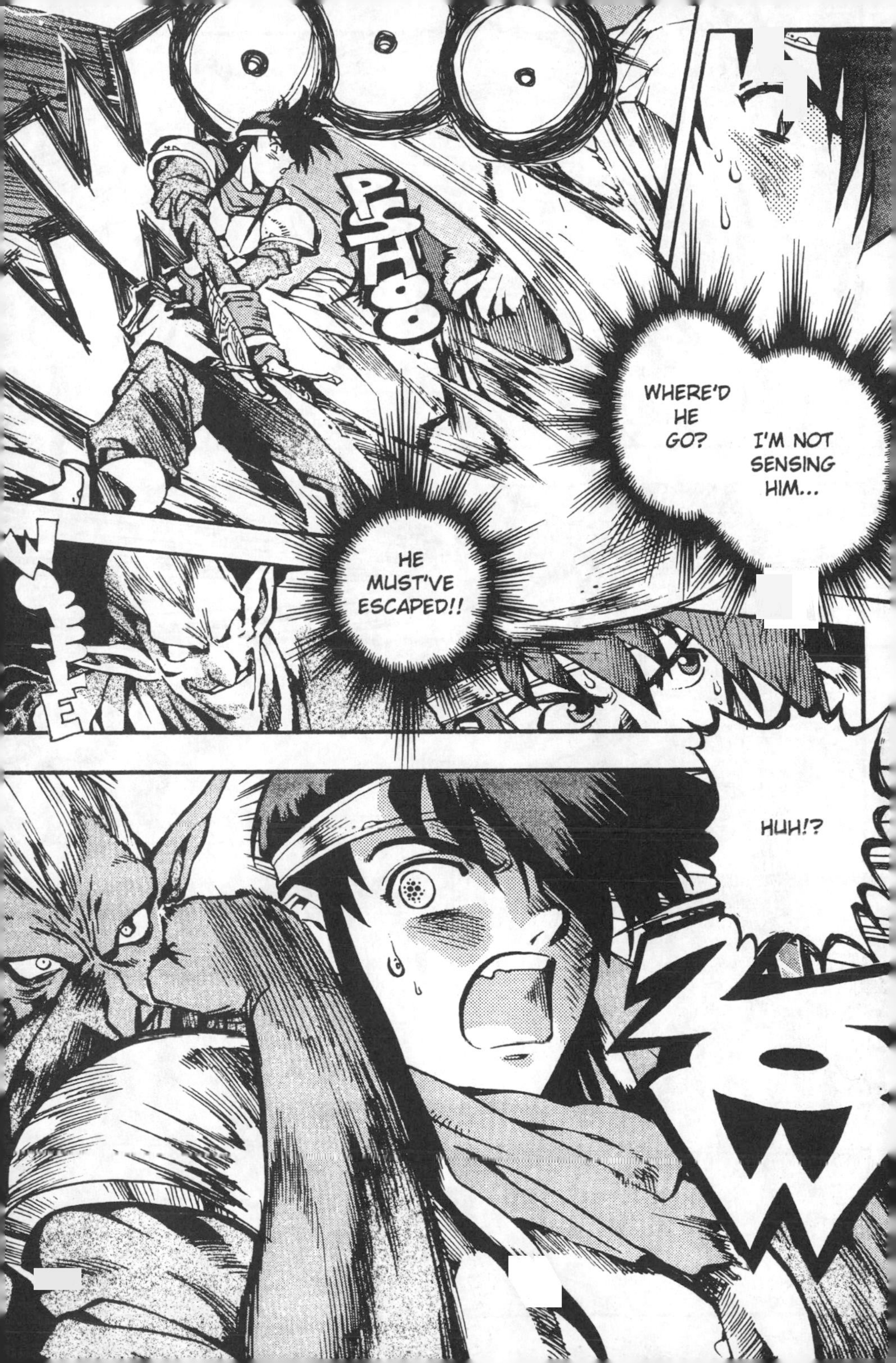

PSHOO
WHERE'D HE GO?
I'M NOT SENSING HIM...
HE MUST'VE ESCAPED!!
HUH!?

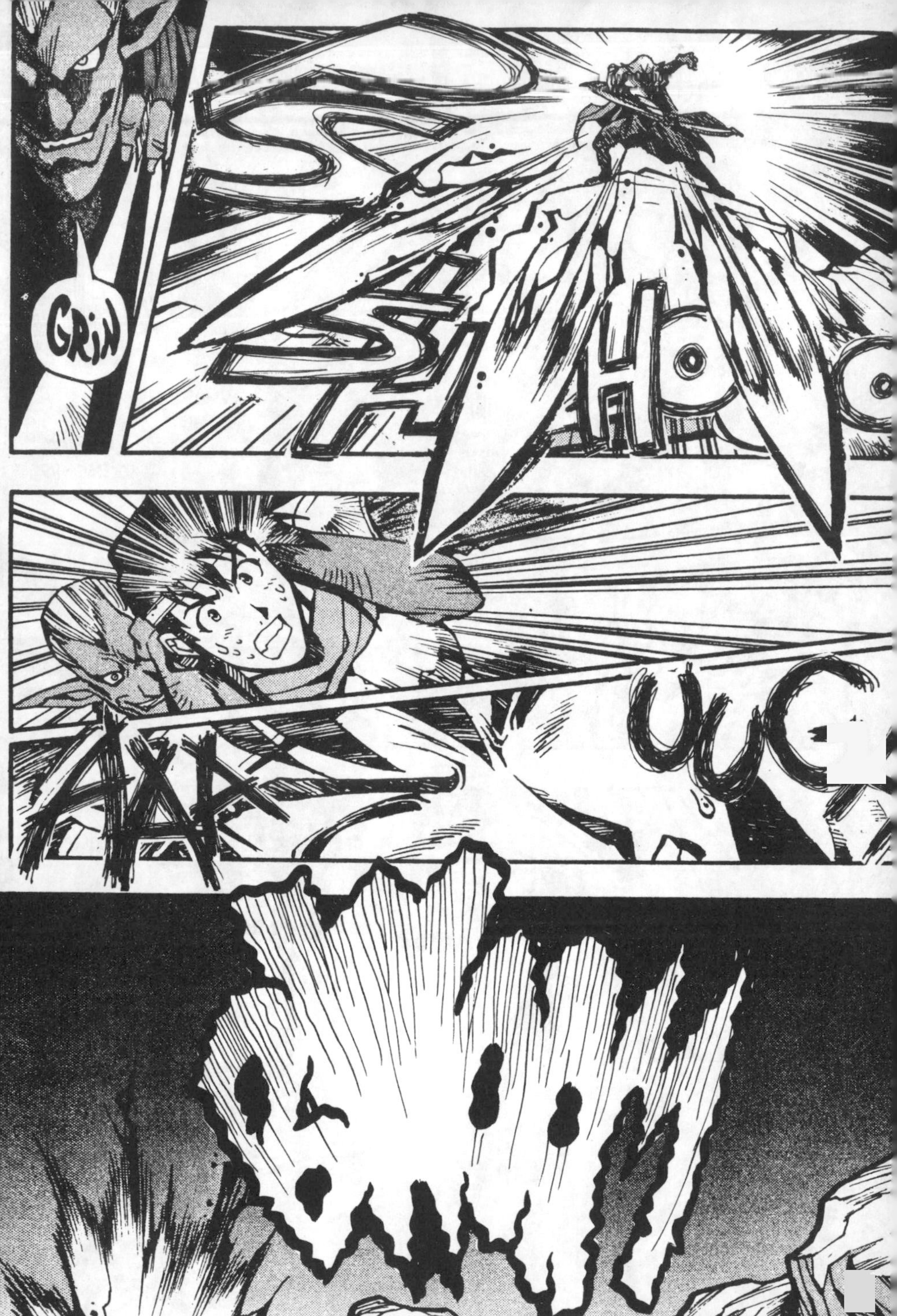
GRIN
UUG

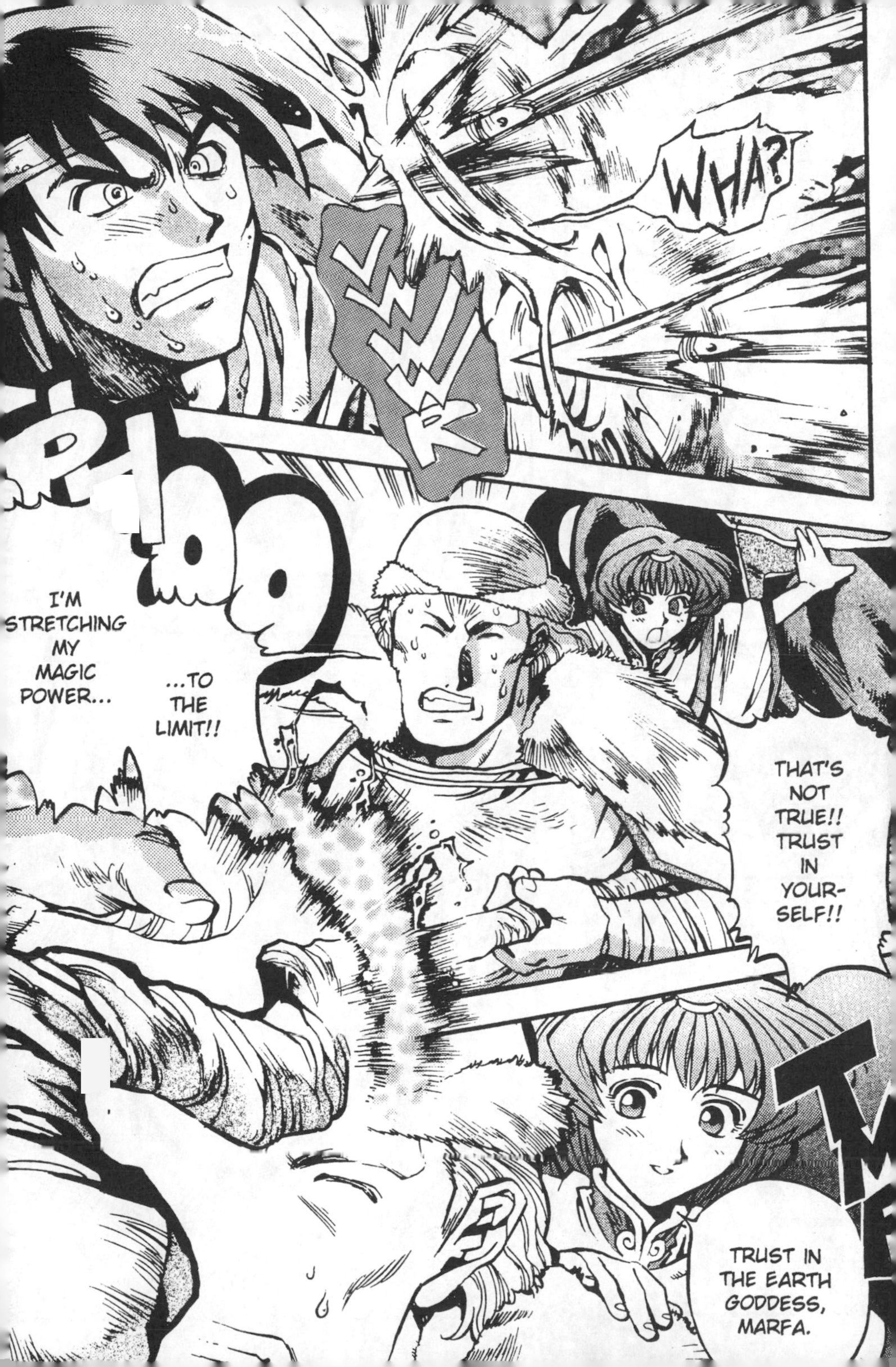

WHA?
I'M STRETCHING MY MAGIC POWER...
...TO THE LIMIT!!
THAT'S NOT TRUE!! TRUST IN YOURSELF!!
TRUST IN THE EARTH GODDESS, MARFA.

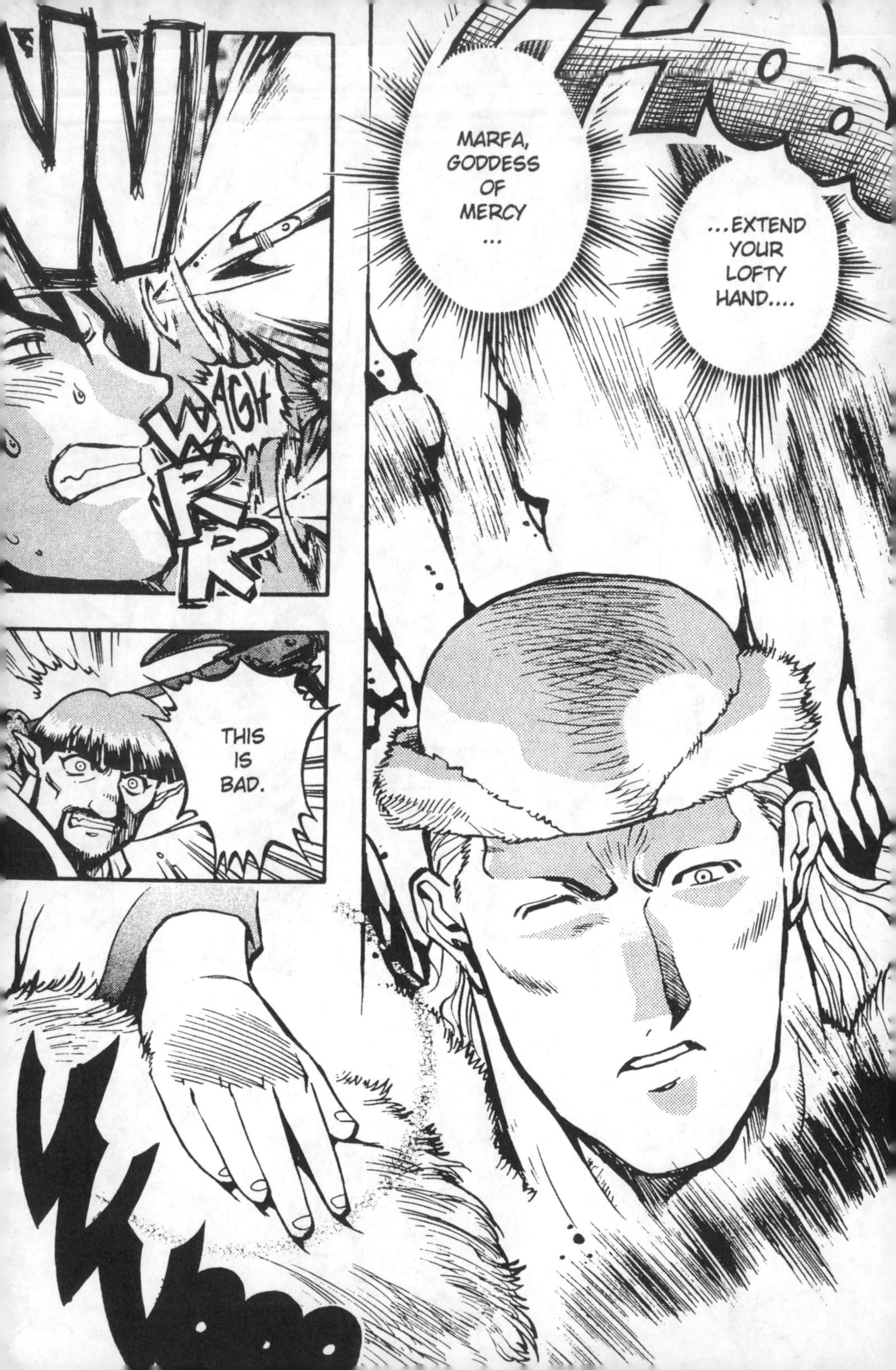
WAGH
THIS IS BAD.
MARFA, GODDESS OF MERCY ...
...EXTEND YOUR LOFTY HAND....

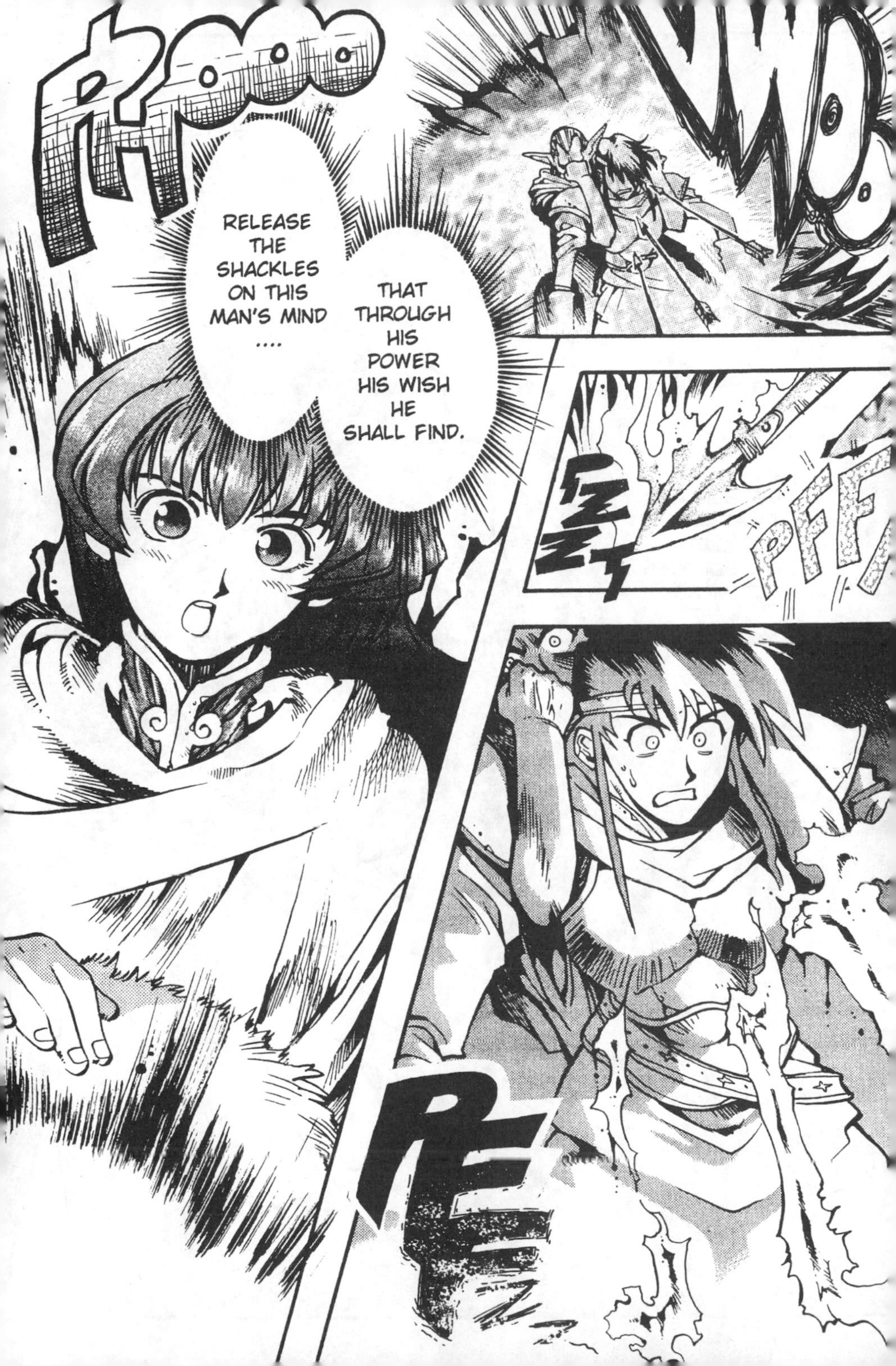
RELEASE THE SHACKLES ON THIS MAN'S MIND ....
THAT THROUGH HIS POWER HIS WISH HE SHALL FIND.

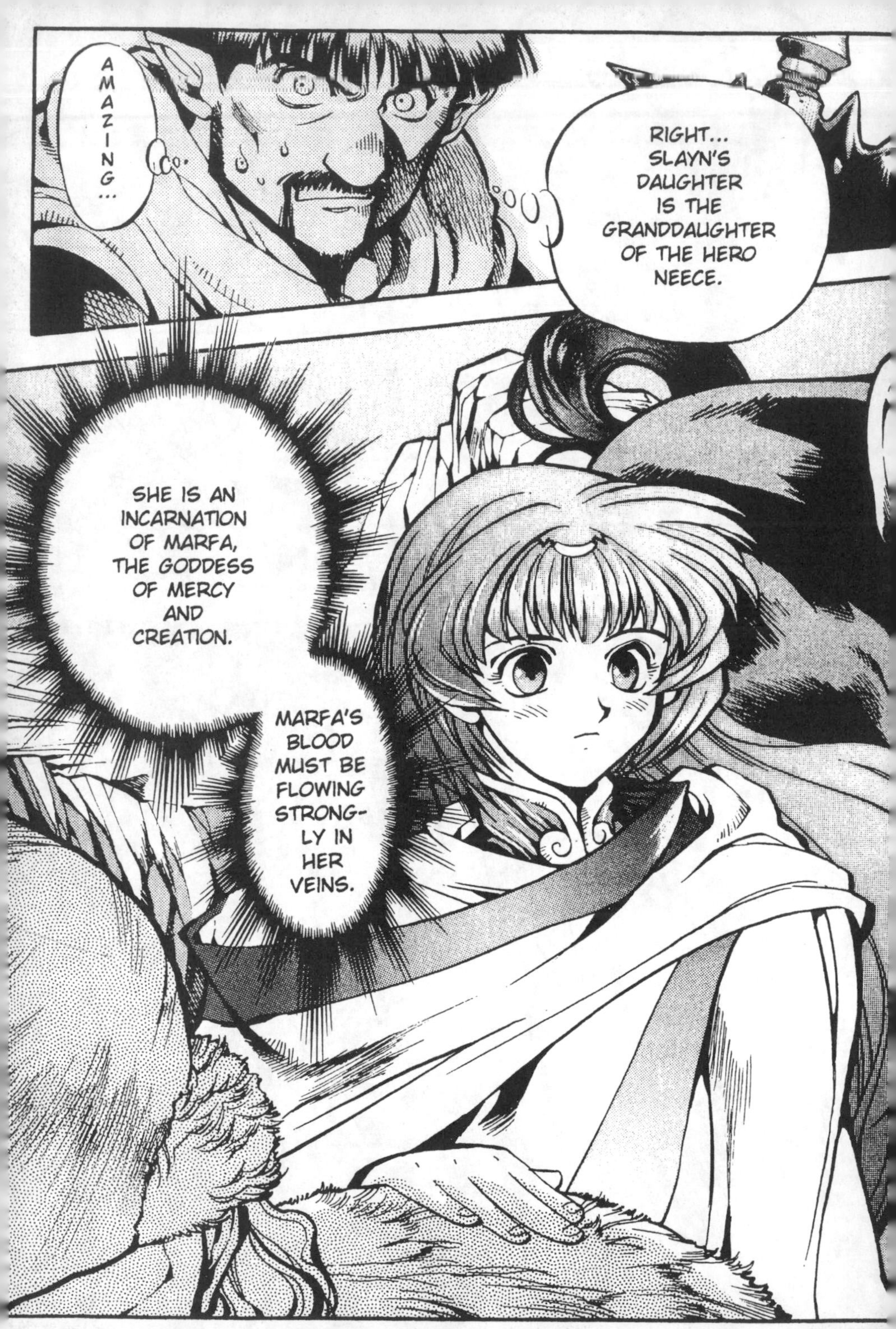
AMAZING...
RIGHT... SLAYN'S DAUGHTER IS THE GRANDDAUGHTER OF THE HERO NEECE.
SHE IS AN INCARNATION OF MARFA, THE GODDESS OF MERCY AND CREATION.
MARFA'S BLOOD MUST BE FLOWING STRONG-LY IN HER VEINS.

# The Spoils Of Battle

EPISODE 10

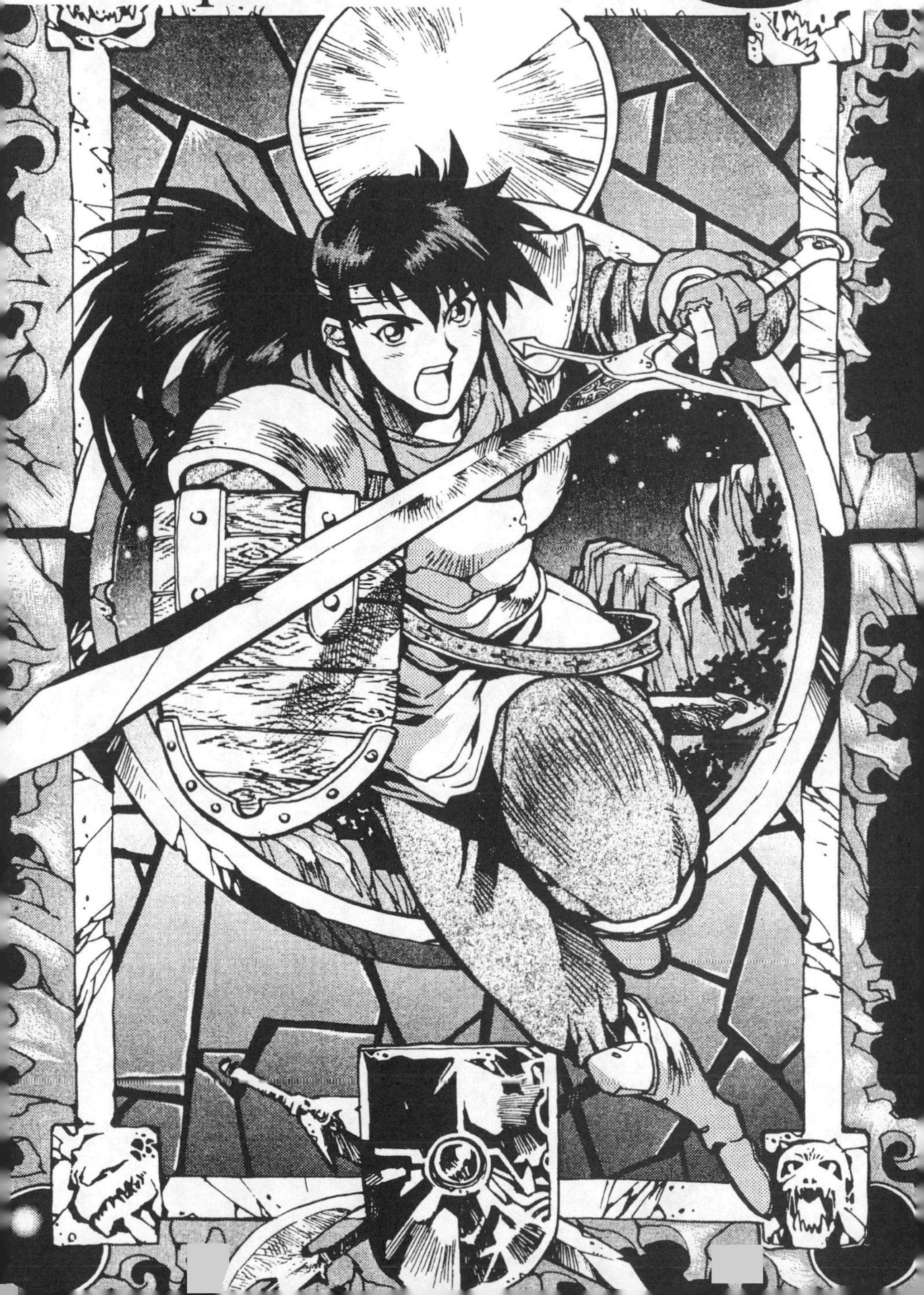

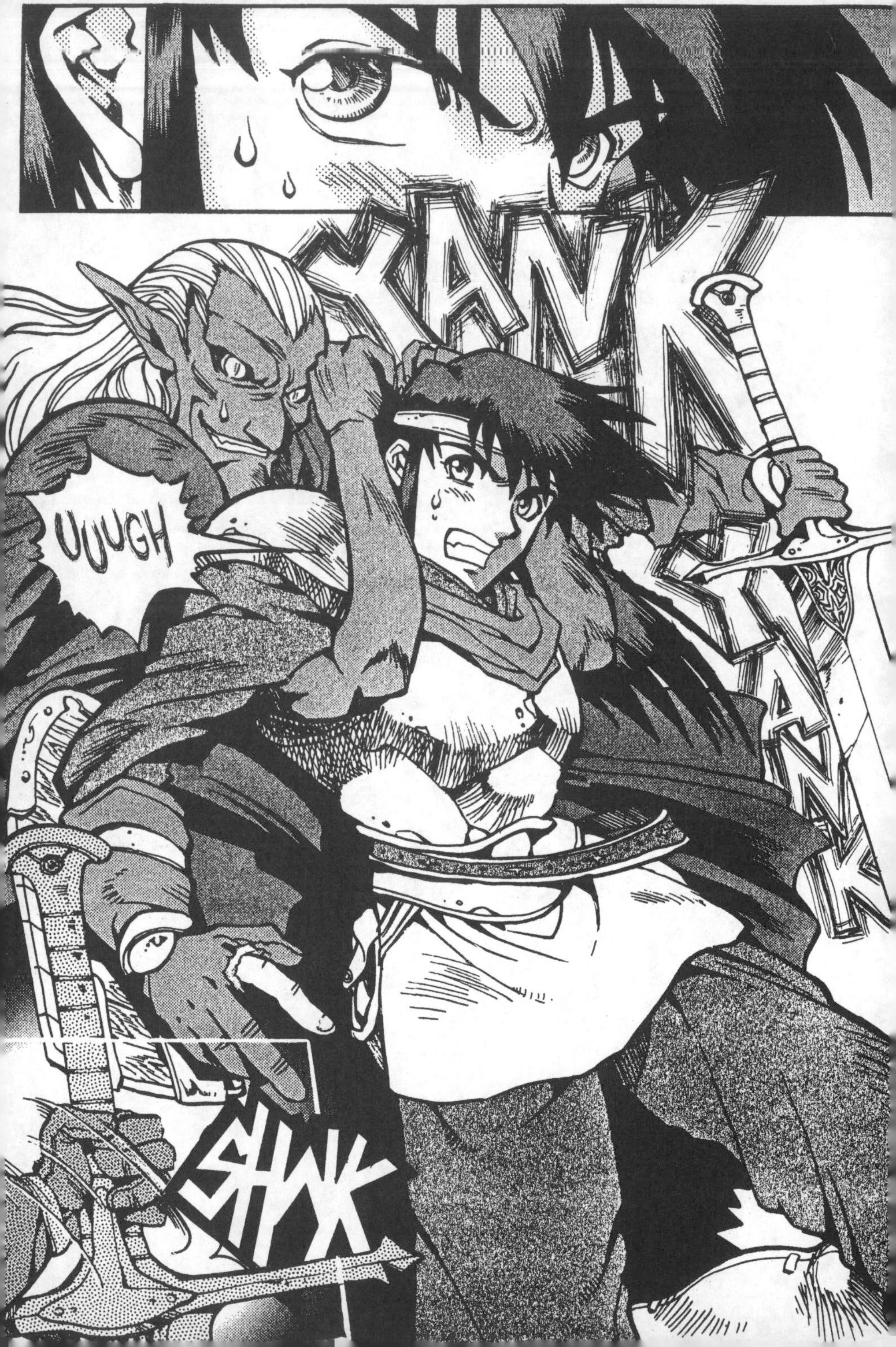
UUUGH

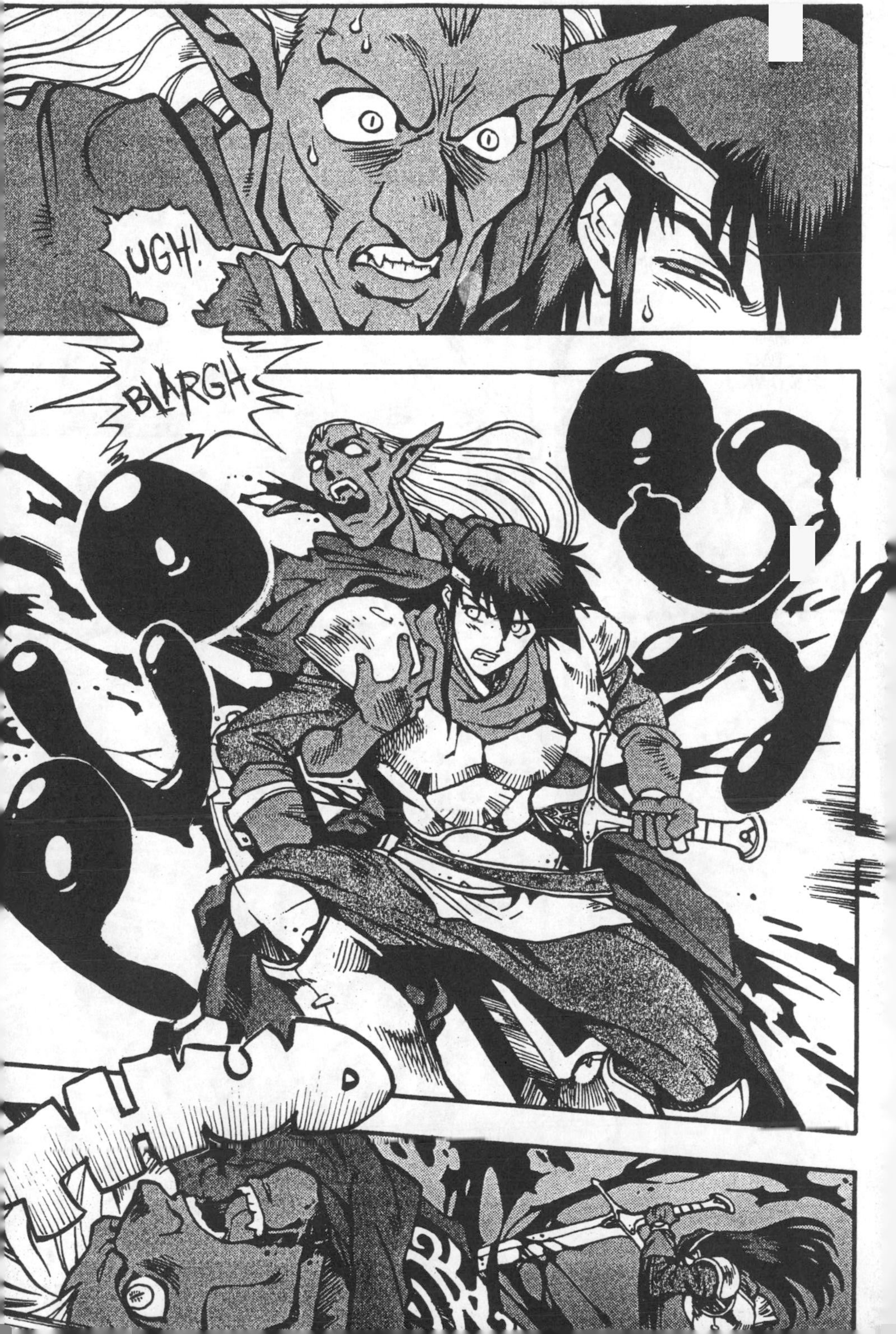
UGH!
BLARGH

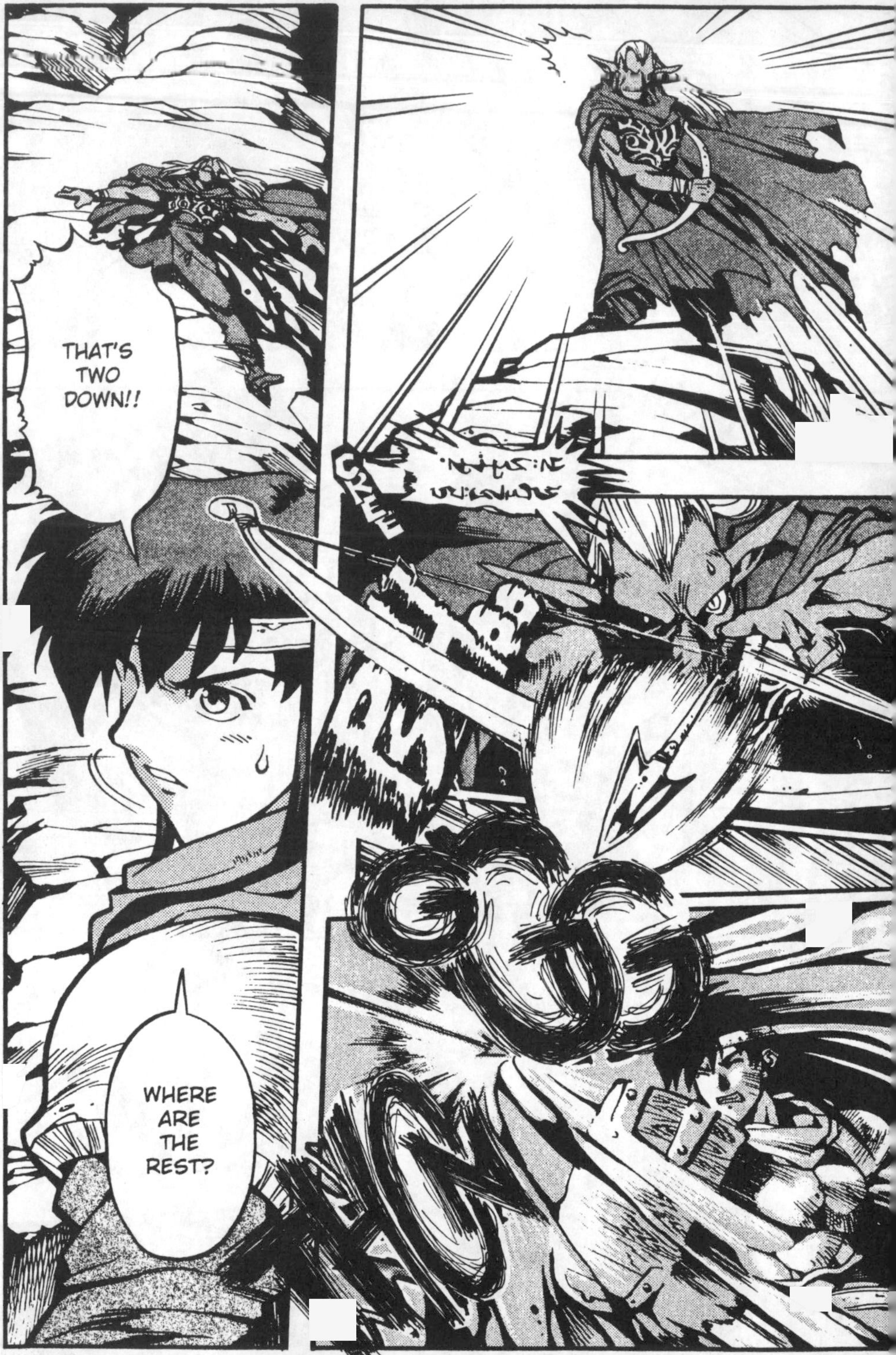
THAT'S TWO DOWN!!
WHERE ARE THE REST?

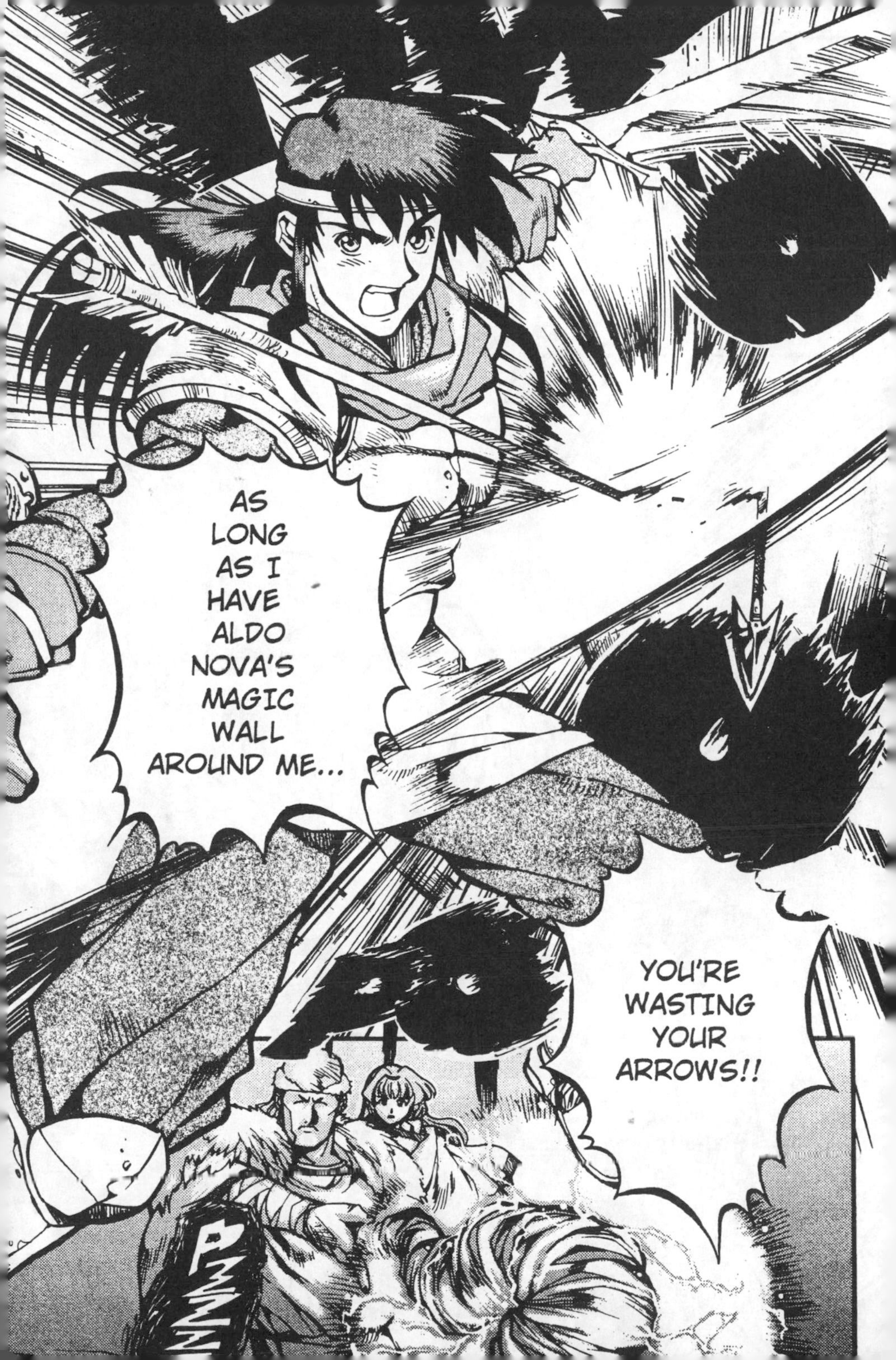
AS LONG AS I HAVE ALDO NOVA'S MAGIC WALL AROUND ME...
YOU'RE WASTING YOUR ARROWS!!

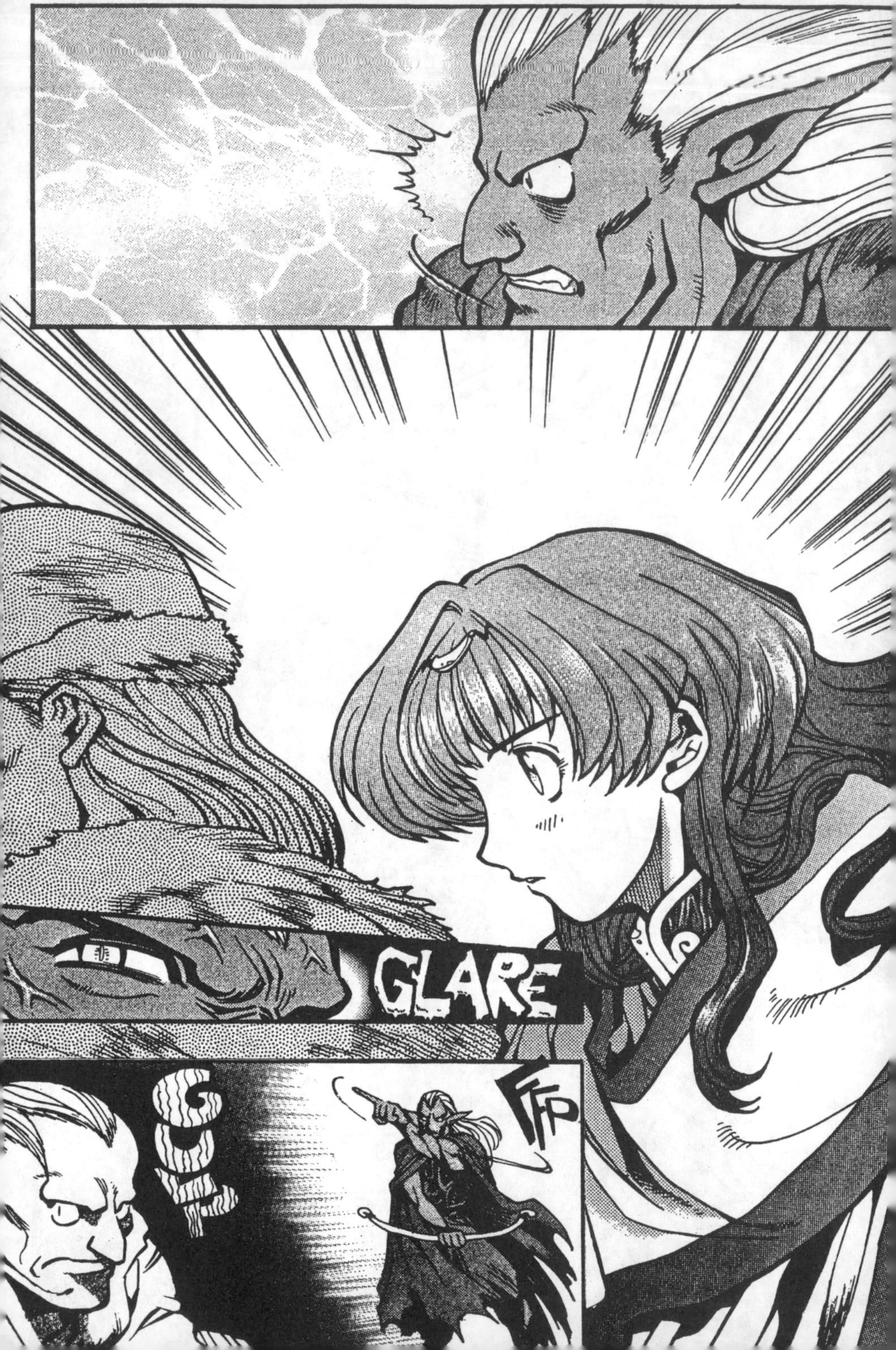
GLARE
G
FFP

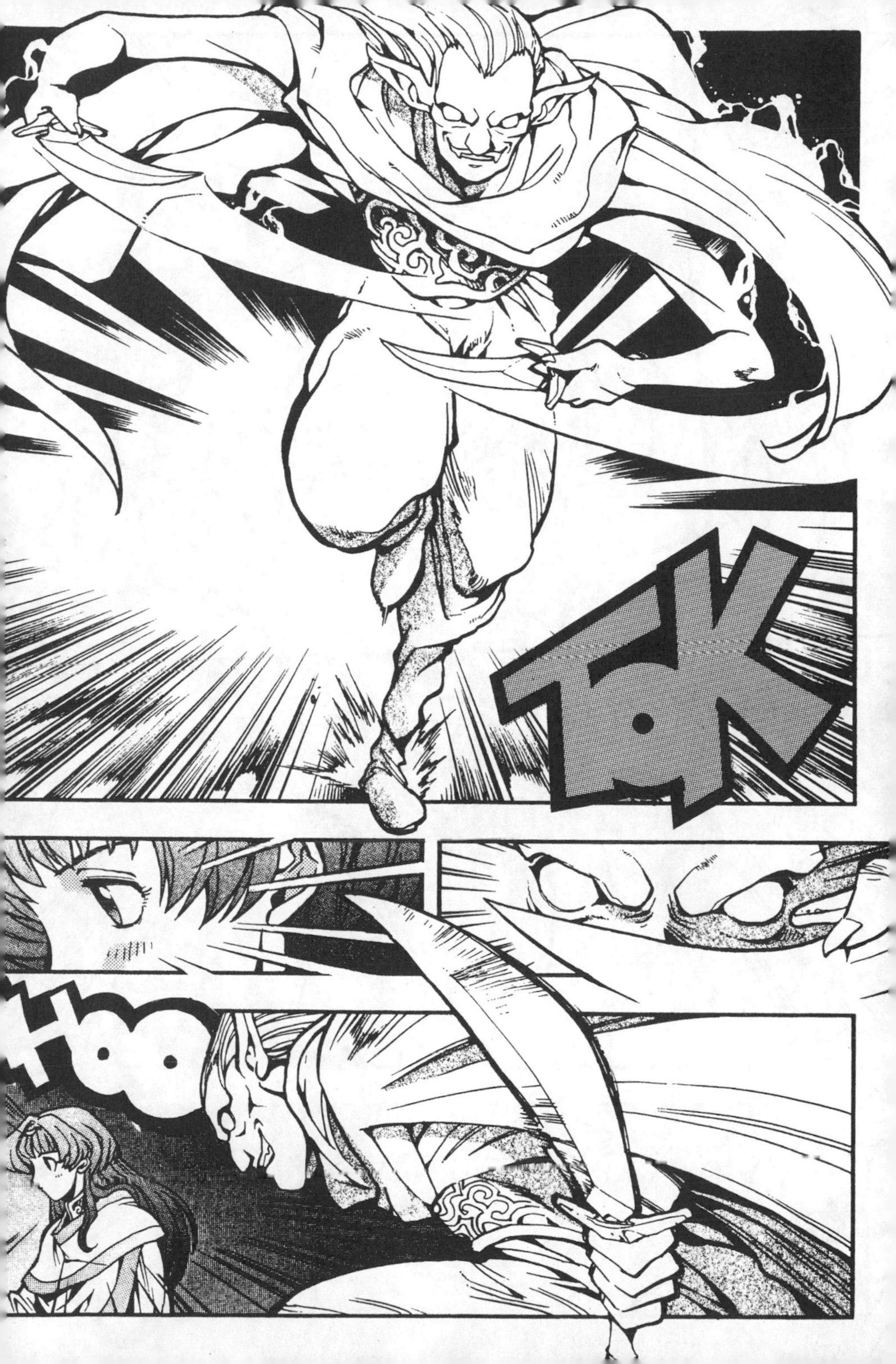
TOK

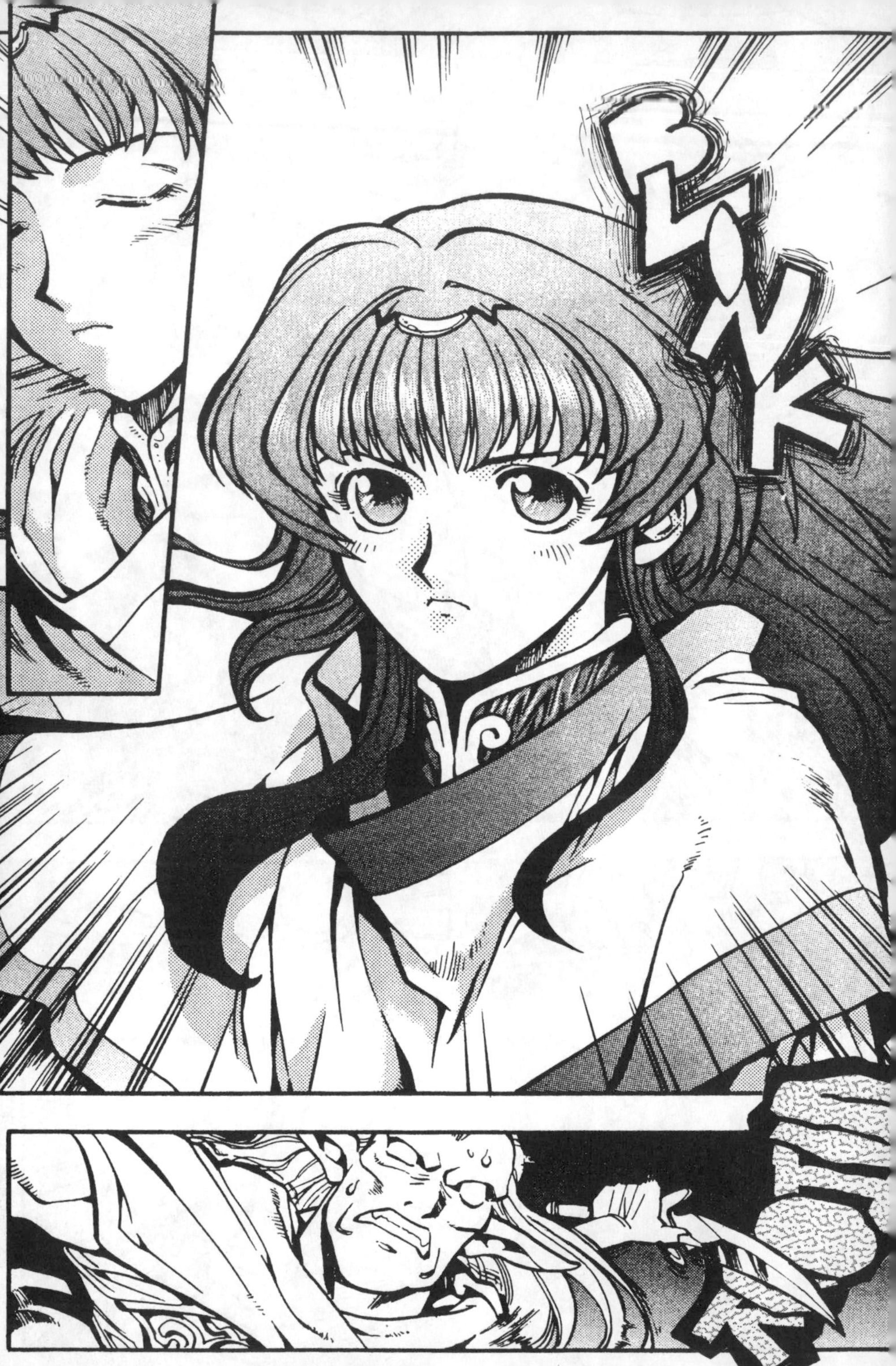
BLINK

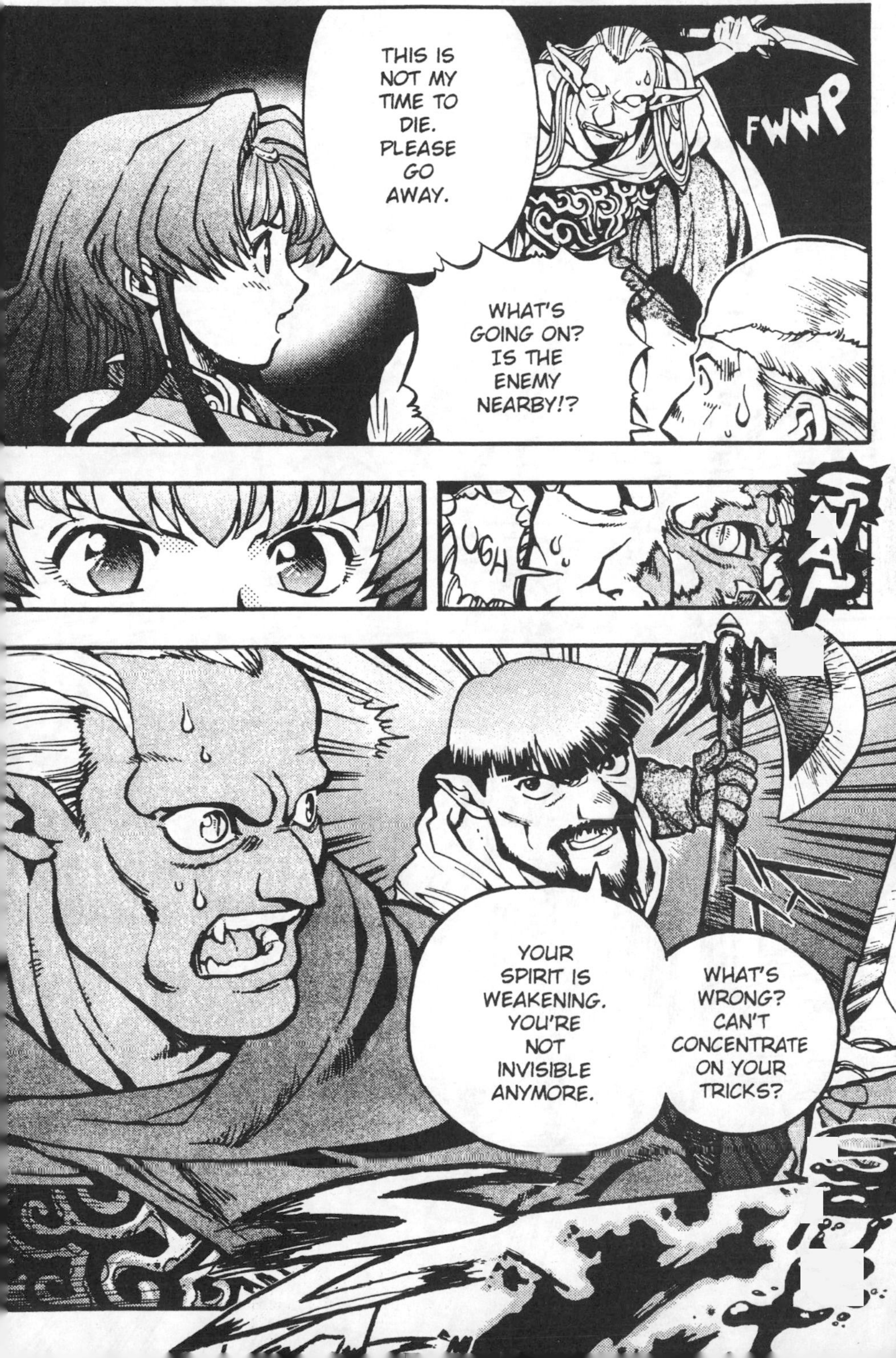
FWWP
THIS IS NOT MY TIME TO DIE. PLEASE GO AWAY.
WHAT'S GOING ON? IS THE ENEMY NEARBY!?
UGH
WHAT'S WRONG? CAN'T CONCENTRATE ON YOUR TRICKS?
YOUR SPIRIT IS WEAKENING. YOU'RE NOT INVISIBLE ANYMORE.

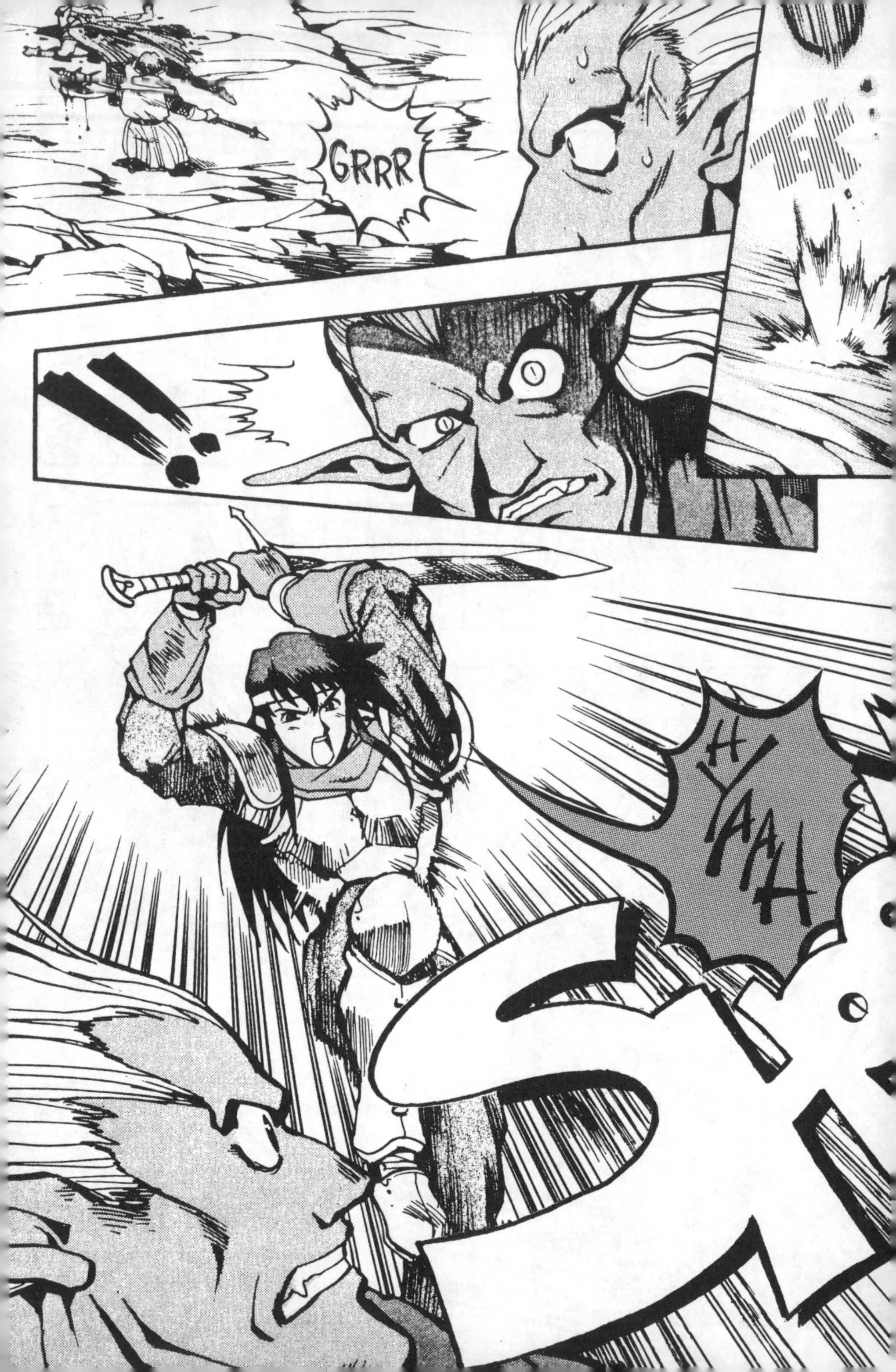
GRRR
!!
HYAAH

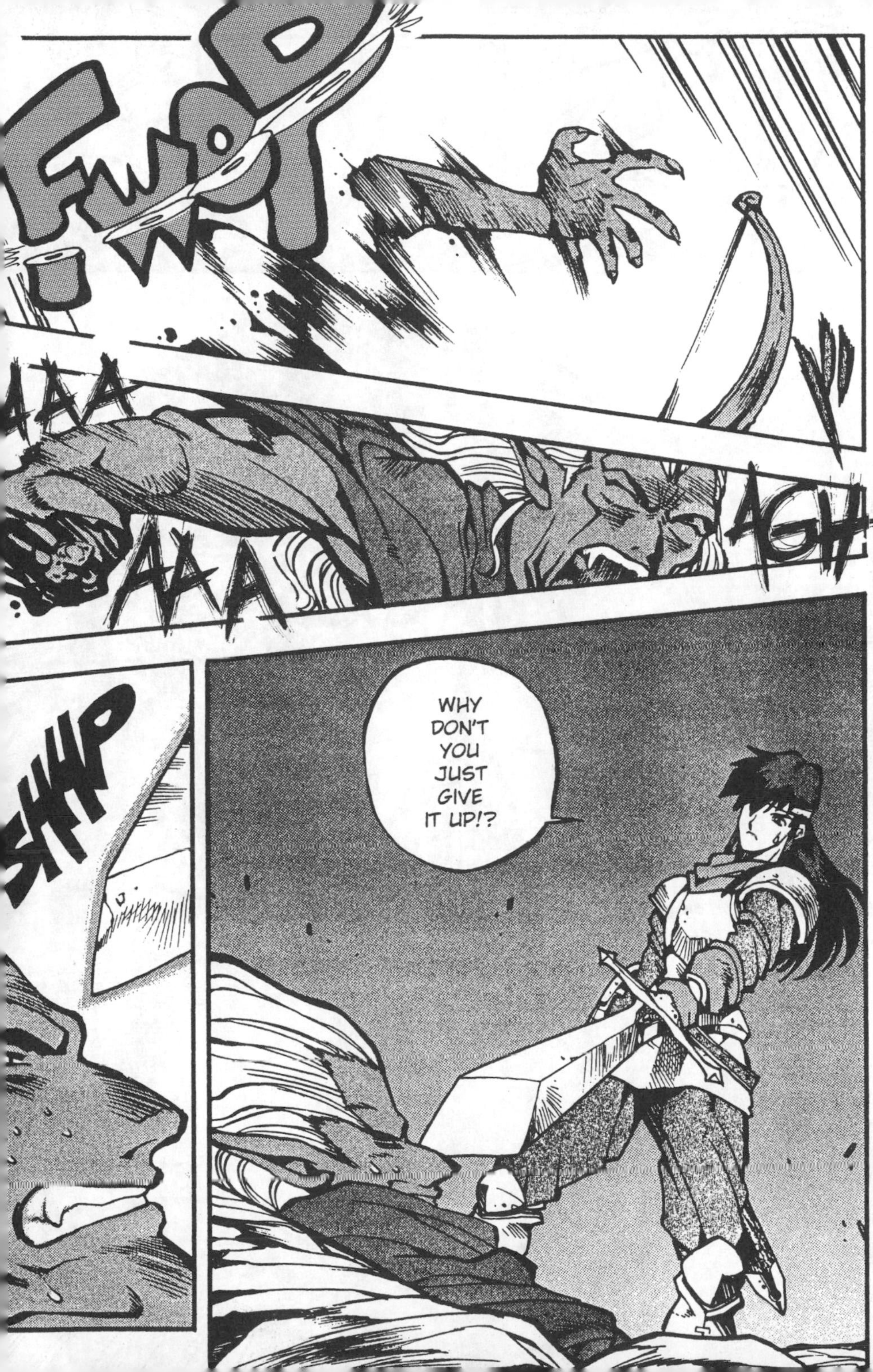
FWOP
AAA
AAA
AGH
SHHP
WHY DON'T YOU JUST GIVE IT UP!?

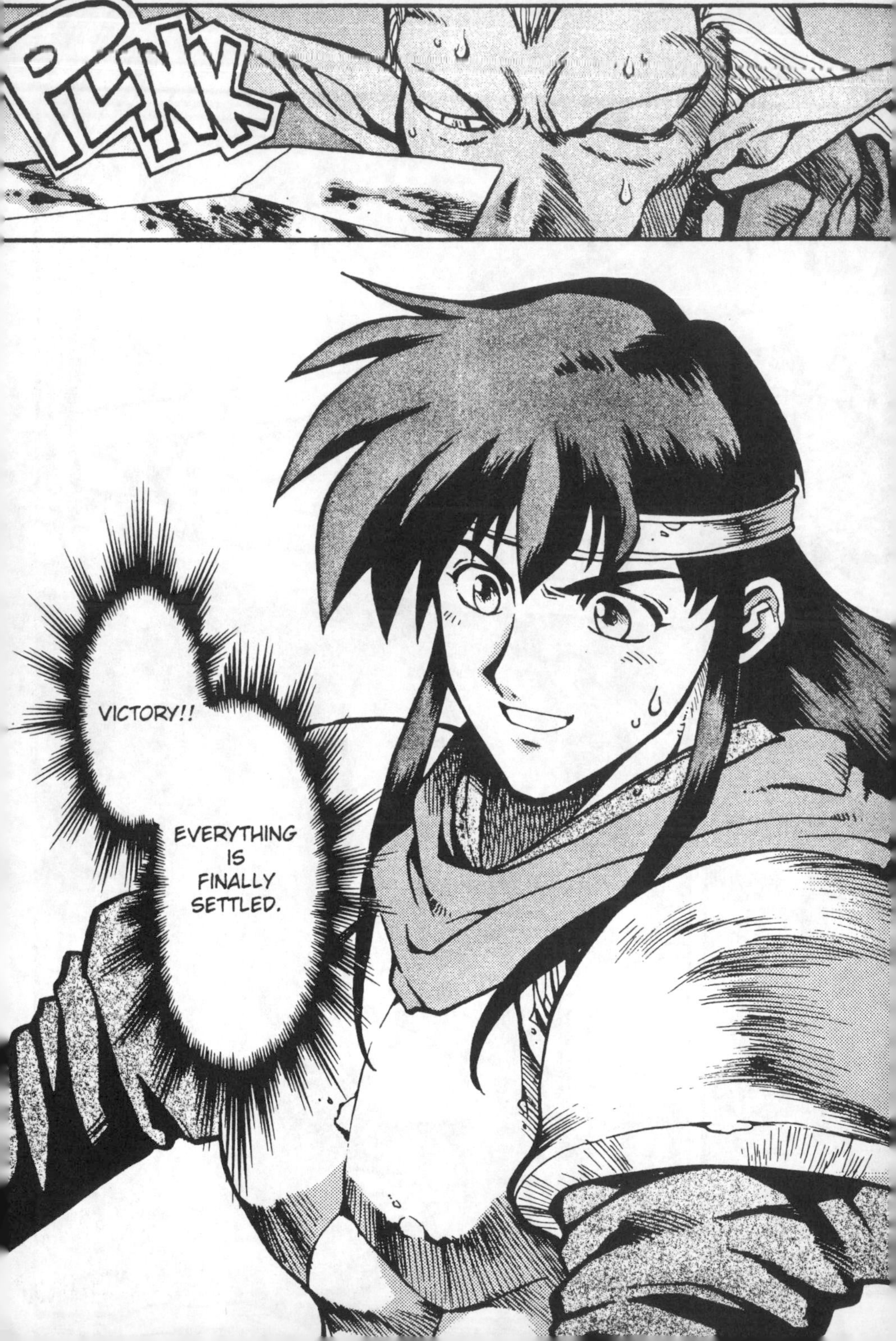
PLINK
VICTORY!!
EVERYTHING IS FINALLY SETTLED.

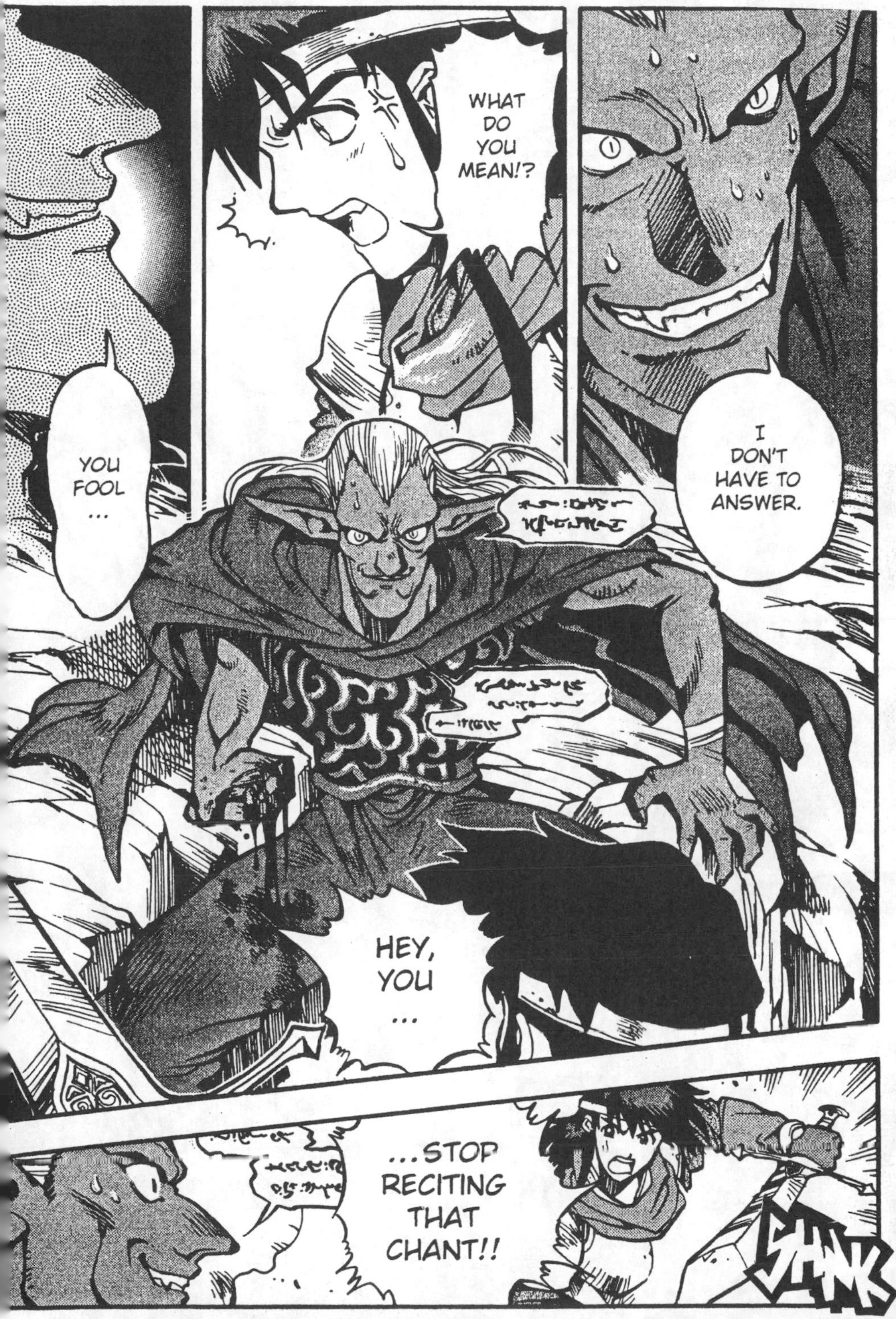
WHAT DO YOU MEAN!?
YOU FOOL ...
I DON'T HAVE TO ANSWER.
HEY, YOU ...
...STOP RECITING THAT CHANT!!
SHINK

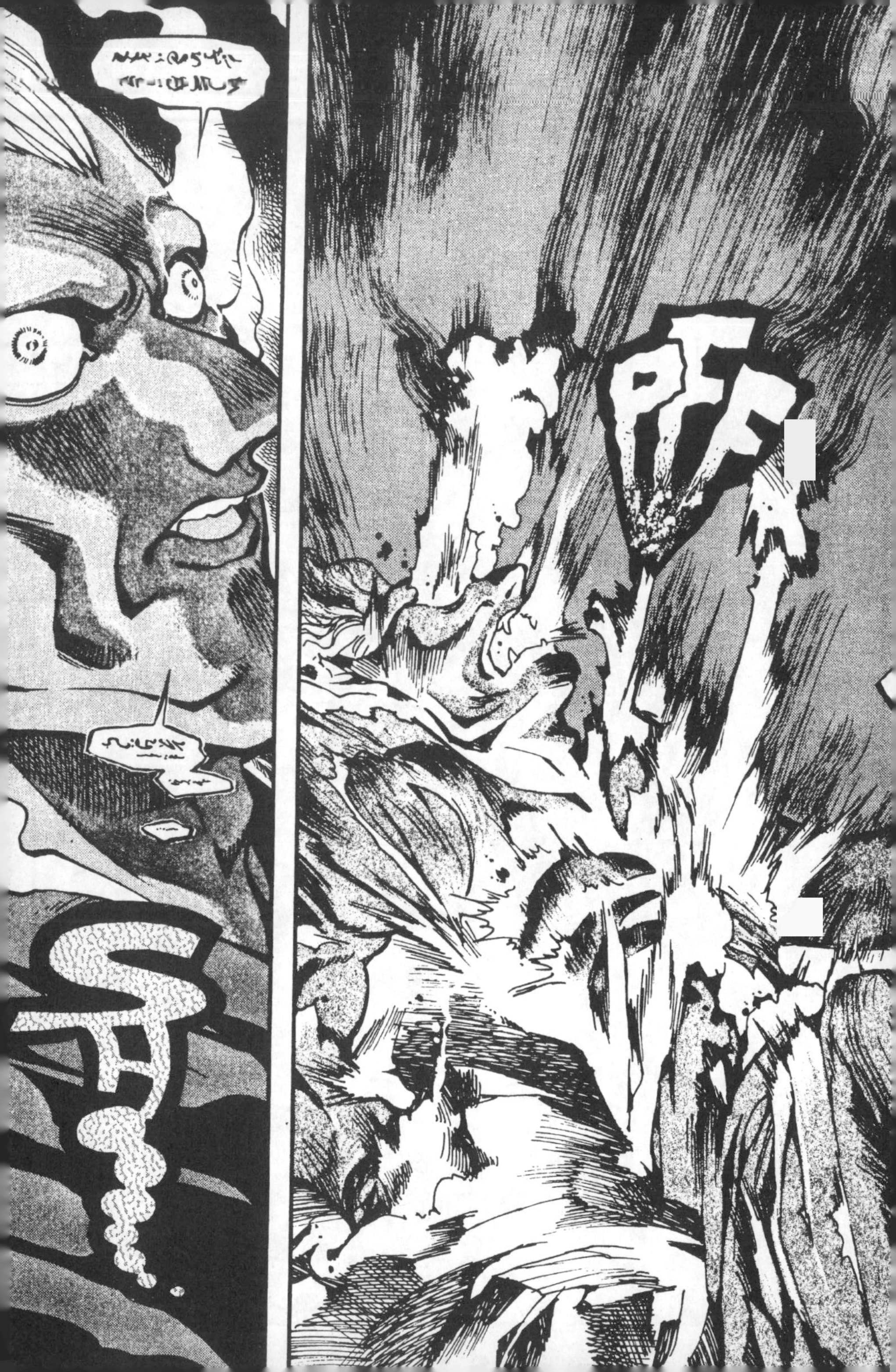
PFF

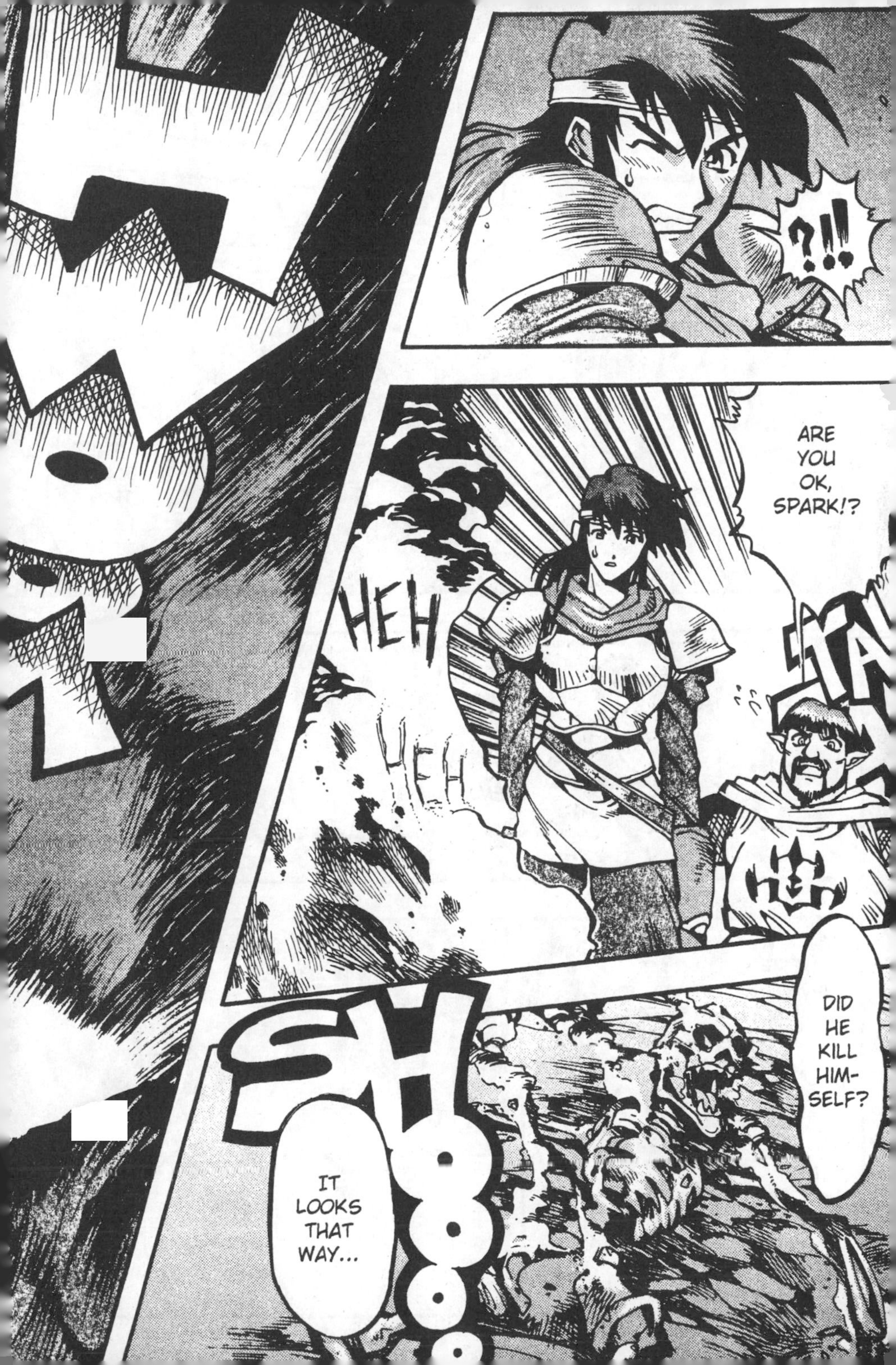
?!!
HEH
HEH
ARE YOU OK, SPARK!?
DID HE KILL HIM-SELF?
IT LOOKS THAT WAY...

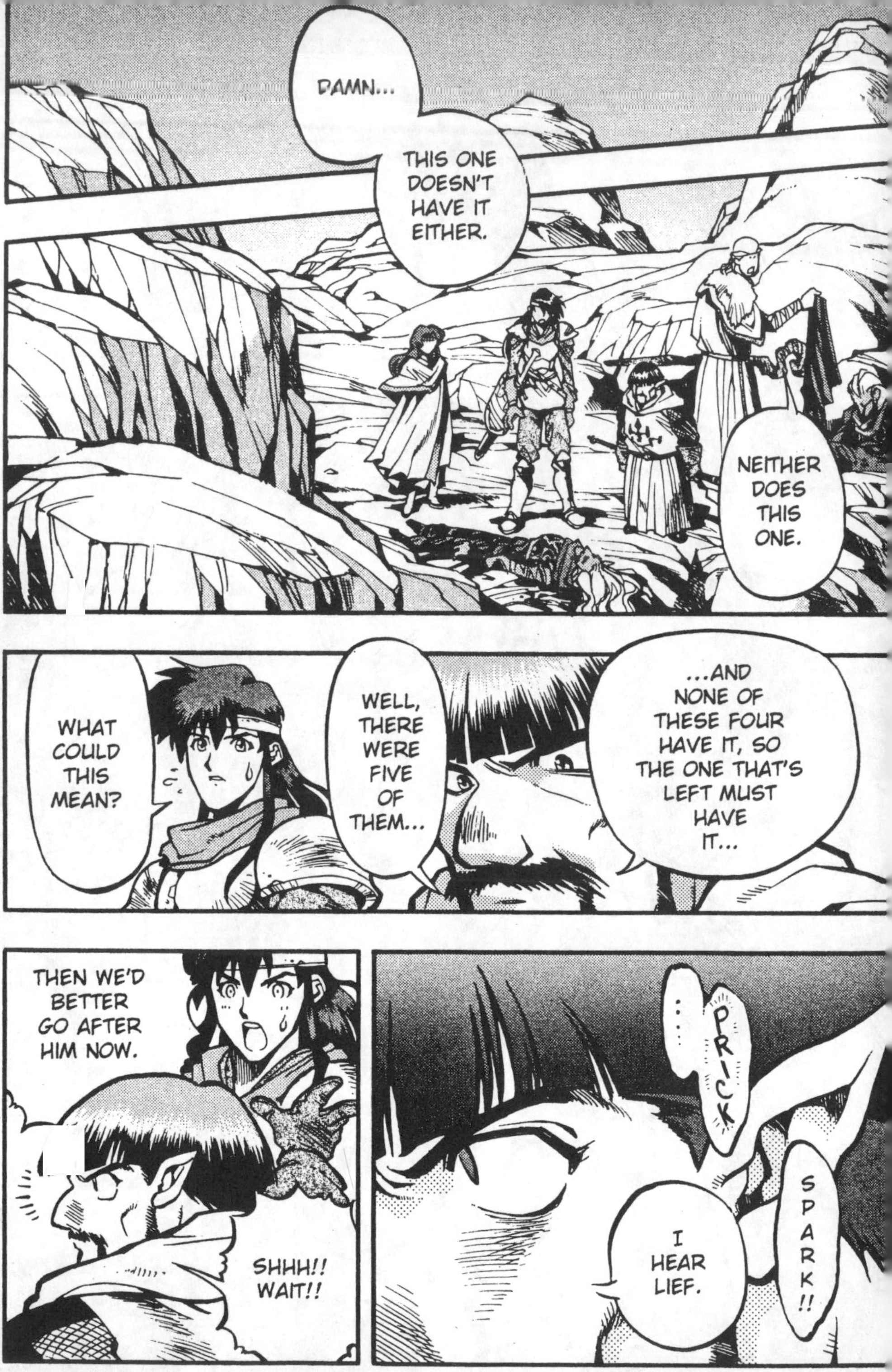
DAMN...
THIS ONE DOESN'T HAVE IT EITHER.
NEITHER DOES THIS ONE.
WHAT COULD THIS MEAN?
WELL, THERE WERE FIVE OF THEM...
...AND NONE OF THESE FOUR HAVE IT, SO THE ONE THAT'S LEFT MUST HAVE IT...
THEN WE'D BETTER GO AFTER HIM NOW.
SHHH!! WAIT!!
...
PRICK
I HEAR LIEF.
SPARK!!

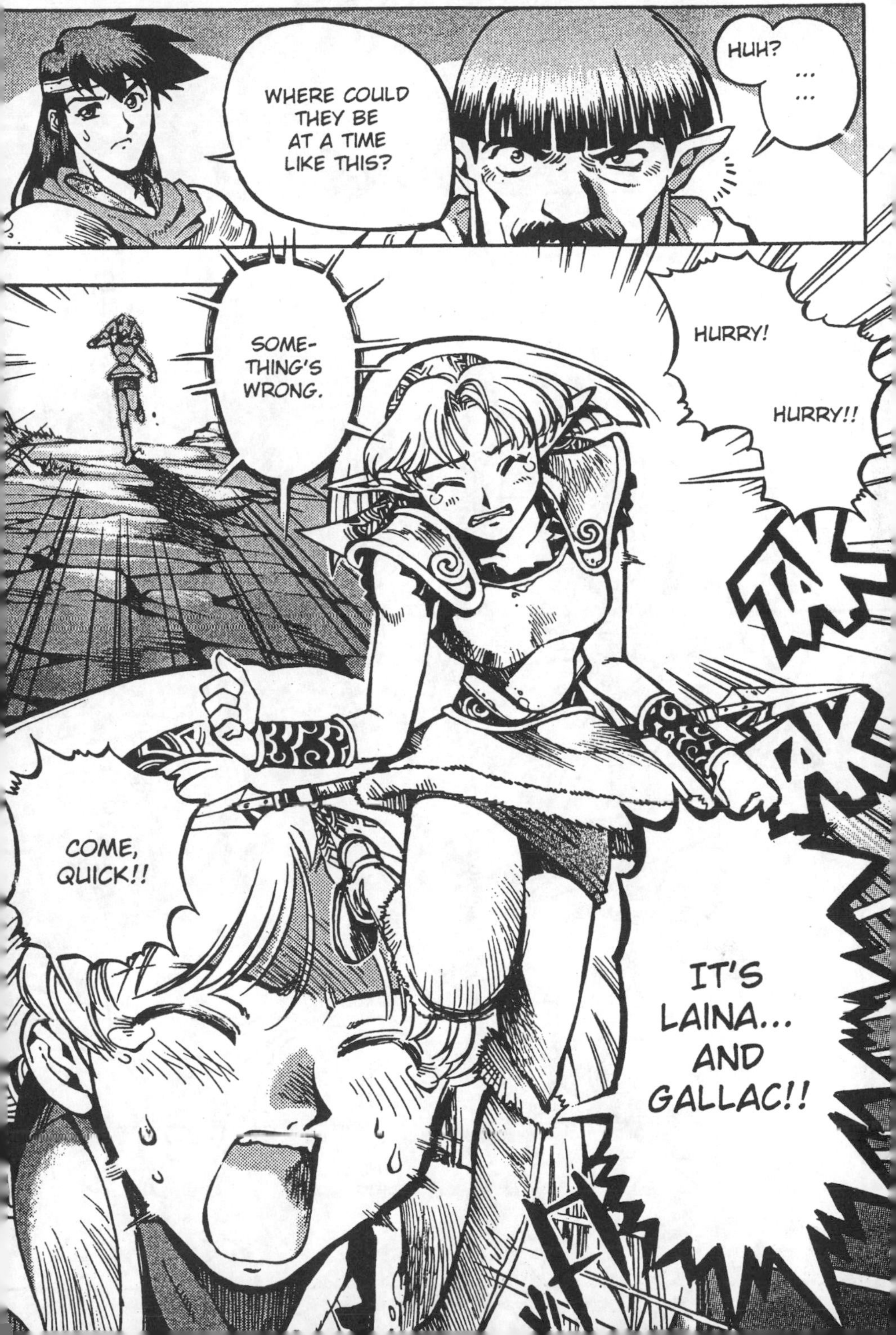
WHERE COULD THEY BE AT A TIME LIKE THIS?
HUH? ... ...
SOME-THING'S WRONG.
HURRY!
HURRY!!
TAK
TAK
COME, QUICK!!
IT'S LAINA... AND GALLAC!!

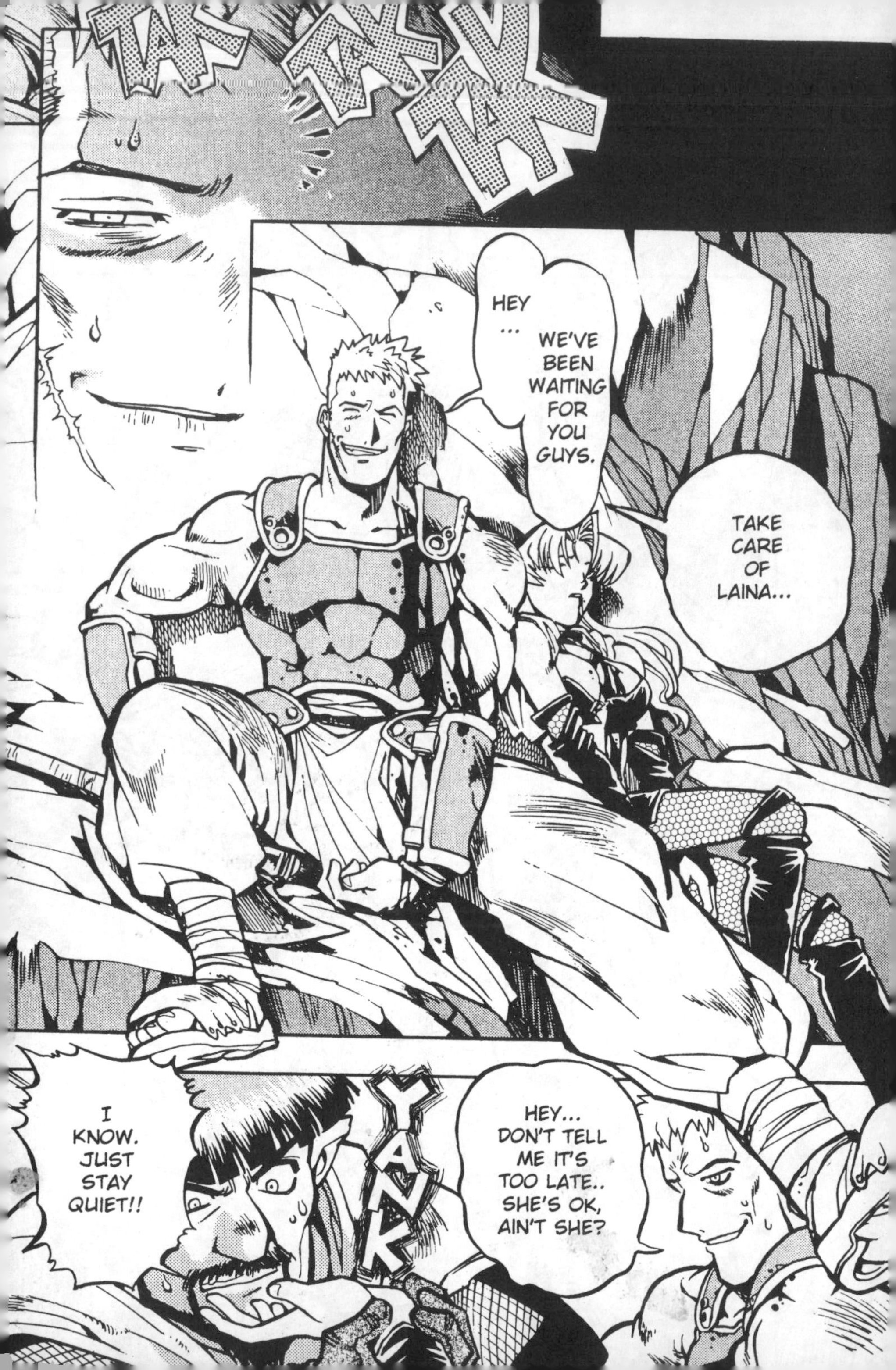
TAK TAK TAK
HEY ... WE'VE BEEN WAITING FOR YOU GUYS.
TAKE CARE OF LAINA...
I KNOW. JUST STAY QUIET!!
YANK
HEY... DON'T TELL ME IT'S TOO LATE.. SHE'S OK, AIN'T SHE?

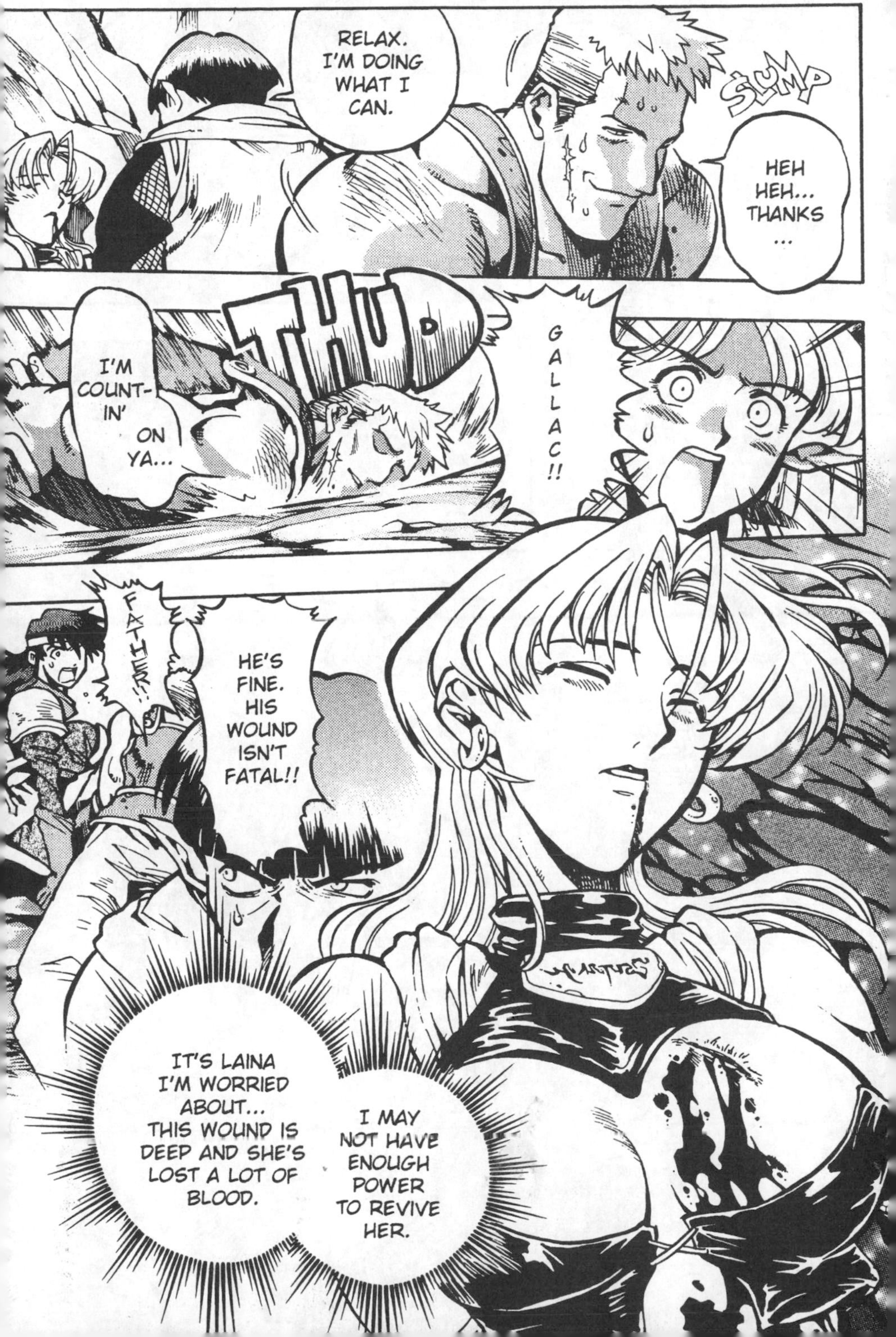
RELAX. I'M DOING WHAT I CAN.
SLUMP
HEH HEH... THANKS ...
I'M COUNT-IN' ON YA...
THUD
GALLAC!!
FATHER!!
HE'S FINE. HIS WOUND ISN'T FATAL!!
IT'S LAINA I'M WORRIED ABOUT... THIS WOUND IS DEEP AND SHE'S LOST A LOT OF BLOOD.
I MAY NOT HAVE ENOUGH POWER TO REVIVE HER.

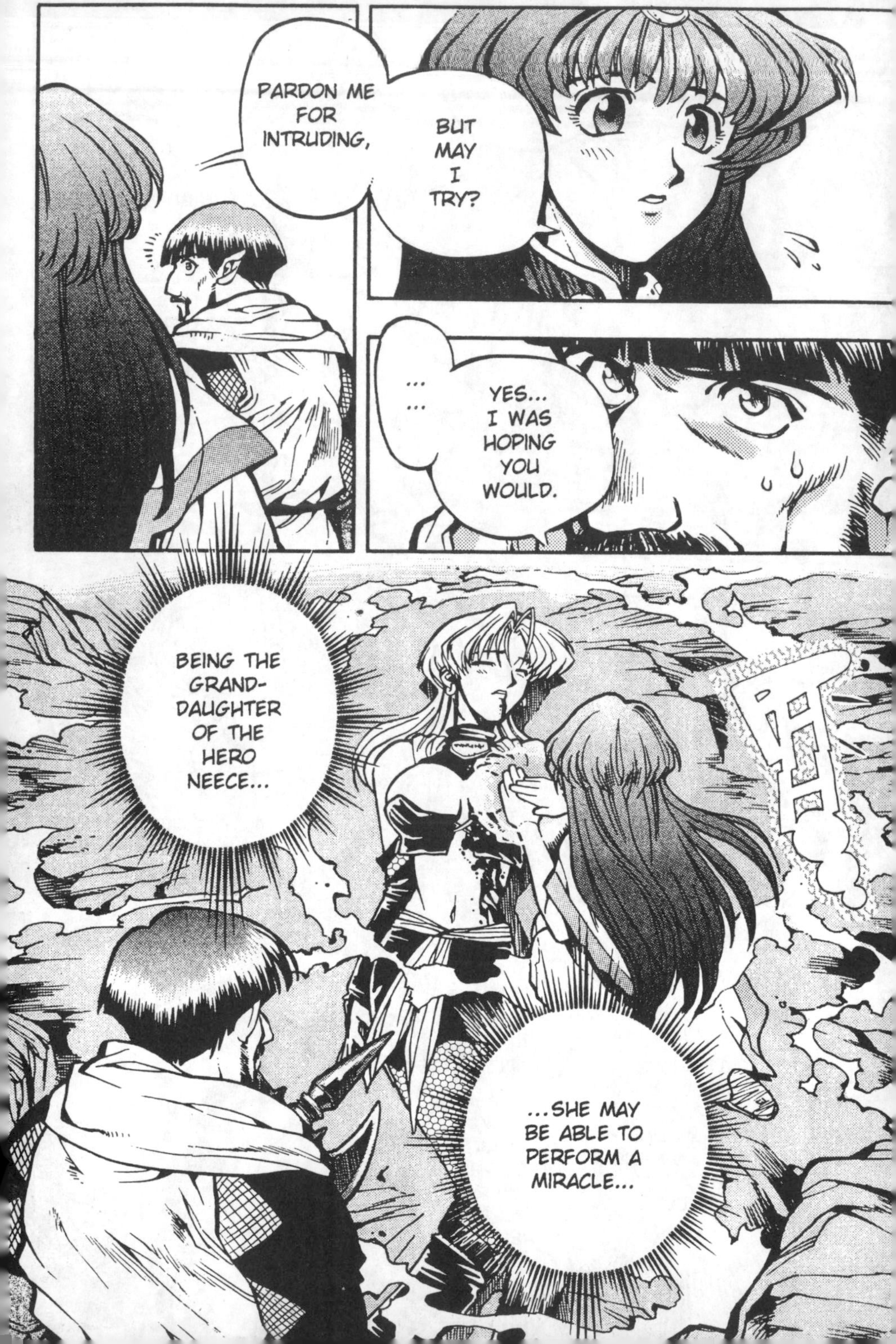
PARDON ME FOR INTRUDING,
BUT MAY I TRY?
...
...
YES... I WAS HOPING YOU WOULD.
BEING THE GRAND-DAUGHTER OF THE HERO NEECE...
...SHE MAY BE ABLE TO PERFORM A MIRACLE...

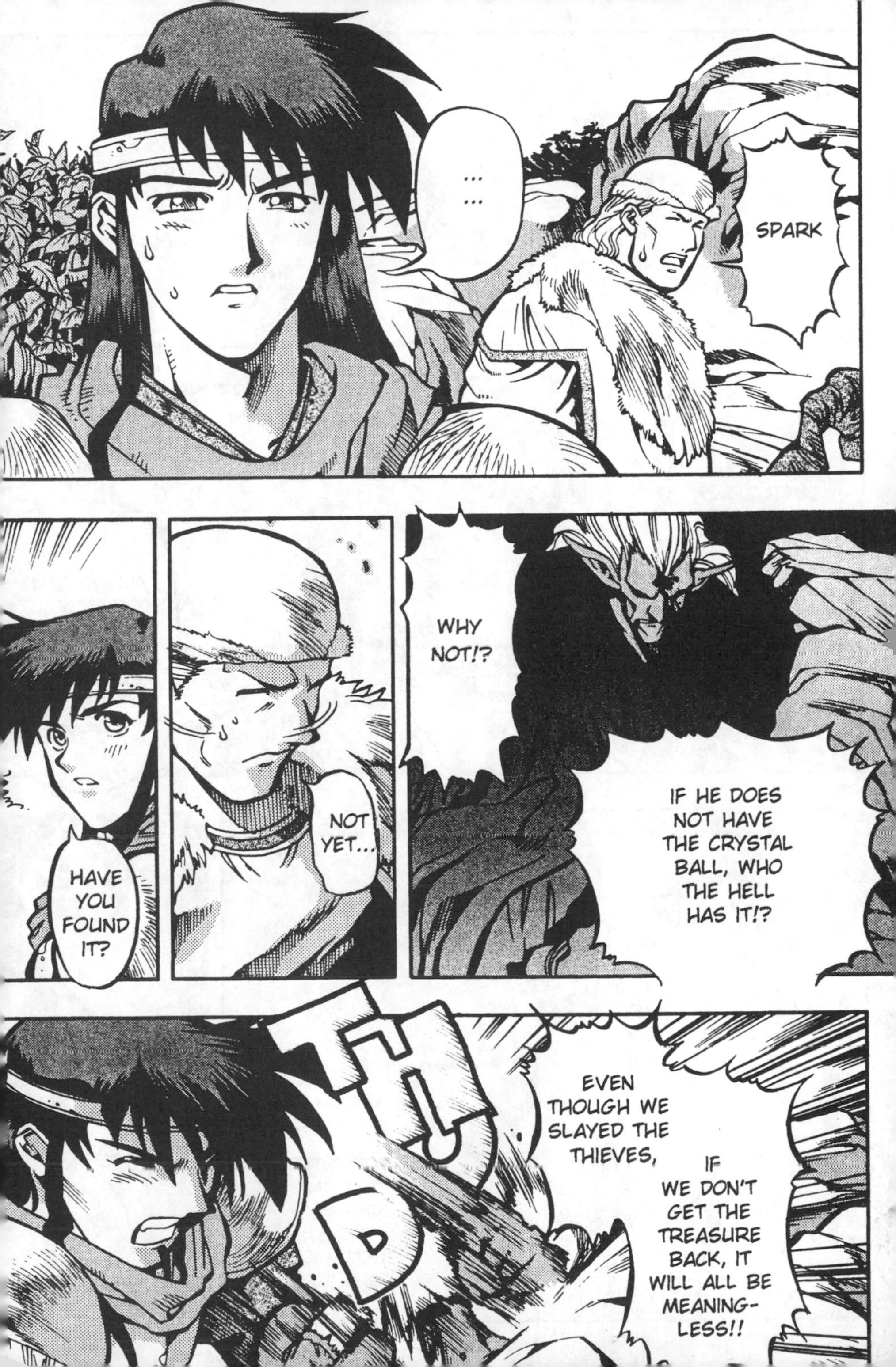

... ...
SPARK
HAVE YOU FOUND IT?
NOT YET...
WHY NOT!?
IF HE DOES NOT HAVE THE CRYSTAL BALL, WHO THE HELL HAS IT!?
THUD
EVEN THOUGH WE SLAYED THE THIEVES,
IF WE DON'T GET THE TREASURE BACK, IT WILL ALL BE MEANING-LESS!!

THAT'S NOT TRUE.

WE'VE KILLED THE THIEVES. WE'VE CARRIED OUT OUR DUTY, HAVEN'T WE?

I'VE DONE EVERYTHING I CAN FOR HER.

ALL WE CAN DO NOW IS WAIT FOR HER TO RETURN TO CONSCIOUSNESS.

ALL I WANT TO DO IS RETRIEVE THE STOLEN TREAURE...

BUT WITHOUT ANY INFORMATION, WE CAN'T MAKE A MOVE.

...
...

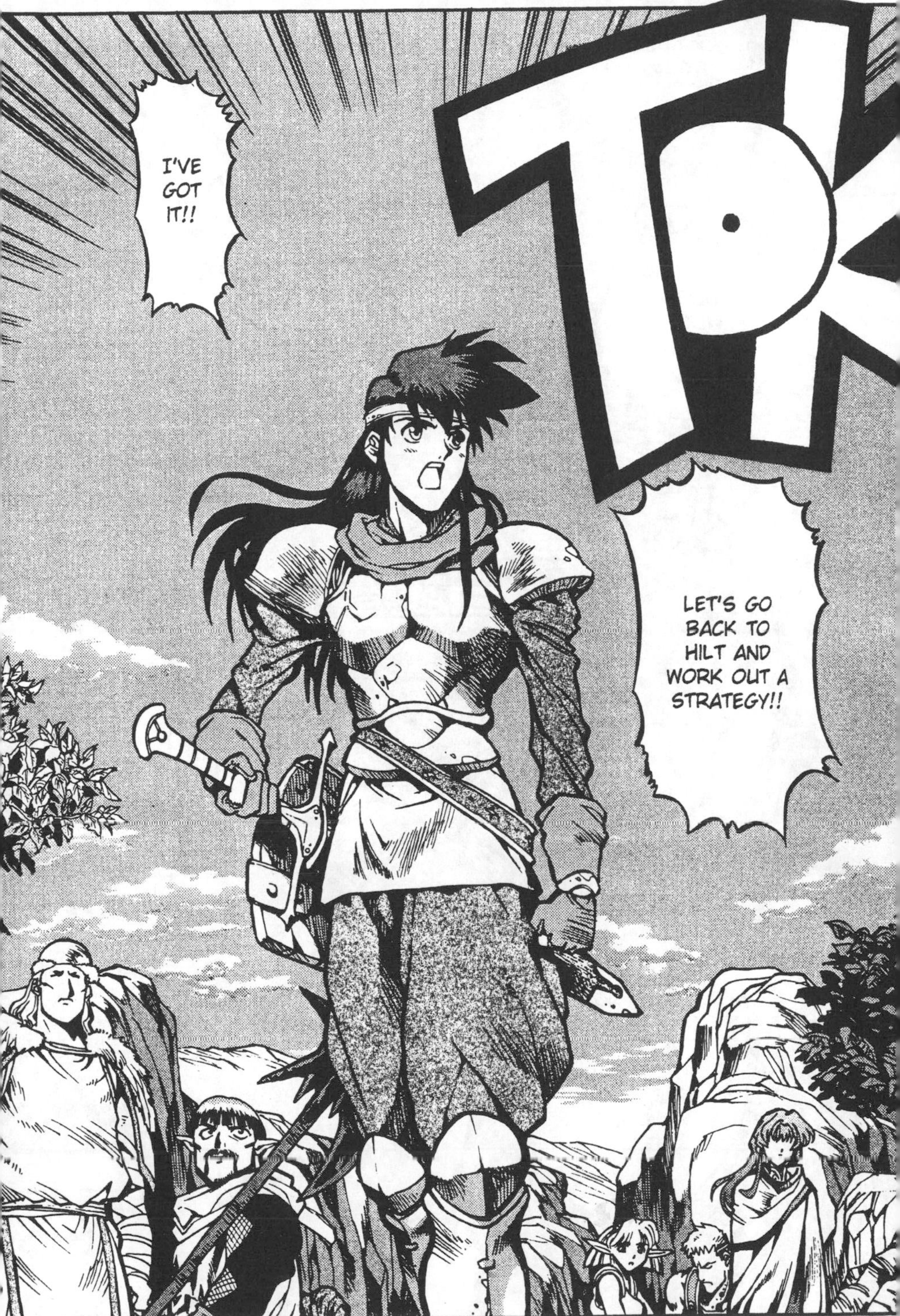
I'VE GOT IT!!
LET'S GO BACK TO HILT AND WORK OUT A STRATEGY!!

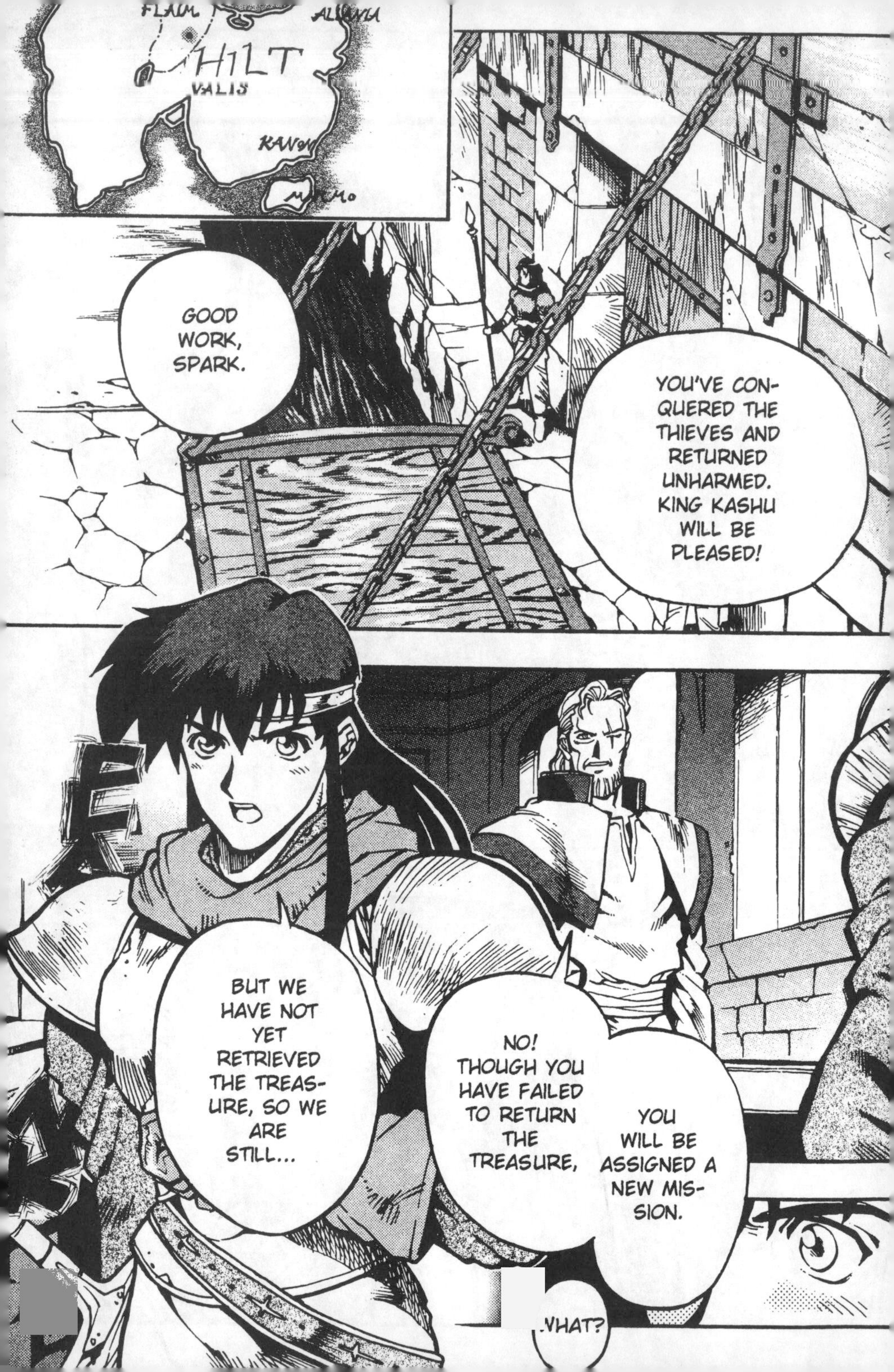
FLAIM
HILT
VALIS
GOOD WORK, SPARK.
YOU'VE CONQUERED THE THIEVES AND RETURNED UNHARMED. KING KASHU WILL BE PLEASED!
BUT WE HAVE NOT YET RETRIEVED THE TREASURE, SO WE ARE STILL...
NO! THOUGH YOU HAVE FAILED TO RETURN THE TREASURE,
YOU WILL BE ASSIGNED A NEW MISSION.
WHAT?

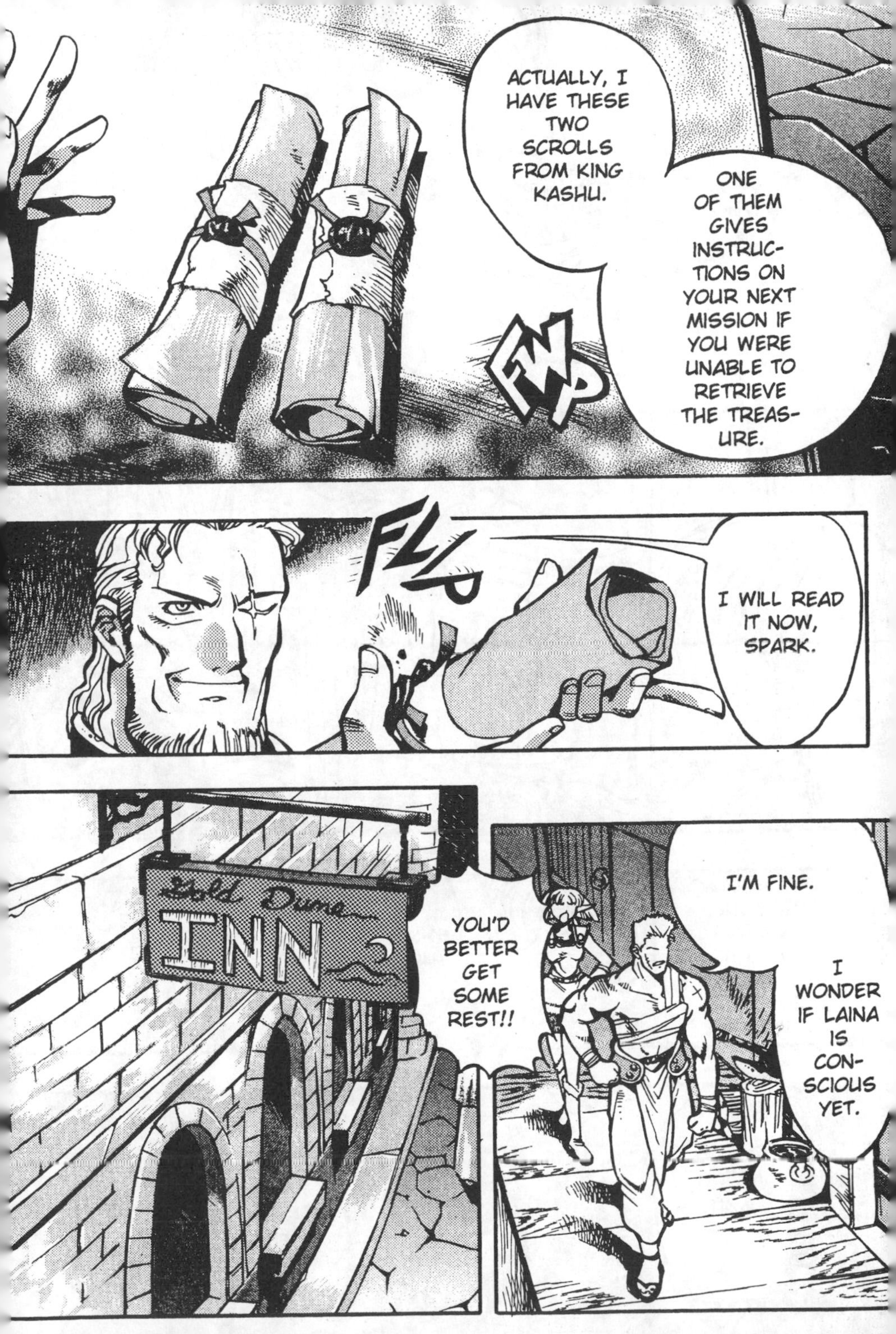
ACTUALLY, I HAVE THESE TWO SCROLLS FROM KING KASHU.
ONE OF THEM GIVES INSTRUCTIONS ON YOUR NEXT MISSION IF YOU WERE UNABLE TO RETRIEVE THE TREASURE.
FWP
FLIP
I WILL READ IT NOW, SPARK.
Gold Dune INN
YOU'D BETTER GET SOME REST!!
I'M FINE.
I WONDER IF LAINA IS CONSCIOUS YET.

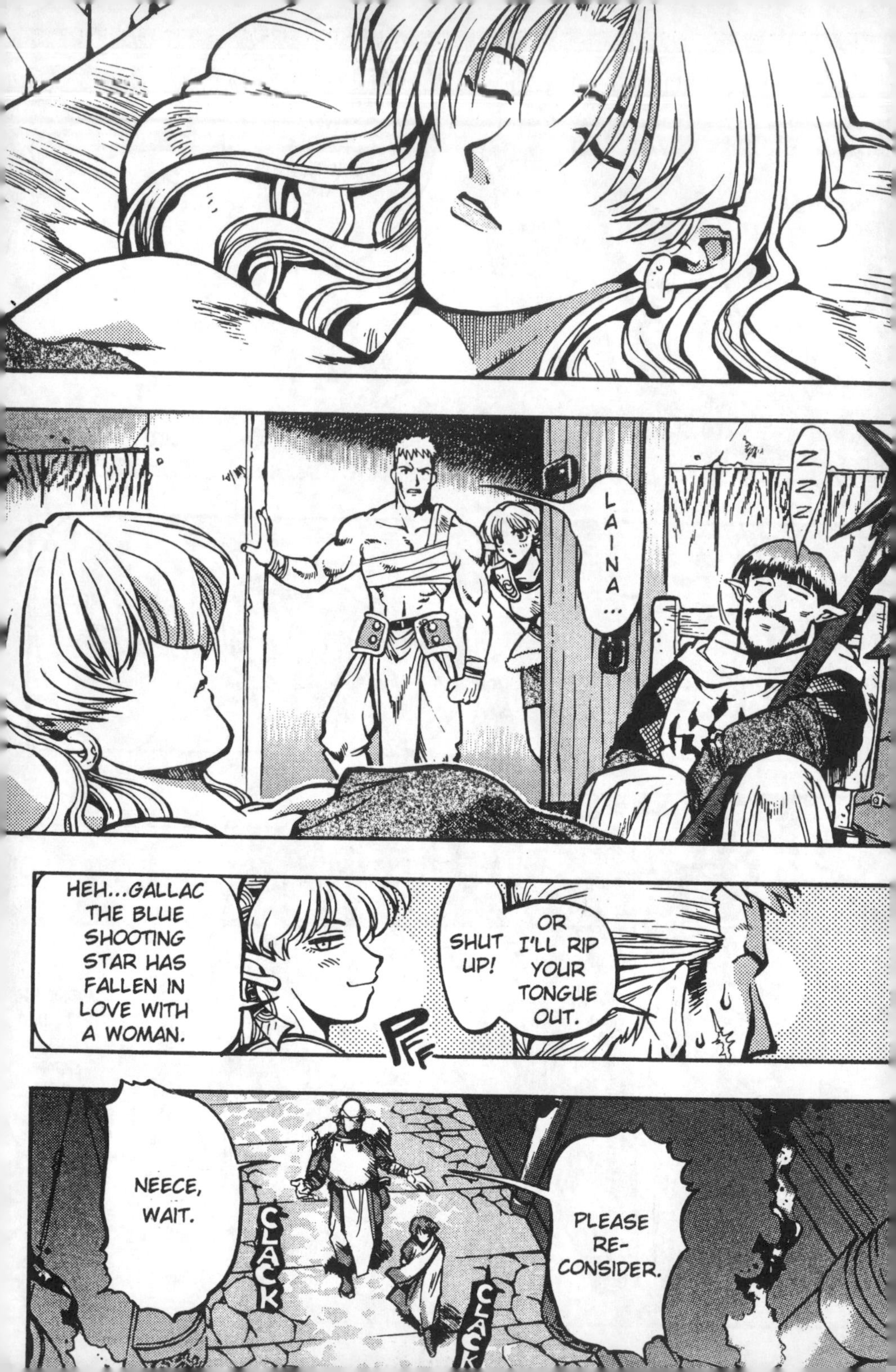
LAINA...
ZZZ
HEH...GALLAC THE BLUE SHOOTING STAR HAS FALLEN IN LOVE WITH A WOMAN.
PFF
SHUT UP!
OR I'LL RIP YOUR TONGUE OUT.
NEECE, WAIT.
CLACK
CLACK
PLEASE RE-CONSIDER.

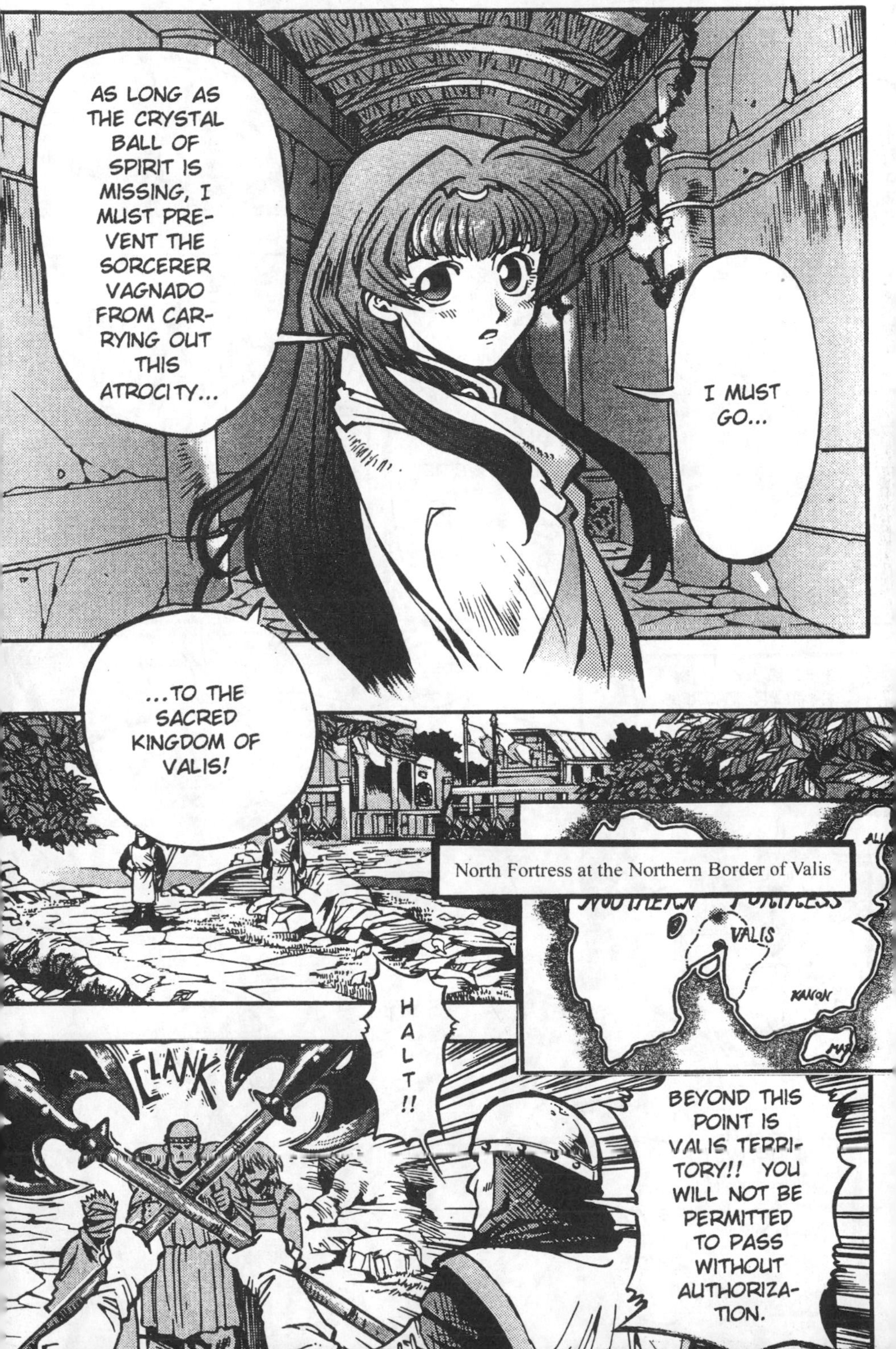
AS LONG AS THE CRYSTAL BALL OF SPIRIT IS MISSING, I MUST PRE-VENT THE SORCERER VAGNADO FROM CAR-RYING OUT THIS ATROCITY...
I MUST GO...
...TO THE SACRED KINGDOM OF VALIS!
North Fortress at the Northern Border of Valis
VALIS
KANON
CLANK
HALT!!
BEYOND THIS POINT IS VALIS TERRI-TORY!! YOU WILL NOT BE PERMITTED TO PASS WITHOUT AUTHORIZA-TION.

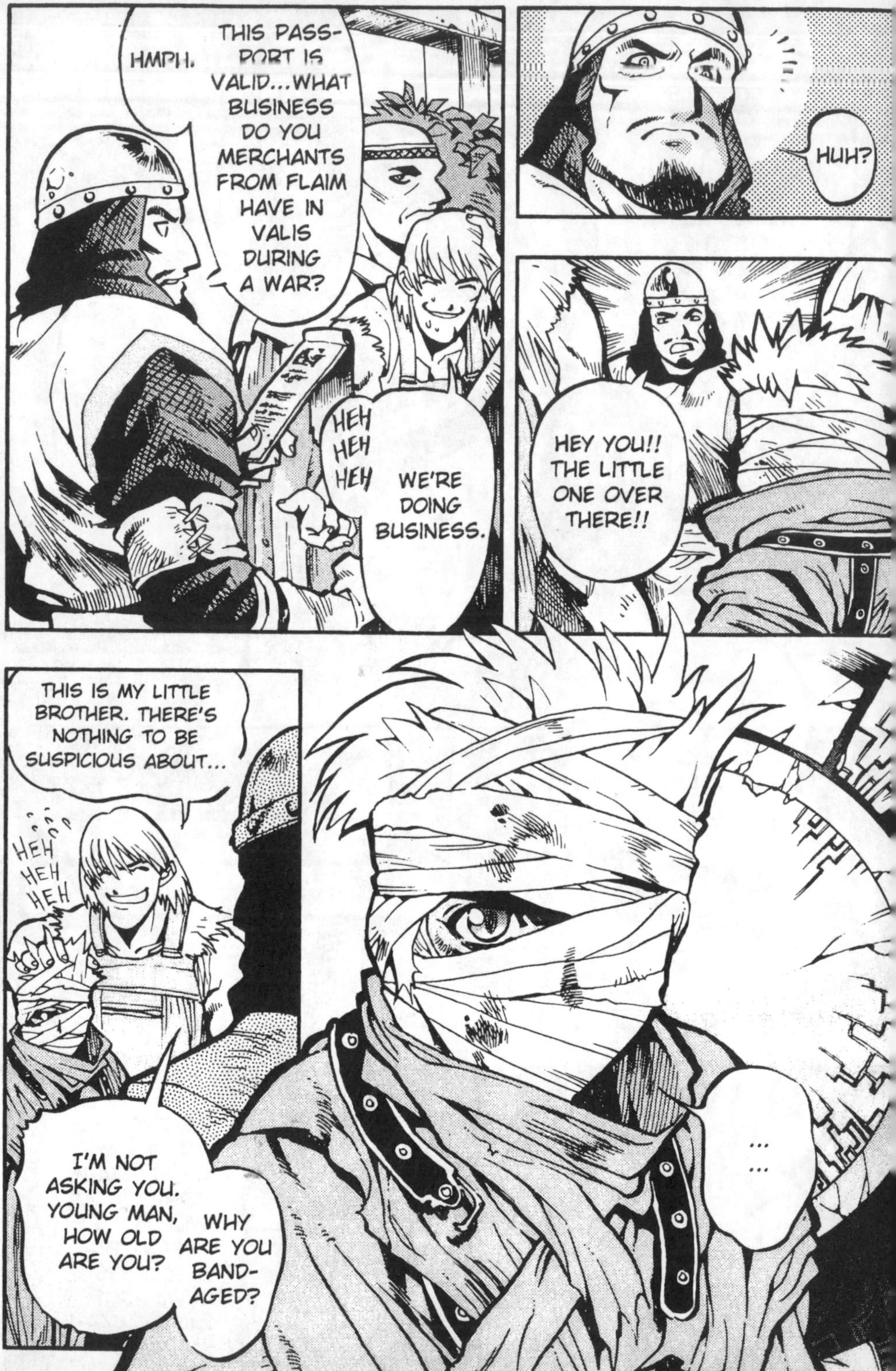
HMPH.
THIS PASS-PORT IS VALID...WHAT BUSINESS DO YOU MERCHANTS FROM FLAIM HAVE IN VALIS DURING A WAR?
HEH HEH HEH
WE'RE DOING BUSINESS.
HUH?
HEY YOU!! THE LITTLE ONE OVER THERE!!
THIS IS MY LITTLE BROTHER. THERE'S NOTHING TO BE SUSPICIOUS ABOUT...
HEH HEH HEH
I'M NOT ASKING YOU. YOUNG MAN, HOW OLD ARE YOU?
WHY ARE YOU BAND-AGED?
... ...

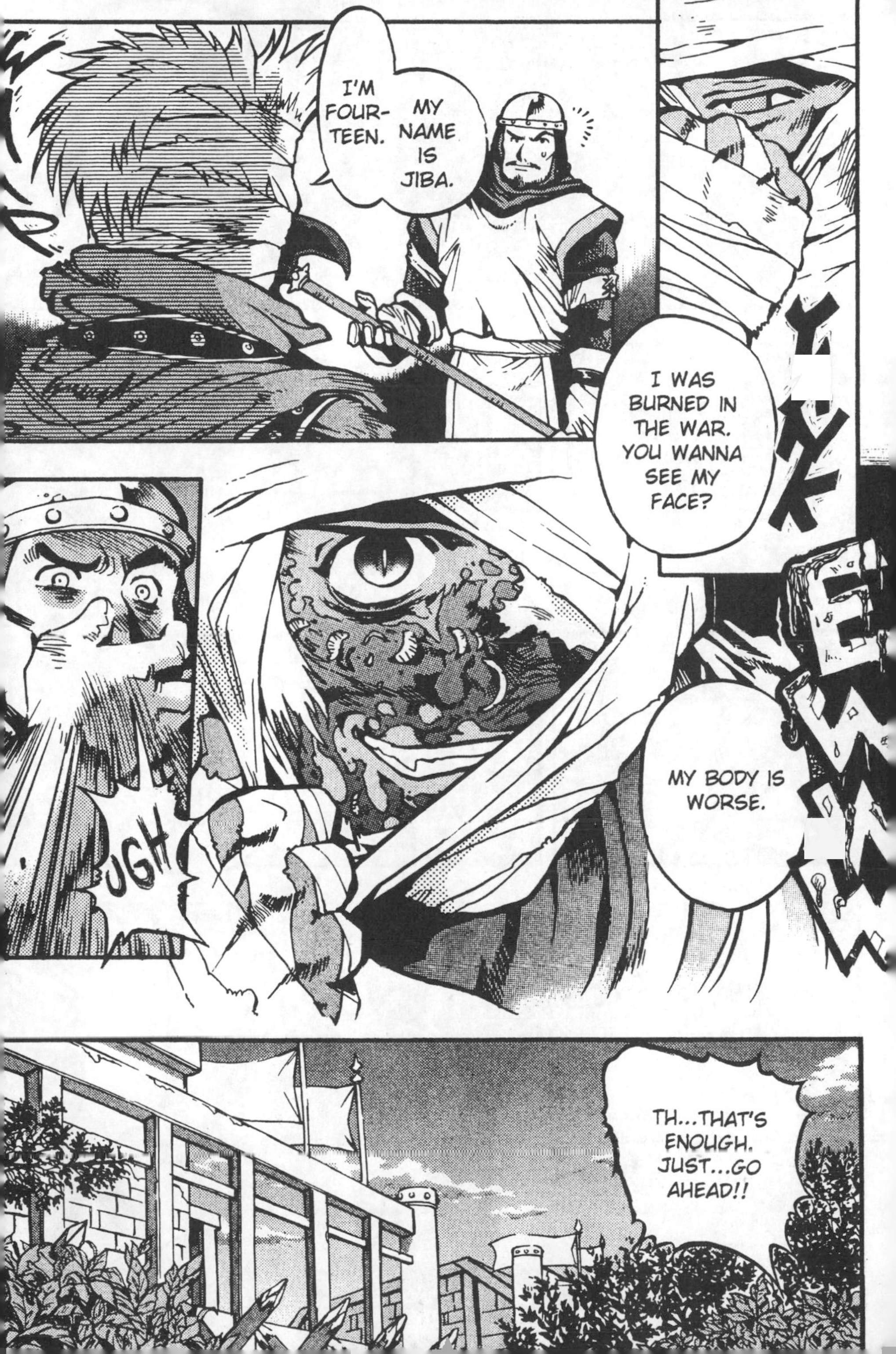
I'M FOUR-TEEN.
MY NAME IS JIBA.
I WAS BURNED IN THE WAR. YOU WANNA SEE MY FACE?
UGH
MY BODY IS WORSE.
TH...THAT'S ENOUGH. JUST...GO AHEAD!!

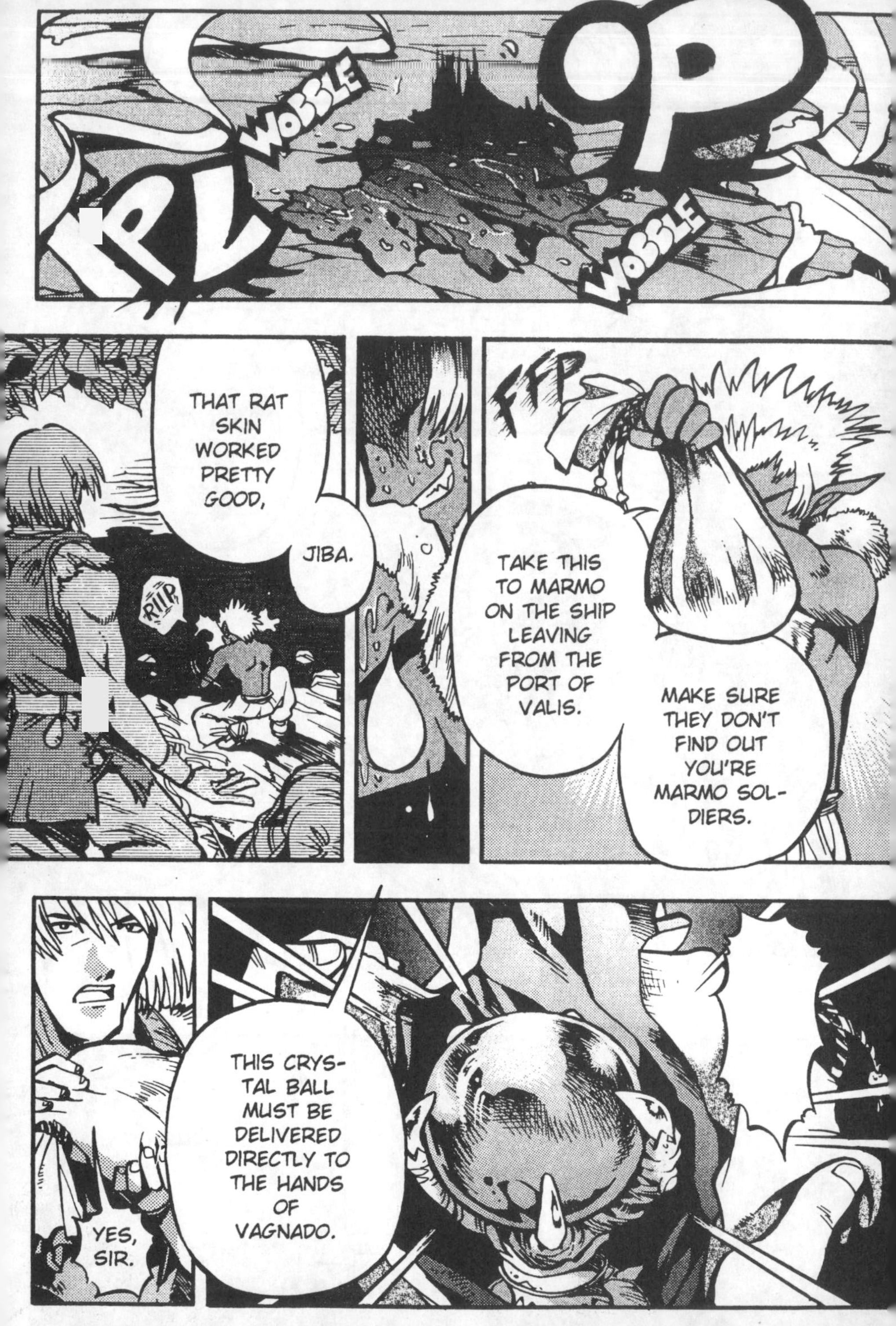
WOBBLE
WOBBLE
THAT RAT SKIN WORKED PRETTY GOOD,
JIBA.
RIIP
FFP
TAKE THIS TO MARMO ON THE SHIP LEAVING FROM THE PORT OF VALIS.
MAKE SURE THEY DON'T FIND OUT YOU'RE MARMO SOL-DIERS.
YES, SIR.
THIS CRYS-TAL BALL MUST BE DELIVERED DIRECTLY TO THE HANDS OF VAGNADO.

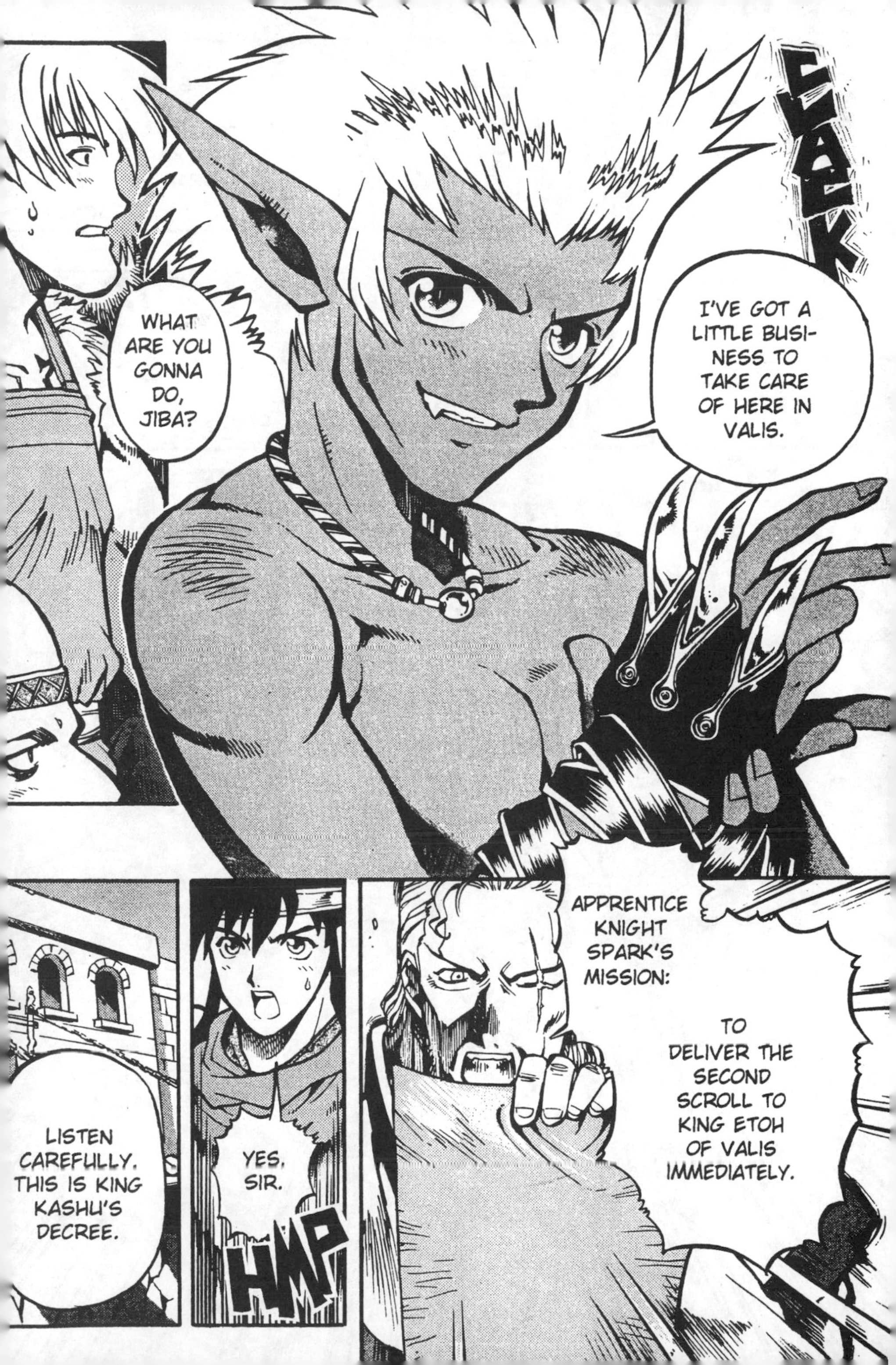
WHAT ARE YOU GONNA DO, JIBA?
CLAK
I'VE GOT A LITTLE BUSI-NESS TO TAKE CARE OF HERE IN VALIS.
LISTEN CAREFULLY. THIS IS KING KASHU'S DECREE.
YES, SIR.
HMP
APPRENTICE KNIGHT SPARK'S MISSION:
TO DELIVER THE SECOND SCROLL TO KING ETOH OF VALIS IMMEDIATELY.

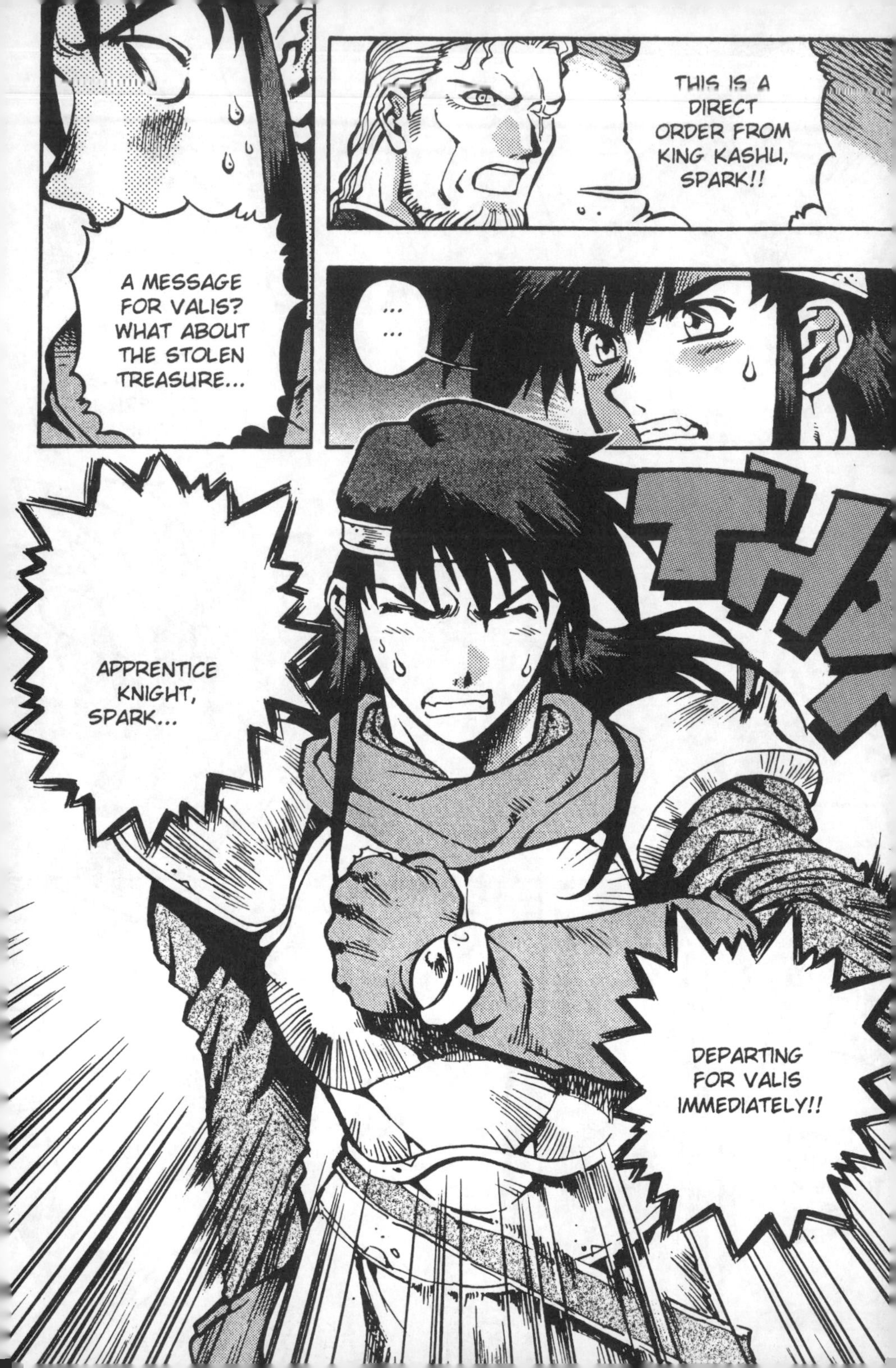
A MESSAGE FOR VALIS? WHAT ABOUT THE STOLEN TREASURE...
THIS IS A DIRECT ORDER FROM KING KASHU, SPARK!!
... ...
APPRENTICE KNIGHT, SPARK...
DEPARTING FOR VALIS IMMEDIATELY!!

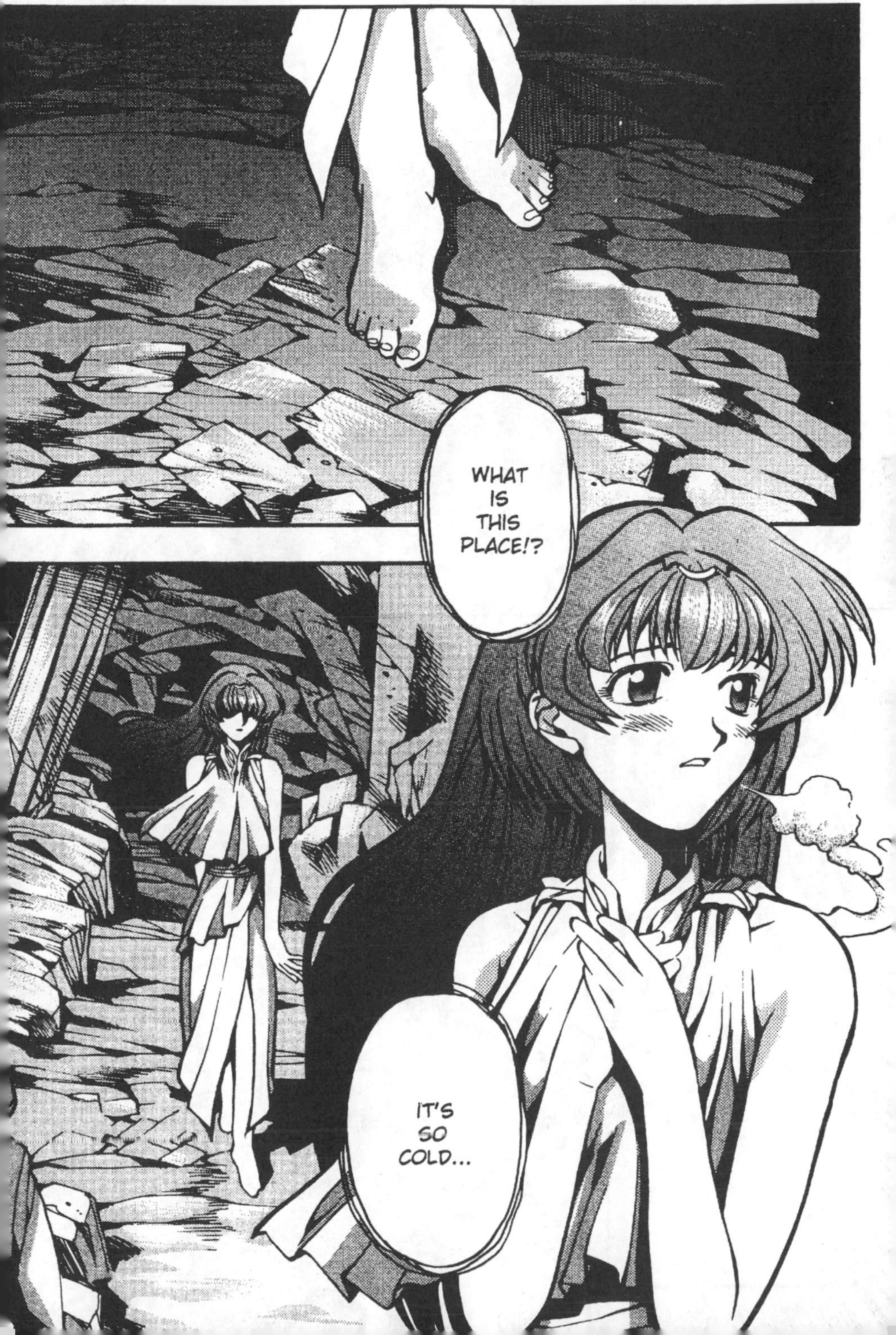
WHAT IS THIS PLACE!?
IT'S SO COLD...

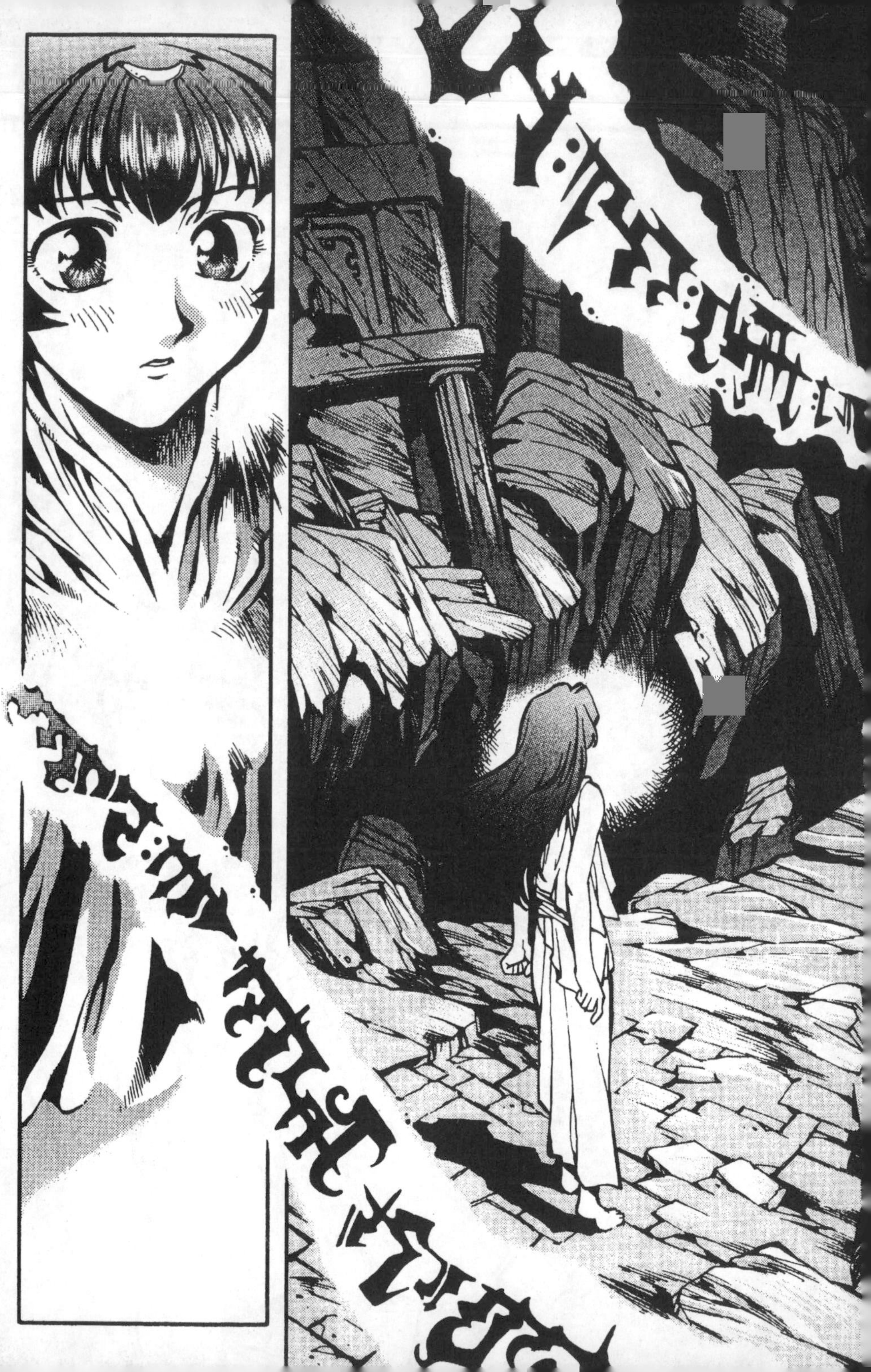

# The One Standing In The Way

EPISODE 11

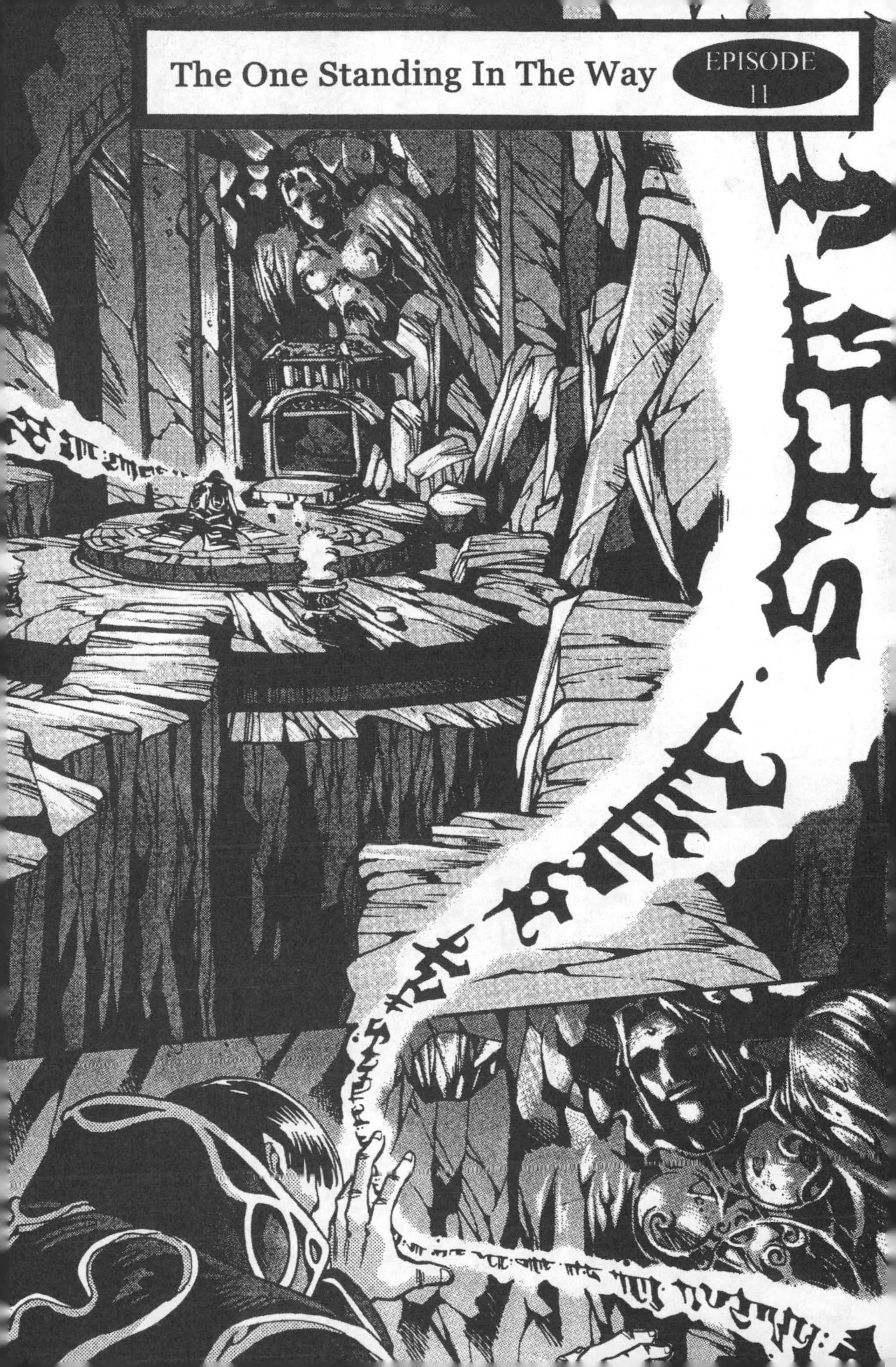

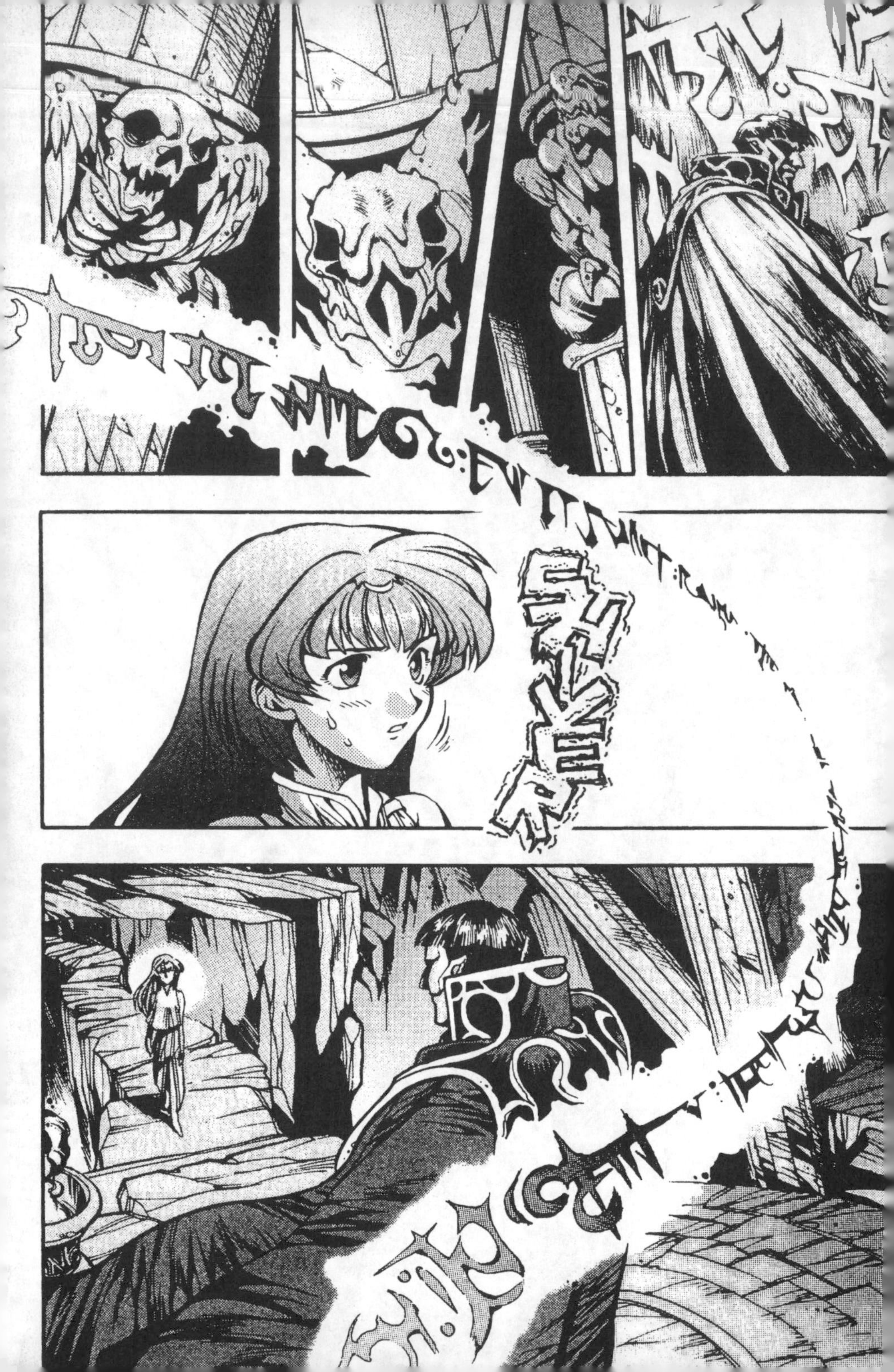

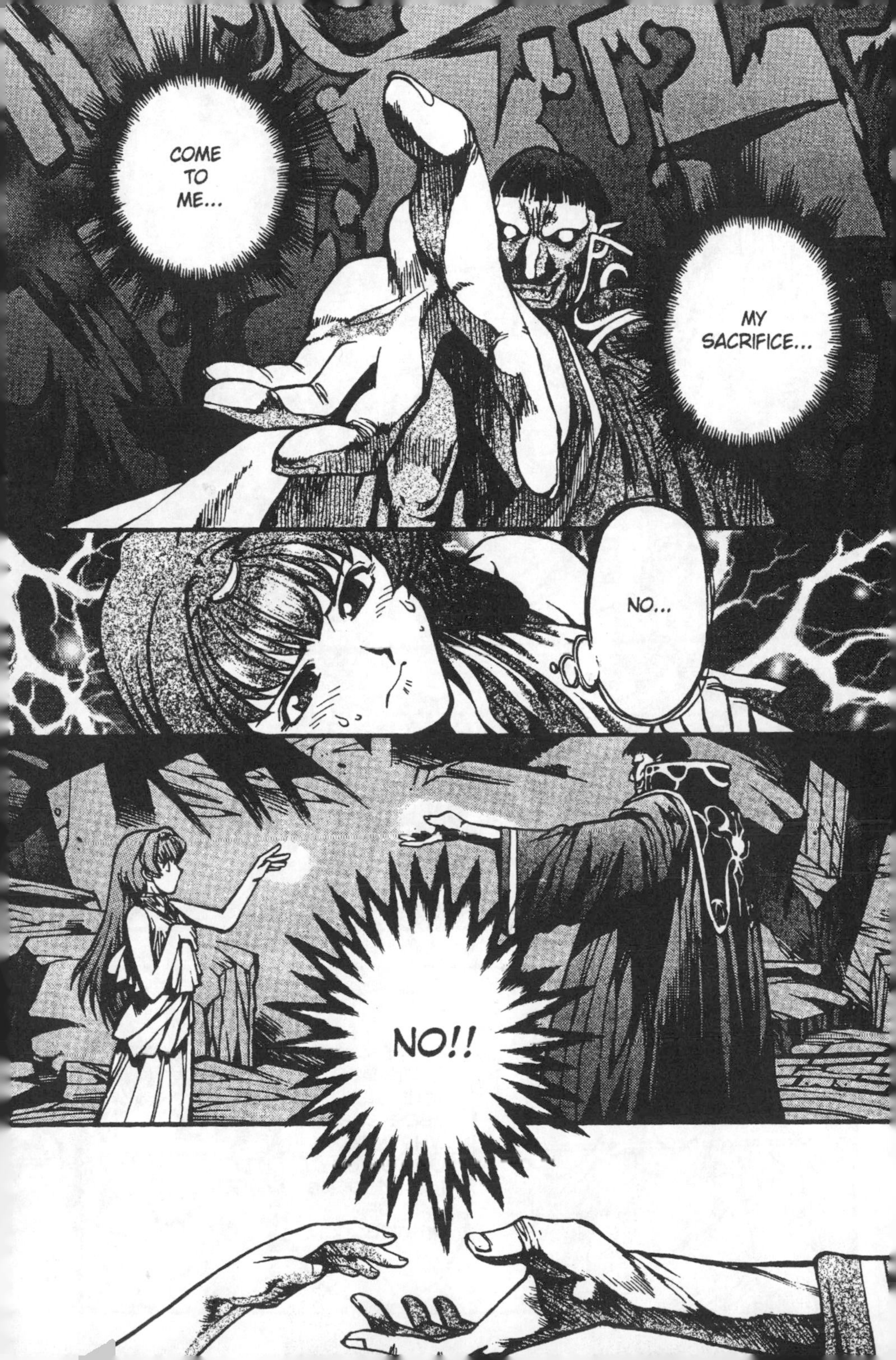
COME TO ME...
MY SACRIFICE...
NO...
NO!!

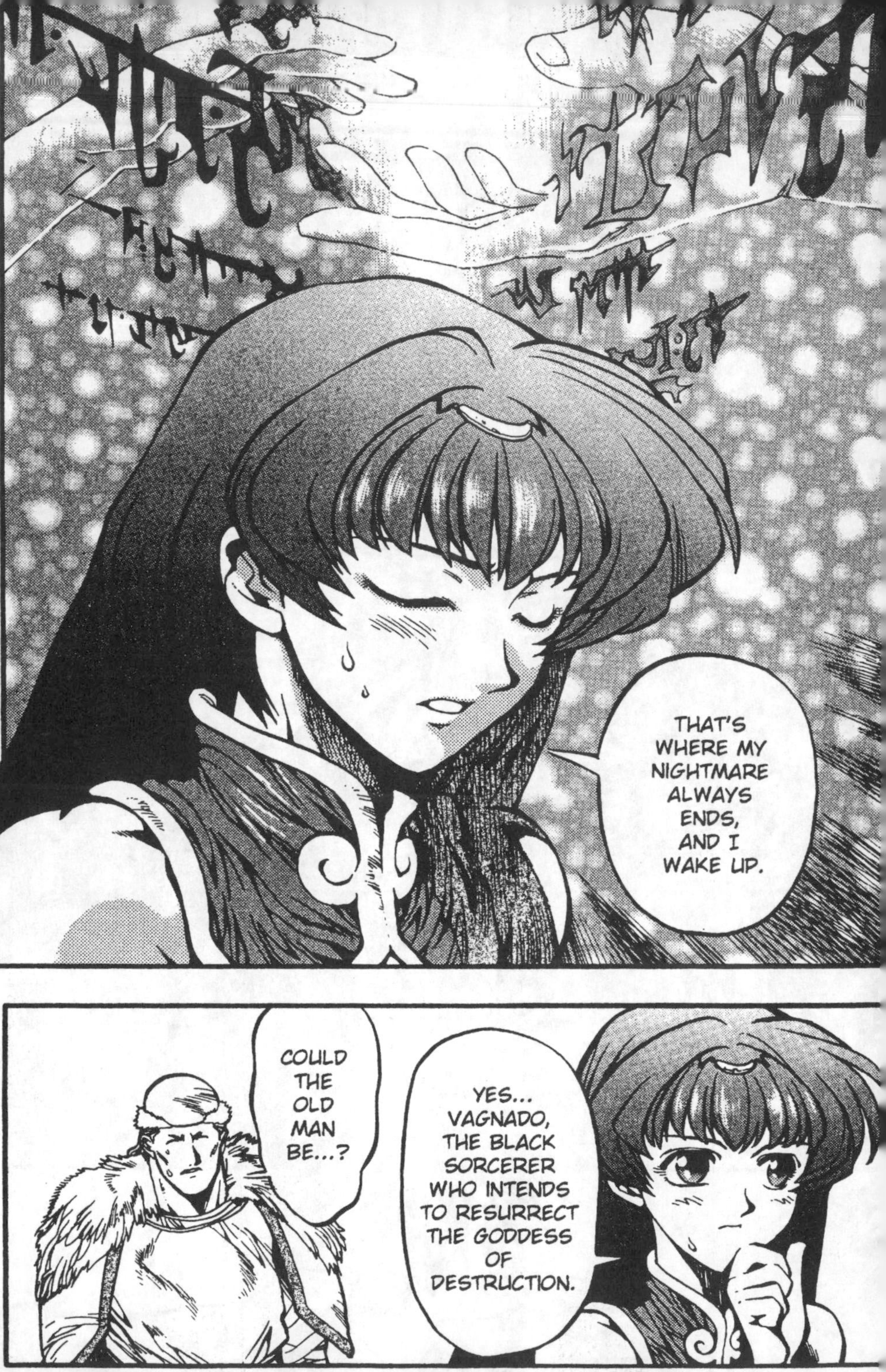
THAT'S WHERE MY NIGHTMARE ALWAYS ENDS, AND I WAKE UP.
COULD THE OLD MAN BE...?
YES... VAGNADO, THE BLACK SORCERER WHO INTENDS TO RESURRECT THE GODDESS OF DESTRUCTION.

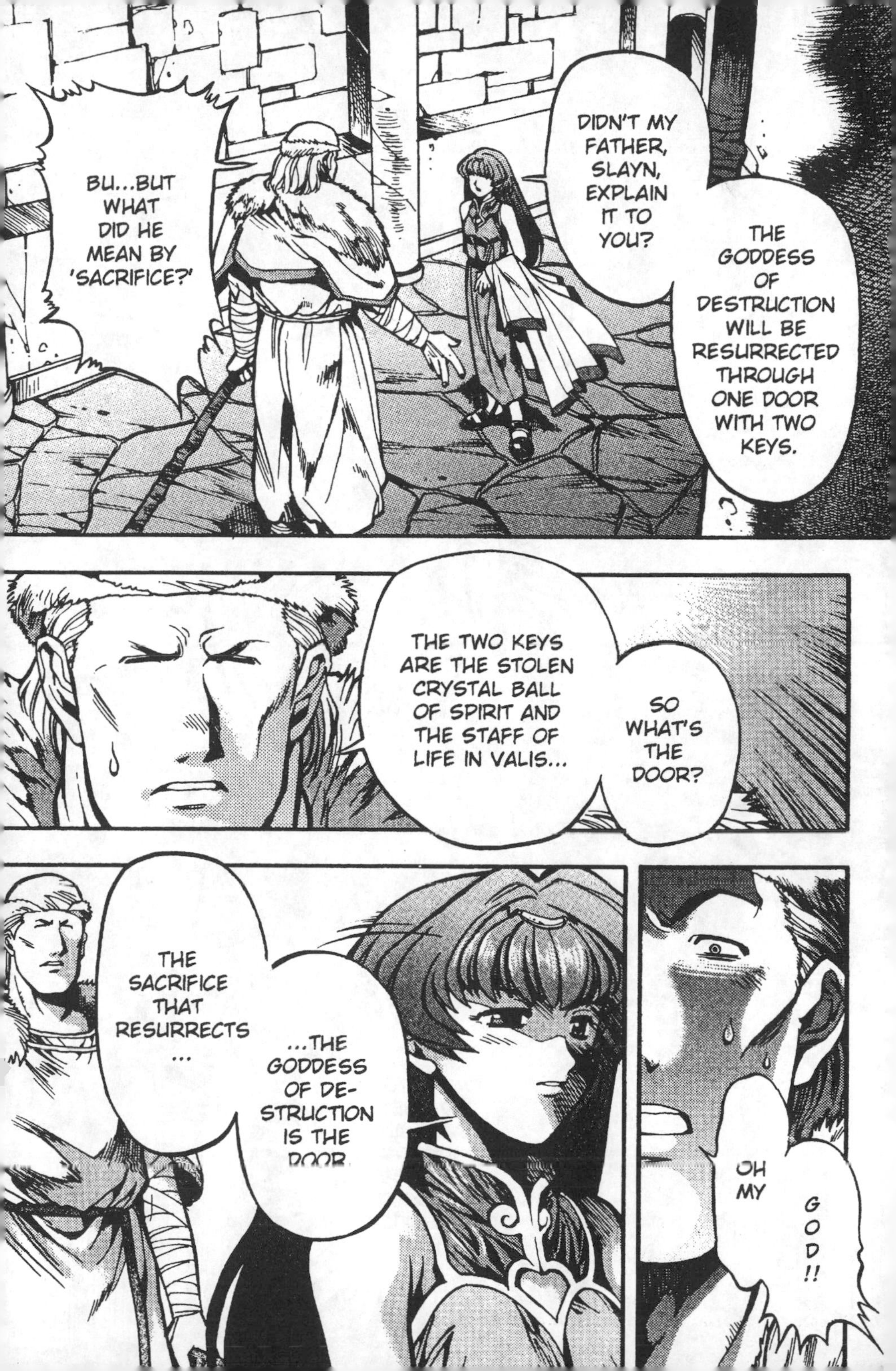
BU...BUT WHAT DID HE MEAN BY 'SACRIFICE?'
DIDN'T MY FATHER, SLAYN, EXPLAIN IT TO YOU?
THE GODDESS OF DESTRUCTION WILL BE RESURRECTED THROUGH ONE DOOR WITH TWO KEYS.
THE TWO KEYS ARE THE STOLEN CRYSTAL BALL OF SPIRIT AND THE STAFF OF LIFE IN VALIS...
SO WHAT'S THE DOOR?
THE SACRIFICE THAT RESURRECTS ...
...THE GODDESS OF DE-STRUCTION IS THE DOOR.
OH MY
GOD!!

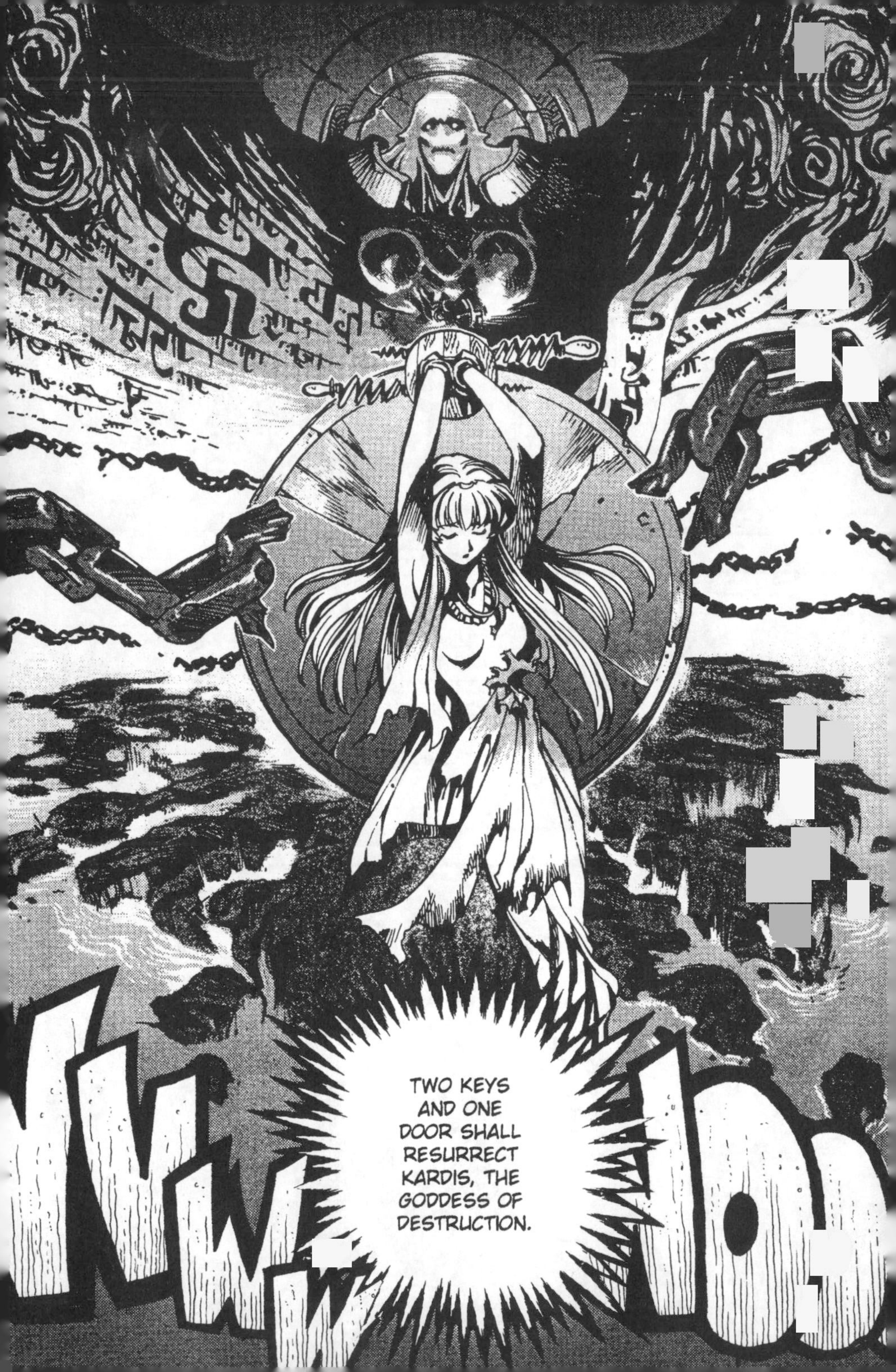
TWO KEYS AND ONE DOOR SHALL RESURRECT KARDIS, THE GODDESS OF DESTRUCTION.

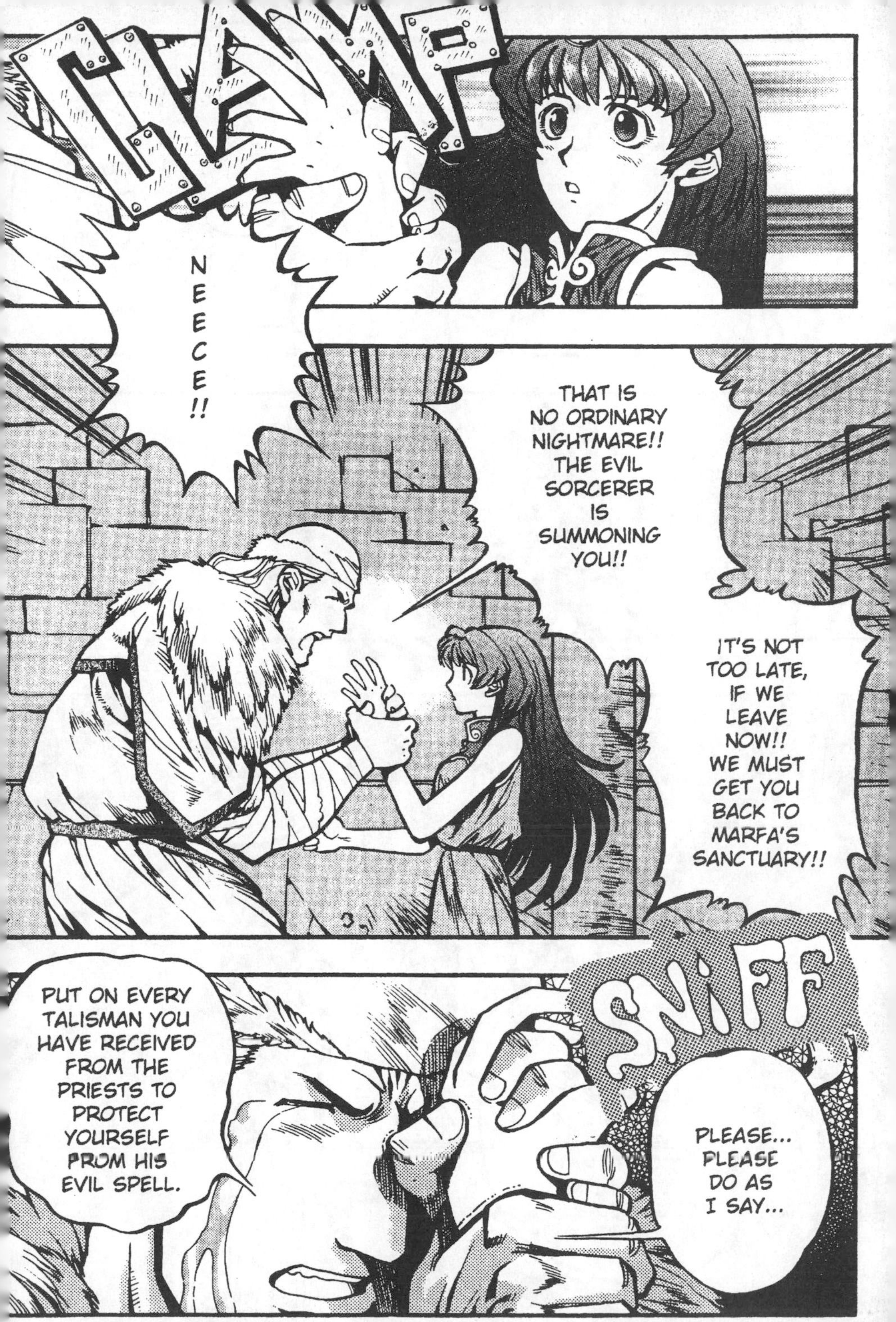
CLAMP
NEECE!!
THAT IS NO ORDINARY NIGHTMARE!! THE EVIL SORCERER IS SUMMONING YOU!!
IT'S NOT TOO LATE, IF WE LEAVE NOW!! WE MUST GET YOU BACK TO MARFA'S SANCTUARY!!
PUT ON EVERY TALISMAN YOU HAVE RECEIVED FROM THE PRIESTS TO PROTECT YOURSELF FROM HIS EVIL SPELL.
SNIFF
PLEASE... PLEASE DO AS I SAY...

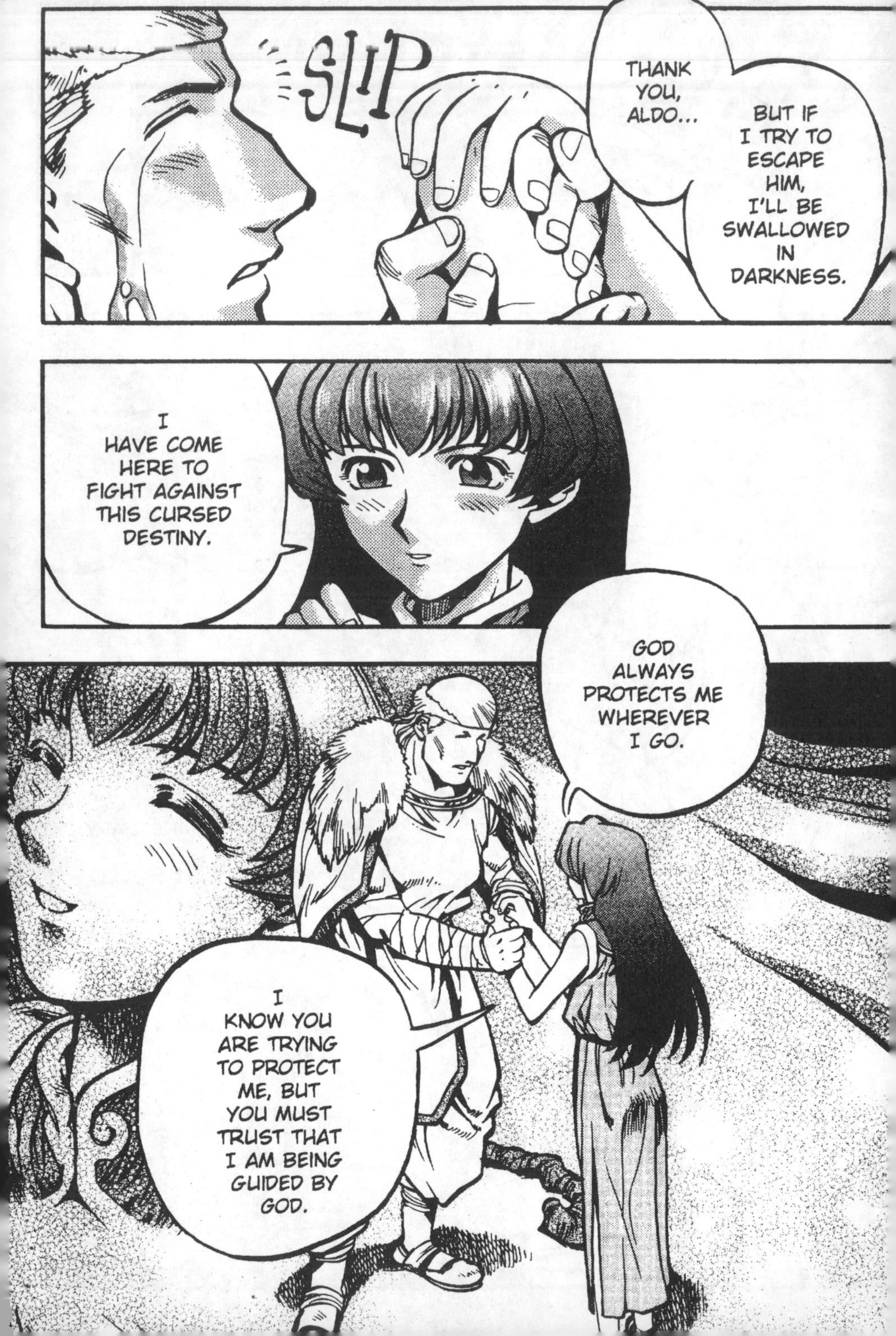
SLIP
THANK YOU, ALDO...
BUT IF I TRY TO ESCAPE HIM, I'LL BE SWALLOWED IN DARKNESS.
I HAVE COME HERE TO FIGHT AGAINST THIS CURSED DESTINY.
GOD ALWAYS PROTECTS ME WHEREVER I GO.
I KNOW YOU ARE TRYING TO PROTECT ME, BUT YOU MUST TRUST THAT I AM BEING GUIDED BY GOD.

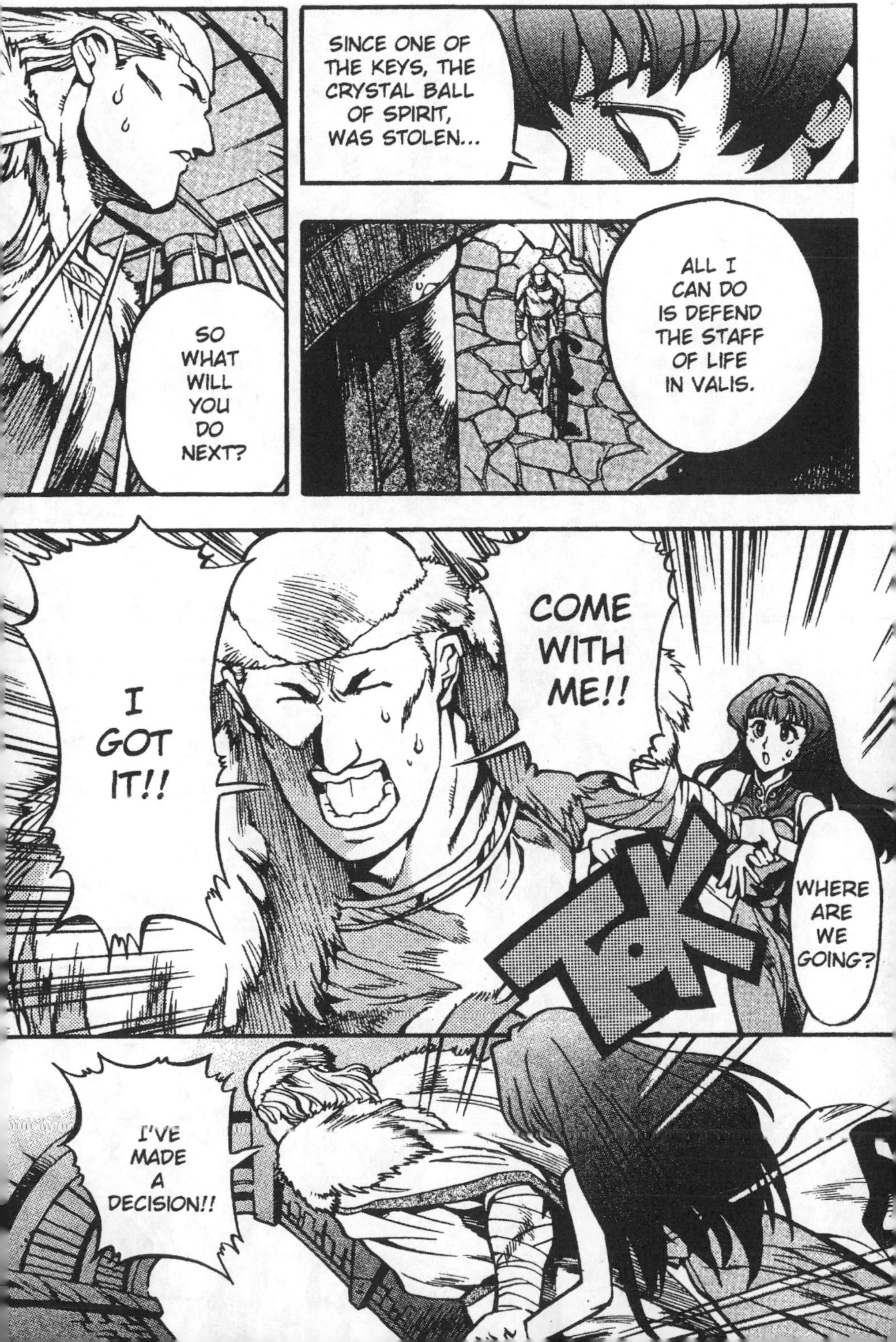
SO WHAT WILL YOU DO NEXT?
SINCE ONE OF THE KEYS, THE CRYSTAL BALL OF SPIRIT, WAS STOLEN...
ALL I CAN DO IS DEFEND THE STAFF OF LIFE IN VALIS.
I GOT IT!!
COME WITH ME!!
WHERE ARE WE GOING?
I'VE MADE A DECISION!!

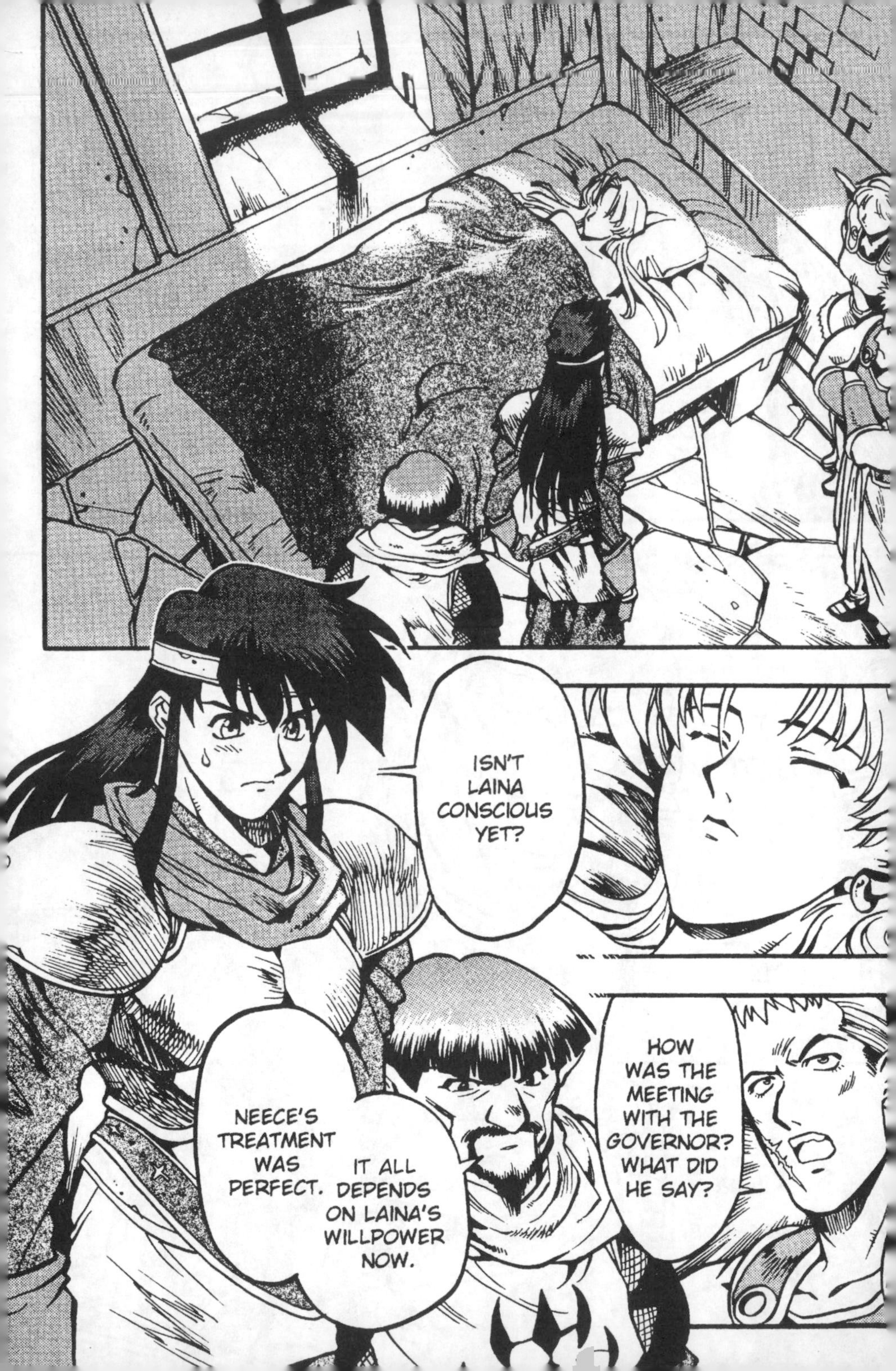
ISN'T LAINA CONSCIOUS YET?
HOW WAS THE MEETING WITH THE GOVERNOR? WHAT DID HE SAY?
NEECE'S TREATMENT WAS PERFECT. IT ALL DEPENDS ON LAINA'S WILLPOWER NOW.

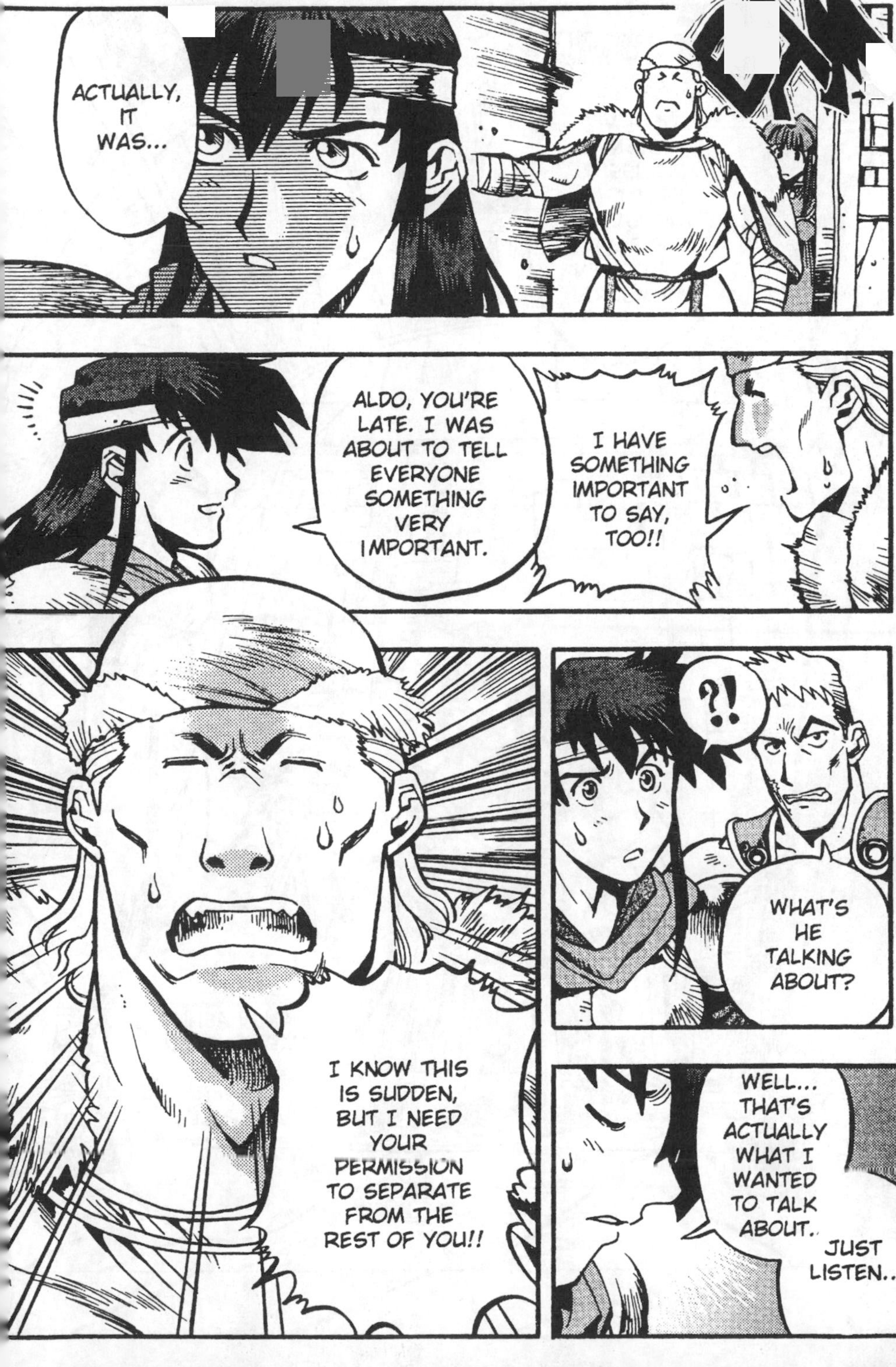

ACTUALLY, IT WAS...
ALDO, YOU'RE LATE. I WAS ABOUT TO TELL EVERYONE SOMETHING VERY IMPORTANT.
I HAVE SOMETHING IMPORTANT TO SAY, TOO!!
I KNOW THIS IS SUDDEN, BUT I NEED YOUR PERMISSION TO SEPARATE FROM THE REST OF YOU!!
?!
WHAT'S HE TALKING ABOUT?
WELL... THAT'S ACTUALLY WHAT I WANTED TO TALK ABOUT..
JUST LISTEN...

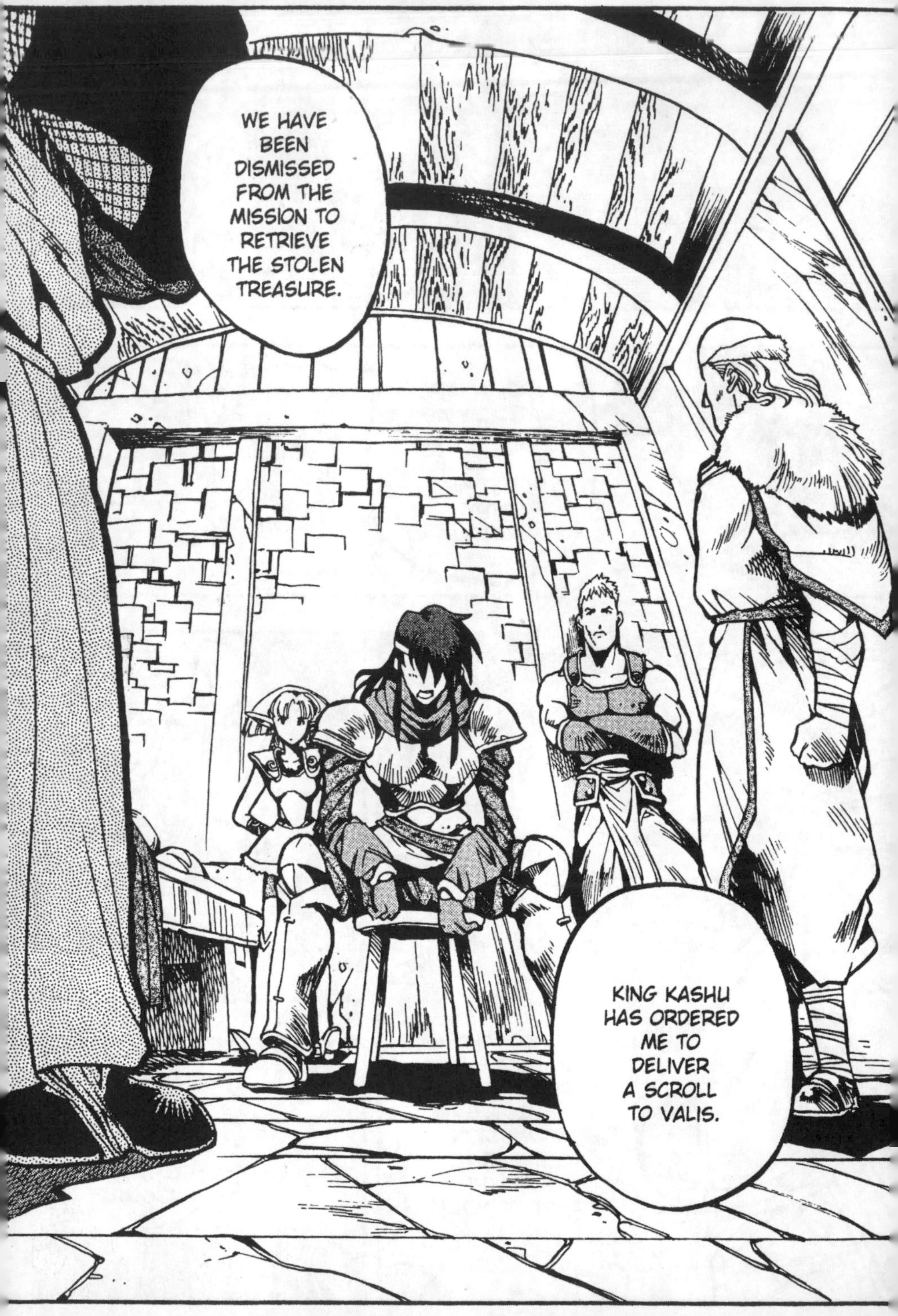
WE HAVE BEEN DISMISSED FROM THE MISSION TO RETRIEVE THE STOLEN TREASURE.
KING KASHU HAS ORDERED ME TO DELIVER A SCROLL TO VALIS.

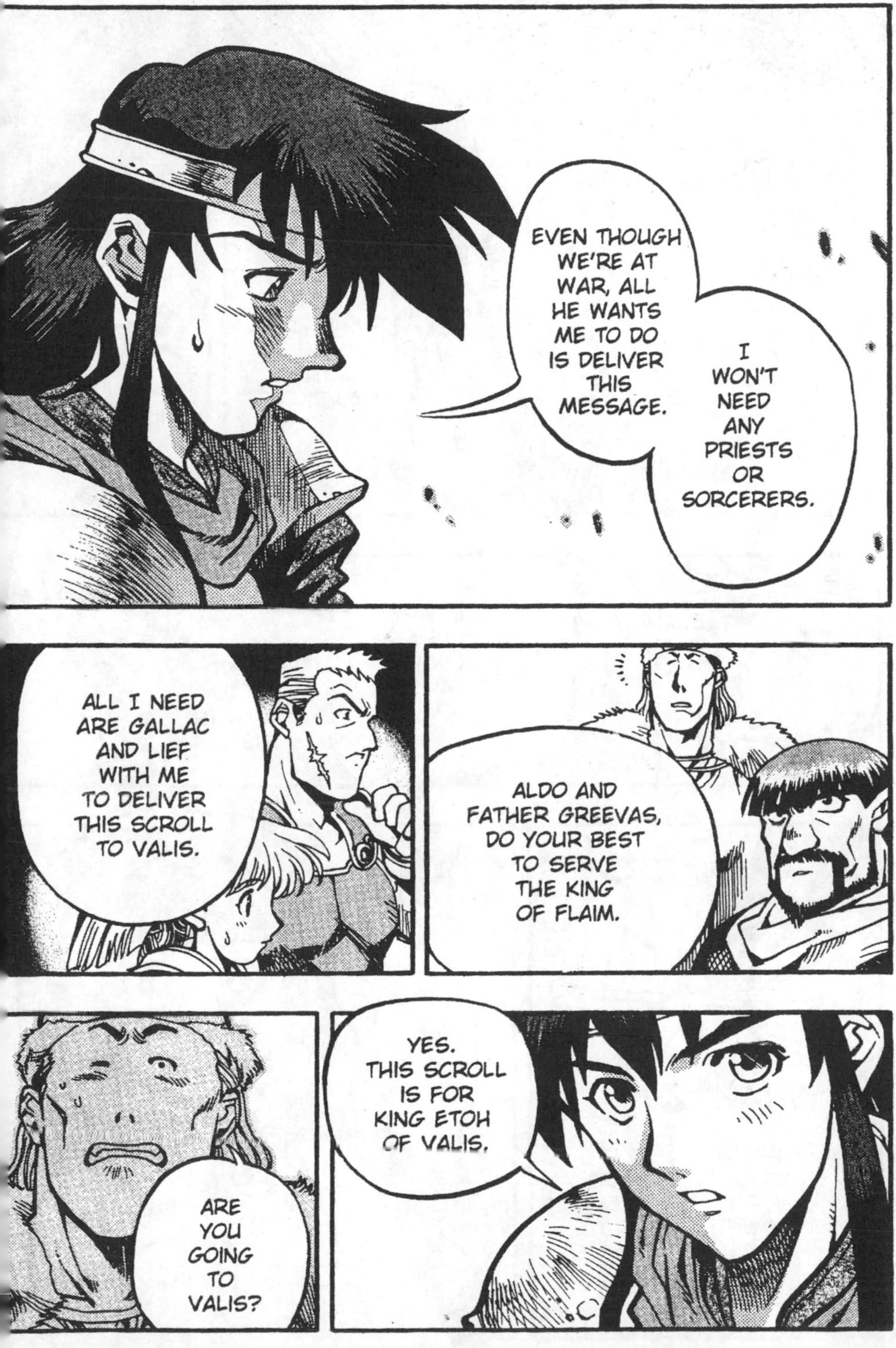
EVEN THOUGH WE'RE AT WAR, ALL HE WANTS ME TO DO IS DELIVER THIS MESSAGE.
I WON'T NEED ANY PRIESTS OR SORCERERS.
ALL I NEED ARE GALLAC AND LIEF WITH ME TO DELIVER THIS SCROLL TO VALIS.
ALDO AND FATHER GREEVAS, DO YOUR BEST TO SERVE THE KING OF FLAIM.
ARE YOU GOING TO VALIS?
YES. THIS SCROLL IS FOR KING ETOH OF VALIS.

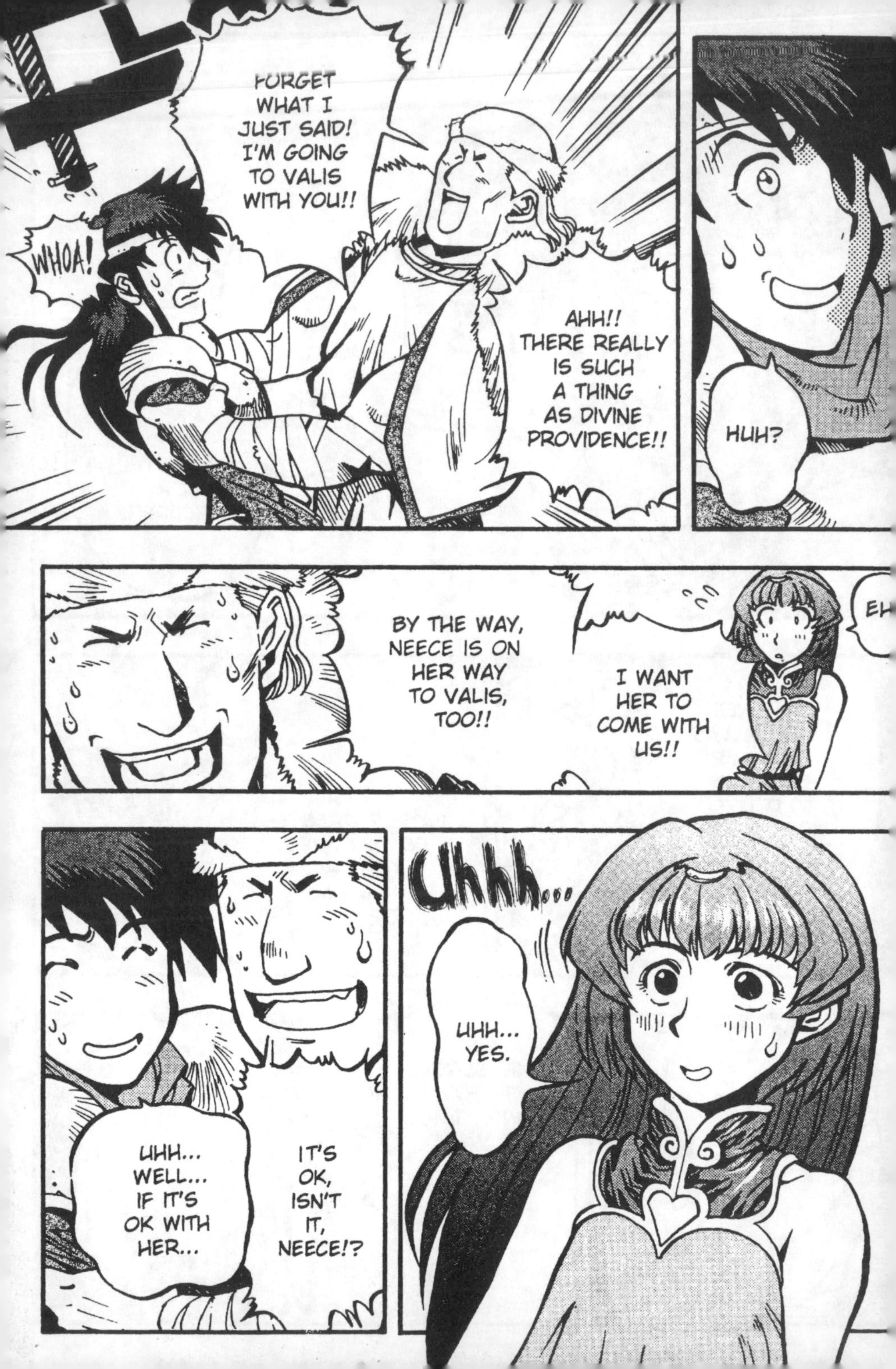

FORGET WHAT I JUST SAID! I'M GOING TO VALIS WITH YOU!!
WHOA!
AHH!! THERE REALLY IS SUCH A THING AS DIVINE PROVIDENCE!!
HUH?
BY THE WAY, NEECE IS ON HER WAY TO VALIS, TOO!!
I WANT HER TO COME WITH US!!
EH
UHH... WELL... IF IT'S OK WITH HER...
IT'S OK, ISN'T IT, NEECE!?
Uhhh...
UHH... YES.

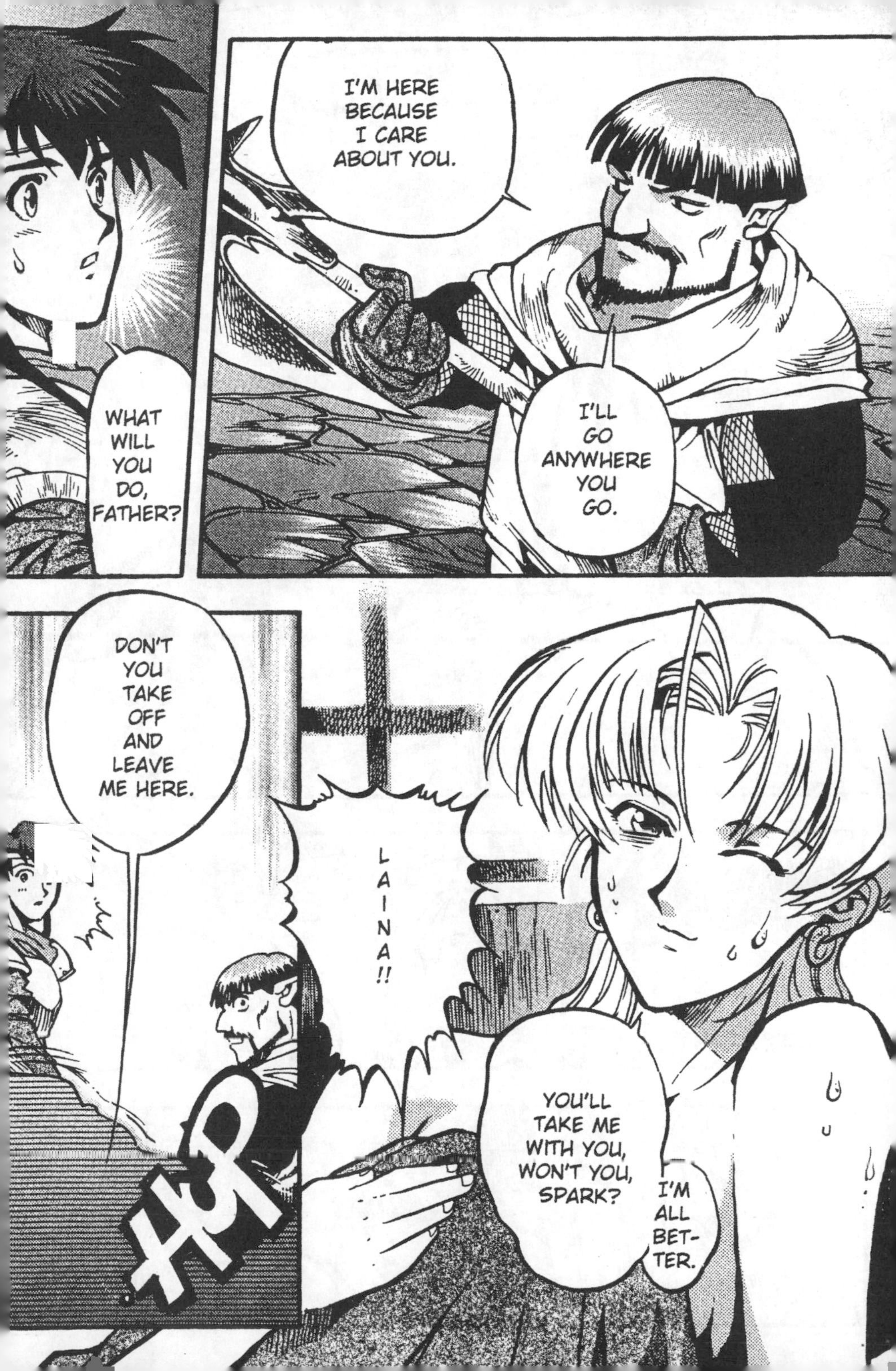
WHAT WILL YOU DO, FATHER?
I'M HERE BECAUSE I CARE ABOUT YOU.
I'LL GO ANYWHERE YOU GO.
DON'T YOU TAKE OFF AND LEAVE ME HERE.
LAINA!!
YOU'LL TAKE ME WITH YOU, WON'T YOU, SPARK?
I'M ALL BET-TER.

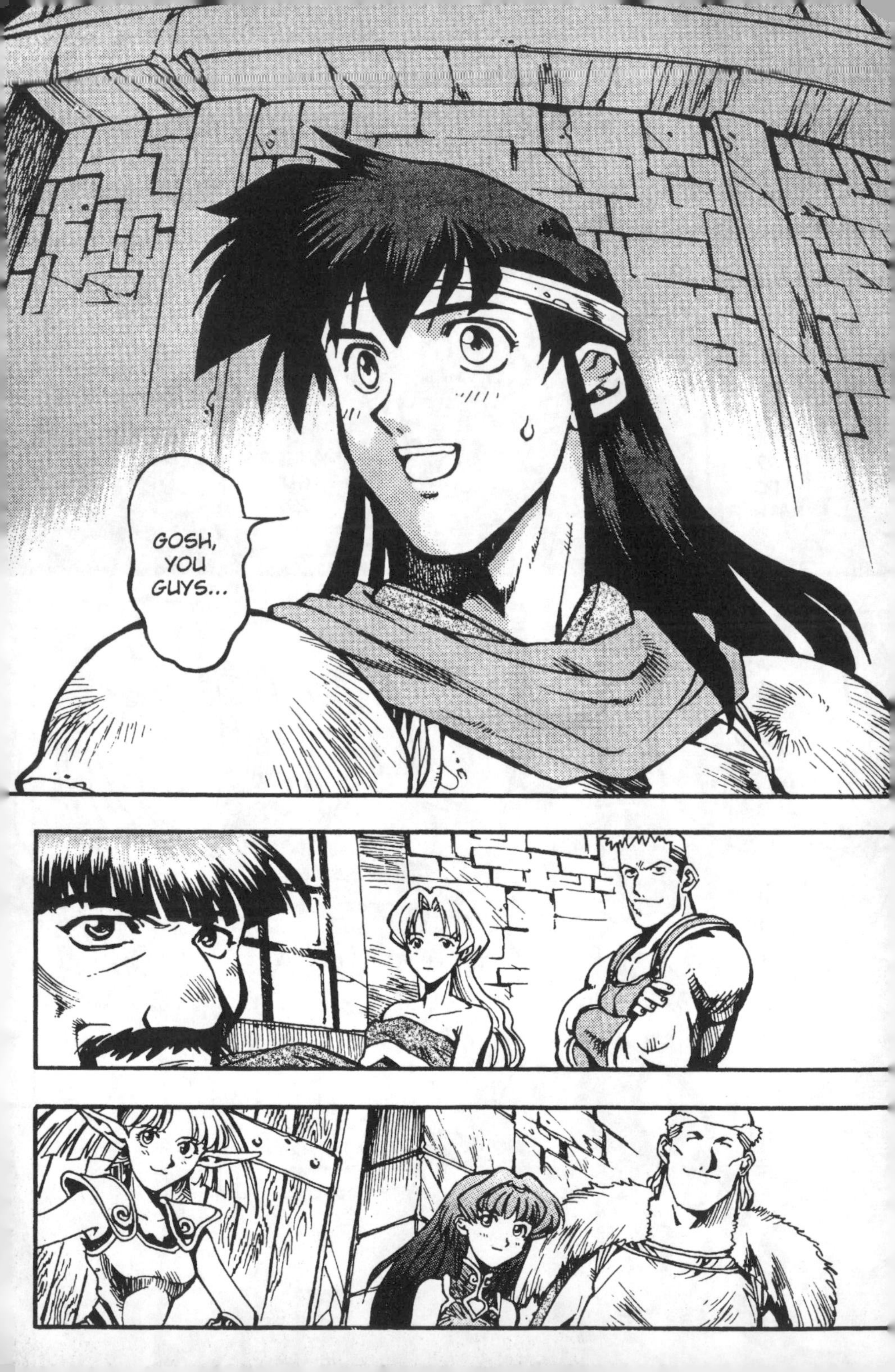
GOSH, YOU GUYS...

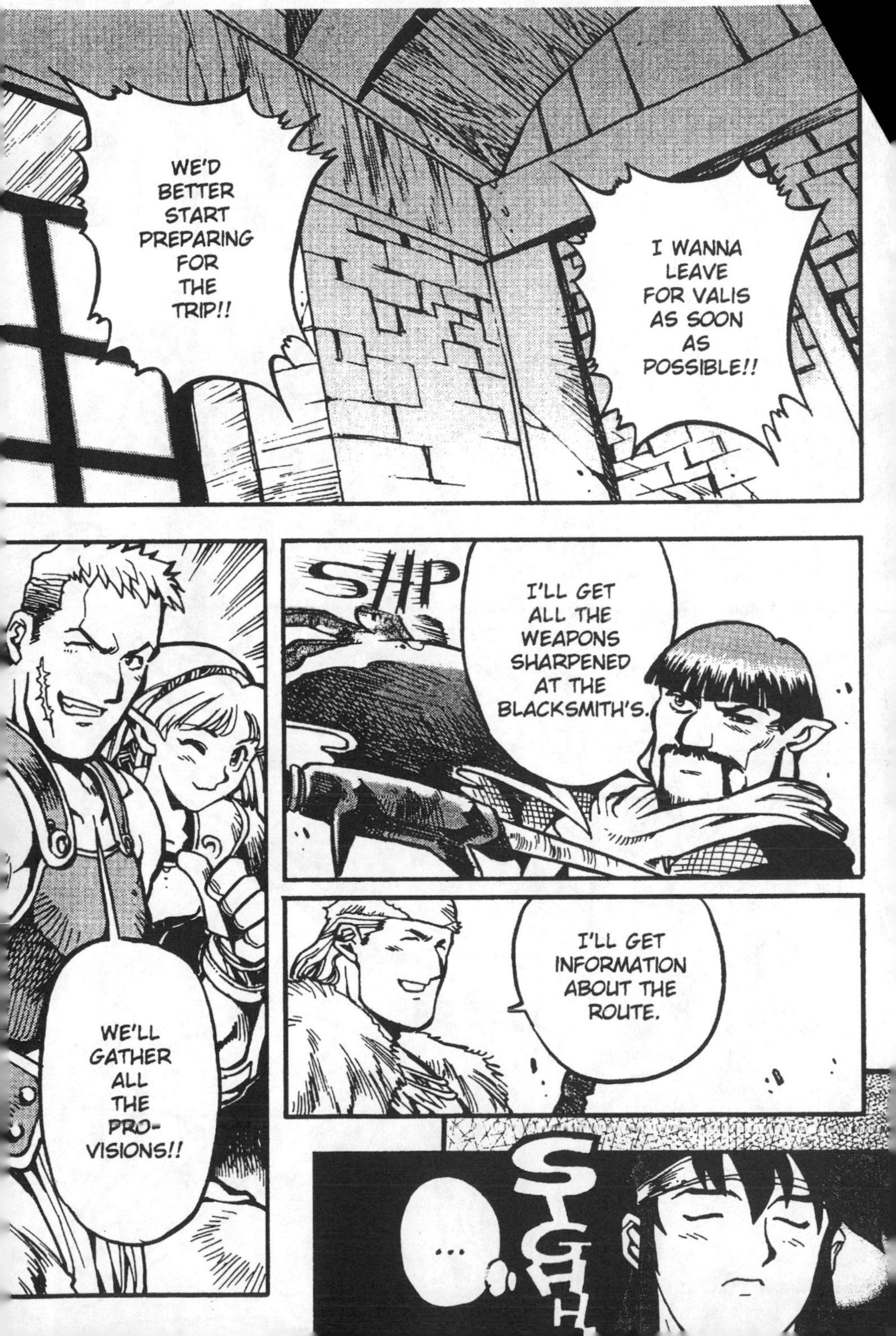
WE'D BETTER START PREPARING FOR THE TRIP!!
I WANNA LEAVE FOR VALIS AS SOON AS POSSIBLE!!
WE'LL GATHER ALL THE PRO-VISIONS!!
SHP
I'LL GET ALL THE WEAPONS SHARPENED AT THE BLACKSMITH'S.
I'LL GET INFORMATION ABOUT THE ROUTE.
...
SIGH

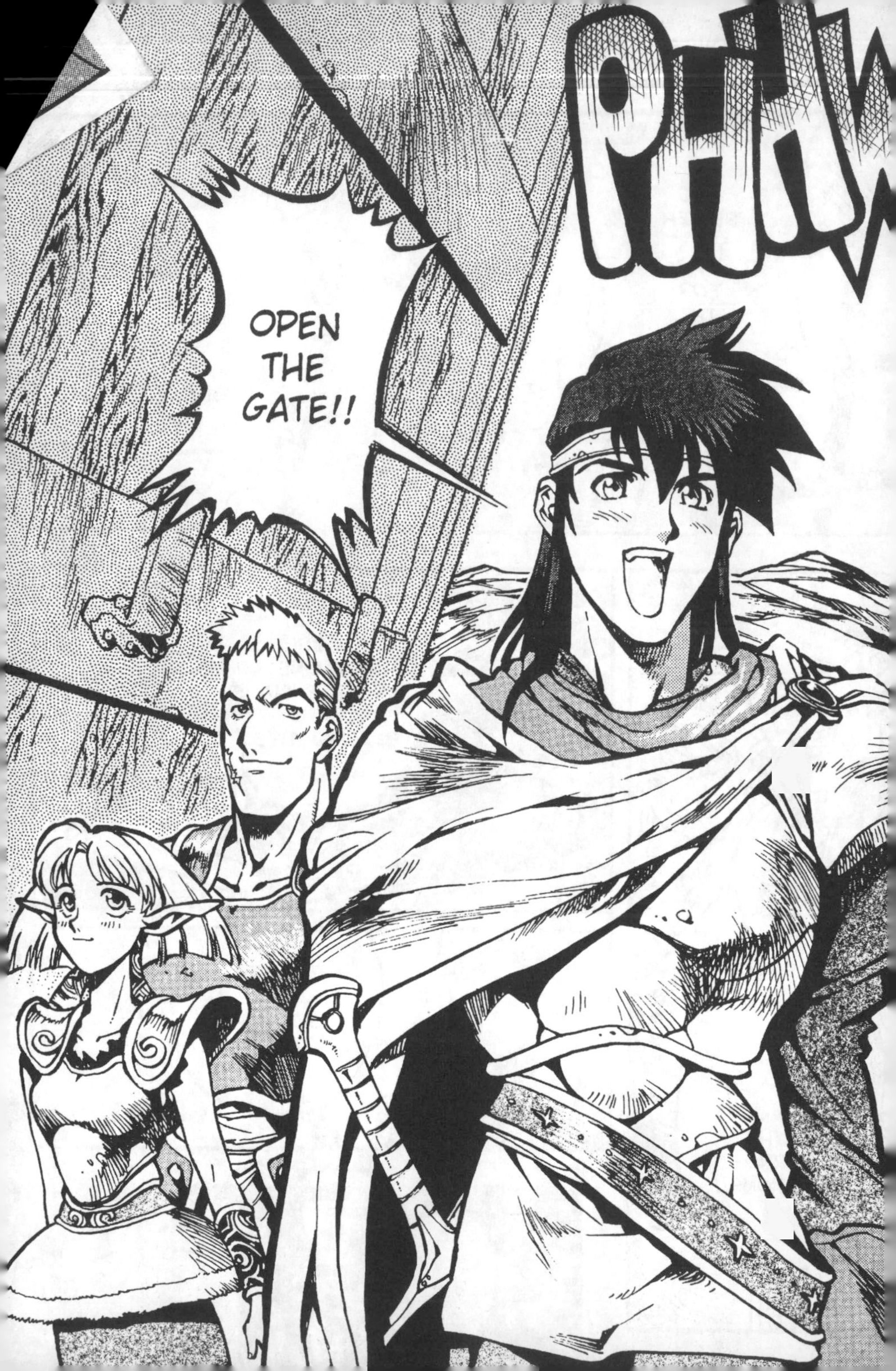
OPEN THE GATE!!

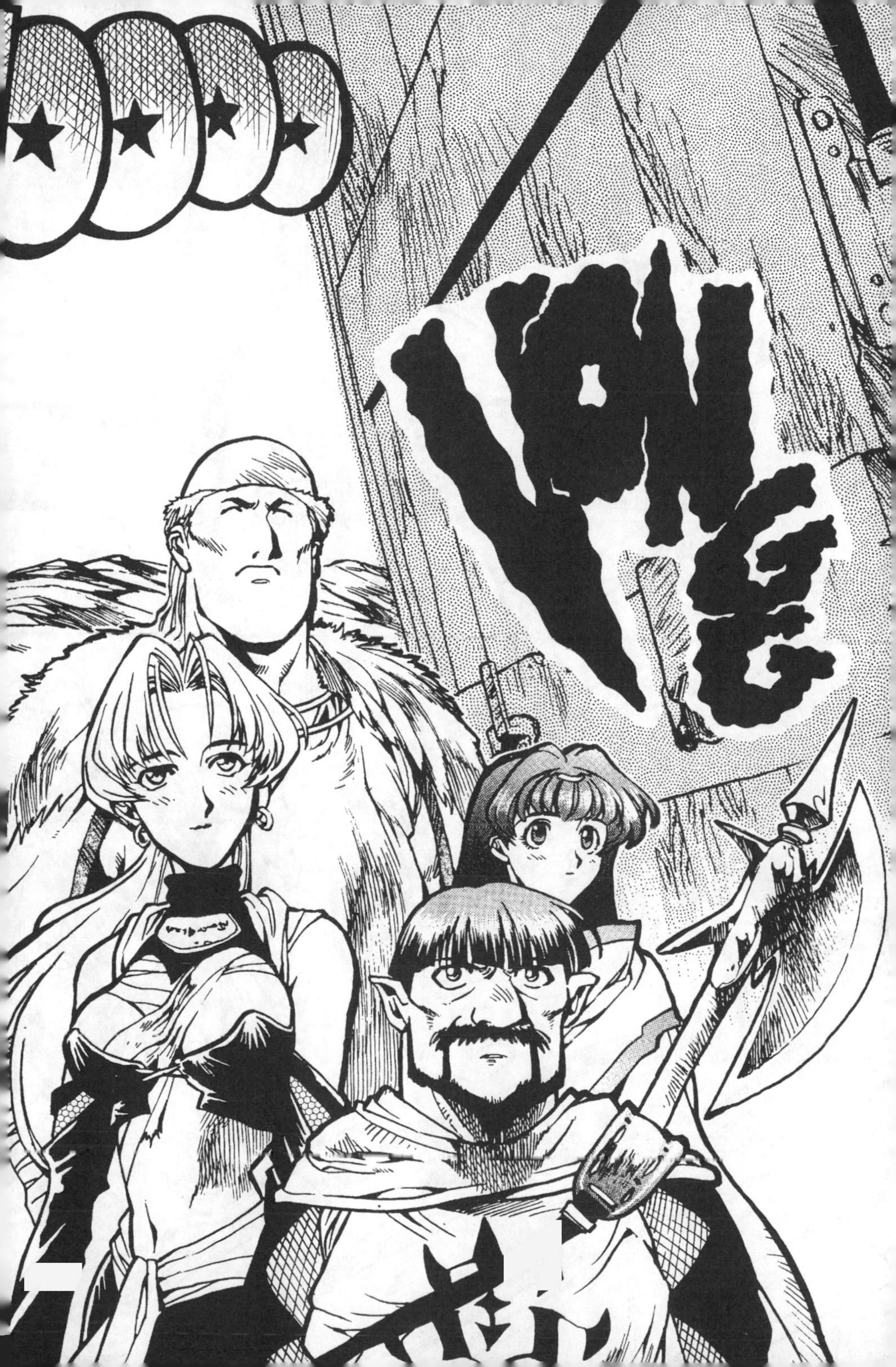

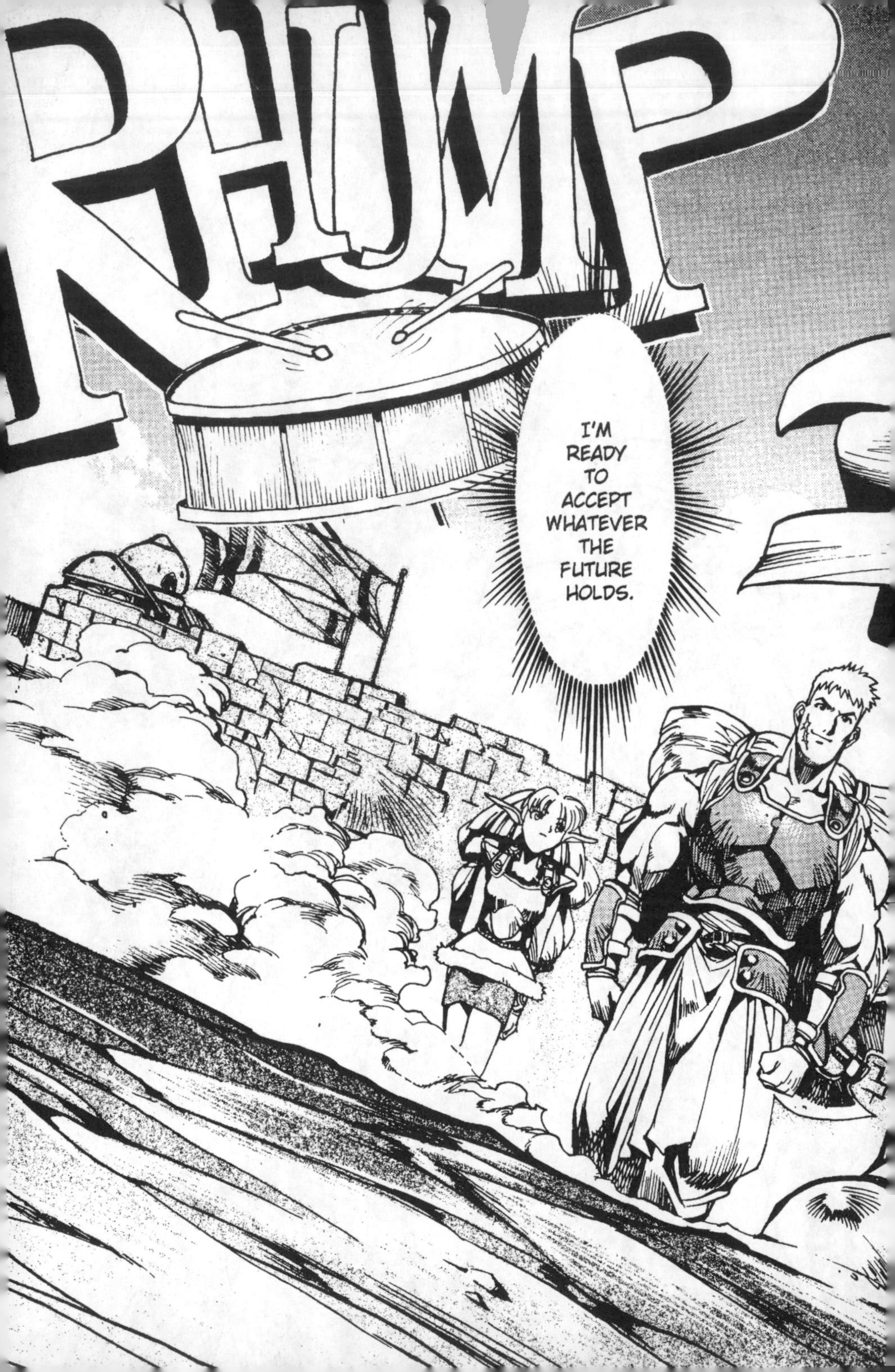
THUMP
I'M READY TO ACCEPT WHATEVER THE FUTURE HOLDS.

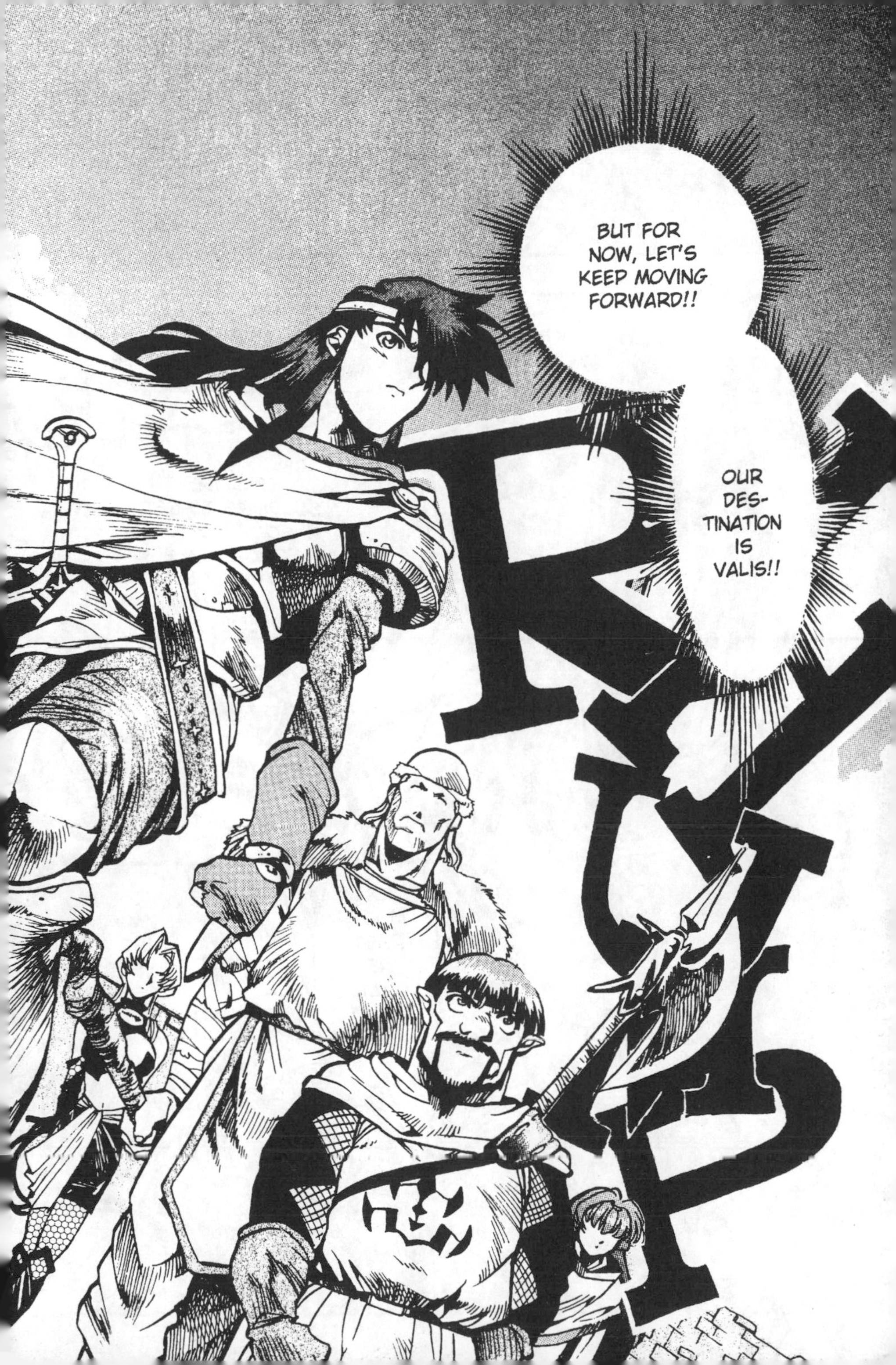
BUT FOR NOW, LET'S KEEP MOVING FORWARD!!
OUR DES-TINATION IS VALIS!!

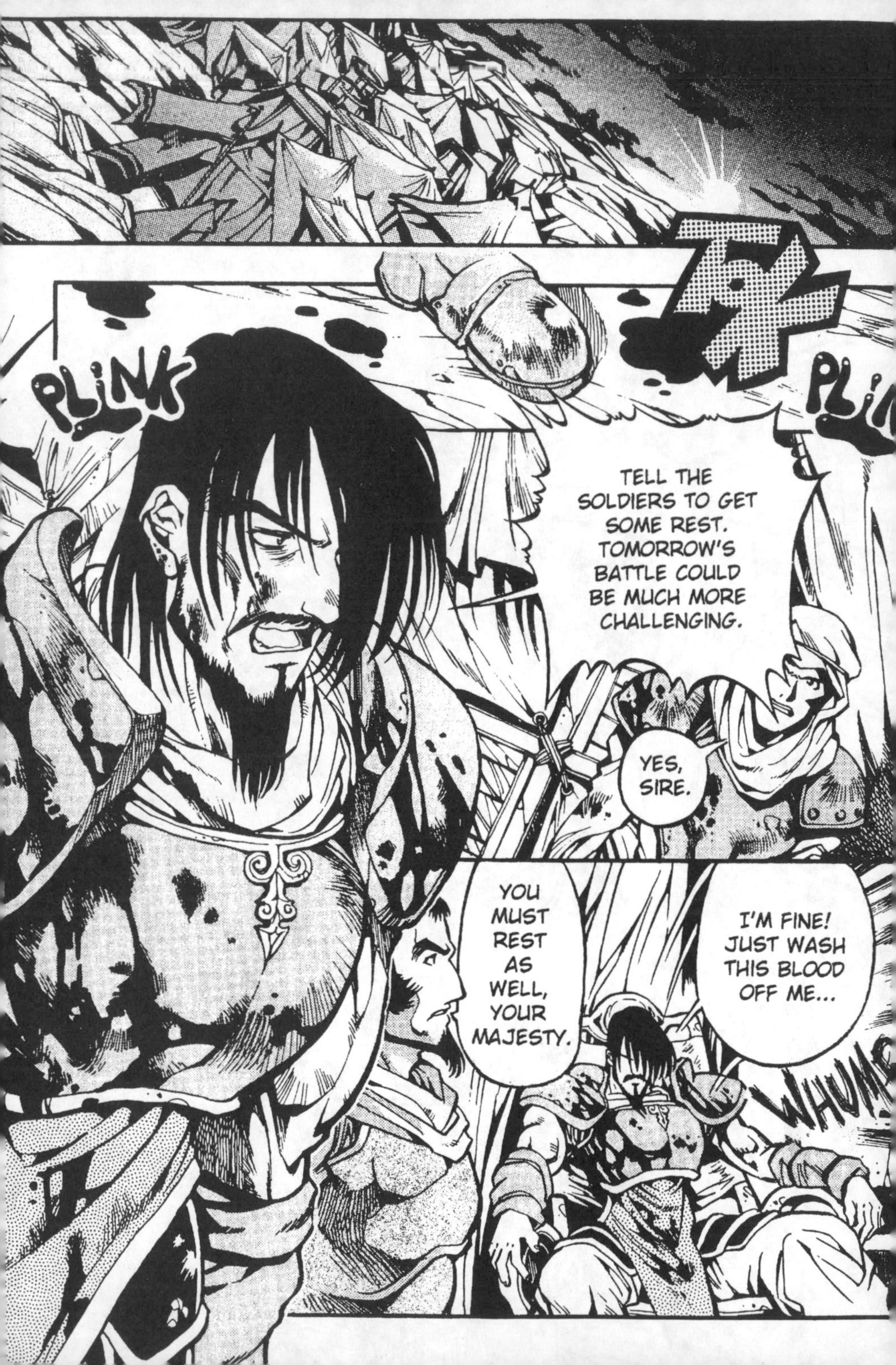
PLINK
PLIN
TELL THE SOLDIERS TO GET SOME REST. TOMORROW'S BATTLE COULD BE MUCH MORE CHALLENGING.
YES, SIRE.
YOU MUST REST AS WELL, YOUR MAJESTY.
I'M FINE! JUST WASH THIS BLOOD OFF ME...
WHUM

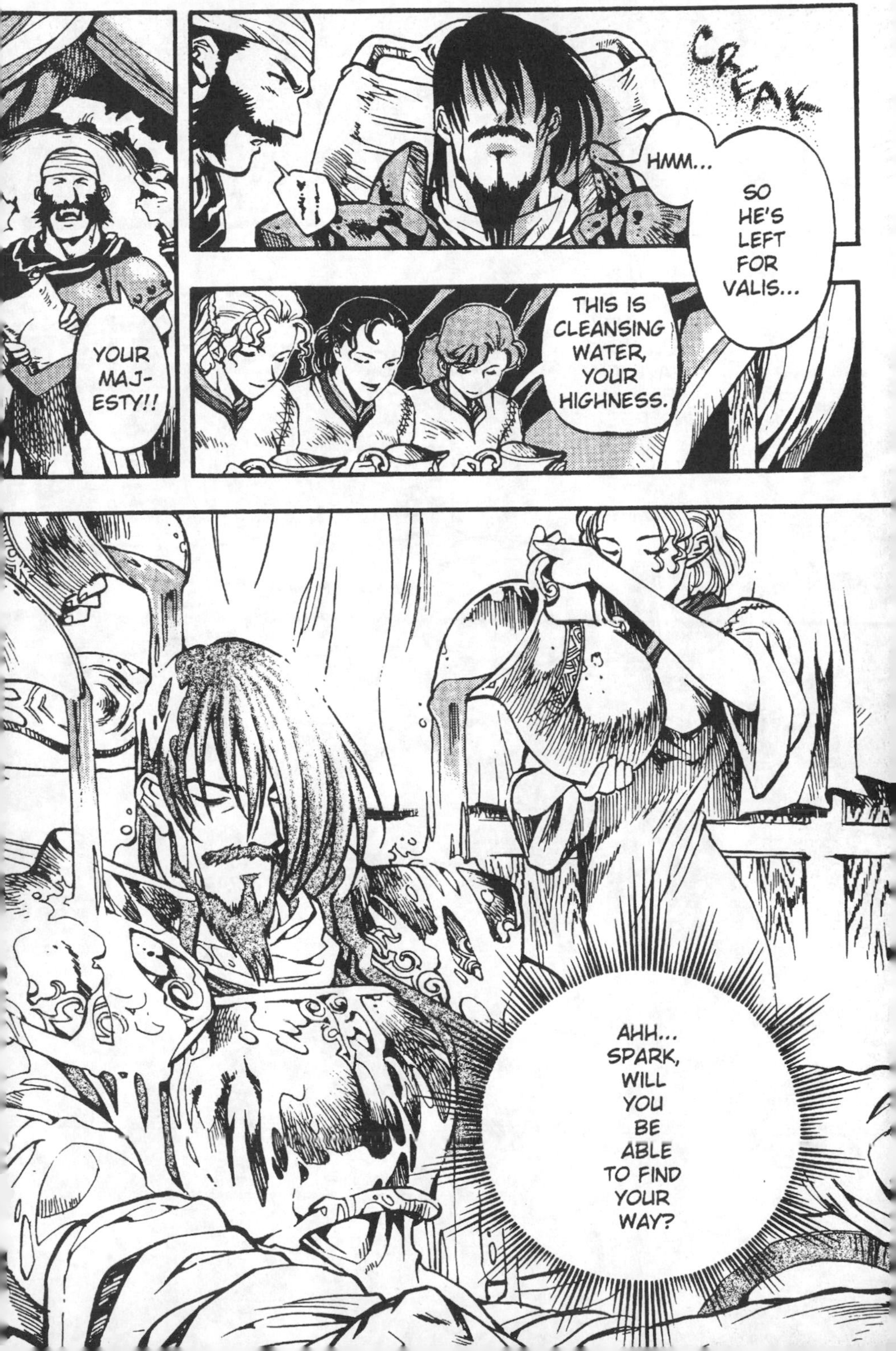
YOUR MAJ-ESTY!!
CREAK
HMM...
SO HE'S LEFT FOR VALIS...
THIS IS CLEANSING WATER, YOUR HIGHNESS.
AHH... SPARK, WILL YOU BE ABLE TO FIND YOUR WAY?

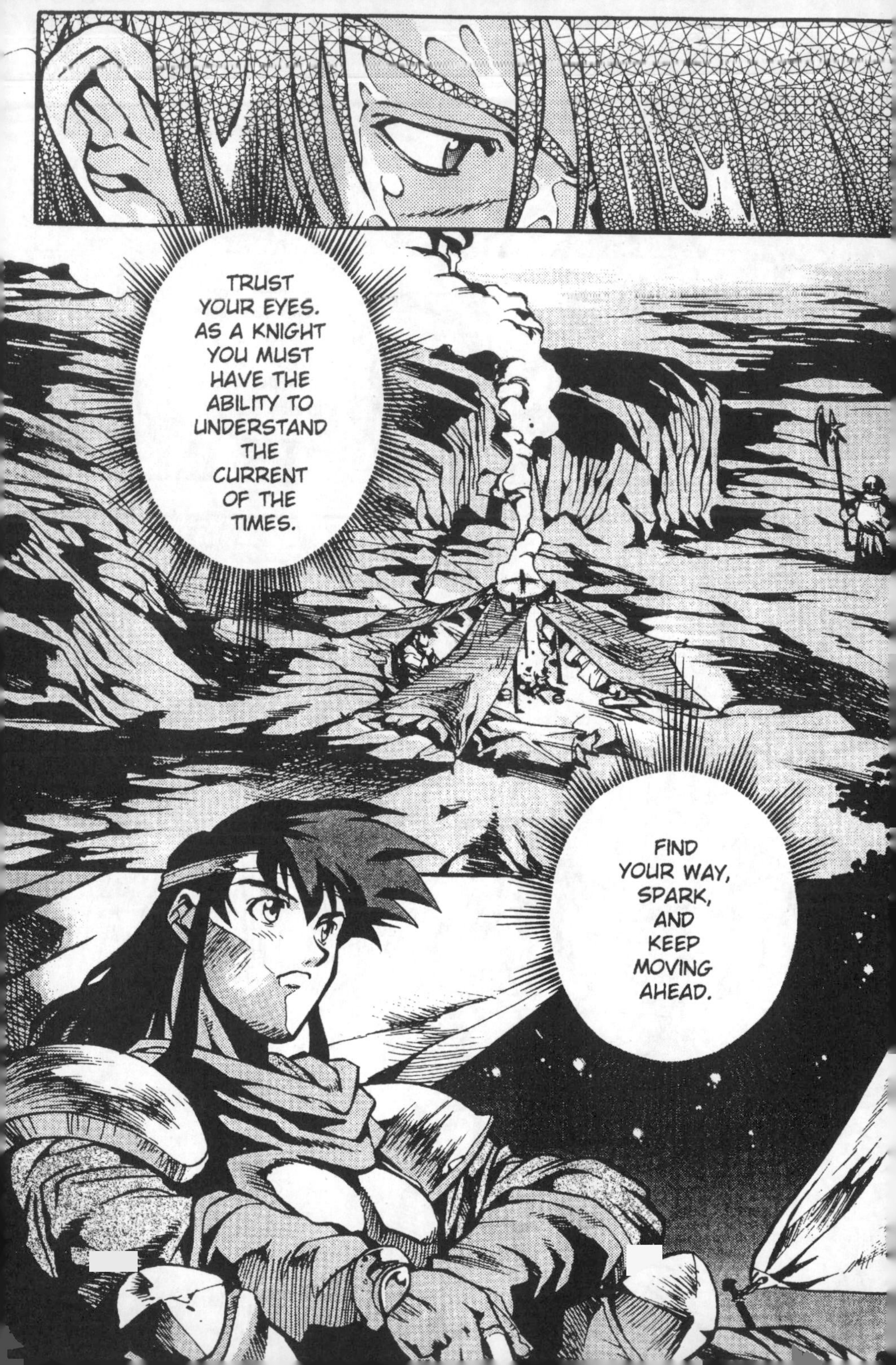
TRUST YOUR EYES. AS A KNIGHT YOU MUST HAVE THE ABILITY TO UNDERSTAND THE CURRENT OF THE TIMES.
FIND YOUR WAY, SPARK, AND KEEP MOVING AHEAD.

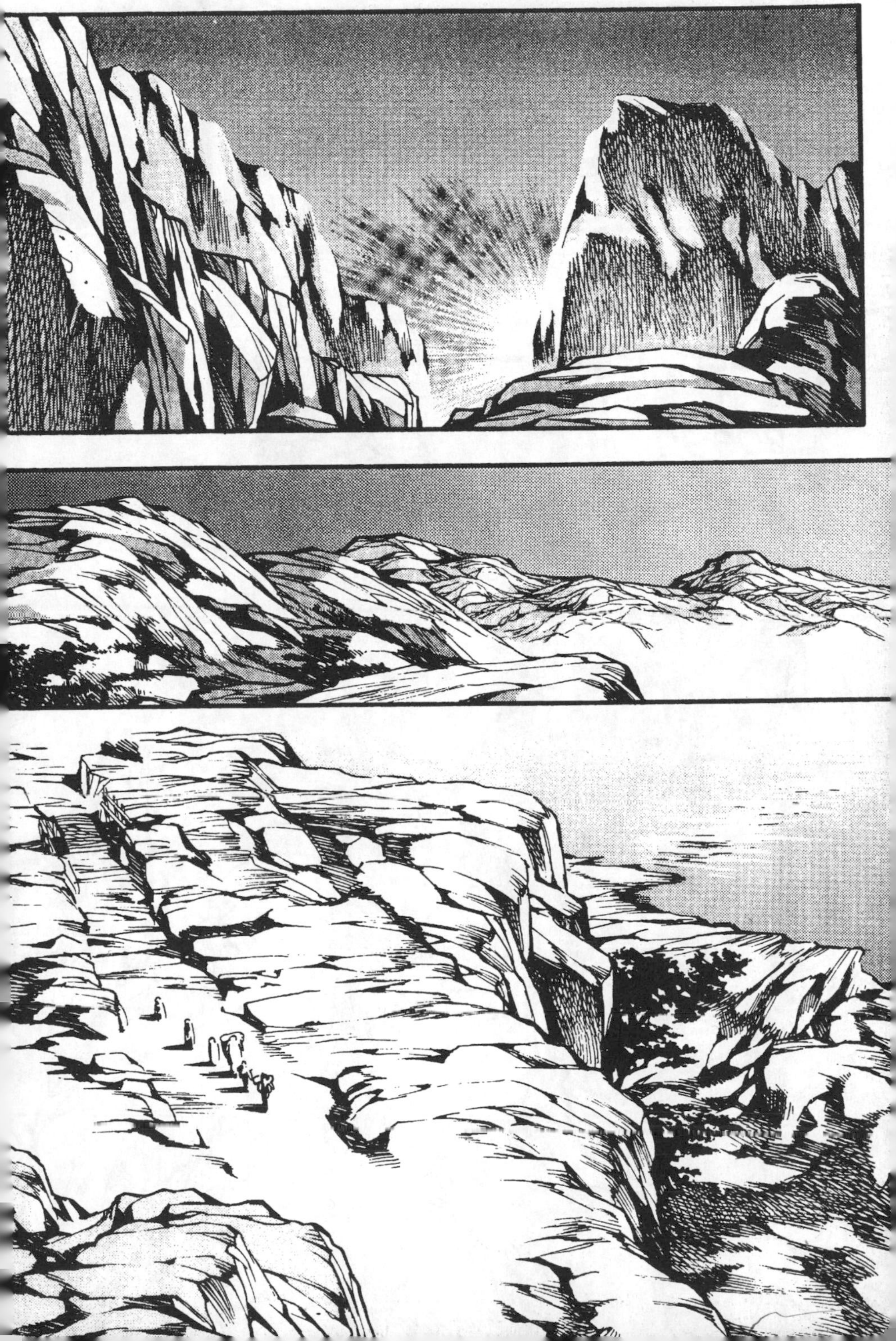

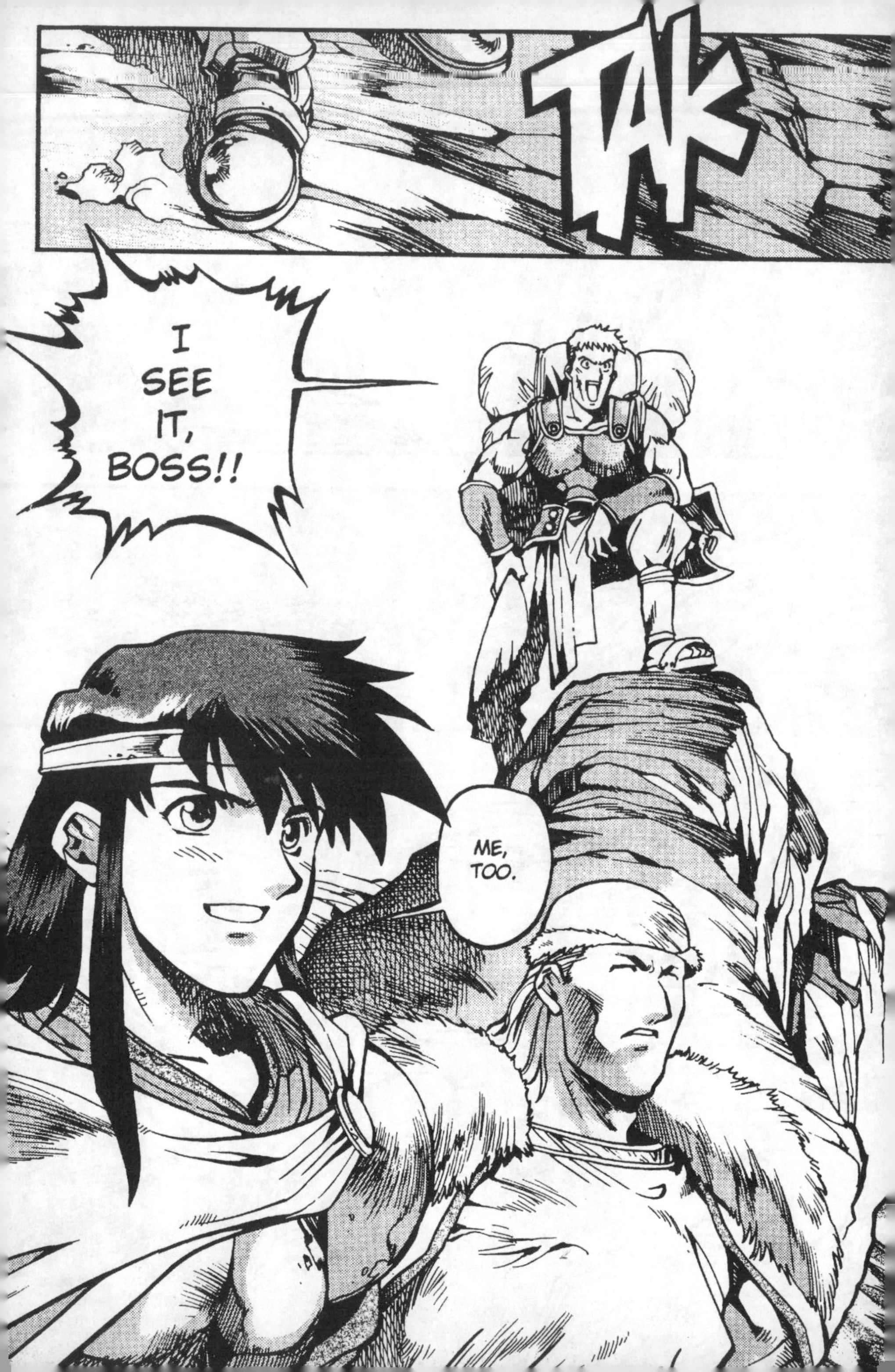
TAK
I SEE IT, BOSS!!
ME, TOO.

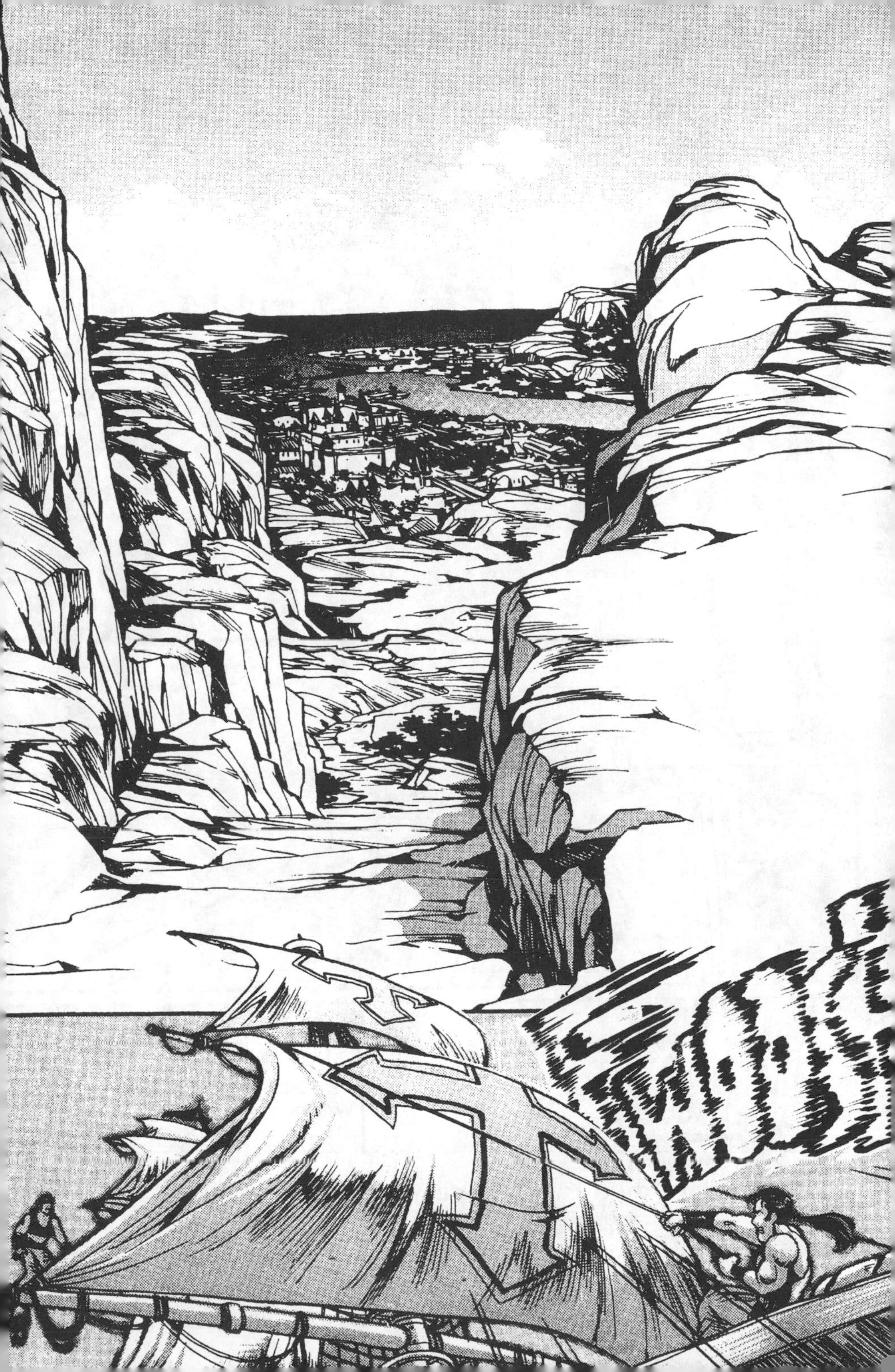

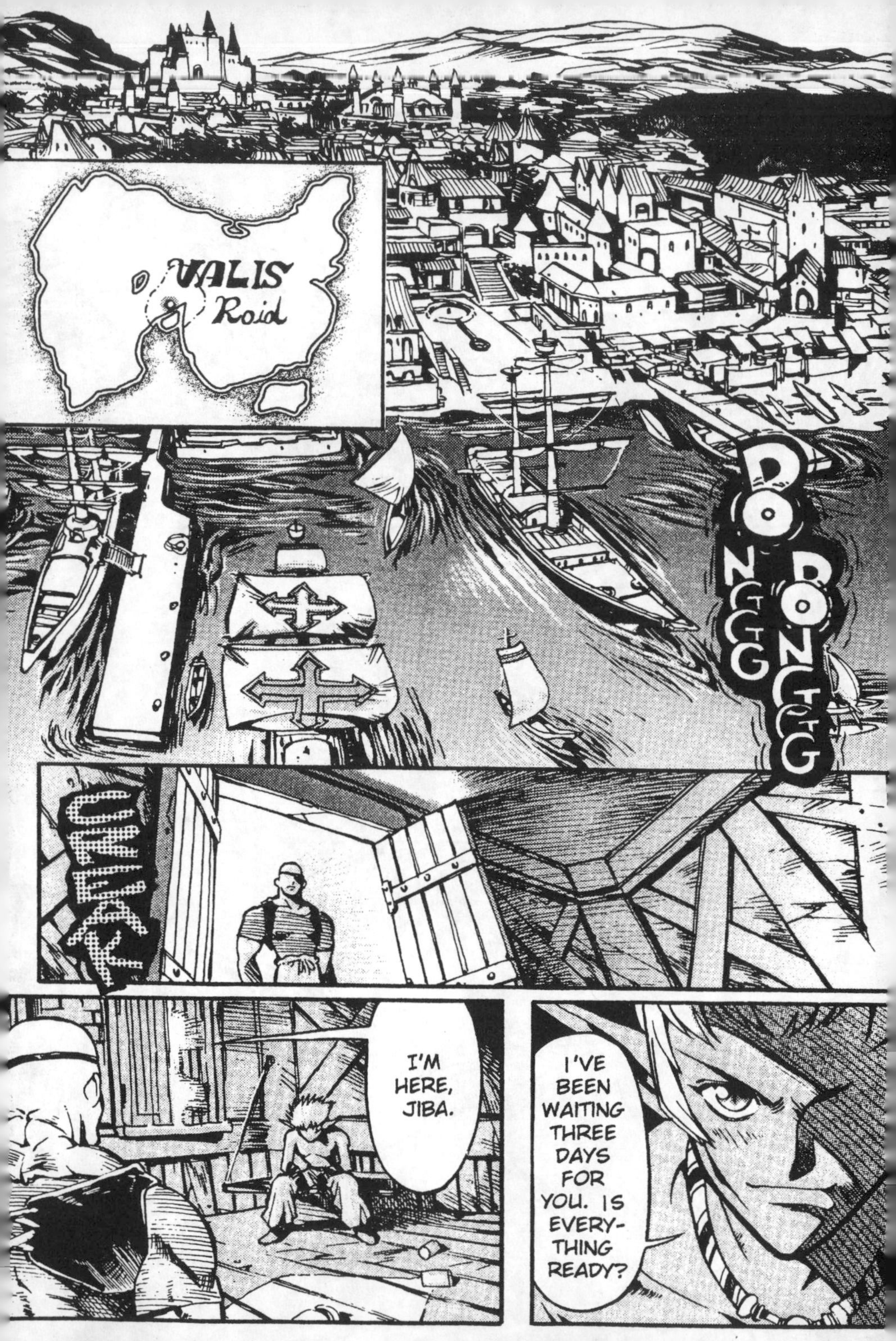
VALIS
Roid
DONG
DONG
CREAK
I'M HERE, JIBA.
I'VE BEEN WAITING THREE DAYS FOR YOU. IS EVERYTHING READY?

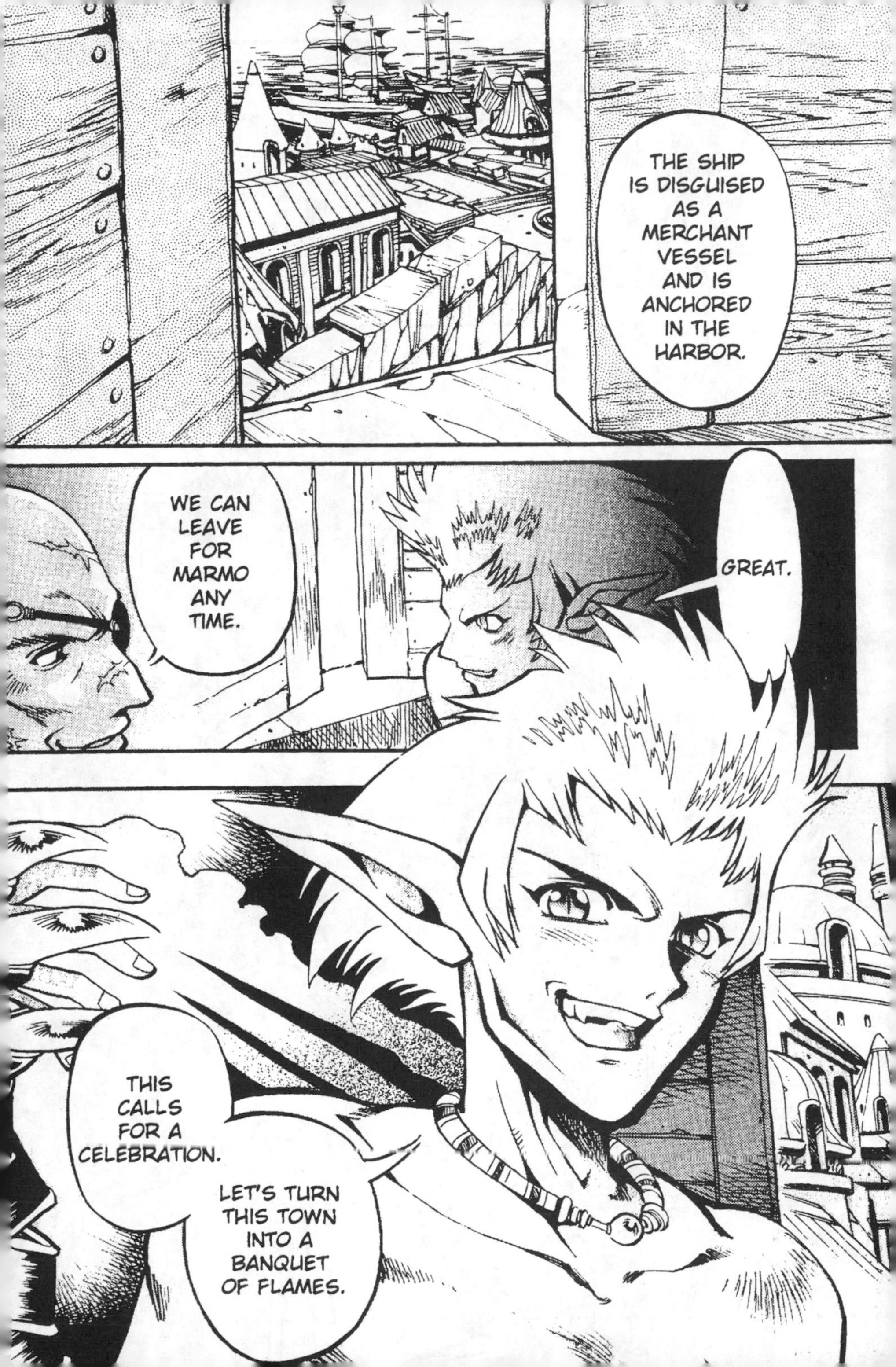
THE SHIP IS DISGUISED AS A MERCHANT VESSEL AND IS ANCHORED IN THE HARBOR.
WE CAN LEAVE FOR MARMO ANY TIME.
GREAT.
THIS CALLS FOR A CELEBRATION.
LET'S TURN THIS TOWN INTO A BANQUET OF FLAMES.

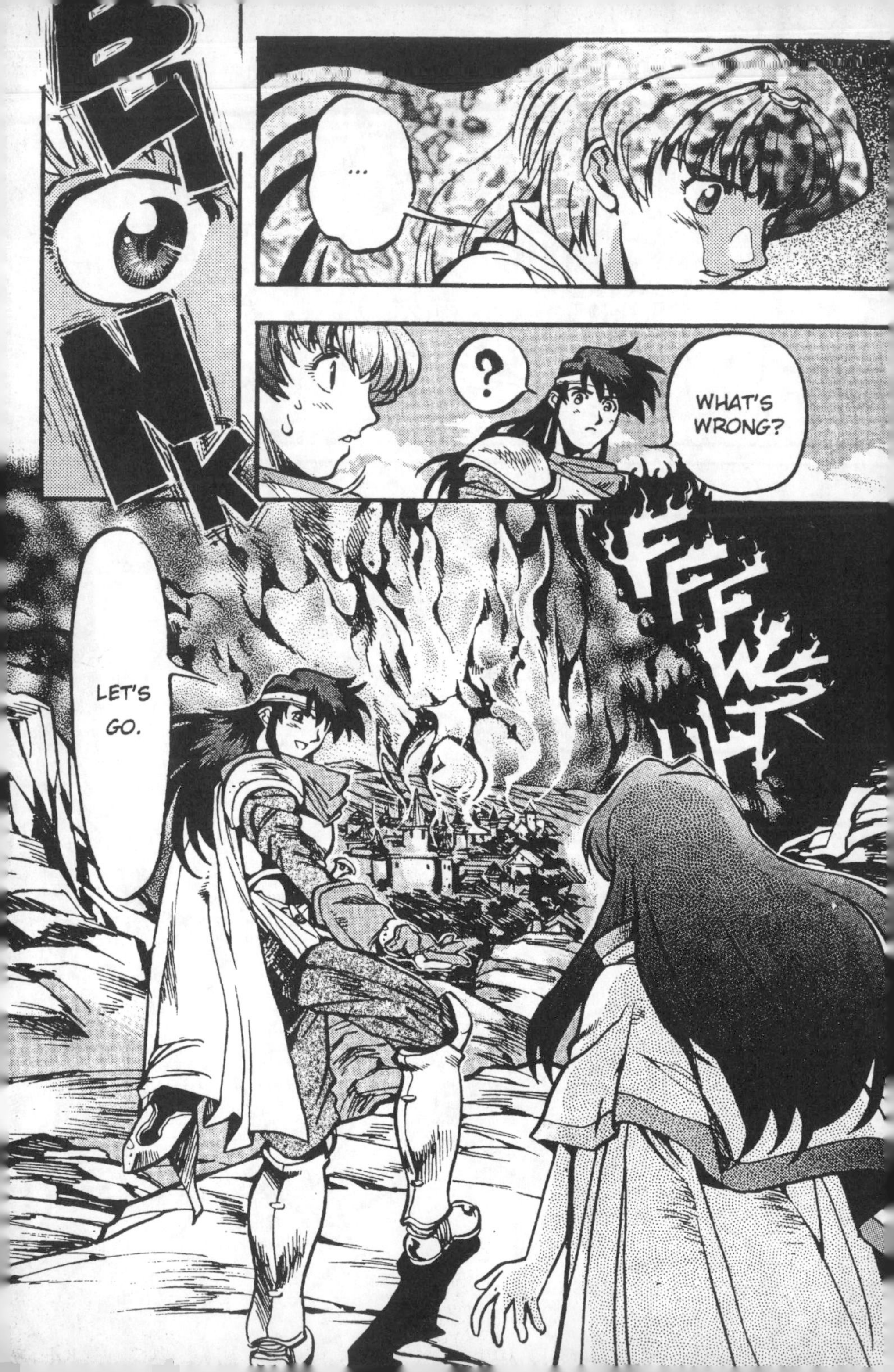
...
?
WHAT'S WRONG?
LET'S GO.

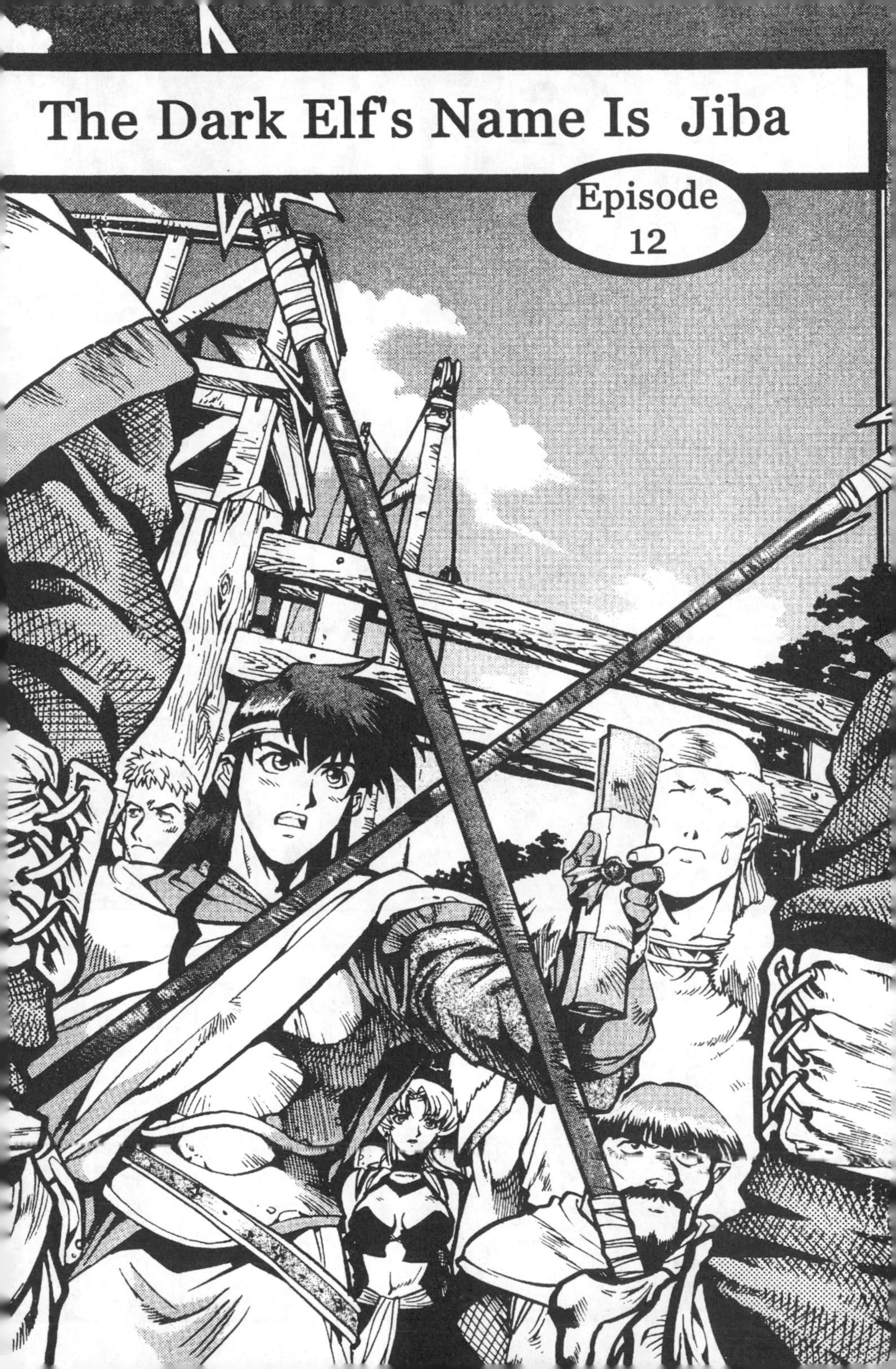
The Dark Elf's Name Is Jiba
Episode 12

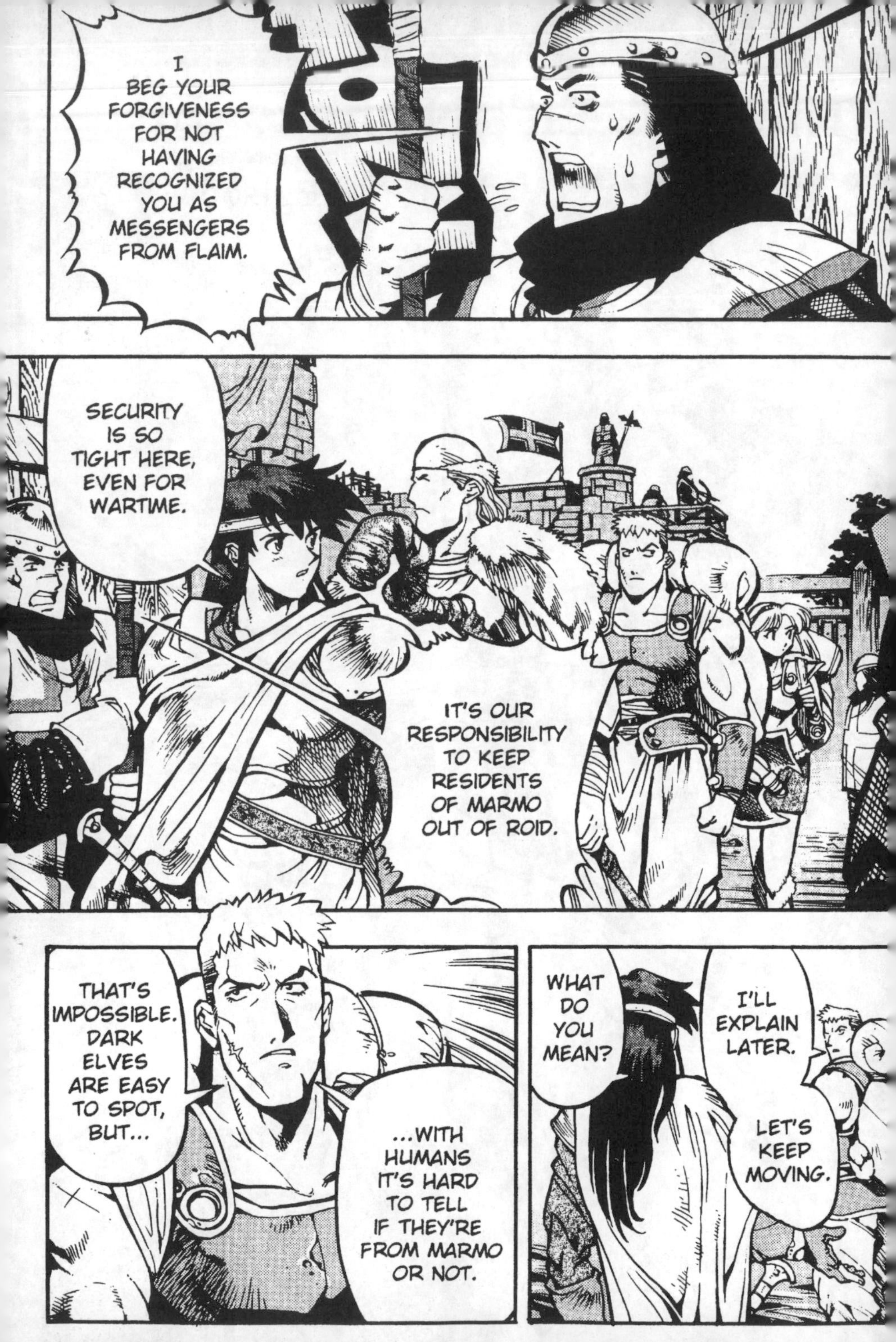
I BEG YOUR FORGIVENESS FOR NOT HAVING RECOGNIZED YOU AS MESSENGERS FROM FLAIM.
SECURITY IS SO TIGHT HERE, EVEN FOR WARTIME.
IT'S OUR RESPONSIBILITY TO KEEP RESIDENTS OF MARMO OUT OF ROID.
THAT'S IMPOSSIBLE. DARK ELVES ARE EASY TO SPOT, BUT...
...WITH HUMANS IT'S HARD TO TELL IF THEY'RE FROM MARMO OR NOT.
WHAT DO YOU MEAN?
I'LL EXPLAIN LATER.
LET'S KEEP MOVING.

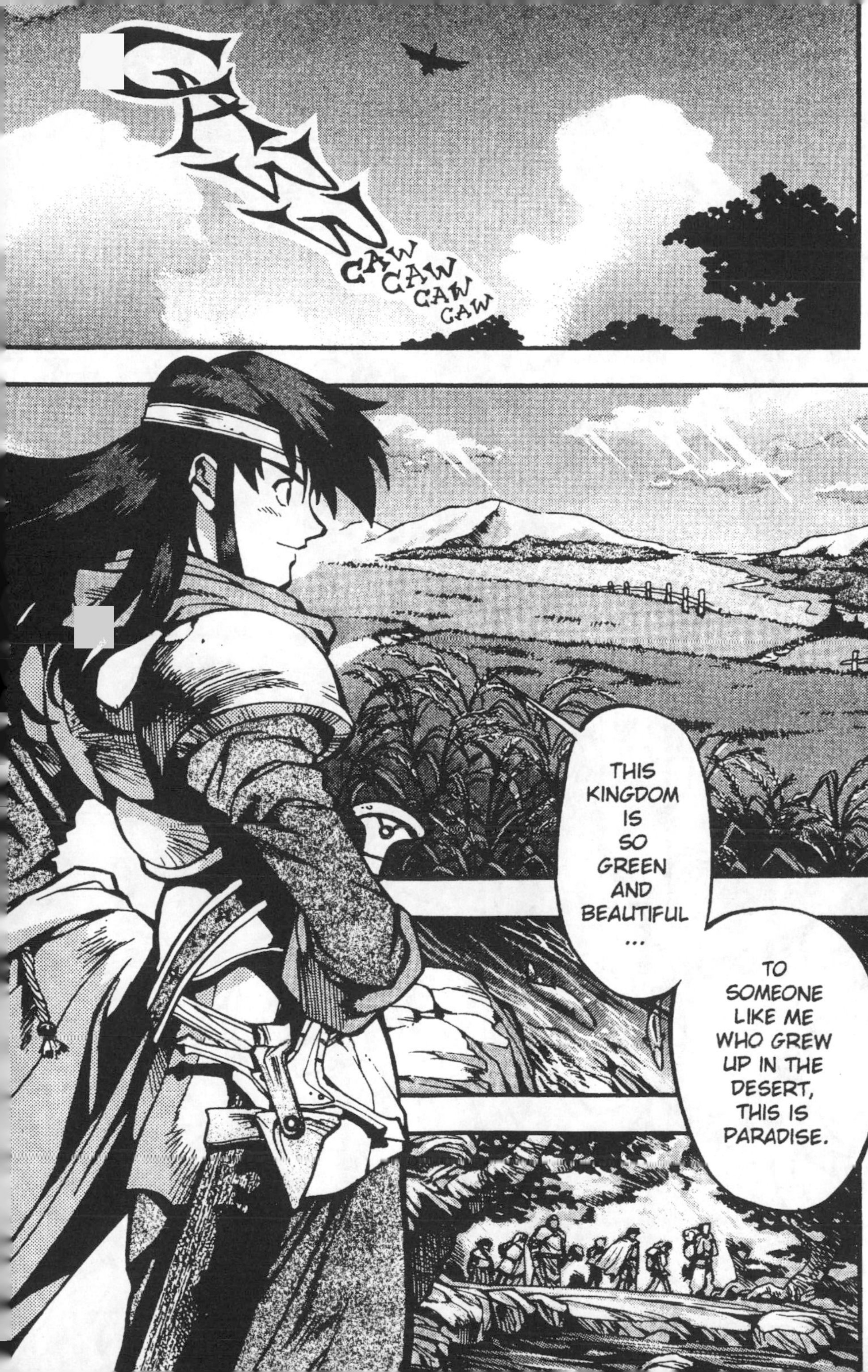
CAW
CAW CAW CAW CAW
THIS KINGDOM IS SO GREEN AND BEAUTIFUL ...
TO SOMEONE LIKE ME WHO GREW UP IN THE DESERT, THIS IS PARADISE.

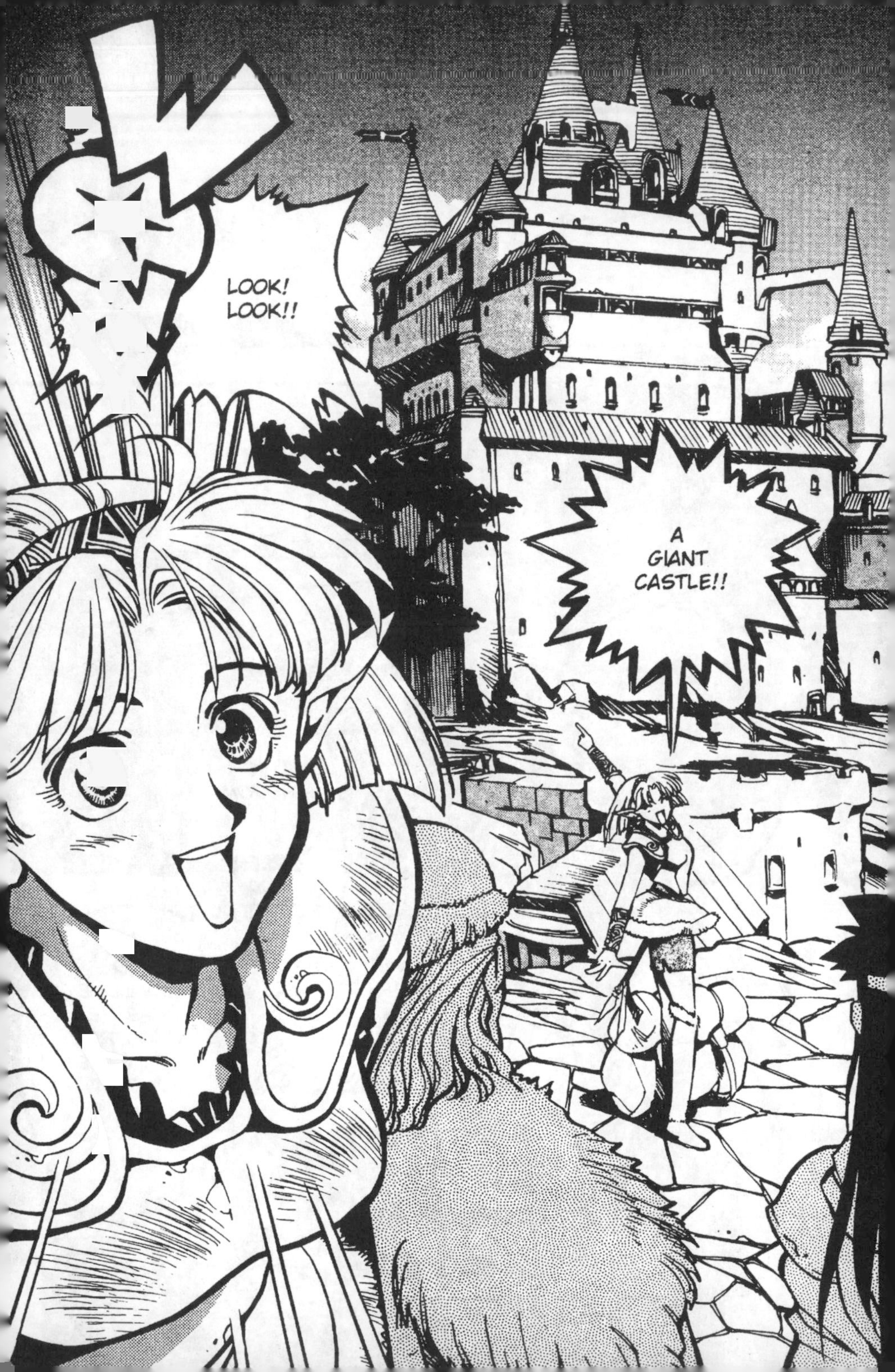
LOOK! LOOK!!
A GIANT CASTLE!!

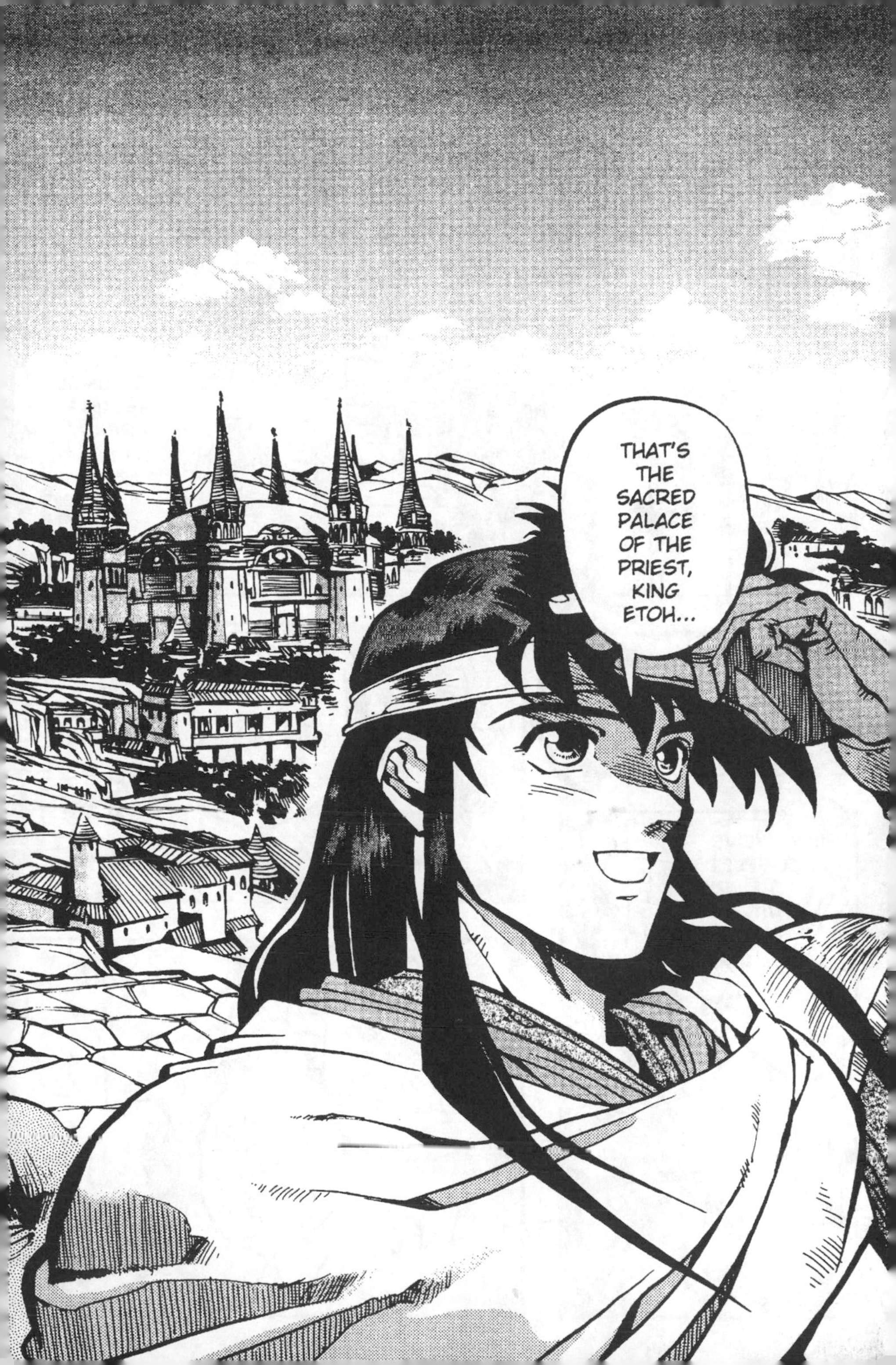
THAT'S THE SACRED PALACE OF THE PRIEST, KING ETOH...

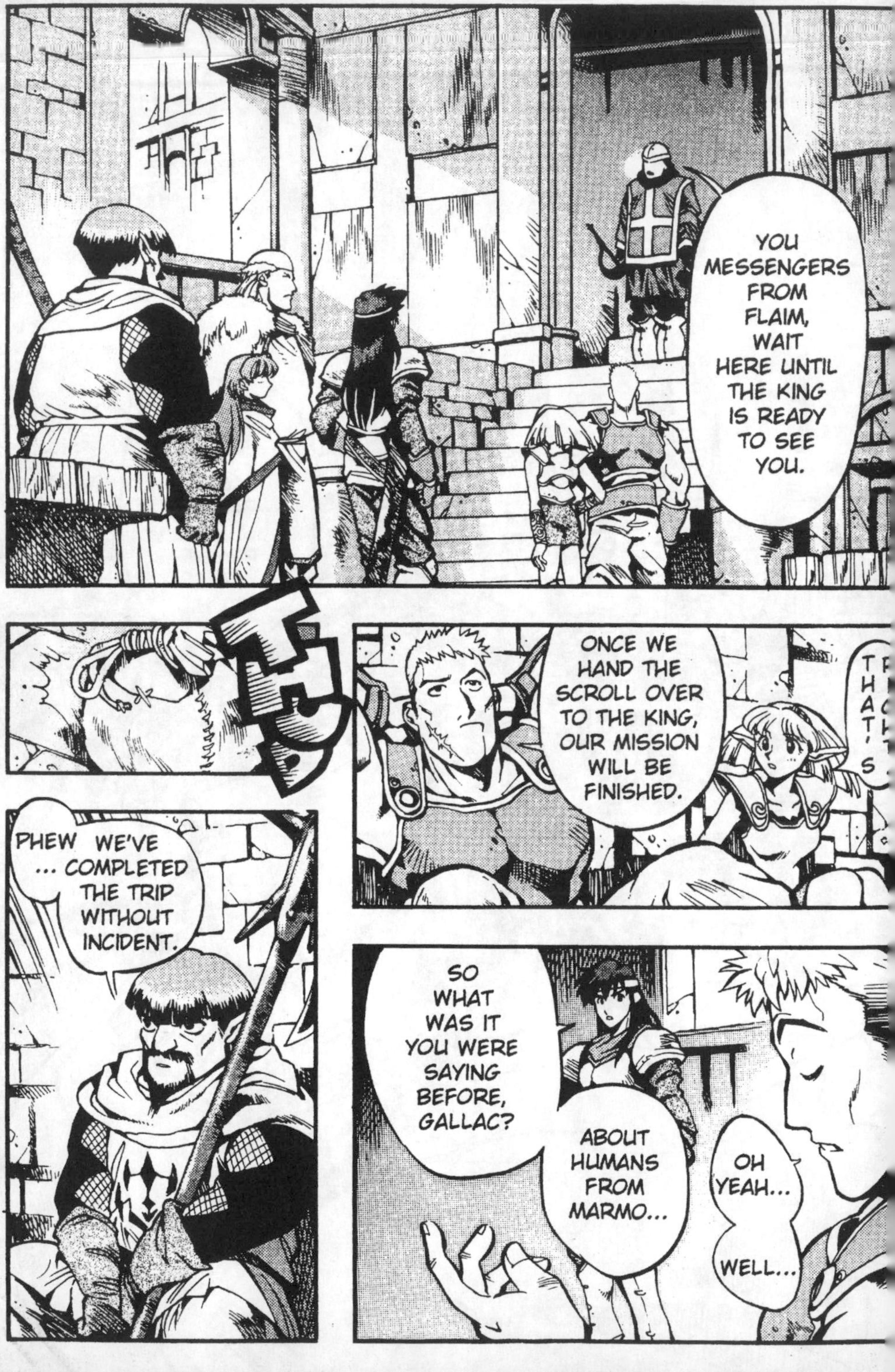

YOU MESSENGERS FROM FLAIM, WAIT HERE UNTIL THE KING IS READY TO SEE YOU.
ONCE WE HAND THE SCROLL OVER TO THE KING, OUR MISSION WILL BE FINISHED.
PHEW ... WE'VE COMPLETED THE TRIP WITHOUT INCIDENT.
SO WHAT WAS IT YOU WERE SAYING BEFORE, GALLAC?
ABOUT HUMANS FROM MARMO...
OH YEAH...
WELL...

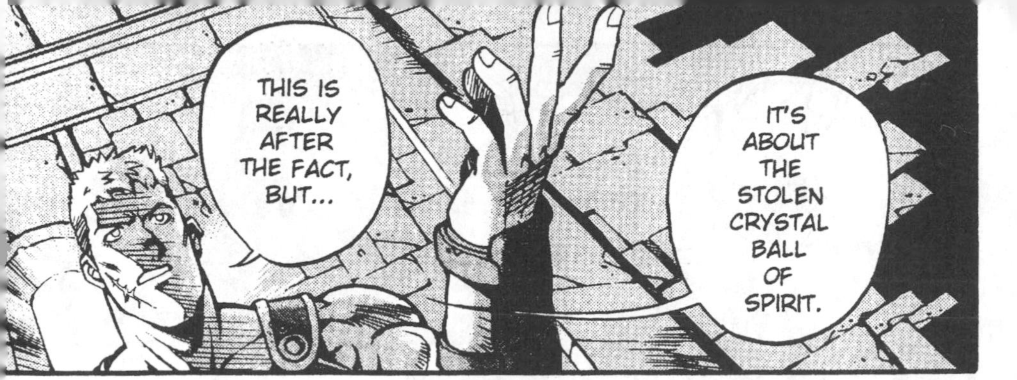
THIS IS REALLY AFTER THE FACT, BUT...
IT'S ABOUT THE STOLEN CRYSTAL BALL OF SPIRIT.

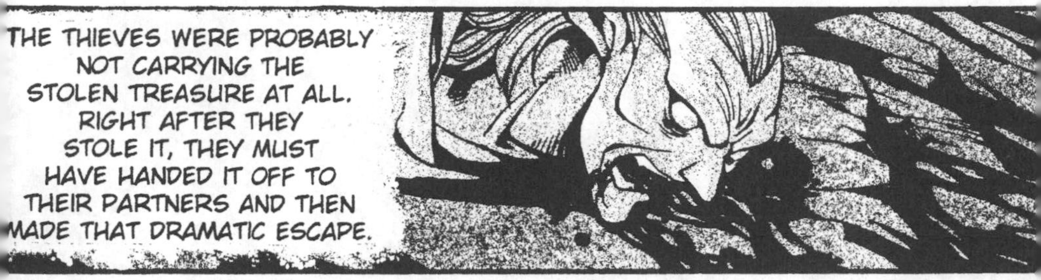
THE THIEVES WERE PROBABLY NOT CARRYING THE STOLEN TREASURE AT ALL. RIGHT AFTER THEY STOLE IT, THEY MUST HAVE HANDED IT OFF TO THEIR PARTNERS AND THEN MADE THAT DRAMATIC ESCAPE.

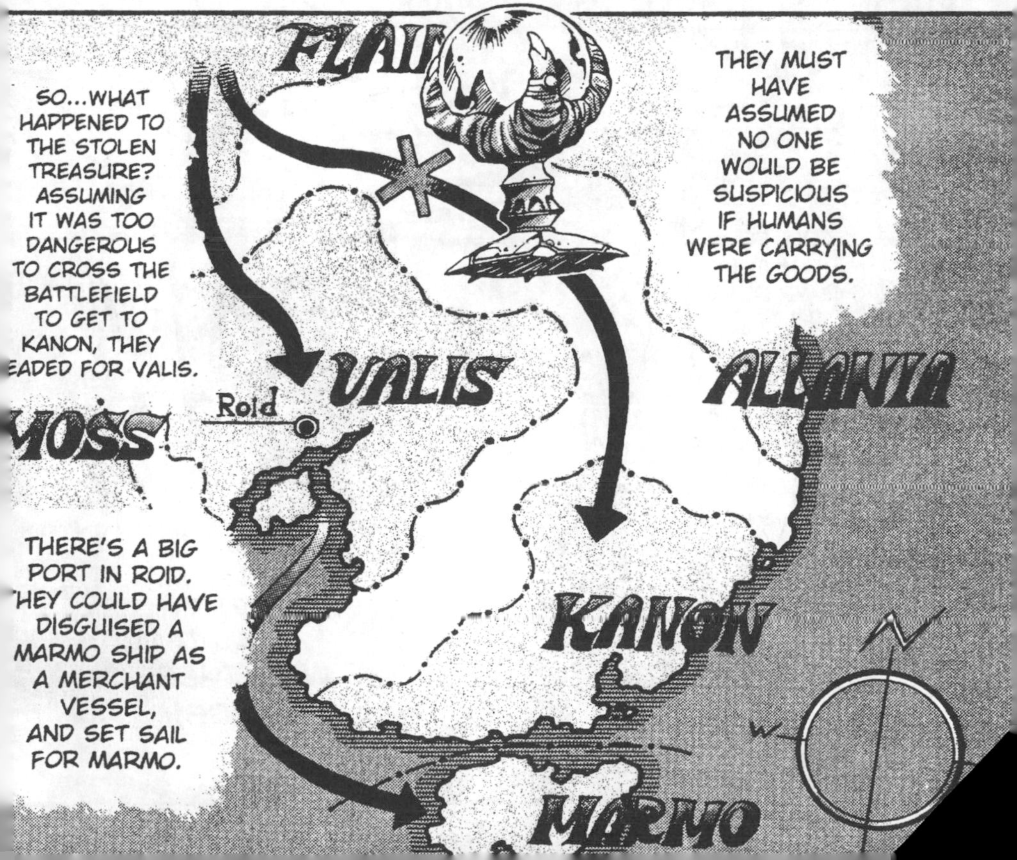
SO...WHAT HAPPENED TO THE STOLEN TREASURE? ASSUMING IT WAS TOO DANGEROUS TO CROSS THE BATTLEFIELD TO GET TO KANON, THEY EADED FOR VALIS.
THEY MUST HAVE ASSUMED NO ONE WOULD BE SUSPICIOUS IF HUMANS WERE CARRYING THE GOODS.
VALIS
Roid
MOSS
KANON
MARMO
THERE'S A BIG PORT IN ROID. HEY COULD HAVE DISGUISED A MARMO SHIP AS A MERCHANT VESSEL, AND SET SAIL FOR MARMO.

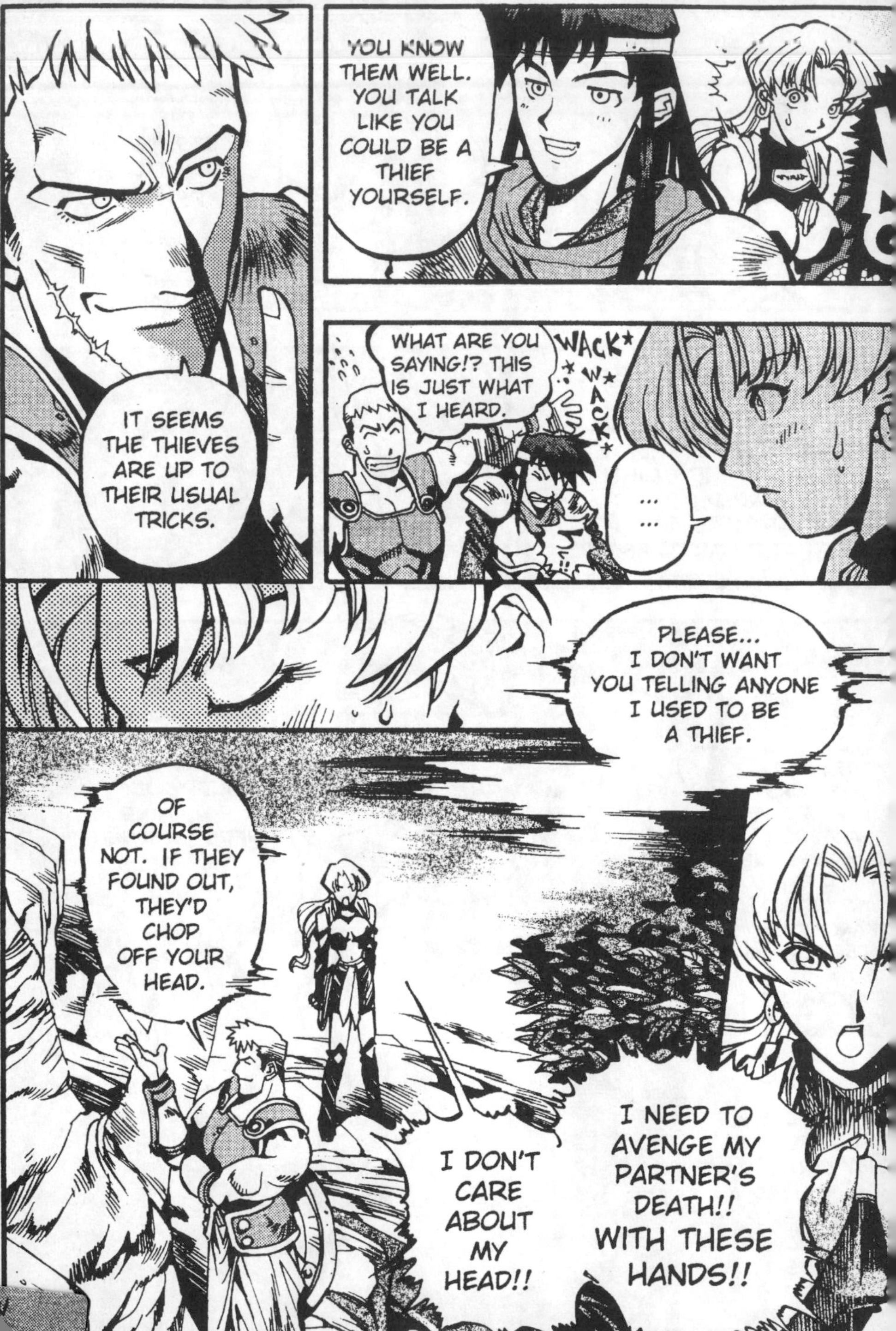
IT SEEMS THE THIEVES ARE UP TO THEIR USUAL TRICKS.
YOU KNOW THEM WELL. YOU TALK LIKE YOU COULD BE A THIEF YOURSELF.
WHAT ARE YOU SAYING!? THIS IS JUST WHAT I HEARD.
WACK* WACK*
... ...
PLEASE... I DON'T WANT YOU TELLING ANYONE I USED TO BE A THIEF.
OF COURSE NOT. IF THEY FOUND OUT, THEY'D CHOP OFF YOUR HEAD.
I DON'T CARE ABOUT MY HEAD!!
I NEED TO AVENGE MY PARTNER'S DEATH!! WITH THESE HANDS!!

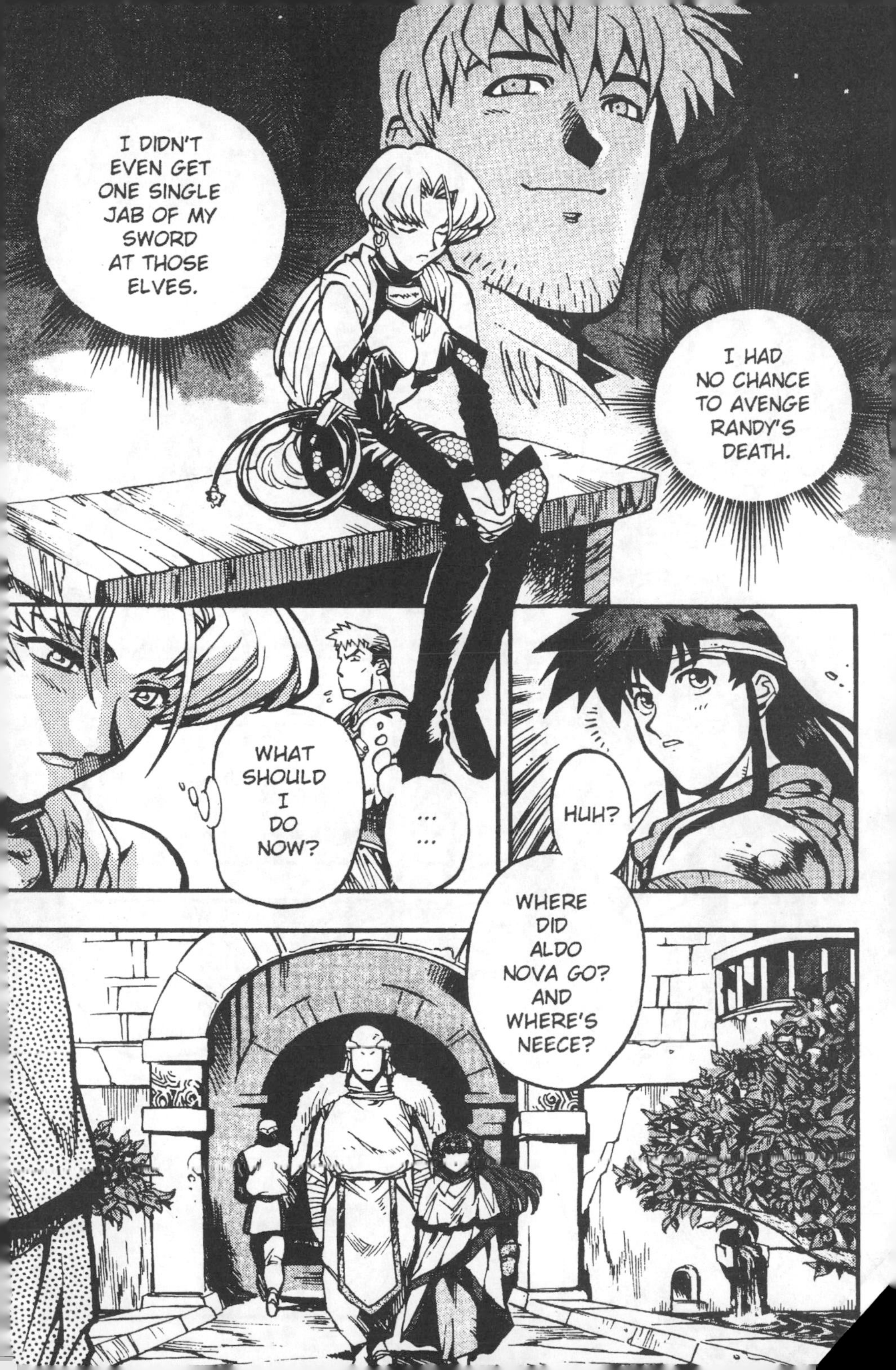
I DIDN'T EVEN GET ONE SINGLE JAB OF MY SWORD AT THOSE ELVES.
I HAD NO CHANCE TO AVENGE RANDY'S DEATH.
WHAT SHOULD I DO NOW?
......
HUH?
WHERE DID ALDO NOVA GO? AND WHERE'S NEECE?

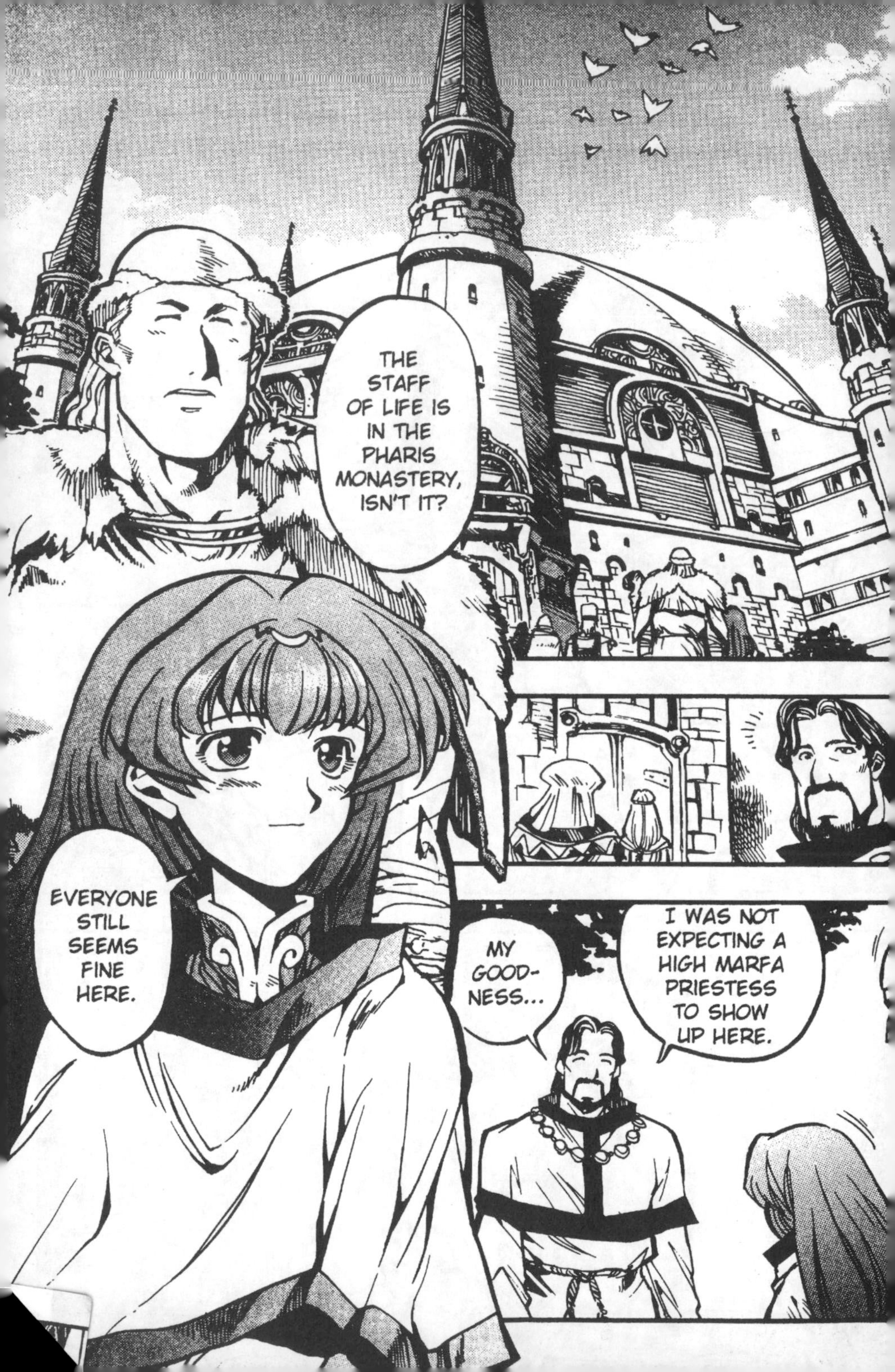
THE STAFF OF LIFE IS IN THE PHARIS MONASTERY, ISN'T IT?
EVERYONE STILL SEEMS FINE HERE.
MY GOOD-NESS...
I WAS NOT EXPECTING A HIGH MARFA PRIESTESS TO SHOW UP HERE.

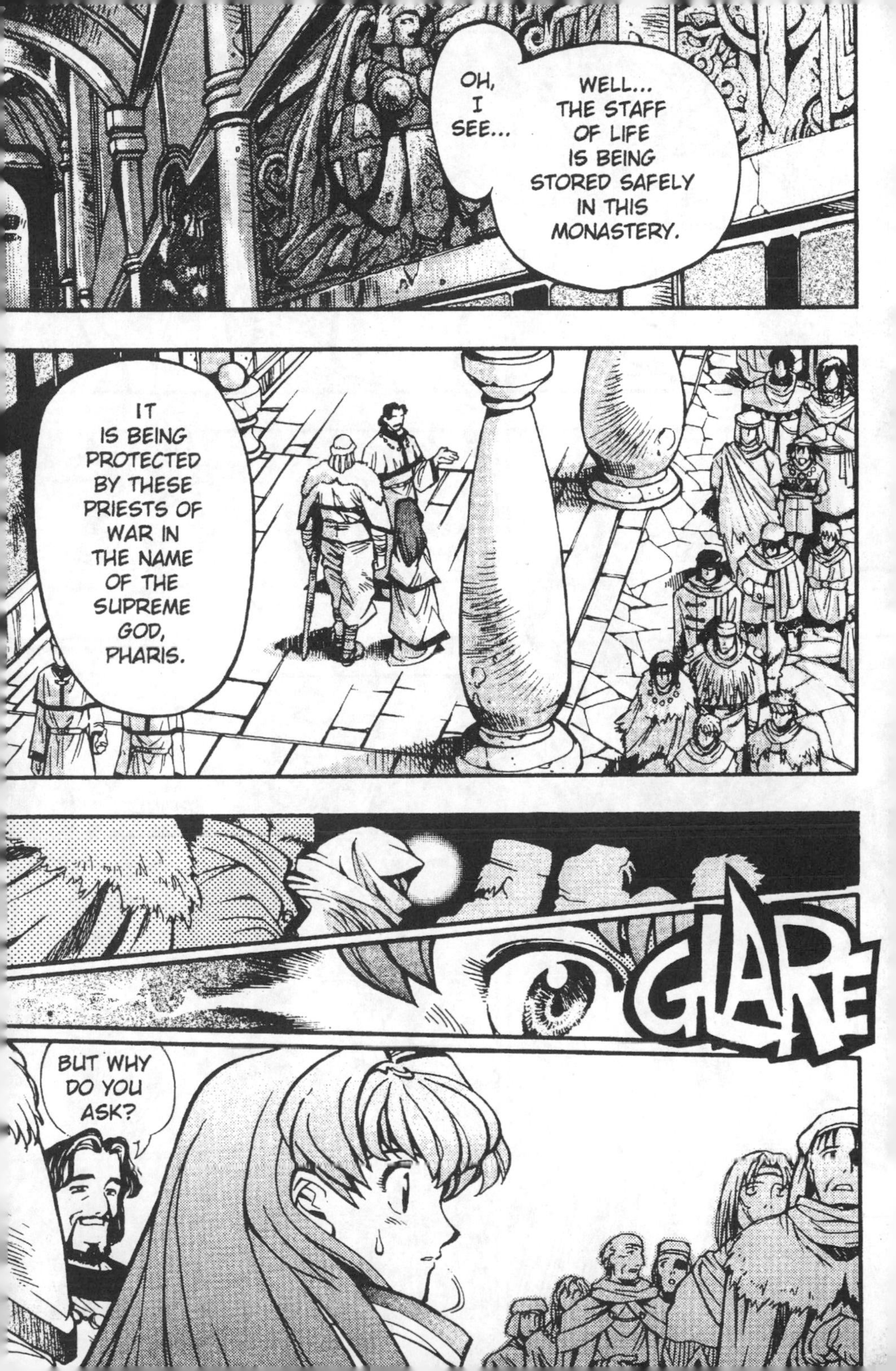
OH, I SEE...
WELL... THE STAFF OF LIFE IS BEING STORED SAFELY IN THIS MONASTERY.
IT IS BEING PROTECTED BY THESE PRIESTS OF WAR IN THE NAME OF THE SUPREME GOD, PHARIS.
GLARE
BUT WHY DO YOU ASK?

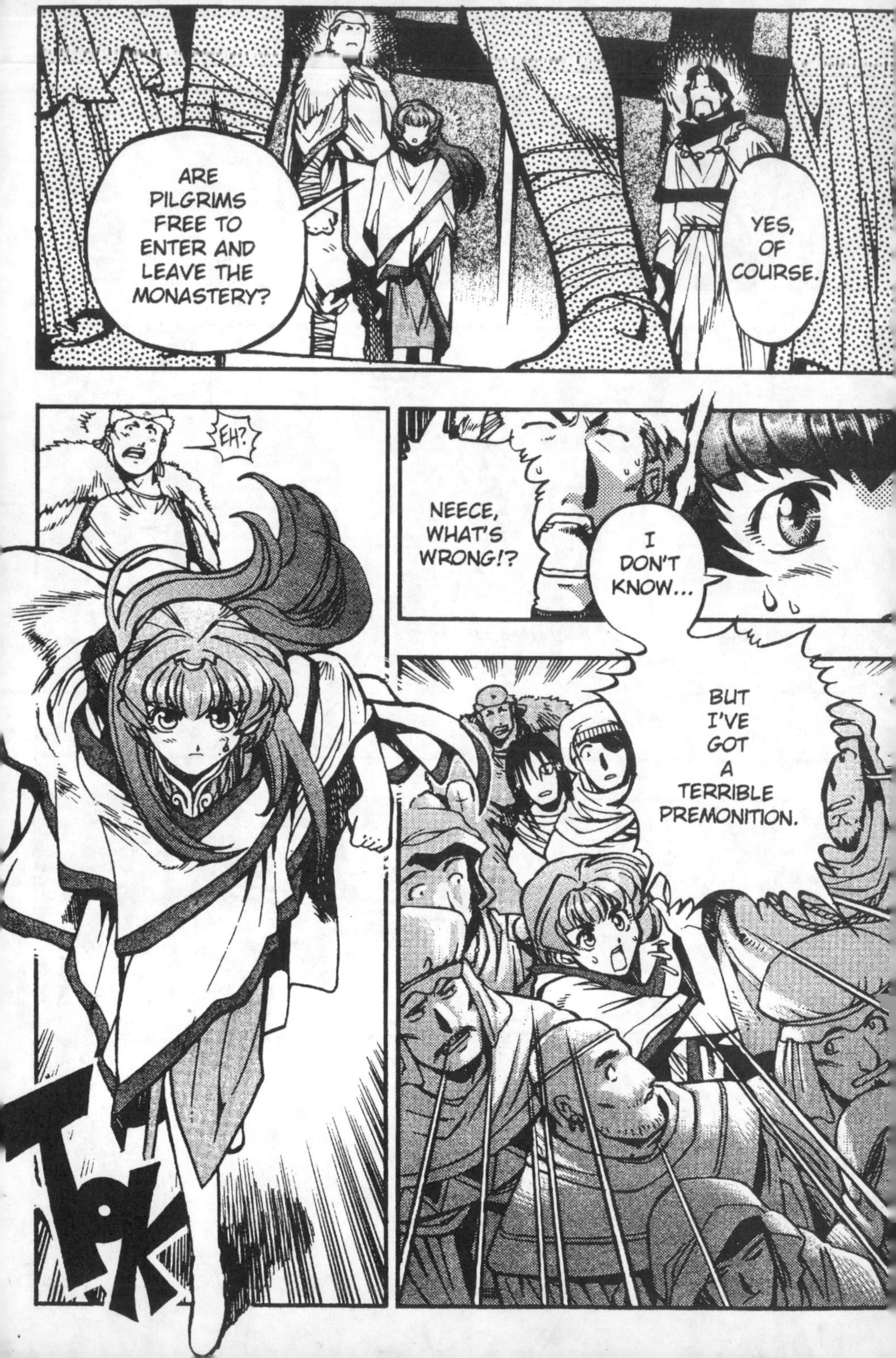
ARE PILGRIMS FREE TO ENTER AND LEAVE THE MONASTERY?
YES, OF COURSE.
EH?
TOK
NEECE, WHAT'S WRONG!?
I DON'T KNOW...
BUT I'VE GOT A TERRIBLE PREMONITION.

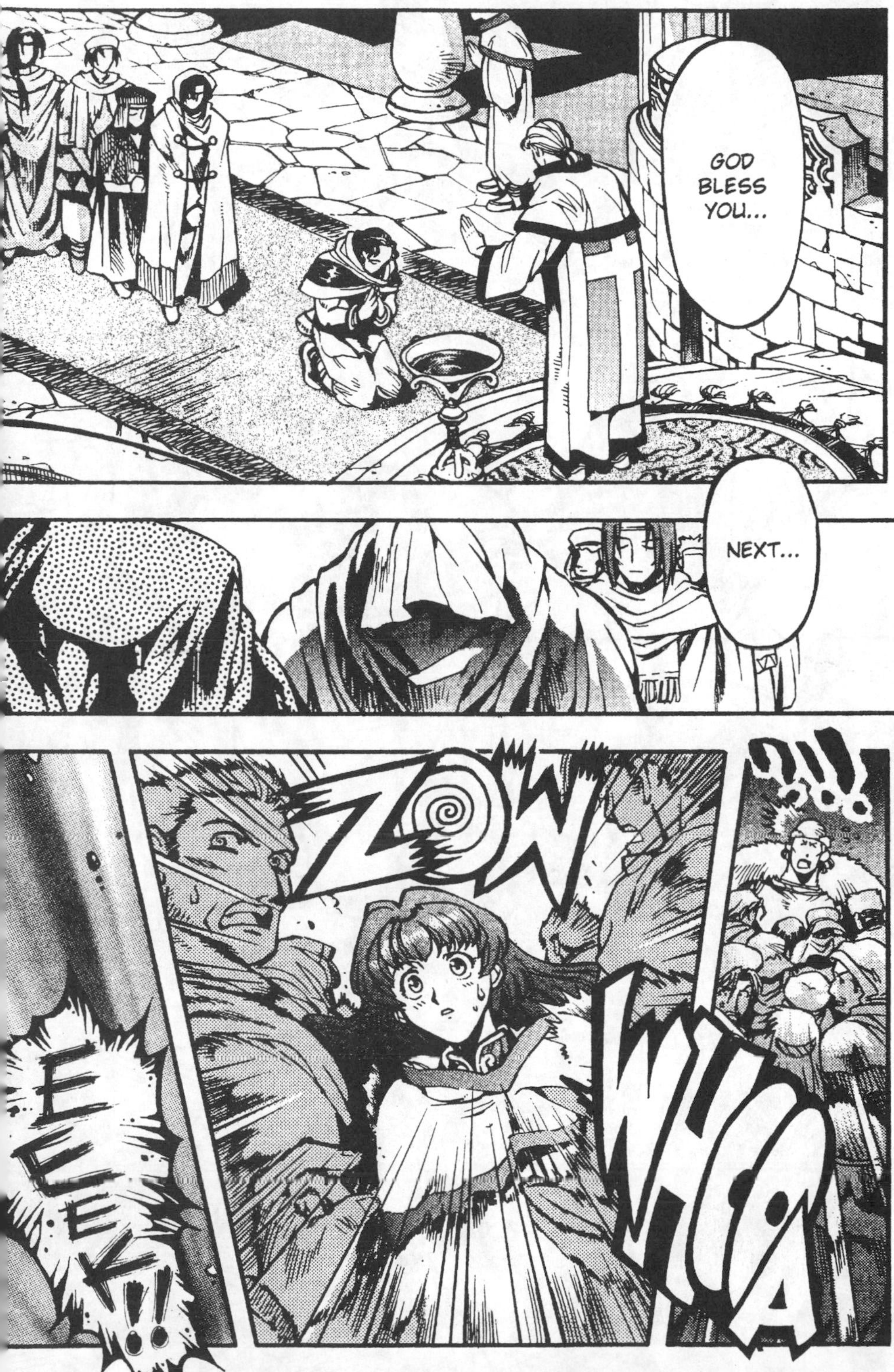
GOD BLESS YOU...
NEXT...
EEEEK!!
ZOW
?!!
WHOA

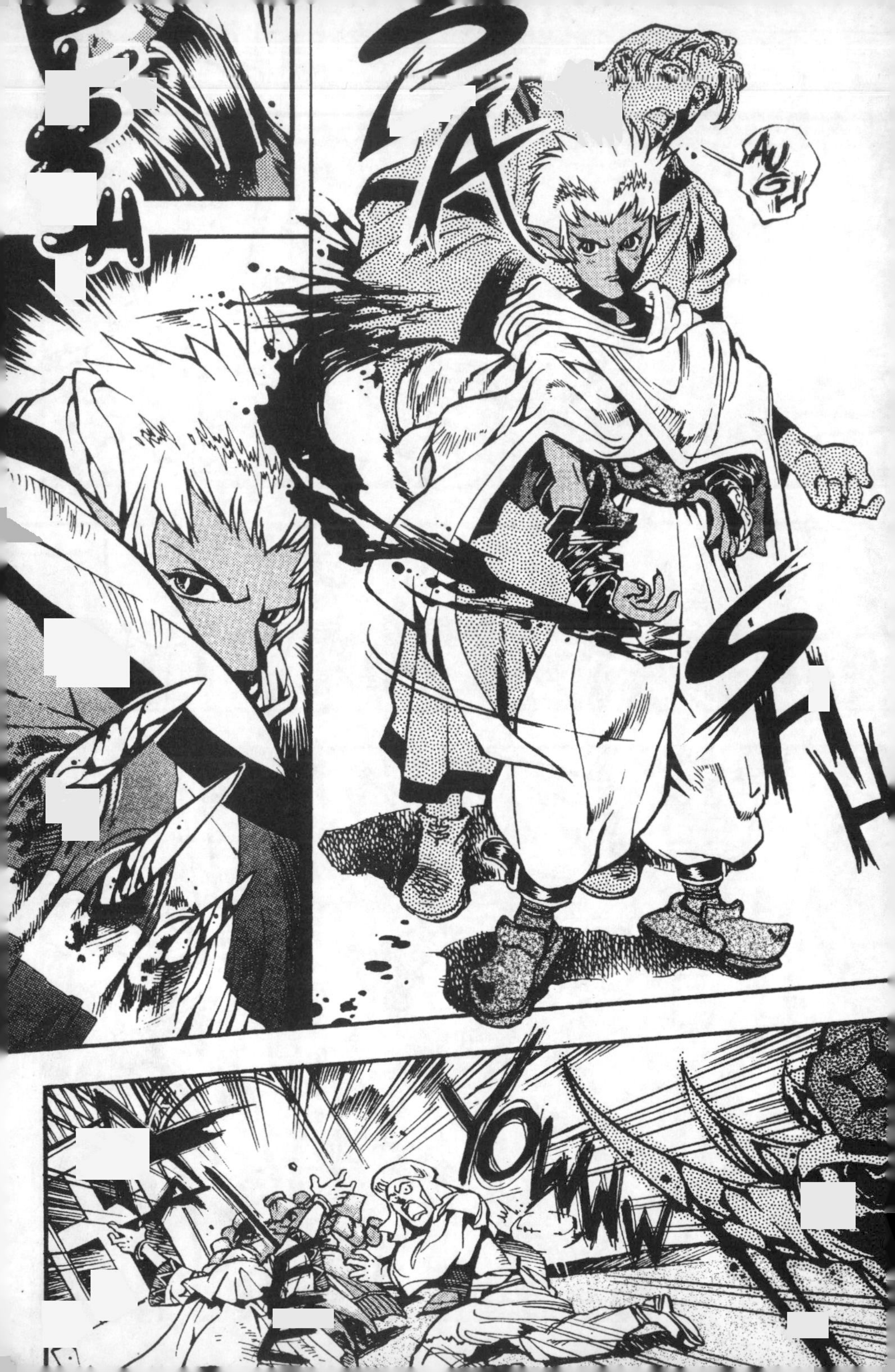
AUGH
YOWWWW

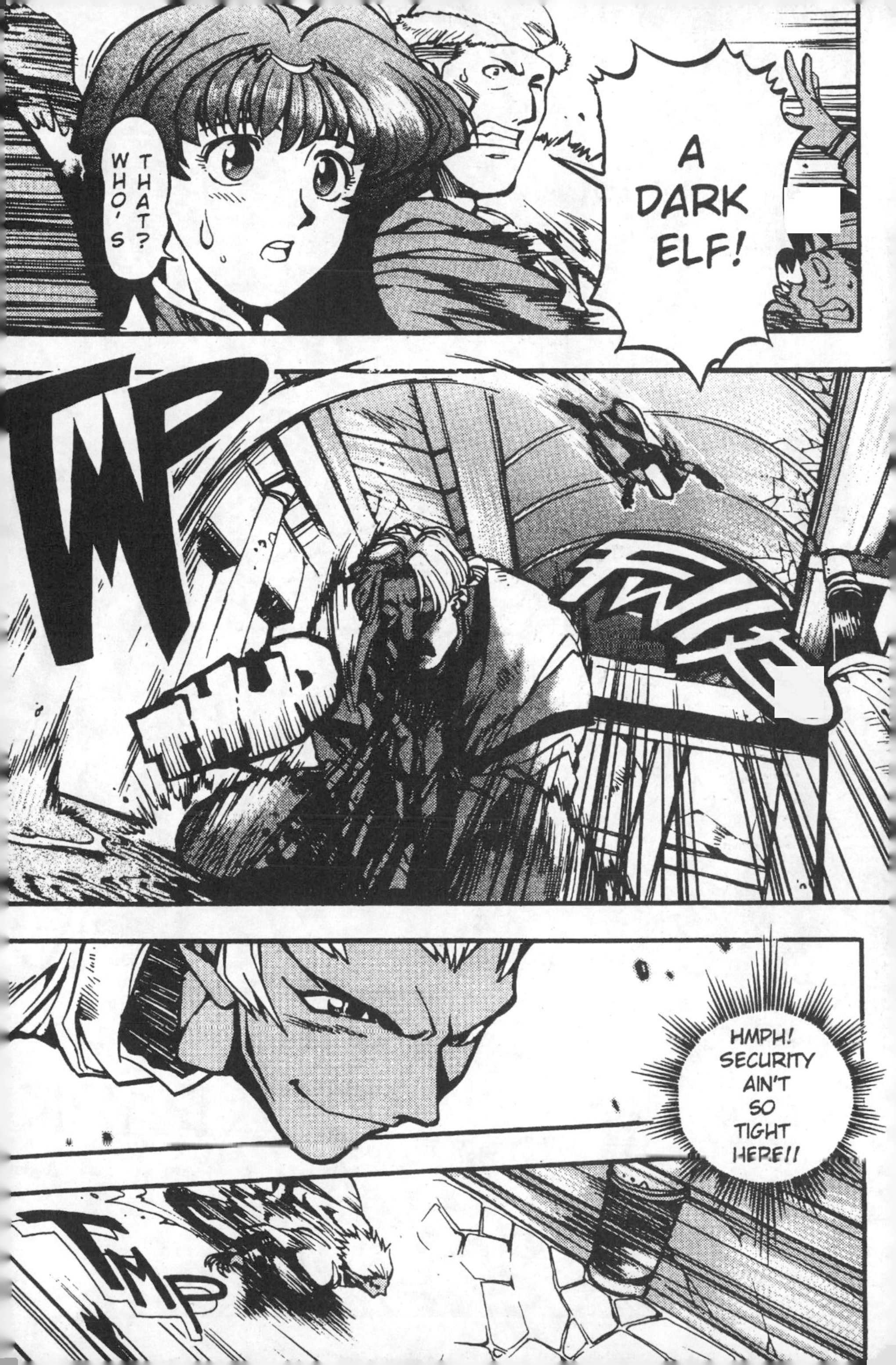
WHO'S THAT?
A DARK ELF!
TMP
HMPH! SECURITY AIN'T SO TIGHT HERE!!
TMP

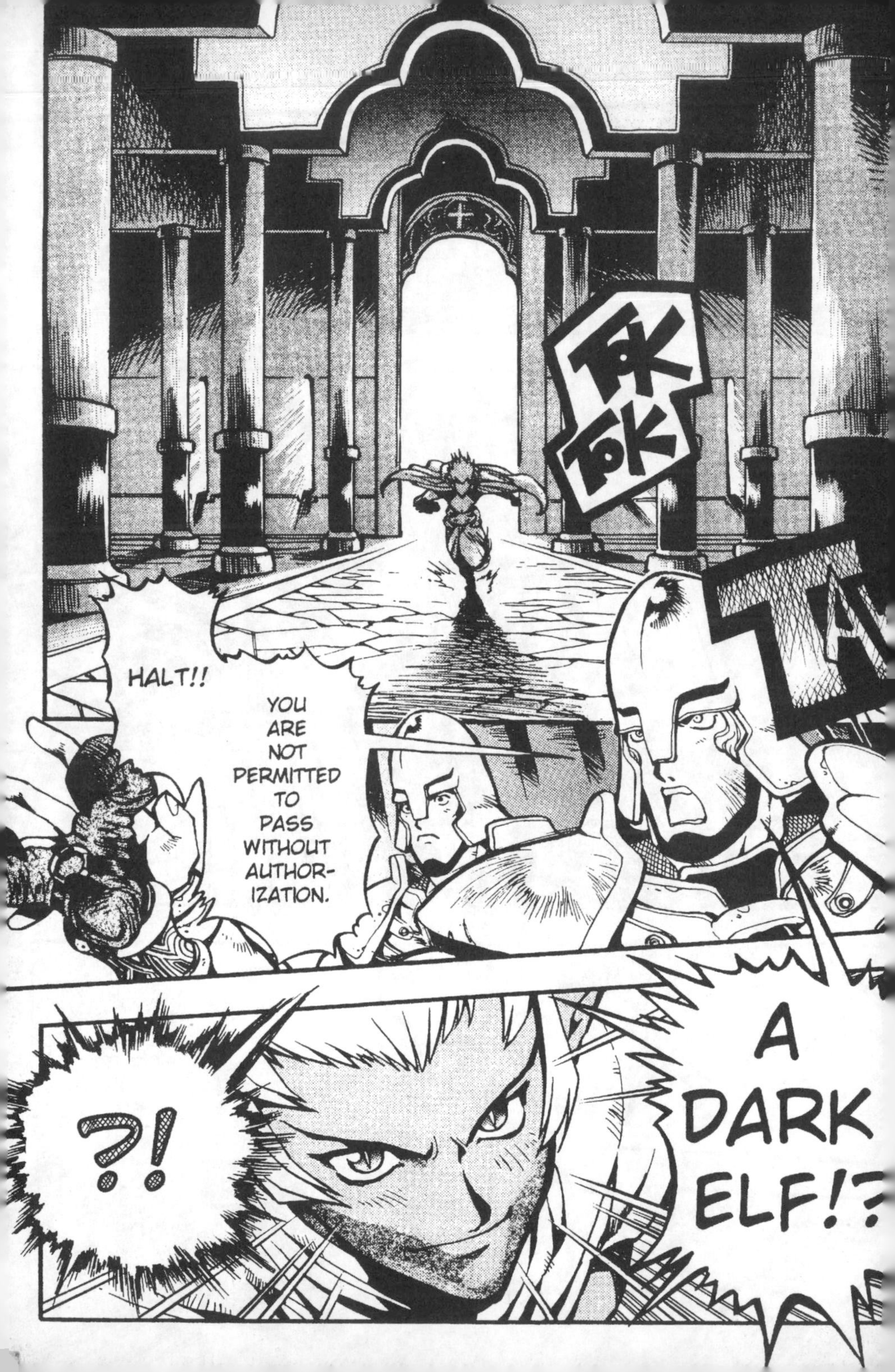
TOK TOK
HALT!!
YOU ARE NOT PERMITTED TO PASS WITHOUT AUTHOR-IZATION.
?!
A DARK ELF!?

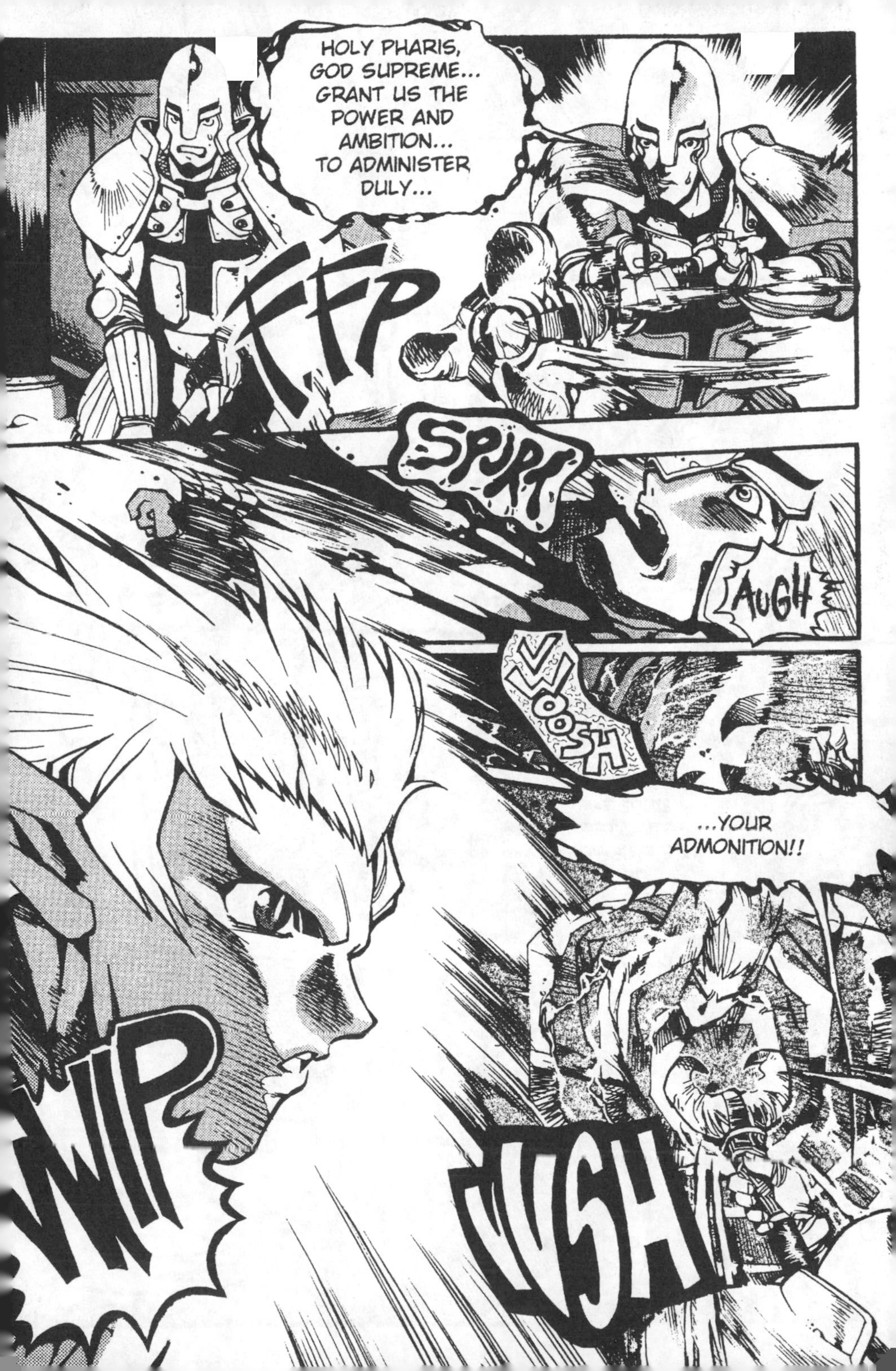
HOLY PHARIS, GOD SUPREME... GRANT US THE POWER AND AMBITION... TO ADMINISTER DULY...
FFP
SPIRT
AUGH
VWOOSH
...YOUR ADMONITION!!
WIP
WUSH

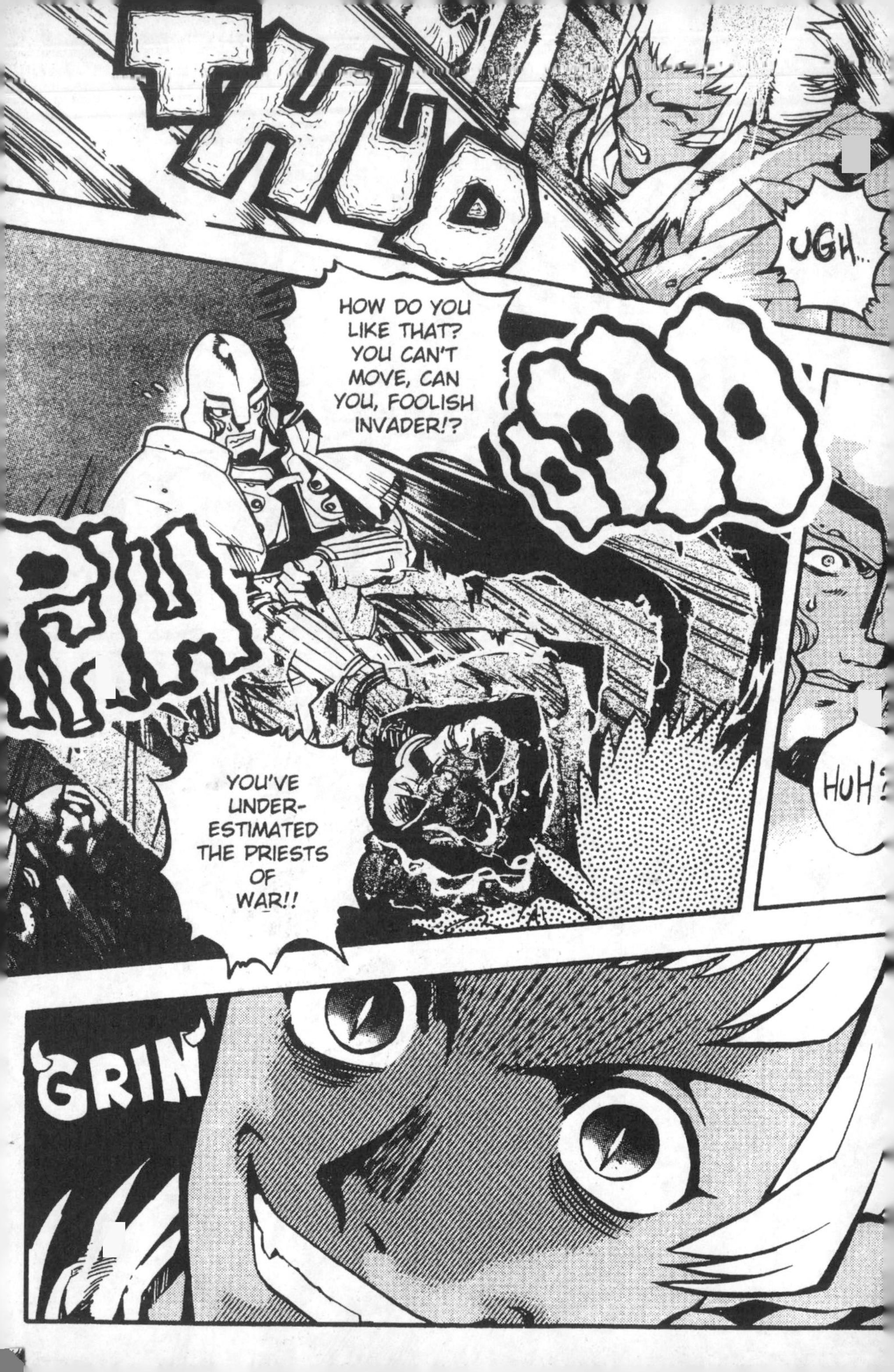
THUD
UGH...
HOW DO YOU LIKE THAT? YOU CAN'T MOVE, CAN YOU, FOOLISH INVADER!?
YOU'VE UNDER-ESTIMATED THE PRIESTS OF WAR!!
HUH?
GRIN

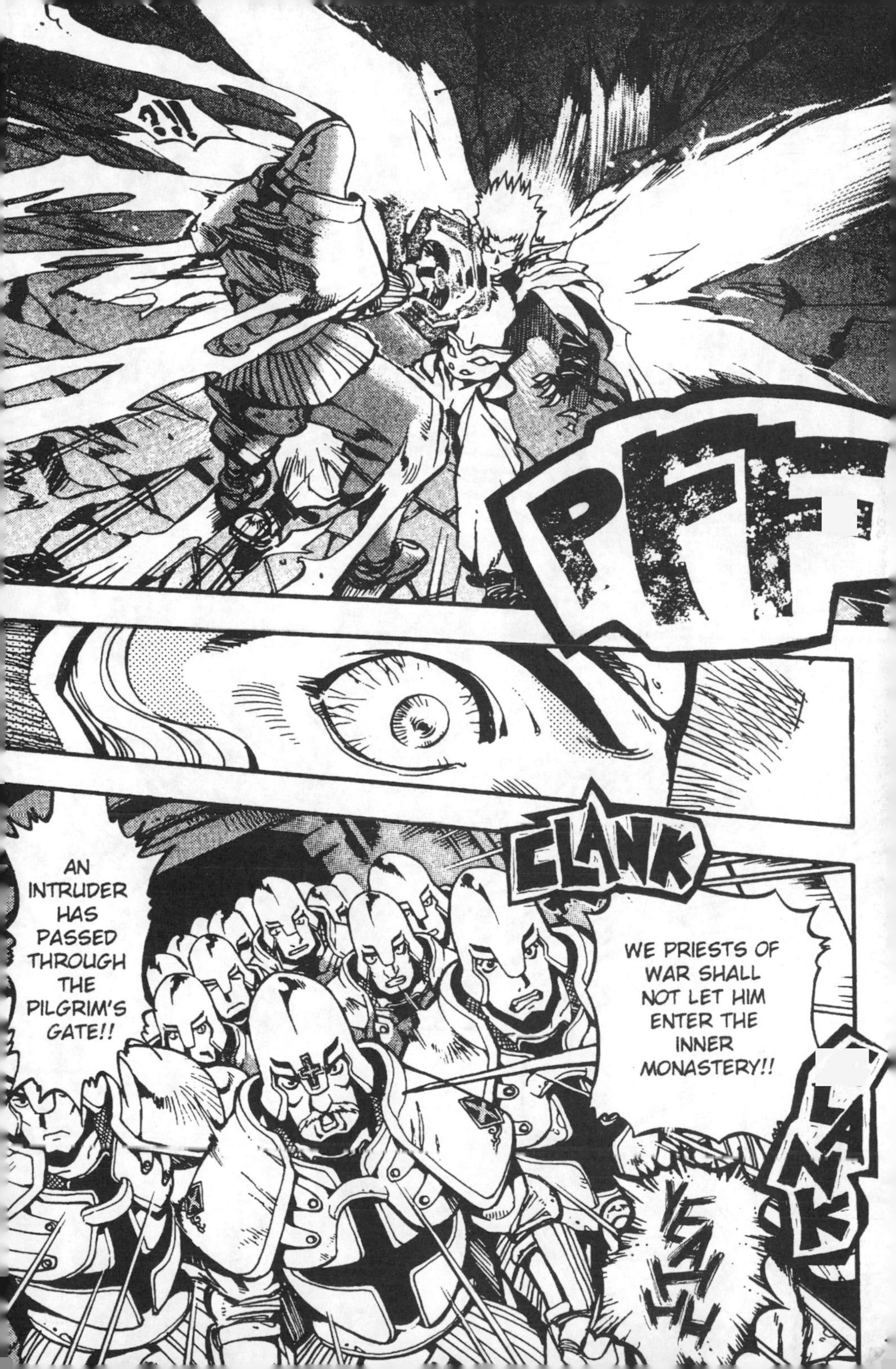

?!!
PFF
CLANK
AN INTRUDER HAS PASSED THROUGH THE PILGRIM'S GATE!!
WE PRIESTS OF WAR SHALL NOT LET HIM ENTER THE INNER MONASTERY!!
YEAHHH
LANK

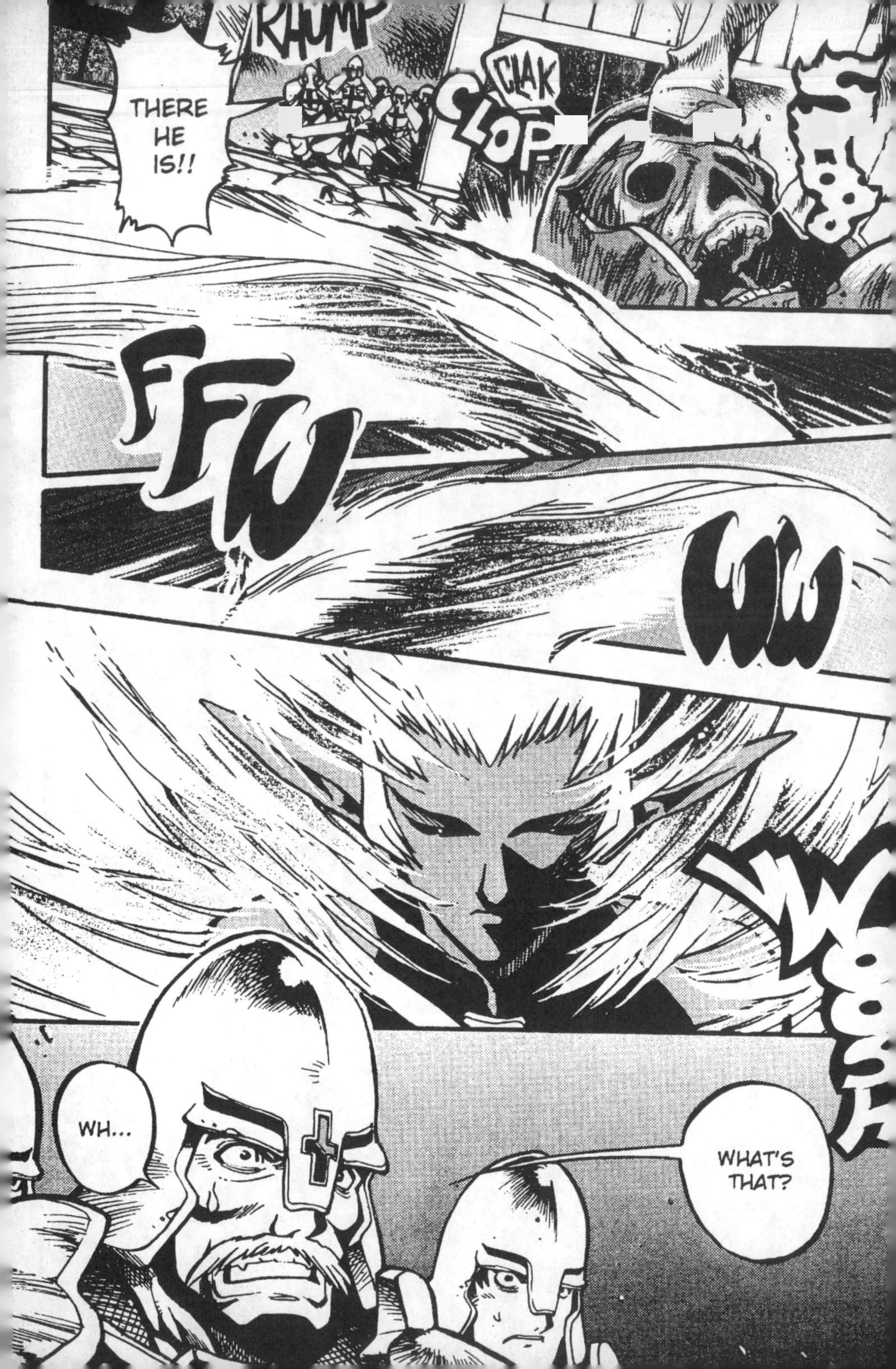
KHUMP
THERE HE IS!!
CLAK
CLOP
FFW
WW
WOOOSH
WH...
WHAT'S THAT?

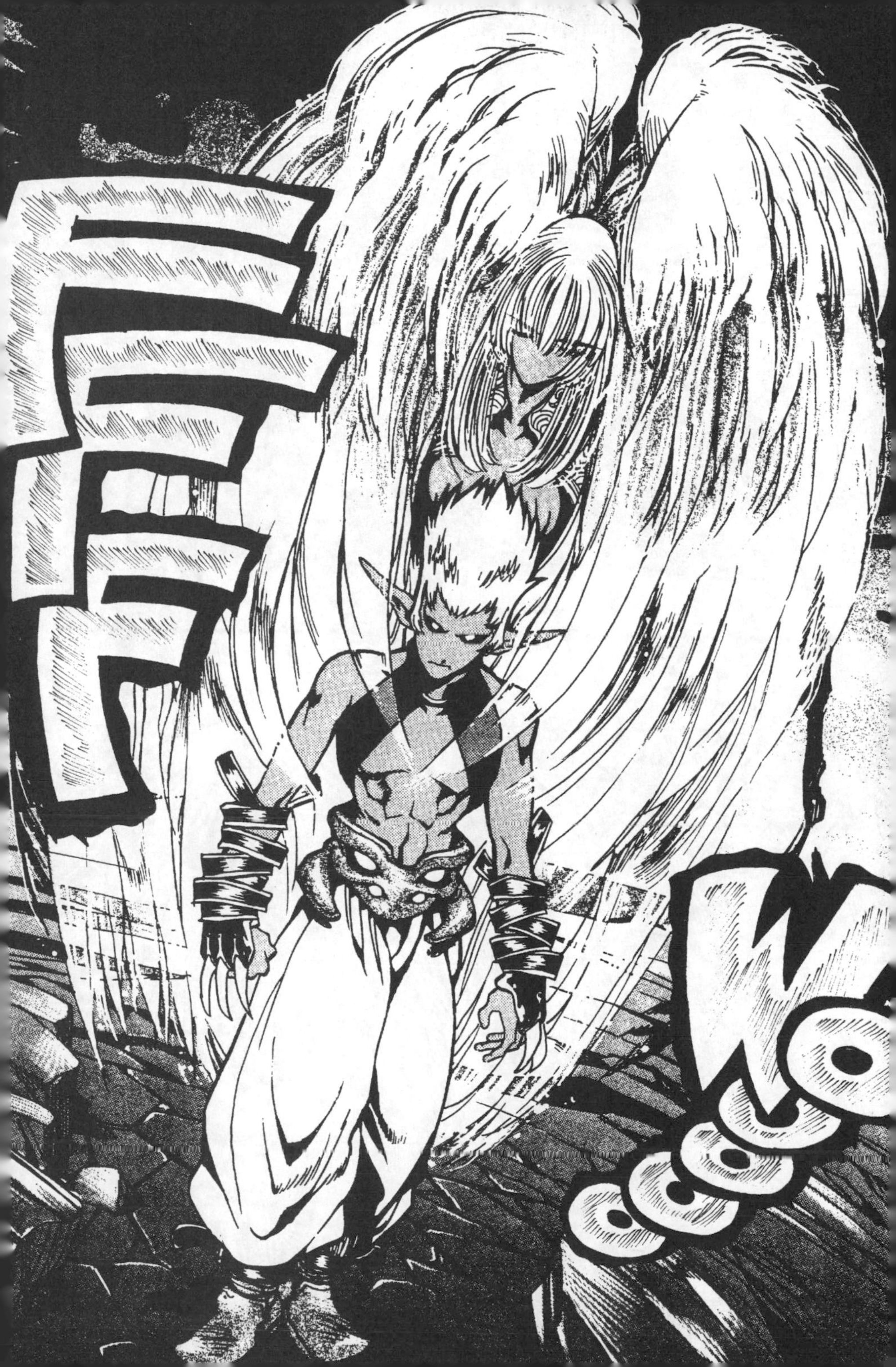
WOOOOOO

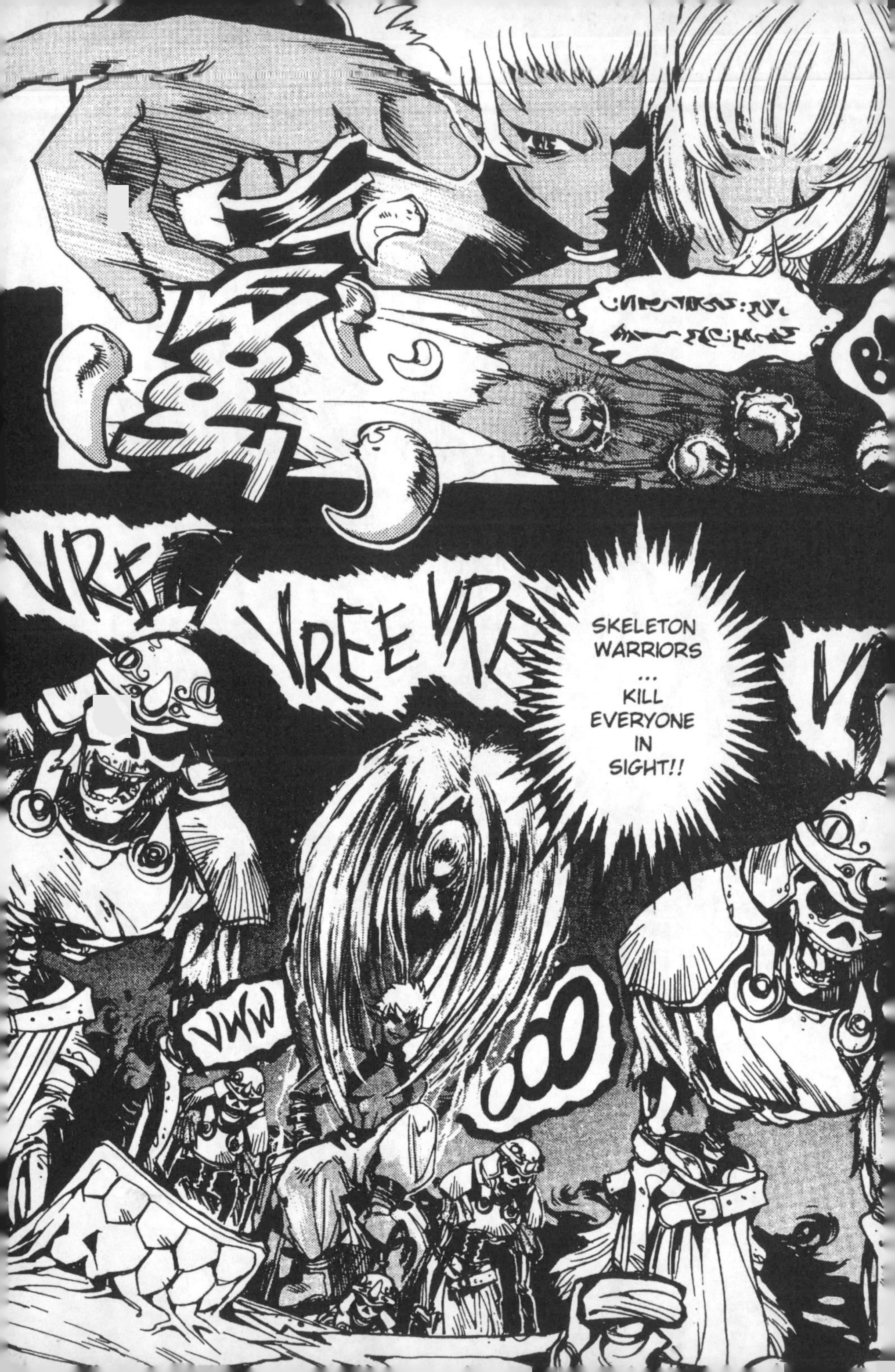
VREE VRE
SKELETON WARRIORS ... KILL EVERYONE IN SIGHT!!
VWW

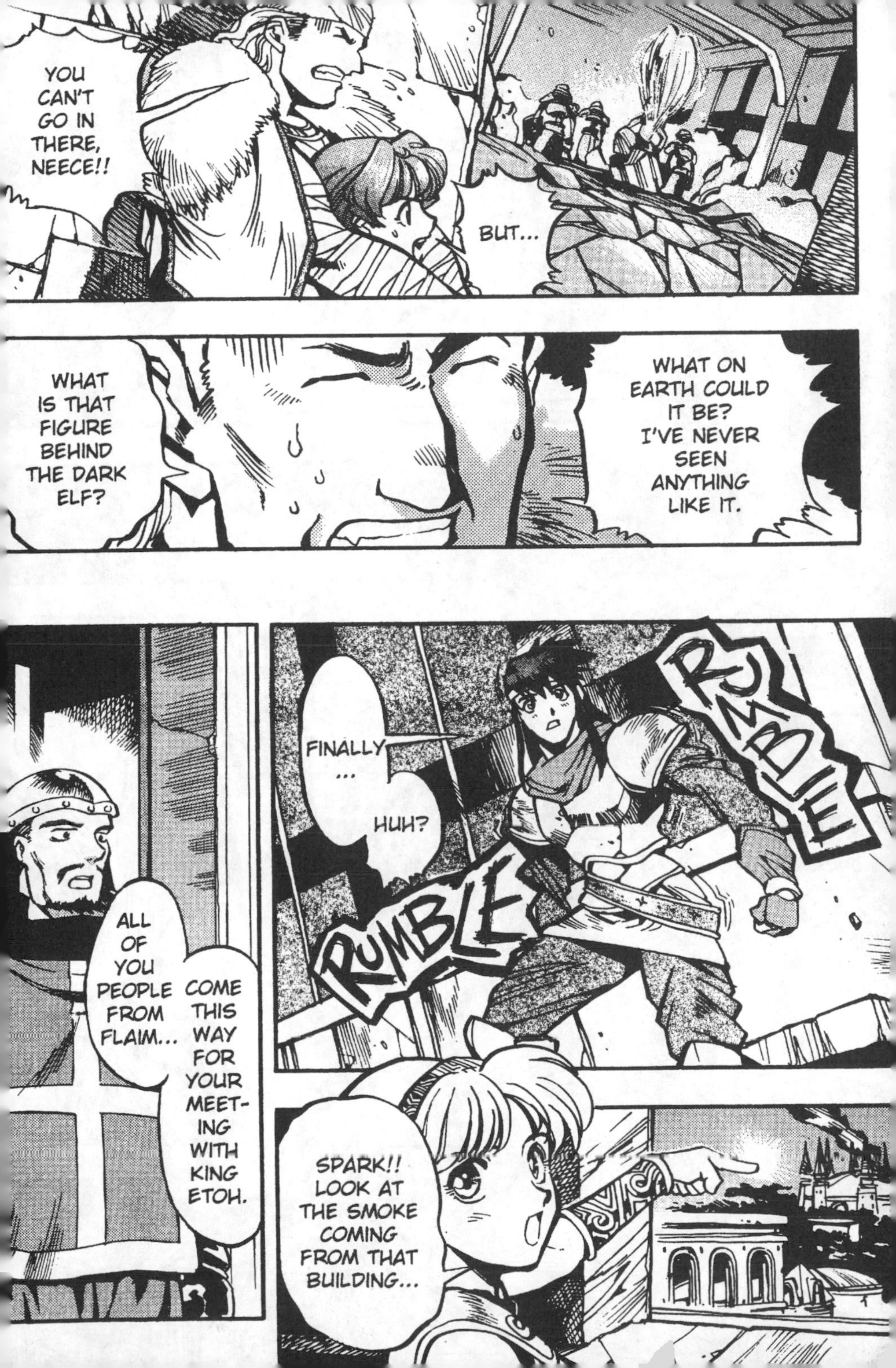
YOU CAN'T GO IN THERE, NEECE!!
BUT...
WHAT IS THAT FIGURE BEHIND THE DARK ELF?
WHAT ON EARTH COULD IT BE? I'VE NEVER SEEN ANYTHING LIKE IT.
ALL OF YOU PEOPLE FROM FLAIM...
COME THIS WAY FOR YOUR MEET-ING WITH KING ETOH.
FINALLY ...
HUH?
RUMBLE
RUMBLE
SPARK!! LOOK AT THE SMOKE COMING FROM THAT BUILDING...

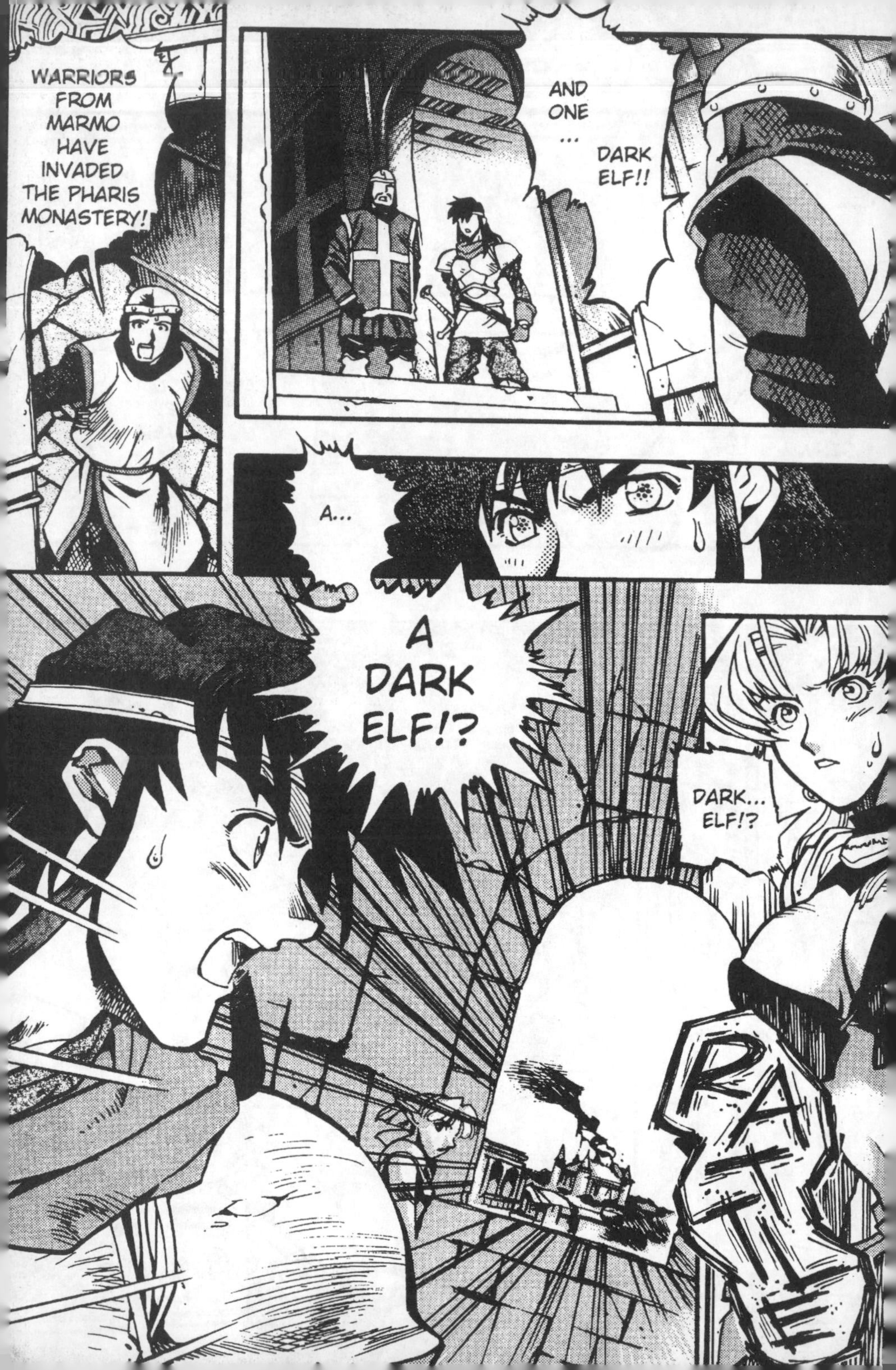
WARRIORS FROM MARMO HAVE INVADED THE PHARIS MONASTERY!
AND ONE ...
DARK ELF!!
A...
A DARK ELF!?
DARK... ELF!?
PAT

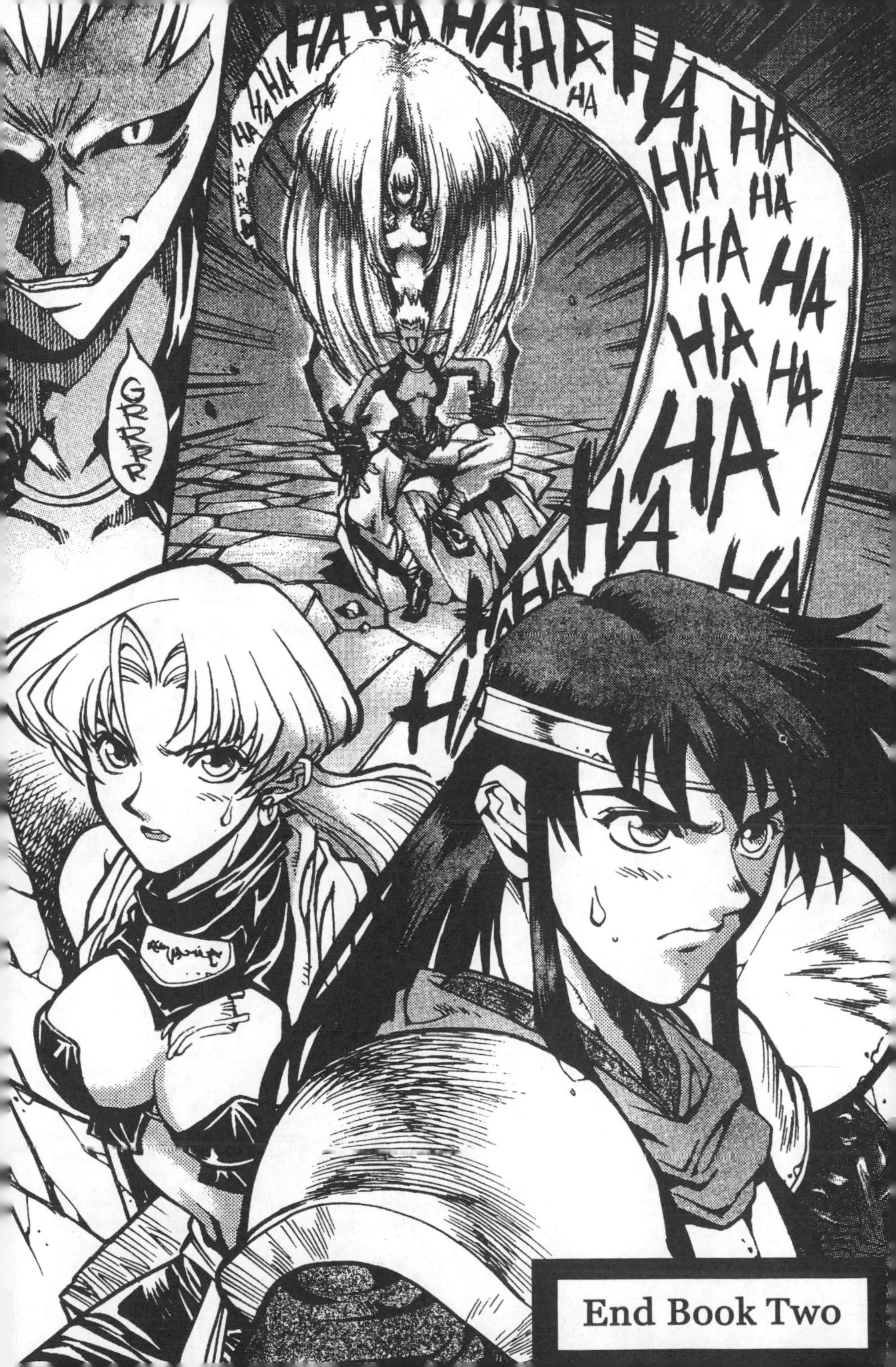
GRRRRR
HA HA HA HA HA HA HA HA HA HA HA HA HA HA HA HA HA HA HA HA HA HA HA HA
End Book Two

# RECORD of LODOSS WAR
## Chronicles of the Heroic Knight

# ROAD TO LODOSS
CHARACTER PROFILES and ROGUES GALLERY.

Road To Lodoss

# Record of Lodoss War
## Chronicles of the Heroic Knight

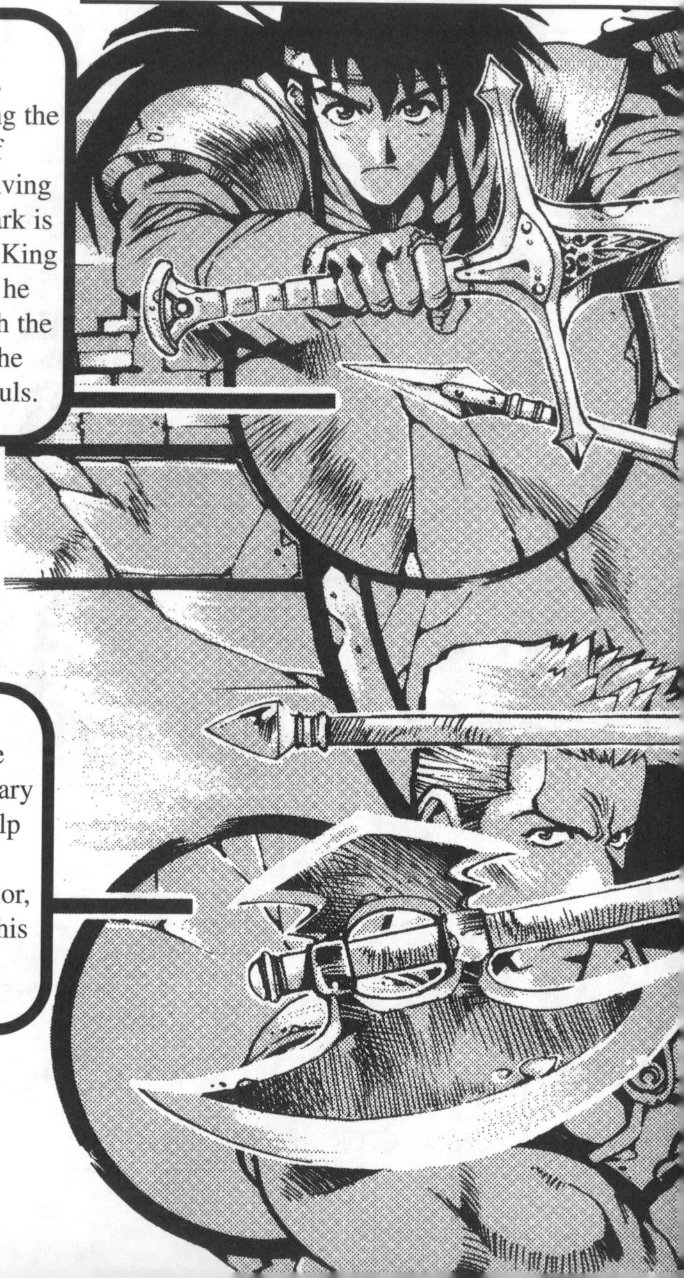

### Spark:
An apprentice knight, enthusiastic about assuming the full responsibilities of knighthood. The last surviving male of the Fire Clan, Spark is in line to become the next King of Flaim, but not before he fulfills his mission to catch the thieves who purloined the sacred Crystal Ball of Souls.

### Gallac:
Also known as the Blue Shooting Star, this mercenary was hired by Kashu to help Spark retrieve Flaim's treasure. A ferocious warrior, Gallac is fiercely loyal to his companions and to the kingdom of Flaim.

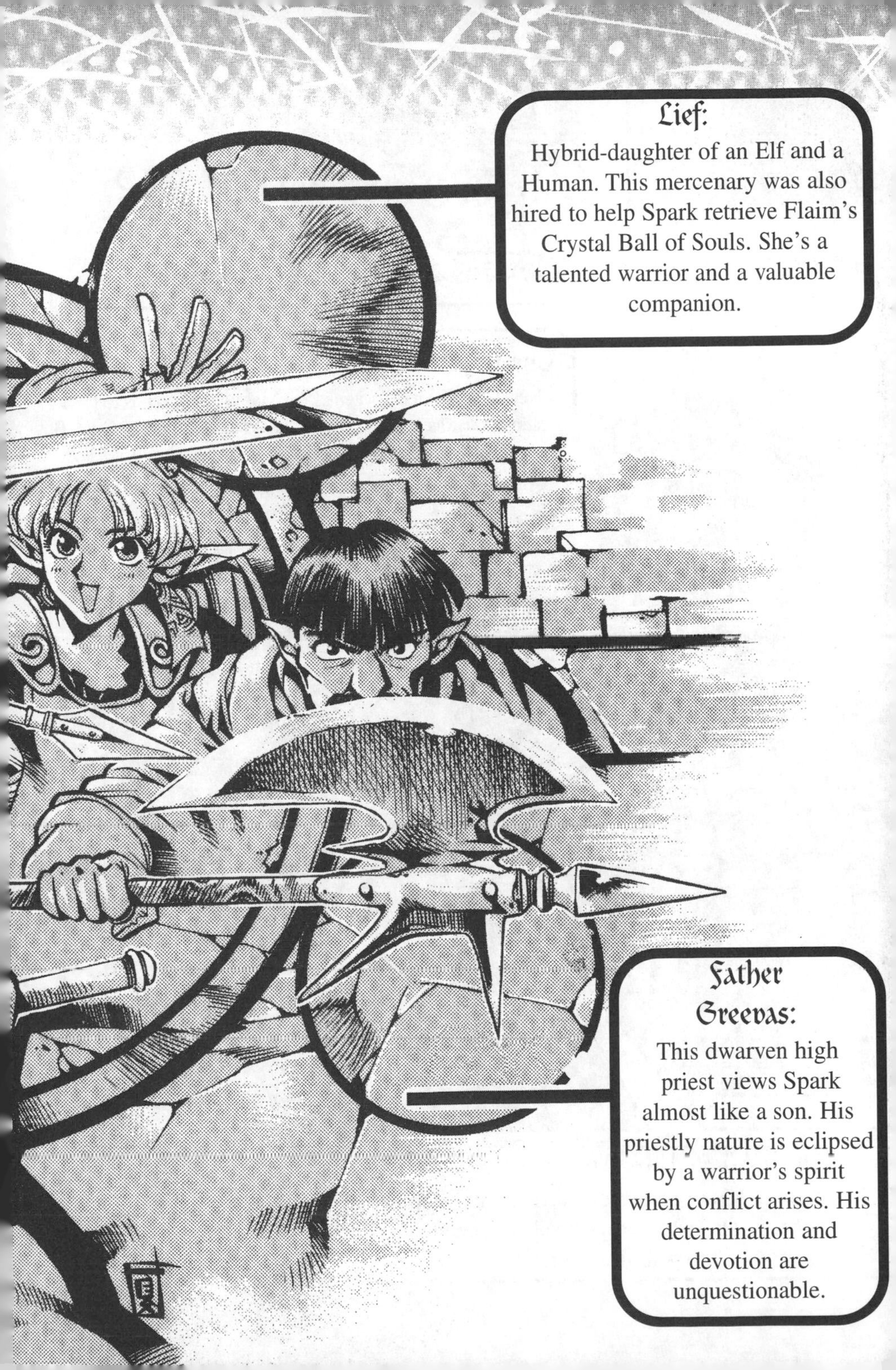
Lief:
Hybrid-daughter of an Elf and a Human. This mercenary was also hired to help Spark retrieve Flaim's Crystal Ball of Souls. She's a talented warrior and a valuable companion.
Father Greevas:
This dwarven high priest views Spark almost like a son. His priestly nature is eclipsed by a warrior's spirit when conflict arises. His determination and devotion are unquestionable.

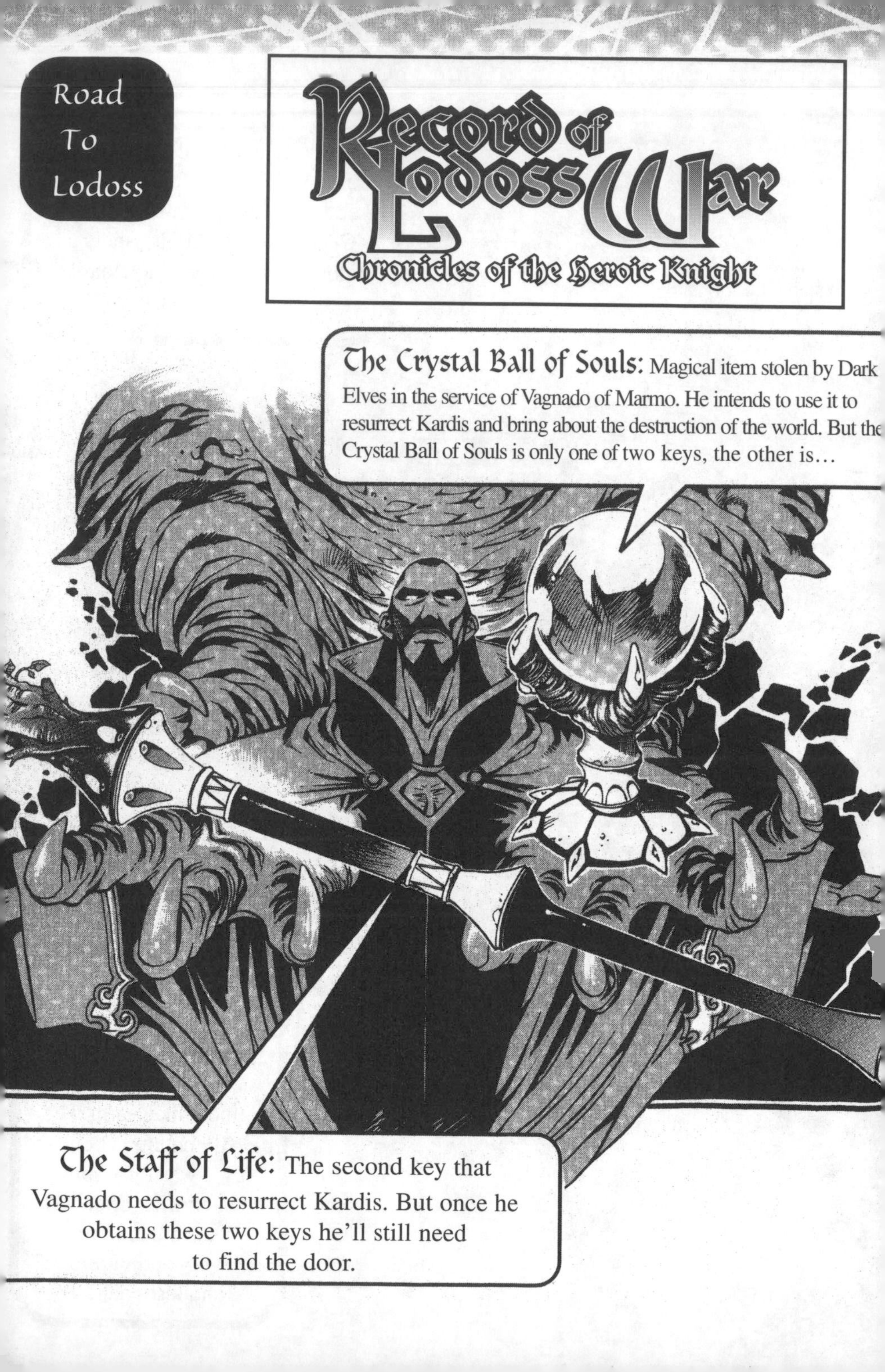

Road To Lodoss
Record of Lodoss War
Chronicles of the Heroic Knight
The Crystal Ball of Souls: Magical item stolen by Dark Elves in the service of Vagnado of Marmo. He intends to use it to resurrect Kardis and bring about the destruction of the world. But the Crystal Ball of Souls is only one of two keys, the other is…
The Staff of Life: The second key that Vagnado needs to resurrect Kardis. But once he obtains these two keys he'll still need to find the door.

## The Dark Emperor, Beld:

Emperor of the Dark Island of Marmo. During the War Against Evil, he was known as the Red Haired Warrior. He fought the War of Heroes guided by his ideal of creating a kingdom where all living creatures are treated equally.

## King Farn:

He is king of the Sacred Kingdom of Valis and, like Beld, he was unrivaled as a swordsman in his youth. Because of his great character and valiance, he is respected by people from not only his kingdom, but other kingdoms as well.

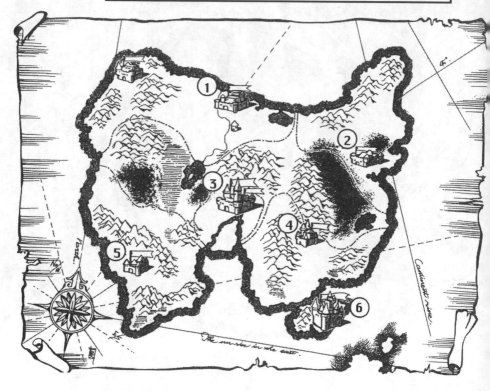

# Island of Lodoss Map

# Record of Lodoss War

## Chronicles of the Heroic Knight

**1. The Kingdom of Flaim**

Ruled by King Kashu, it is the strongest of all the kingdoms of Lodoss. King Kashu settled the long-standing battle between the Wind Clan and the Fire Clan. Spark is a direct descendant of the Fire Clan.

**2. The Kingdom of Allania**

Ruled by the Duke of Rastar, it is the oldest of the kingdoms of Lodoss. The Duke of Rastar is an ambitious, cold-hearted ruler who assassinated the former leader, King Kadomos VII.

**3. The Sacred Kingdom of Valis**

Valis is ruled by the priest, King Etoh. King Etoh was a companion to Parn and Deedlit during the War of the Heroes. Parn and King Etoh have been friends since childhood.

**4. The Kingdom of Kanon**

Kanon is currently ruled by a man in black from the Marmo Empire known as General Ashram. A local war is developing in Kanon with the free knight, Parn, leading the Kanon Freedom Army.

**5. The Kingdom of Moss**

Moss is a kingdom ruled by Duke Jester. Moss is not actually one kingdom, but a group of smaller nations united as allies. This alliance is bound under an agreement known as the "Treaty of Dragons," stipulating a united front against any external enemy. There has, however, been internal fighting in Moss for hundreds of years.

**6. The Dark Island of Marmo**

What mysteries lie on this enchanted isle? No one knows for sure.

## Island of Lodoss Map

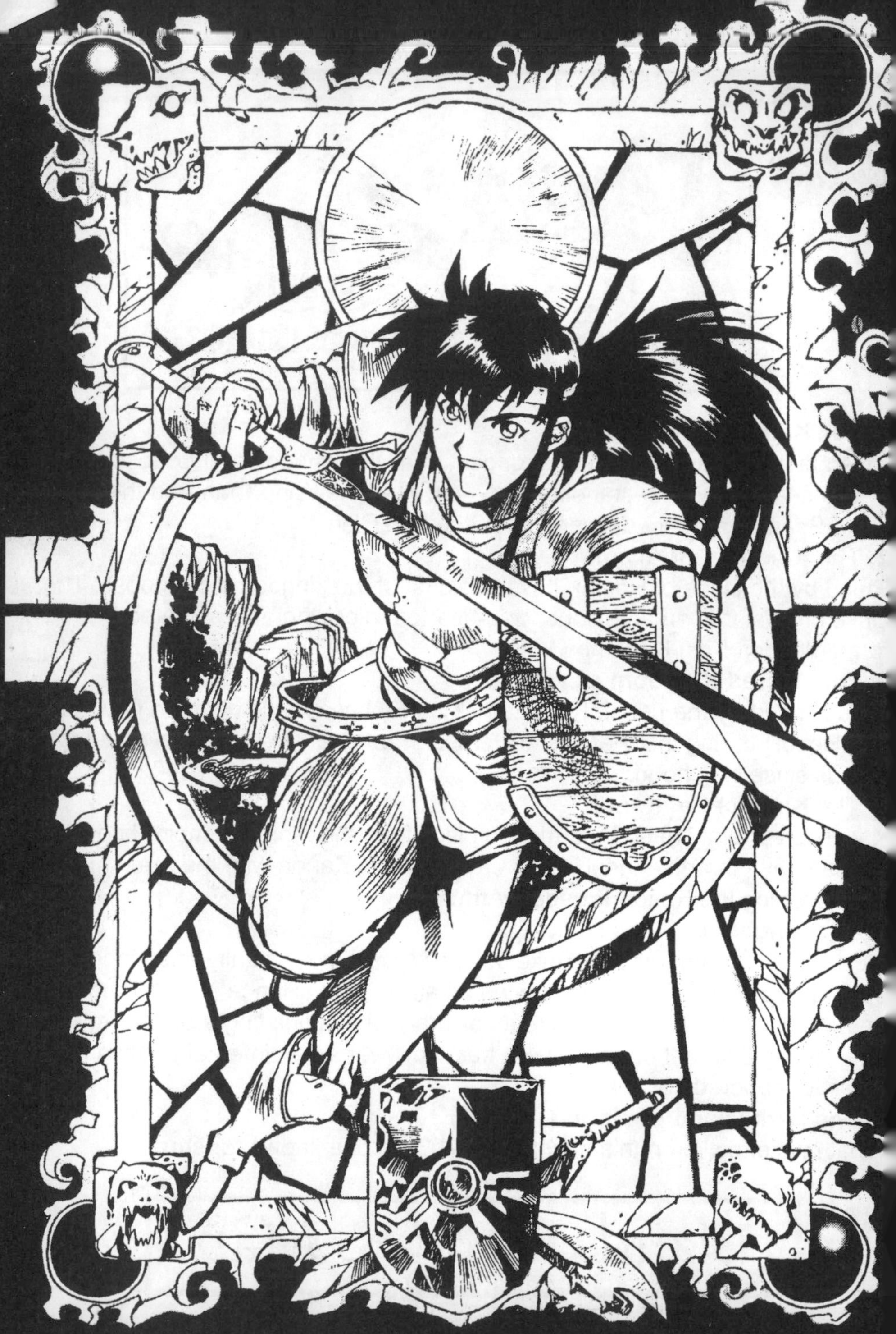

# Creators' Bios

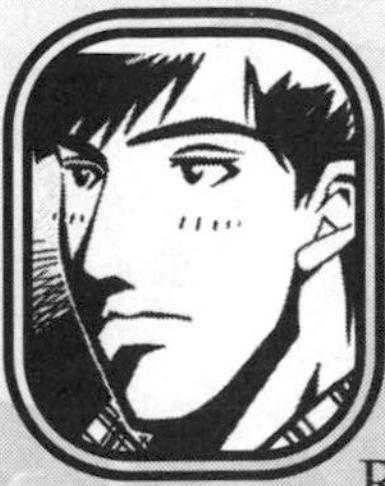

## Ryo Mizuno

Ryo Mizuno is the world-renowned creator of the *Record of Lodoss War* universe. In addition to writing the manga, he has written best-selling novels and created popular role-playing games based on the Lodoss world. His other *Record of Lodoss War* works that are available from CPM Manga include: *The Grey Witch Trilogy,* the first Lodoss story Mr. Mizuno ever wrote; *The Lady of Pharis,* a graphic novel that delves deeply into the history of Lodoss; and *Deedlit's Tale*, a romantic Lodoss story drawn by the famous shoujo artist Setsuko Yoneyama (*Endless Waltz)*. Regarding the creation of *Heroic Knight*, Mr. Mizuno observed, "It's been ten years since I started writing *Record of Lodoss War.* I can't ell if it's a long time or a short time, but thanks to your continued support I am able to publish this new book."

## Masato Natsumoto

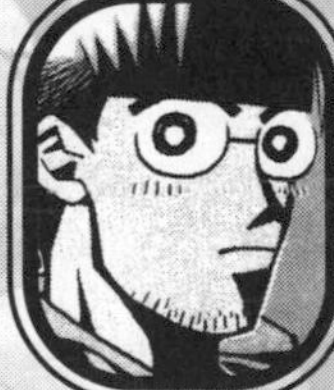

Masato Natsumoto, creator of the lynamic and action-packed artwork for *Chronicles of the Heroic Knight,* was born in Tokyo in 1970. Among his best-known manga creations are the manga based on a popular video game series, *King of Fighters (KOF)*. His well-egarded KOF manga titles are *King of Fighters: KYO '95* and *King of Fighters: KYO '96.* Regarding his experience of working on *Chronicles of the Heroic Knight,* Mr. Natsumoto said, "*Record of Lodoss War* is a truly epic fantasy with a long history. I never expected to be working on the creative end of it, but here I am. The high ideals of the story present a variety of difficulties, but I'm doing my best to keep it fun and interesting."

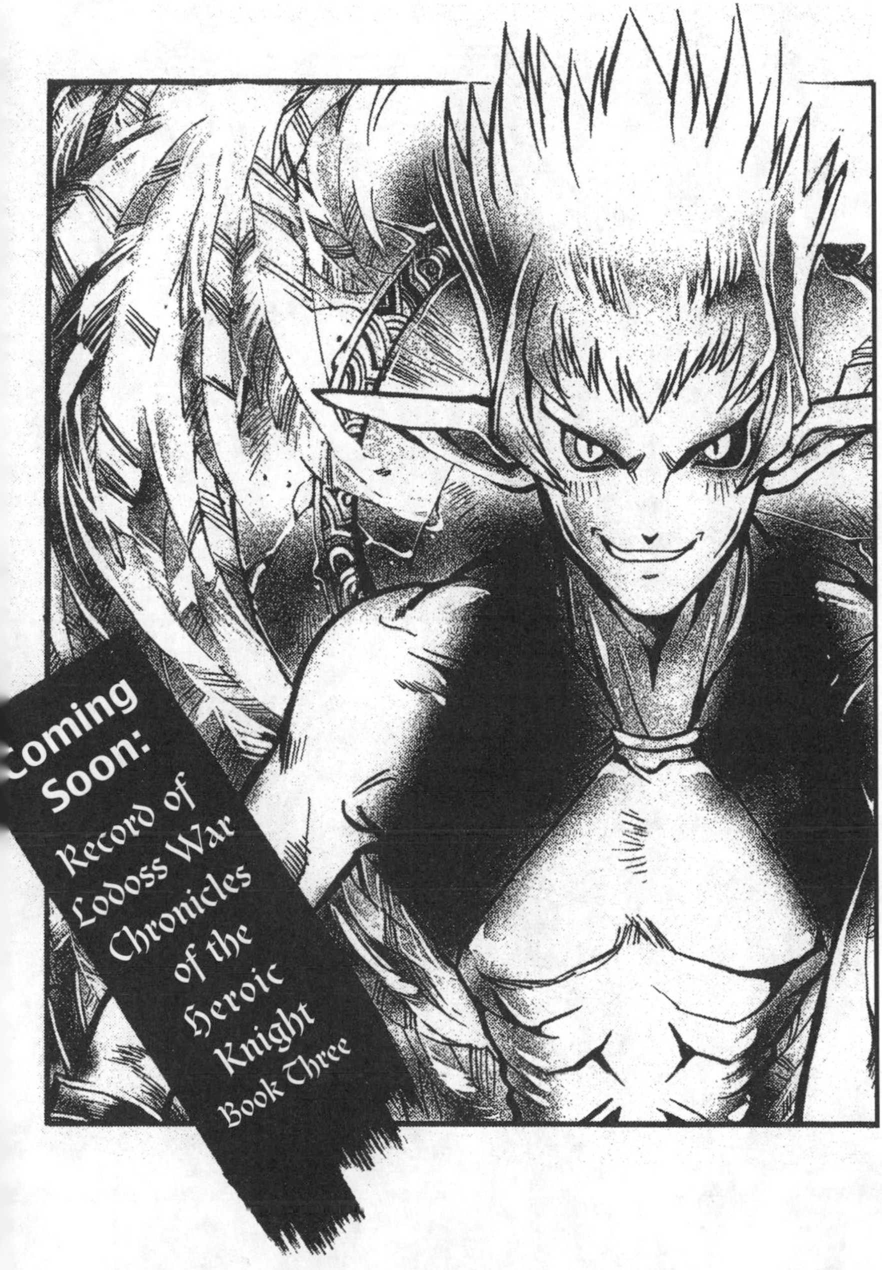
Coming Soon:
Record of Lodoss War Chronicles of the Heroic Knight
Book Three

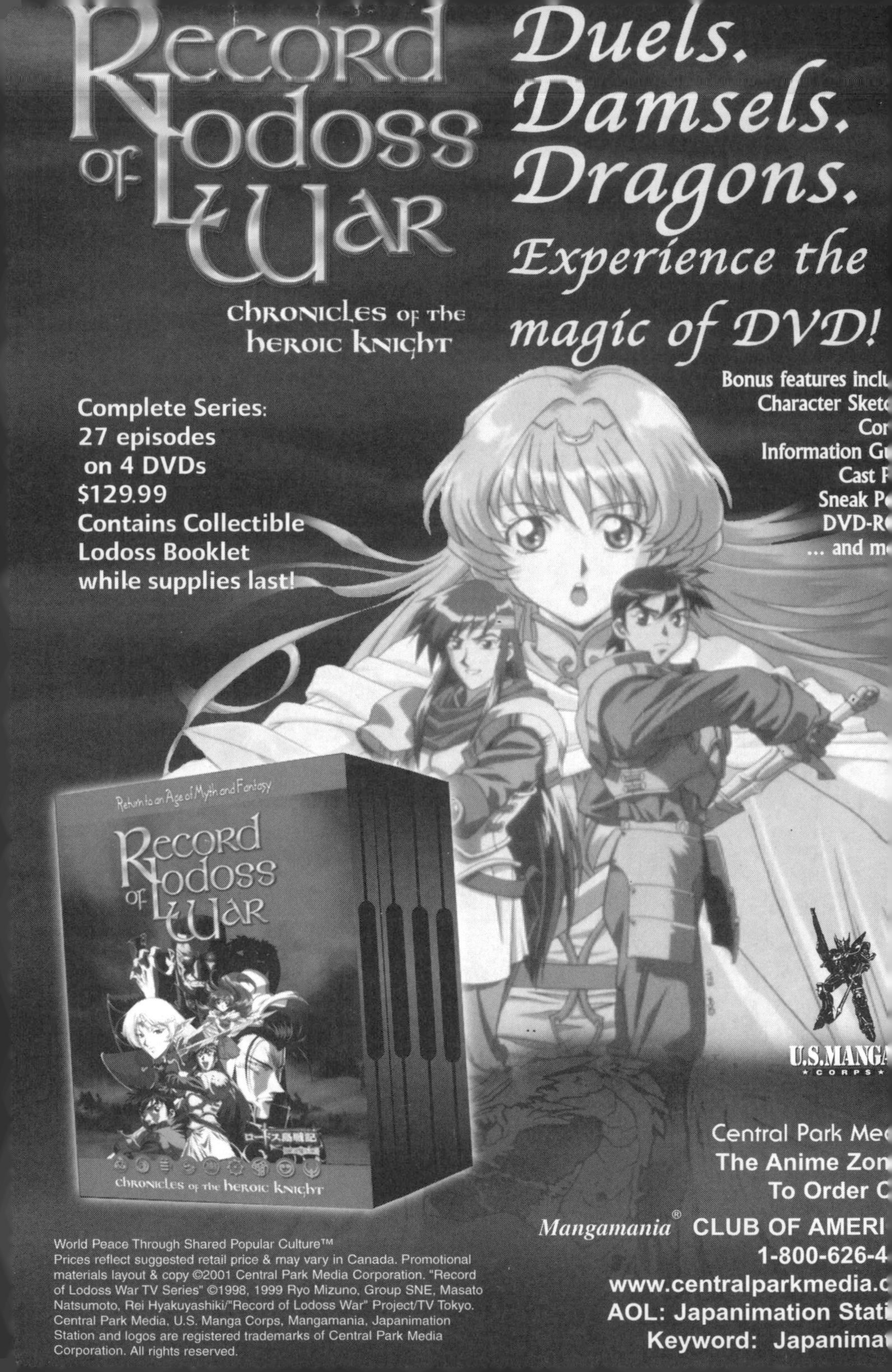
Record of Lodoss War
Chronicles of the heroic knight
Duels.
Damsels.
Dragons.
Experience the
magic of DVD!
Bonus features inclu
Character Sketc
Cor
Information Gu
Cast F
Sneak Pe
DVD-RO
... and mo
Complete Series:
27 episodes
on 4 DVDs
$129.99
Contains Collectible
Lodoss Booklet
while supplies last!
Return to an Age of Myth and Fantasy
Record of Lodoss War
ロードス島戦記
Chronicles of the heroic knight
U.S.MANGA
CORPS
Central Park Med
The Anime Zon
To Order C
Mangamania® CLUB OF AMERI
1-800-626-4
www.centralparkmedia.c
AOL: Japanimation Stati
Keyword: Japanima
World Peace Through Shared Popular Culture™
Prices reflect suggested retail price & may vary in Canada. Promotional materials layout & copy ©2001 Central Park Media Corporation. "Record of Lodoss War TV Series" ©1998, 1999 Ryo Mizuno, Group SNE, Masato Natsumoto, Rei Hyakuyashiki/"Record of Lodoss War" Project/TV Tokyo. Central Park Media, U.S. Manga Corps, Mangamania, Japanimation Station and logos are registered trademarks of Central Park Media Corporation. All rights reserved.

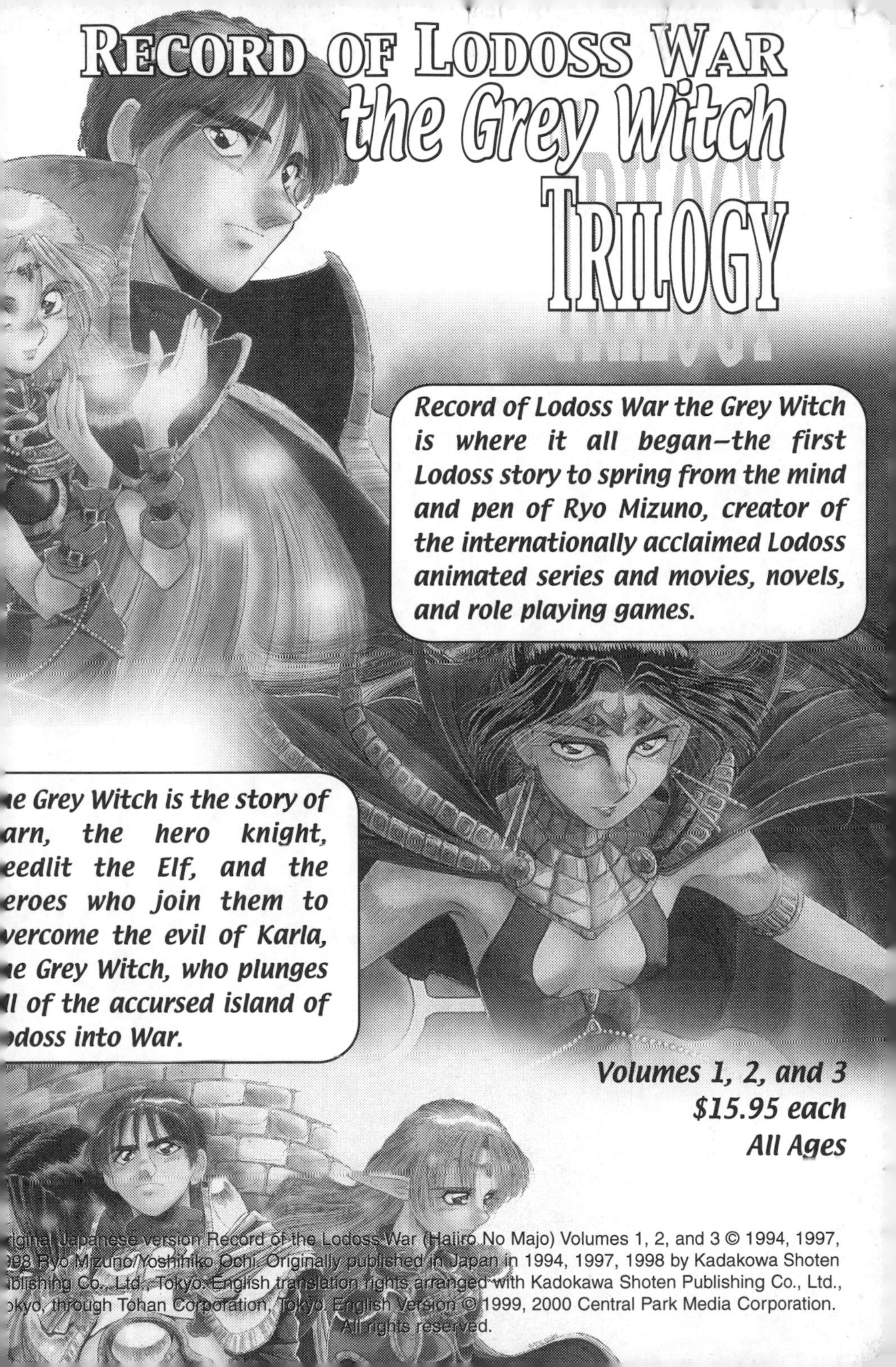
RECORD OF LODOSS WAR
the Grey Witch
TRILOGY
Record of Lodoss War the Grey Witch is where it all began—the first Lodoss story to spring from the mind and pen of Ryo Mizuno, creator of the internationally acclaimed Lodoss animated series and movies, novels, and role playing games.
ne Grey Witch is the story of arn, the hero knight, eedlit the Elf, and the eroes who join them to vercome the evil of Karla, ne Grey Witch, who plunges ll of the accursed island of odoss into War.
Volumes 1, 2, and 3
$15.95 each
All Ages
riginal Japanese version Record of the Lodoss War (Haiiro No Majo) Volumes 1, 2, and 3 © 1994, 1997, 998 Ryo Mizuno/Yoshihiko Ochi. Originally published in Japan in 1994, 1997, 1998 by Kadakowa Shoten ublishing Co., Ltd., Tokyo. English translation rights arranged with Kadokawa Shoten Publishing Co., Ltd., okyo, through Tohan Corporation, Tokyo. English Version © 1999, 2000 Central Park Media Corporation. All rights reserved.

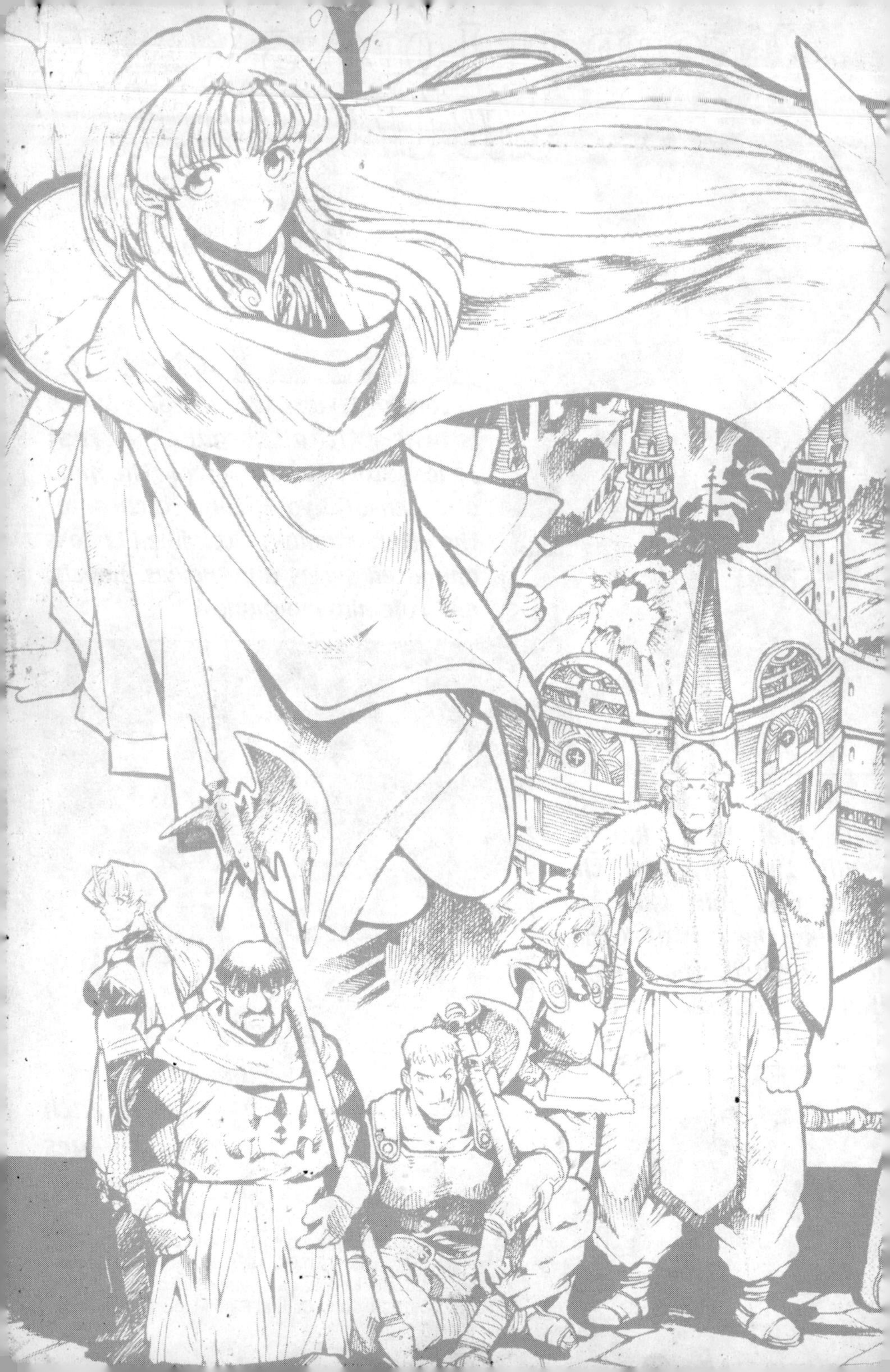